Multicultural Religious Education

Multicultural Religious Education

edited by

Barbara Wilkerson

1997

Religious Education Press
Birmingham, Alabama

Library of Congress Cataloging-in-Publication Data

Multicultural religious education / edited by Barbara Wilkerson.
   Includes bibliographical references and index.
   ISBN 0-89135-101-9 (pbk.: alk. paper)
   1. Christian education.   2. Multiculturalism—Religious aspects—Christianity.
   3. Christian education—United States.
I. Wilkerson, Barbara.
BV1471.2.M85 1997
268'.0973–dc21   97–6735
                                                       CIP

Religious Education Press
5316 Meadow Brook Road
Birmingham, Alabama 35242–3315
10 9 8 7 6 5 4 3 2

Religious Education Press publishes books exclusively in religious education and in areas closely related to religious education. It is committed to enhancing and professionalizing religious education through the publication of serious, significant, and scholarly works.

PUBLISHER TO THE PROFESSION

CONTENTS

TABLES AND FIGURES

INTRODUCTION

Throughout the world no trend is more evident, more unequivocal, and more predictive of the future than the trend toward cultural change. Nonwhite groups represent the growing edge of global population figures. As recently as 1950 25 percent of the world's people lived in Europe and North America. By 1989 that figure had decreased to 12 percent, and demographers predicted that by the year 2000 it could be a mere 6 percent.[1]

In the United States the statistics are well known—early in the 1990s students of color were already a majority in twenty-five of the nation's largest school districts and in the state of California; by the middle of the twenty-first century half the nation's population will be people of color.[2] These populations represent not simply racial or cultural differences— African-American, Asian, Hispanic—but ethnic groups and subgroups that are global in scope: West Indian, African and African-American blacks; Chinese, Indian, Vietnamese, and Korean Asians; Mexican, Puerto Rican, and Central American Hispanics; whites from Eastern Europe and the Middle East; all in addition to a growing population of Native Americans of many Native nations. In the midst of this social change the realities of racial and ethnic conflict in major cities—ongoing inequity in housing, employment, and education, lack of political power—all challenge a nation built on democratic values.

The spiritual needs of this diverse population, and in particular of the young who represent the greatest percentage of social change, are the focus of concern for religious educators, clergy, and congregations. If the church of Jesus Christ hopes to reach the population of North America in coming decades, it must reach an increasing array of cultural groups. Yet, with the exception of so-called ethnic congregations, few American churches have addressed this reality or have adjusted their programs in any serious way

---

1. Curtiss Paul DeYoung, *Coming Together: The Bible's Message in an Age of Diversity* (Valley Forge, Pa.: Judson, 1995), p. xvii. DeYoung quotes from *American Demographic Desk Reference Series*, no. 1, July 1995, p. 5.

2. James A. Banks, "National Council on Social Studies Curriculum Guidelines for Multicultural Education," *Social Education*, September 1992, p. 274.

to reflect it. In fact, the controversies surrounding adoption or rejection of school curricula labeled "multicultural" may have caused many churches to look the other way. This means that churches will lose opportunities for religious education among significant portions of society. We need to ask whether the failure to attend to human difference all around us is not also a failure to attend to the theological imperatives of Christian faith.

The task of this book is to explore the consequences of multiculturalism for Christian faith and church ministry and to help churches design a religious education that responds to the call of the gospel in a culturally diverse society. In using the descriptor culturally diverse I wish to underscore the scope and focus of the book's discussion. The term *multicultural* can mean different things to different people. It is important that we clarify how the term is understood in this book, as well as how other key terms are defined.

DEFINITIONS

Multicultural

Carl Grant, an educator and specialist in multicultural education, says that a lack of clarity in definitions has been a barrier to multicultural research. "Authors do not clearly define what they mean by the term. . . . This lack of definition allows critics to either ignore multicultural education or view it as an idea without meaning and structure."[3] Geneva Gay acknowledges multiple definitions, but argues that this need not impede theoretical development. Most scholars of multiculturalism, Gay finds, agree that multicultural education includes both a philosophical viewpoint and criteria for making decisions that best serve the educational needs of culturally diverse student populations.[4]

The term *multicultural* originally referred to the cultures of particular racial or ethnic groups, and some scholars continue to refer to multicultural education as only or chiefly for those considered marginal to the dominant culture. On the other hand, some scholars extend the definition of multicultural education to include differences of gender, region, social class, sexual orientation, and handicapping or other exceptional conditions.[5]

---

3. Carl A. Grant, *Research and Multicultural Education: From the Margins to the Mainstream* (Washington, D.C.: Falmer, 1992), p. 8.

4. Geneva Gay, "Curriculum Theory and Multicultural Education," in *Handbook of Research on Multicultural Education,* ed. James A. Banks and Cherry A. McGee Banks (New York: Macmillan, 1995), p. 28.

5. See Christine E. Sleeter and Carl A. Grant, *Making Choices for Multicultural Education: Five Approaches to Race, Class, and Gender* (New York: Merrill, 1993), pp. 41–61, 167–84.

In this volume *multicultural* and *multiethnic* are used interchangeably to refer to all races and ethnic origins, not simply minority populations. Extending *multicultural* to include gender, class, and other differences creates a definition so broad as to be beyond the scope of this volume. Nevertheless, since issues of class and gender cut across all racial and ethnic lines, and often interrelate with cultural factors, discussions in some chapters embrace these issues as well.

Culture

The term *culture*, emerging from anthropological studies, refers less to a group's distinctive artifacts, food, clothing, and customs and more to its distinctive values and ways of viewing reality. When residents of East Harlem or Chinatown or any of the thousands of ethnic enclaves across North America leave their neighborhoods of homes, markets, and places of worship to go to work or school, they may leave the external distinctives of their culture, but they carry with them the experiences, norms, and perspectives of that culture. While we appear to pay homage to many cultures by celebrating their food or music or national costumes, clashes may nevertheless occur in the less obvious domain of attitude and cognitive style.

Multicultural Religious Education

Educational historian Lawrence Cremin maintains that education is not simply a matter of classrooms and schools, but is a much broader social activity. If we accept Cremin's definition that education is the "deliberate, systematic, and sustained effort to transmit, evoke, or acquire knowledge, attitudes, values, skills or sensibilities,"[6] and if we define the term *religious education* as education for knowing, valuing, and living one's religion, then *multicultural religious education* becomes the effort to develop multicultural knowledge, attitudes, values, and skills in the process of learning a lived Christian faith. While this book specifically addresses Christian religious education, it is hoped that religious educators of all other faiths will find many principles applicable to their own efforts to promote a multicultural religious education.

GUIDING PRINCIPLE

The guiding principle in this discussion of multicultural religious education is to avoid reflecting a particular political ideology or a relativistic approach

---

6. Lawrence A. Cremin, *American Education: The Metropolitan Experience, 1876–1980* (New York: Harper and Row, 1988), p. x.

to religion. While it speaks from a strongly Christian perspective, it avoids identifying with any specific political or ideological agenda. The book promotes the view that "religious education which is authentically Christian should be as wide as the arms of Christ and embrace with equal warmth persons of every ethnic and cultural group."[7] The contributors believe that God's revelation in Christ is so immeasurably rich that no one Christian religion in any of its cultural expressions totally contains it. Instead, Christians from various cultures, learning from each other, can help bring Christian faith to a fullness that its immersion in a particular culture is unable to achieve.

OVERVIEW

Each section and chapter of the book seeks to support and expand the concept of multiculturalism in its educational and religious context. Part 1 addresses the principles and goals of the movement, its theoretical basis in the social sciences and in the biblical-theological foundations. Part 2 presents chapters by religious educators in four major North American cultural groups—African–American, Asian–Pacific American, Hispanic, and Native American. Part 3 addresses the implications of multiculturalism for instruction and curriculum in religious education, and part 4 offers a concluding vision for a comprehensive, multicultural approach.

The chapter authors make up an ethnically diverse group of women and men, Protestant and Catholic, who represent a broad range of theological perspectives and geographical regions. Readers are encouraged to read or at least peruse the entire volume rather than focus on specific chapters. As in a truly intercultural conversation, the contributors address important issues from their own perspective, each speaking in a somewhat different voice. The value of the conversation lies in hearing all the voices.

Chapter 1 explores the historical and philosophical streams that have fed into the multicultural education movement, identifying major principles and proponents. Many of the concepts introduced in the chapter are picked up and elucidated later in the book. Sociologists Carol Jenkins and Dale Kratt in chapter 2 discuss the socialization of voluntary and involuntary immigrant groups in our society—an illuminating analysis for anyone wanting to understand the distinctly different responses of various cultural groups to the dominant culture. In chapter 3 Donald Ratcliff mines the field of psychology for constructs that are helpful to the multicultural religious educator. He draws from relevant research to help the reader interpret emerging theories concerning learning style, culture, and individual differences.

---

7. The quote was made by James Michael Lee in a personal communication.

Concluding part 1, Randolph Crump Miller, in the first part of chapter 4, presents the historical Jesus as the center and source of a Christology for multicultural religious education. Summarizing many twentieth-century studies of Jesus, Miller states that "a return to the historical Jesus assists us greatly" in our effort to free the teaching of the gospel from cultural baggage. He then considers five current theologies in relation to the resources they provide for establishing a basis for unity and tolerance in multicultural dialogue.

Part 2 provides a window on the experiences of ethnic and multiethnic churches, as well as on the extraordinary activity of religious education in many of these churches and the diocesan and denominational structures that support them. Change, struggle, creativity, and faithfulness mark the work of religious education in these churches. In chapter 5 Harold Dean Trulear sees religious education as central to African-American life, involving the dimensions of identity formation, relationship to God and humanity, and social context. Trulear calls black, middle-class churches to eschew an "uncritical integration into prevailing American values" by restoring through religious education the "holistic vision for ministry" of African-American tradition.

In chapter 6 Greer Anne Wenh-In Ng brings her many years of research and leadership in religious education to bear on the experience of Pacific-Asian North American churches in their search for and contributions to effective religious education on the continent. Surveying the history and the cultural contexts of North America's pluralistic Asian immigration, Ng discusses important issues in their religious life and development. The final section explores resources and current programs for Asian-Pacific and other religious-education practice and also offers a compelling look at the future for multicultural religious education.

Hispanic religious education has surmounted social, cultural, and language barriers to grow and flourish in North America. In chapter 7 Esperanza Ginoris details the struggle and perseverance of Hispanic Christians striving to overcome obstacles, bring their own gifts and values to Christian spiritual renewal, and "celebrate their faith at a personal and communitarian level."

In chapter 8 Jace Weaver jolts our thinking out of stereotypical assumptions into recognition of what a Native American religious education can contribute to the Christian understanding of the Creator and the created order. Rejecting what he calls the "reductionist paradigm" of the past, Weaver reflects on a Native conceptualization of "a whole picture of experience" that, to this reader at least, resonates better with the Hebraic worldview than with the Cartesian model Western Christianity has accommodated. For Weaver, as for other writers in this section, the issue becomes "how to integrate alternative models of discourse" into religious education. Mainstream, dominant-culture Christians surely cannot fail to hear the prophetic voice speaking to the larger church from the pain and triumph North America's ethnic churches have experienced.

Part 3 brings multicultural issues into the instructional process. In chapter 9 Deborah Bainer and Jeffrey Peck examine recent research on cognitive style and on the impact that community forces have on learning within cultural groups. The authors espouse a "culturally responsible pedagogy" that applies meaningfully in the religious education context.

Concluding part 3, Laura Lewis, Ronald Cram, and James Michael Lee bring their expertise in religious-education curriculum to the multicultural arena. Defining curriculum as "the interplay of 'texts' that intentionally communicate attitudes, values, and behaviors," Lewis and Cram reflect on the multiple perspectives of a particular biblical example. James Michael Lee articulates a structure for defining and building a multicultural religious-education curriculum. Together the authors explore historical antecedents in religious and multicultural education, and they present a basis for religious educators of all ethnic (including European-American) varieties to begin the disciplined task of forming a curriculum that is truly multicultural.

Virgilio Elizondo closes the volume fittingly with a personal statement from a pioneer in the work of multicultural religious education. Elizondo's visionary essay calls for a grace-filled religious education to guide Christians through the disciplines of repentance and confession to unity and true celebration. Such a process offers the hope of a transformed church that has gone "beyond the sacrilized divisions of the past" to become "one very diverse and beautiful human family."

Having come to the end of the volume, we still have not brought closure to all the questions. Will Christians respond to the multicultural challenge? Will a focus on ethnicity keep us segregated in our own churches at the expense of Christian unity? Should multicultural parishes and congregations, with their imaging of unity in diversity, be advanced as the ideal toward which all should move? If not, what of the future for ethnic churches? Will second- and third-generation children of the new immigration continue to prefer worship with their elders or will they seek the mainstream? Much remains to be discovered.

The work of editing this book has been for me both a personal multicultural experience and a journey toward hope. In conversation and correspondence with religious educators of many cultures and Christian traditions, I have felt the energy and commitment of each one to a shared purpose: to make evident through all our diverse and distinct particularities our solidarity in faith. That was, after all, our Savior's criterion for authentic discipleship: "By this everyone will know you are my disciples, if you have love for one another."[8]

---

8. John 13:35

Thanks are always in order at the end of a journey. Mine go to James Michael Lee, who encouraged me to take on and (many times) to persist in and perfect this project; to Nancy Vickers at Religious Education Press, always a very present help in trouble; to Alliance Theological Seminary, which provided both a wonderfully multicultural milieu in which to work and an invaluable sabbatical semester; to the patient and understanding staff of the Korean American Presbyterian Church where I served, worshiped, and learned during much of this time, and to my husband, Fort H. Wilkerson, whose loving attention to and support of my every endeavor has given new meaning to that gracious word *partner*.

Barbara Wilkerson
Nanuet, New York

PART I

FOUNDATIONS OF
MULTICULTURAL
RELIGIOUS EDUCATION

1

GOALS OF MULTICULTURAL
RELIGIOUS EDUCATION

Barbara Wilkerson

Beginning in the mid-1960s, migration from one country to another began to accelerate around the world. Multiculturalism became a global phenomenon. On the North American continent, as the impact of large numbers of immigrants began to be felt, the character of life in the United States took the form of an identity crisis. Americans struggled for continuity between the past and the future. They had long pictured their country as a melting pot, a nation of immigrants melted down and poured into a common mold. Now the pot and the mold were often discredited, exposed by contemporary historians as caricatures that never reflected reality for many citizens.[1] Americans suddenly seemed unsure about what they were; they were sure only that they were changing.

After the 1990 census revealed the dramatic increase in people of color in the United States, the term *multiculturalism* quickly achieved the status of a buzzword. The corporate world adjusted rapidly to changes in the ethnic profile of the American population. In response to predictions that by the year 2000 two-thirds of the workforce would be people other than white males, managers received crash courses to promote cross-cultural understanding in the workplace. By 1991 three-quarters of the companies surveyed by a consulting firm had established diversity training programs.[2]

---

1. Lawrence Cremin, *American Education: The Metropolitan Experience, 1876–1980* (New York: Harper & Row, 1988), pp. 144–45.
2. Kathleen Murray, "The Unfortunate Side Effects of 'Diversity Training,'" *New York Times*, 1 August 1993, p. 5F.

A major cosmetics firm developed a new spectrum of 115 shades and hues of makeup "from palest ivory to deepest ebony." The spokesman for Benetton North America claimed, "We *own* multiculturalism."[3]

Meanwhile the debate over multicultural curriculum raged through academia, grabbing headlines in newspapers and attention from other media. As public schools and universities tried to adapt to a one-third increase in minority populations,[4] criticism, value clashes, and confrontation marked educational efforts to accommodate a sudden multiplicity of worldviews.[5]

Where is the church in this tidal wave of change? How have churches responded in their religious education programs to the implications of a major cultural shift in the nation's population? Or have they responded at all? How do biblical, theological, and religious categories inform Christians concerning their efforts to teach the gospel in a multicultural society? What about the deep bonds between ethnicity and faith? Can such bonds be overcome in the interests of a truly multicultural church? Should they be? Given the complexities of the situation, is there any hope that religious educators, a largely volunteer group, can take on this new challenge? Will the church—*should* the church—be able to say, "We own multiculturalism?"

This chapter reflects the writer's conviction that multicultural religious educational aims are theologically and religiously rooted, sociologically imperative, and educationally effective. All churches, not only those with ethnically diverse parishes, can and should train their leaders and modify their religious education programs to accommodate a multicultural society.

At the same time it is recognized that multicultural education, particularly in its religious context, is a new (if vigorous) movement. Attempts to define the theoretical and philosophical foundations of any current social phenomenon are risky at best, but particularly so for the development of an educational field that, by the admission of its proponents, has not excelled in explaining itself.[6] Nevertheless, multicultural religious education does have a history to be examined, goals to be considered, theoretical models and research for reflection. And, in the writings of some theorists, there are philosophical roots to be tapped. These are the tasks of this chapter.

---

3. Penelope Green, "World Hues," *New York Times Magazine*, 18 August 1991, p. 38.

4. "New Faces at School: How Changing Demographics Reshape American Education," *Report on Education Research*, Special Supplement, 13 November 1991, p. 1.

5. Christine E. Sleeter summarizes major criticisms of the left, which finds multicultural education too conservative, and of the right, which finds it too radical, in "An Analysis of the Critiques of Multicultural Education," in *Handbook of Research on Multicultural Education*, ed. James A. Banks and Cherry A. McGee Banks (New York: Macmillan, 1995), pp. 81–94.

6. Christine E. Sleeter and Carl A. Grant, "An Analysis of Multicultural Education in the United States," *Harvard Educational Review* 57 (November 1987): 436–37.

ORIGINS AND GOALS OF
MULTICULTURAL EDUCATION

Three historical streams fed into the movement now called multicultural education. Although one stream eventually drained off and dried up, it laid paths in writing and research that later were accessed by two more powerful streams.

In the earliest years of the twentieth century, educators gave increasing attention to the challenge of ethnic diversity. American public and parochial schools were absorbing large numbers of students of eastern and southern European ancestry whose parents had immigrated in the previous century.[7] At the same time, for the children of North America's oldest ethnic groups, conflicting philosophies concerning the education of black and Native American children locked most of them into schooling experiences that were both segregated and educationally inferior. The prevailing educational philosophy fit the melting pot metaphor popularized by Israel Zangwill in his 1908 stage play by the same name. Educational historian Ellwood Patterson Cubberley set forth the doctrine in 1909: "Our task is to break up these groups or settlements [of immigrants], to assimilate and amalgamate these people as part of our American race, and to implant in their children, as far as can be done, the Anglo-Saxon conception of righteousness, law and order, and popular government, and to awaken in them a reverence for our democratic institutions and for those things in our national life which we as a people hold to be of abiding worth."[8]

Cubberley seems to have missed entirely the irony that racially segregated schooling *prevented* African-American and Native American children from "assimilating" or "amalgamating," even if they had wanted to. These children were made to feel permanently marginalized by an educational system that assumed the superiority of whiteness. Martin Marty cites Ruth Miller Elson's study of nineteenth-century textbooks, *Guardians of Tradition*, as indicating how schoolbooks "instinctively graded racial and ethnic groups, using as a measure 'the white race, the normal race,' as one book put it."[9] Churches bought into these assumptions, as demonstrated in the work of church historian Robert Baird. Writing in 1843, Baird ranked ethnic groups in America *downward* from Anglo-Saxon, maintaining that "our national

---

7. Lawrence A. Cremin documents this period in "Patterns of Diversity," chap. 3 in *American Education: The Metropolitan Experience, 1875–1980* (New York: Harper & Row, 1988), pp. 115–50.

8. Ellwood P. Cubberley, *Changing Conceptions of Education* (Boston: Houghton Mifflin, 1909), pp. 15–16, quoted in *Multiethnic Education: Theory and Practice*, by James A. Banks, 2d ed. (Boston: Allyn & Bacon, 1988), p. 4.

9. Martin Marty, "History, Education, and Policy: A Review," *Religious Education* 82 (summer 1987): 504.

character is that of the Anglo-Saxon race." Says Marty, "The themes of [white, Anglo-Saxon Protestant] ethnicity and superiority which had been explicit in the nineteenth century became implicit and taken for granted in the twentieth."[10] In 1911 a forty-one volume report of the congressionally appointed Dillingham Commission was published, purporting to document the "inferiority" of the "new" immigration. According to Lawrence Cremin, the report influenced Congress to reduce immigration drastically in succeeding years. Cremin describes the surge of public school "Americanization" programs emerging in the wake of the Dillingham Report. These programs involved a complex process of socialization far exceeding ordinary instruction in English and civics. It included training in personal cleanliness, middle-class values, industrial-style discipline, and in many cases "the inculcation of disdain for the immigrant heritage."[11]

Looking back on this period, James Banks points out that voices from inside and outside ethnic communities were calling for change and envisioning American democracy as a mosaic that allowed each group to contribute its unique strengths to the whole. But American educational leaders generally ignored these voices.[12] In the second decade of the twentieth century, Horace Kallen defended a new concept for American democracy, coining the term *cultural pluralism*. Except for his fellow intellectuals, however, few people showed interest in Kallen's vision. The nationalistic movement gained strength in wartime and impelled the Immigration Acts of 1917 and 1924, effectively halting immigration to the United States of all but northern and western Europeans.[13]

Between World War I and II, and partly in response to racial conflicts in America, a movement arose known as intergroup or intercultural education. This movement devised educational principles and practices aimed at reducing racial prejudice and misunderstanding. Proponents of the intergroup movement assumed that an informed citizenry, knowledgeable about the backgrounds of various American culture groups, would live in greater harmony. Religious as well as public educators promoted these goals and propelled the intergroup education movement into the 1950s. According to James Banks, this movement became the first stream of education for diversity. But it failed to become institutionalized, partly because it was seen as important mainly for schools experiencing open conflict, and partly because the movement never developed "a well articulated

---

10. Idem, "Ethnicity: The Skeleton of Religion in America," in *The Immigrant Religious Experience*, American Immigration and Ethnicity Series, vol. 19 (New York: Garland, 1991), p. 240.

11. Cremin, "Patterns of Diversity," 1988, p. 237.

12. Banks, *Multiethnic Education*, p. 5.

13. E. Allen Richardson, *Strangers in This Land: Pluralism and the Response to Diversity in the United States* (New York: Pilgrim, 1988), pp. 114–15.

and coherent philosophical position" vis-à-vis American educational and political values.[14]

In spite of the efforts of interculturalists, the goal of assimilation prevailed through most of the twentieth century and eventually worked well for white immigrant groups, for example Irish, Italian, and Polish, who, while suffering discrimination initally, were able in the second and third generations to climb the social and economic ladders. Some of these children of immigrants lost their ethnic identity along the way, while others maintained it alongside their mainstream identity. But persons of color—African Americans, Asian Americans, Native Americans—did not have the same assimilationist options. Their ethnic identity, whether they wished to embrace it or not, was stamped on their physical appearance and tended to marginalize them from the dominant culture.

Following after the intergroup education movement, the second stream to influence multicultural education was the civil rights movement of the 1960s. This struggle effected revolutionary changes in the institutionalized racial segregation that had characterized every level of American life. African Americans overturned discriminatory practices, not only in education but also in housing, travel, and employment. Subsequently, other ethnic groups also fought successfully against many forms of discrimination. The black civil rights movement legitimized ethnicity, and as other victimized groups searched for their own ethnic roots, they began to demand more civil and human rights.[15]

The third stream began with the Immigration Reform Act, which was enacted in 1965 and became effective in 1968. In the decade that followed, the number of immigrants entering the United States increased almost 80 percent over the number entering between 1951 and 1960. Not only the number but the ethnicity of immigrants changed. Whereas Europeans had accounted for almost 60 percent of immigrants during the 1950s, they made up only 18 percent of immigrants between 1971 and 1980.[16] The number of Asians and Latin Americans dramatically increased. Political upheavals in some countries propelled immigration from Cuba, Vietnam, Cambodia, and Laos. Mexican and Latin American immigration also grew. Between 1981 and 1989 about 85 percent of immigrants to the United States came from Asia (47 percent) and Latin America (38 percent).[17] A declining birthrate among white Americans combined

---

14. Banks, *Multiethnic Education*, p. 9. See also William E. Vickery and Stewart G. Cole, *Intercultural Education in American Schools* (New York: Harper, 1943).

15. Banks, *Multiethnic Education*, p. 11.

16. Ibid.

17. James A. Banks, "National Council on Social Studies Curriculum Guidelines for Multicultural Education," *Social Education*, September 1992, p. 275. The trends in immigration continued into the 1990s. A special issue of *Time* reported that while

with the new immigration to drastically alter the demographic picture of the United States and focus attention on the demands of diversity. Encouraged by funding provided by the 1968 Bilingual Education Act,[18] public school districts with large immigrant populations initiated bilingual programs and sought ways to promote learning for children from new cultural groups.[19] Many churches and community agencies became involved in sponsoring families of refugees, and worked to help them settle into their new environment.

The Multicultural Education Movement

By the 1970s a growing body of professional literature was emerging on multicultural educational issues, sometimes called "multiethnic education," "multiracial education, "education for equity," or "education for cultural pluralism."[20] Writing in 1976, anthropologist Margaret Gibson described multicultural education as "that process whereby a person develops competencies in multiple systems of standards for perceiving, evaluating, behaving, and doing." She identified the following core ideas:

1. Culture and ethnic group are not equated; instead, diversity within an ethnic group is recognized.
2. Education includes out-of-school learning.
3. Ethnic isolation is antithetical to education, since the development of competencies in a new culture requires intensive interaction with people who are already competent.
4. Individuals need not reject their cultural identity to function in a different cultural milieu.
5. Divisive dichotomies between cultures are avoided, bringing about an increased awareness of multiculturalism as "the normal human experience."[21]

---

in 1940 70 percent of immigrants came from Europe, in 1992 15 percent came from Europe, 37 percent from Asia, and 44 percent from Latin America and the Caribbean. *Time*, (Special Issue, Fall 1993), p. 14.

18. M. Hussein Fereshteh, "Multicultural Education in the United States Historical Review," *MultiCultural Review* 4 (June 1995): 42.

19. Christine E. Sleeter and Carl A. Grant, *Making Choices for Multicultural Education: Five Approaches to Race, Class, and Gender* (New York: Merrill, 1993), p. 56.

20. Although the focus of this volume is on the multicultural education movement in the United States, it is important to note that multicultural education has had a significant history in Canada, Great Britain, and Australia, and much scholarly research conducted in those countries has informed the movement in the United States. For a comparison of the issues in British and American understandings of multicultural education, see *Cultural Diversity and the Schools: Volume I, Education for Cultural Diversity Convergence and Divergence*, ed. James Lynch, Celia Modgil, and Sohan Modgil (London: Falmer, 1992), pp. 83–123.

21. Summarized from Christine I. Bennett, *Comprehensive Multicultural Education: Theory and Practice* (Boston: Allyn & Bacon, 1986), pp. 53–54.

In 1987 Christine Sleeter and Carl Grant reviewed the professional literature on multicultural education. Describing multicultural education as a reform movement aimed at changing the content and processes within schools (compare Gibson's description), Sleeter and Grant identified five distinct approaches to multicultural education discernible in the literature they reviewed. The authors reviewed a selection of eighty-nine articles and thirty-eight books published in the 1970s and 1980s, analyzing them according to the following typologies: teaching the culturally different, the human-relations approach, single-group studies, multicultural education, and lastly, education that is multicultural and social reconstructionist.

According to Sleeter and Grant, "teaching the culturally different" is an assimilationist approach aimed at helping minority students develop competence in "the public culture of the dominant group" and at helping educators teach "culturally different" students. This approach assumes that multicultural education is for students of color only and that its main purpose is to equip them to compete in the dominant culture.

The "human-relations" approach seeks to promote communication and good human relations among students of different backgrounds. Helping students feel good about themselves is also a primary goal. Sleeter and Grant find this approach long on practical ideas for teachers, but short on well-grounded theory and long-term goals. The review critiques the lack of attention to issues of social stratification: "Advocates may hope that eventually better communication will lead, for example, to cooperation among Blacks and Whites to reduce the incidence of poverty among Blacks." But they found that issues such as poverty, institutional discrimination, and powerlessness are seldom addressed in the human-relations literature.[22] Educational books and articles tend to apply the human-relations approach rather than give a theoretical base for it. This author notes that many of the "idea" books suggesting multicultural activities for children's classes seem to reflect the human-relations approach.

The next category described in the review, called "single-group studies," tends to focus on the cultural experience of a single ethnic group. Special attention is given to curriculum and instruction, with stress on the contributions and experiences of the ethnic group. Sleeter and Grant criticize this approach in two respects: it tends to avoid discussion of oppression experienced by the group, and it ignores social stratification within the group. The result may be that teachers and learners are not sensitized to the need for social change

The title "multicultural education" was applied to the fourth approach, which was the one most widely represented in the professional literature. Proponents of the multicultural-education approach shared a significant core of common goals. Diane Gollnick's summary of the five major goals of

---

22. Sleeter and Grant, "An Analysis of Multicultural Education," pp. 421–23, 427.

this approach includes (1) promotion of the strength and value of cultural diversity, (2) respect for human rights and cultural diversity, (3) alternative life choices, (4) social justice and equal opportunity for all, and (5) equitable distribution of power among all ethnic groups.[23]

The literature that advocates the multicultural-education approach focuses mainly on race and ethnicity, the cultures of American racial groups, and, in some cases, culture as an anthropological concept. Proponents disagree on whether to expand the meaning of *multicultural* to include differences other than race and ethnicity. The multicultural-education approach seems to have the strongest theoretical base, and several well-developed models are offered to help teachers implement multicultural goals. Sleeter and Grant also find multicultural education the most popular of the five approaches, but one that has not dealt seriously with pedagogy or with systemwide educational practices that need changing. "By failing to address pedagogy, multicultural education can remain trapped in those instructional patterns that predominate in our schools." The two authors further maintain that a lack of reports showing examples of the approach in operation indicates that it has yet to be widely applied.[24]

Finally, Sleeter and Grant describe a more recent approach identified as "education that is multicultural and social reconstructionist." This is the approach that Sleeter and Grant themselves espouse. It extends the term *multicultural education* to mean "education that prepares young people to take social action against social structural inequality." Goals of this approach, sometimes called by its proponents "transformational education" or "emancipatory education," include changing teaching practices so that classrooms become more democratic and students "learn to use power for collective betterment, rather than mainly learning obedience." Some of the literature emanating from the social-reconstructionist approach criticizes what its proponents see as an unhelpful emphasis on culture in the other approaches. One writer is quoted as warning that the social issues of racism, sexism, and inequality are frequently overlooked or forgotten when culture is overemphasized. The strength of this approach is its aim of "reducing racism and building a more just society." A weakness is a lack of material on ways to achieve its goals for education. Sleeter and Grant also observed that their literature review led them to the disturbing conclusion that there was a general paucity of empirical studies on multicultural education. They recommended scholarly research that goes beyond advocacy and discussion of issues.[25]

In the book that resulted from their initial research, Sleeter and Grant described the philosophical orientation of education that is multicultural and social reconstructionist as based in Theodore Brameld's call in the

23. Ibid., p. 429.
24. Ibid., p. 434.
25. Ibid., pp. 435–38.

mid-1950s for an educational reconstructionism that could critique modern culture. Attention to issues of social conflict and social justice also emerge from the writings of Paulo Freire, Henry Giroux, and other critics of what are seen as institutionalized and oppressive social structures.[26]

Sleeter and Grant's five categories are widely used to analyze the many strands of multicultural education practiced in schools and evident in curriculum materials. Leonard and Patricia Davidman propose a "synthesis conception" that integrates elements from several approaches. They define multicultural education as a multifaceted, change-oriented strategy aimed at six interrelated goals: educational equity; empowerment of students and parents; cultural pluralism in society; intercultural, interethnic, and intergroup harmony in the learning environment; expanded knowledge of cultural and ethnic groups; and the development of learners, parents, and educators whose ideas and actions are guided by an informed and inquisitive multicultural perspective.[27]

Considering the breadth and scope of the goals presented so far, it is important to make clear that most advocates of multicultural education do not see it as a panacea for all educational ills. Motivating learners, increasing parent involvement, improving instructional practice, and making curriculum more relevant are issues that will continue to pose challenges to public, private, and religious education programs. Nevertheless, pursuing the goals of multicultural education can, as Sonia Nieto maintains, lead to more productive learning environments, more varied instructional strategies, and a greater awareness of the role culture and language play in the learning process.[28] Such outcomes would represent significant changes.

Common threads in the various approaches described above are the understanding that diversity is enriching rather than threatening, and a goal of creating mutual and equitable relations among all groups in society. Viewed this way, the goals of multicultural education seem consistent with the aims of the church as a redemptive, reconciling community.

The Church and Multicultural Goals
Religious educator and theologian Marina Herrera points out that the failure (according to Acts 15) of the earliest apostolic community to grasp the

---

26. Sleeter and Grant, *Making Choices*, pp. 209, 210.

27. Leonard Davidman with Patricia T. Davidman, *Teaching with a Multicultural Perspective: A Practical Guide* (New York: Longman, 1994), p. 2. A comprehensive resource available for use with this book is the award-winning video *Multicultural Education* featuring James Banks and Carlos Cortés, and an accompanying facilitator's guide. Order from the Association of Supervisors and Curriculum Developers, Alexandria, Va., 1-800-933-ASCD.

28. Sonia Nieto, *Affirming Diversity: The Sociopolitical Context of Multicultural Education* (New York: Longman, 1992), p. 207.

universal dimension of the salvation message led to an identity crisis in
the early church. Repeated failures of this kind have plagued the work of
Christian missions since the first century.[29]

Yet an examination of the New Testament documents shows how clearly
the universal dimension of salvation was portrayed. If there had been
any doubt in the minds of Jesus' twelve disciples that the gospel was a
transcultural message, his final command to "Go . . . make disciples of all
nations" (Mt 28:19–20) should have made it clear. The first chapter of Acts
records Jesus' further instructions that his disciples be witnesses beyond
their country's borders to the ends of the earth. Peter (Acts 10), James
(Acts 15), and Paul (Gal 3) learned that there was to be no favored nation or
people, no preferred class or cultural style, no "Jew nor Greek, bond nor free,
male nor female" (Gal 3:28). All were one in Christ Jesus. The "oneness"
did not mean "sameness." Wesley Woo observes that the meaning of "one
in Christ" is not that Christians deny their particularities, but rather that
particularities do not block anyone from full participation in God's reign.[30]

The New Testament offers powerful and positive images of human
diversity. At Pentecost the Holy Spirit empowered different kinds of human beings—men, women, old, young—to proclaim the message in many
tongues to those "from every nation under heaven." The presence of the Holy
Spirit united a diverse population, but the Spirit recognized and sustained
their diversity by communicating in their own tongues (Acts 2:5–11). The
image of the body of Christ is constantly brought to bear on the church's consciousness through passages in the apostle Paul's letters (1 Cor 12; Eph 4).
Members of the one body are distinct, having different characteristics, lo-
calities, nationalities, gifts. What is desired is that there be "many members,
yet one body" (1 Cor 12:12). The unity of the body is fulfilled in John's
revelation of the heavenly assembly, where the national origins of believers
seem to be distinct: the "great multitude" is "from every nation, from all
tribes and peoples and languages" (Rev 7:9). From these biblical images
and those developed more fully by Randolph Crump Miller (chap. 4), it is
evident that if any institution on earth could claim to be multicultural, called
to value the diversity God has created among groups and individuals, the
church can make that claim. Whether the church's educational philosophy
and practice in recent times have reflected that claim is another question.

Religious educators in many Christian traditions call the church to recognize its cultural pluralism. Affirming that the message of the gospel does
not change, Marina Herrera maintains nevertheless that it cannot be fully

---

29. Marina Herrera, "Theoretical Foundations of Multicultural Catechesis," in *Faith
and Culture: A Multicultural Catechetical Resource* (Washington, D.C.: Dept. of Education, United States Catholic Conference, 1987), p. 11.

30. Wesley S. Woo, "Theological Dimensions," in *Asian Pacific American Youth
Ministry*, ed. Donald Ng (Valley Forge, Pa.: Judson, 1988), p. 17.

expressed or understood in any one cultural form, but requires a multicultural community to convey its universal message.[31] Church history supports Herrera's contention, recording the regularity with which messengers of the gospel conflated their message with the patterns and norms of their own cultures, imposing them on converts as though Christ and their own culture were inseparable. Thus in the sixteenth century the Spanish conquered and colonized the peoples of Latin America even as they evangelized them, and in the nineteenth century British and American missionaries planted Western social, economic, and educational institutions in China and Korea along with churches. Through much of the twentieth century, American churches of the cultural mainstream, both Protestant and Catholic, continued on a local scale the assumptions of their own cultural primacy. Claiming to be color-blind, many churches welcomed members of other groups, but expected them to worship and learn exclusively in the mainstream way. Herrera reminds religious educators that the gospel "challenges the attitudes of the mainstream cultures towards other expressions of the Gospel."[32]

In the latter half of the twentieth century the growing problems of race in American cities, the dynamic of the civil rights movement, and the influence of the new immigration—the same forces that fed into the multicultural education movement—impelled religious educators to critique the churches' history regarding cultural dominance. In major American cities many churches had already led the way. Responding to pressing social needs, urban churches created new educational and community structures. They forged new partnerships as immigrant groups revitalized declining local churches and as Hispanic, West Indian, Korean, and Vietnamese congregations shared facilities. Ethnic churches called for bilingual curriculum and denominational programs that recognized their cultural style. In these churches, as often in the history of religious education, practice had preceded theory.[33]

In 1987 a slim but significant volume challenged what editor Charles Foster called "the myth of homogeneity" in church education. *Ethnicity in the Education of the Church* contrasted the cultural diversity of American churches with the monocultural and monolingual nature of published curriculum materials and programs for religious education. In his introductory chapter Foster states bluntly that in the United States cultural assumptions

---

31. Herrera, "Theoretical Foundations," p. 11.
32. Ibid., p. 12.
33. Authors who discuss the growth of new urban churches include David Claerbaut, *Urban Ministry* (Grand Rapids, Mich.: Zondervan, 1983), pp. 31–47; Joseph P. Fitzpatrick, *One Church, Many Cultures: The Challenge of Diversity* (Kansas City, Mo.: Sheed & Ward, 1987); and Robert E. Jones, "Learning to Face Diversity in Urban Churches," in *Urban Church Education*, ed. Donald B. Rogers (Birmingham, Ala.: Religious Education Press, 1989), pp. 84–101.

associated with northern Europe and England have dominated not only
the general society but also the educational institutions of the church. "All
cultural and ethnic communities that do not share this common heritage,"
Foster said, "have had to define themselves in relation to it."[34]

In 1992 David Ng reviewed the progress of multicultural religious
education and found great impetus for multiculturalism at work in religious
communities. Besides the pressure of social realities and the growing
awareness of our diverse contexts, Ng observed a new awareness that the
time for multiculturalism had come, along with a consciousness of a new
way to interpret tradition, texts, and contexts. Finding in familiar Bible
passages "a multicultural vision," Ng cited the story of the Tower of Babel
as an example of a passage traditionally taught as providing negative lessons
on usurping God's prerogatives, but coming to be seen as showing the folly
of expecting any one language or culture to dominate in the varied world
of peoples that God created. The lesson is: "What God has put asunder let
no one try to melt into one pot or tower or domicile."[35]

Ng's analysis then specifies three kinds of churches that must be considered in any discussion of multicultural religious education. These general
categories are also reflected in the writings of others concerned with multiculturalism in Christian communities.

Cultural Minority Churches: Ng defines the tasks for multicultural
education in two types of churches—racial, or ethnic "minority," churches
and white, or "majority," churches. The former need to recognize the identity
focus of minority people in a majority culture and assist their members
to identify themselves as full human beings—people with experiences,
histories, and aspirations, with their own validity and integrity. Religious
education in such settings must identify study themes that are especially
relevant to that ethnic group. Drawing upon Paulo Freire, Ng contends that
"banking methods of education," which impose a hierarchy of teacher over
learner, need to be replaced with participatory strategies to which learners
contribute their knowledge and experience. Finally, Ng insists on a strategy
of leadership development for ethnic churches. Asserting that developing
leaders is more valuable than developing curricula, he calls for leaders
equipped both to communicate with their own people and to develop their
own local curricula.[36]

Cultural Majority Churches: Majority parishes or congregations, on
the other hand, need to learn cultural awareness, including awareness of
what Ng identifies as their own "invisible, weightless, knapsacks of cultural
imperialism" that must be unpacked. These churches need to affirm each

---

34. Charles R. Foster, ed., *Ethnicity in the Education of the Church* (Nashville:
Scarritt, 1987), p. 4.

35. David Ng, "Impelled toward Multicultural Religious Education," *Religious Education* 87 (spring 1992): 193–94.

36. Ibid., pp. 196–98.

person's cultural heritage and teach attitudes of respecting and appreciating other cultures. Ng stresses that such affirmation includes participating in the cultures of others as a way of respecting their values.

Multicultural Churches: Ng acknowledges the existence of multicultural churches, that is, churches where large percentages of different ethnic groups are present and active in the congregation. These churches can experience community in new ways as "unity in diversity" transforms relationships and understandings. "To be multicultural," Ng holds, "is to take a giant step toward fulfilling community."[37]

Ng's analysis raises again the questions framed in the introduction to this volume: Is a multicultural church the ideal church? Can majority-culture and minority-culture churches be valid forms of Christian community in American society? The answers are complex. While multicultural churches may, as Ng says, be increasing in number, they remain the exception. Robert Jones describes the journey of one urban church that set out to become multiracial and multicultural. As white members fled the increasingly black neighborhood, a majority of the congregation (not including the pastor and elders, who wanted to move the church) deliberately set out to reflect the new ethnic makeup of the community. They determined "to seek, to have, and to maintain an ongoing integrated leadership—black, white, male and female at all levels of the congregation."[38] Jones describes the trials of the journey into multiculturalism after the church's decision in 1977. Finding pastoral leadership for the congregation was not easy. Both black and white ministers preferred to devote their energies to stable, monocultural churches that seemed to offer more economic and vocational security. Conflicts within the congregation emerged, but members discovered that when they faced conflicts rather than avoiding them, they were able to craft change and promote growth. Nevertheless, white members became anxious as black membership climbed to 50 percent, reflecting the neighborhood population. The enthusiasm of older members, black and white, declined. In spite of these discouraging experiences the church continued to progress, stressing four essentials—training for leadership, a diverse style and form of worship, religious education aimed at promoting Christian community beyond Sunday-morning settings, and outreach through projects that create bonds between people of diverse backgrounds. In 1987 the congregation's cultural makeup was approximately 50 percent black, 47 percent white, 3 percent Asian, and 1 percent Hispanic. Jones summarizes the unique ministry of the multicultural church as "teaching what we are," helping each different group to retain its identity. "Such a church has a profoundly relevant lesson to teach to our world, for congregations that are mixed racially and culturally

---

37. Ibid., p. 201.
38. Robert E. Jones, "Learning to Face Diversity in Urban Churches," in *Urban Church Education*, ed. Donald Rogers (Birmingham, Ala.: Religious Education Press, 1989), p. 94.

proclaim dramatically Paul's words to the Corinthians: 'Therefore if anyone
is in Christ he [or she] is a new creation; the old has passed away. Behold,
the new has come.' (2 Cor 5:17) Racially and culturally mixed churches
teach by their life that reconciliation with one another can follow from
reconciliation with God."[39]

In the years ahead the first two types of churches identified by Ng—
ethnic or minority churches—will probably continue to outnumber multicultural churches. This is not surprising. When the New Testament speaks
of discipling "the nations" (Mt 28:19; Lk 24:47) and of those from "every
nation" gathered before the heavenly throne (Rev 7:9), the Greek term used
is *ethnos*, from which we draw the words *ethnic* and *ethnicity*, meaning
the collective identity of a people.[40] This identity, bonded to religious
faith, mitigates against the probability of inclusive, ethnically diverse religious communities, especially where large numbers of first-generation
immigrants seek to worship in their own language. Worshiping outside that
warm, supportive social climate may prove stressful, even when people are
motivated to try. Distinctive ways of worshiping, communicating, marrying,
burying, eating, working, and relaxing become familiar through repeated
experiences at home and in the ethnic church. As many authorities attest,
religious faith is commonly transmitted from adults to young people through
intimate family and other primary relationships.[41] The nurturing provided
by home and church through common language and lifestyle tends to bond
together family, faith, and culture.

The bonding of faith and ethnicity is not a recent phenomenon. Religion among American immigrant groups has always reinforced ethnicity,
and vice versa. In New York City neighborhoods of the nineteenth century, German Catholic and Irish Catholic children walked by each other's
churches on the way to their separate parochial schools. Commenting on this
phenomenon, church historian Jay Dolan states that religion and ethnicity
were bonded together in the national parish, with one supported by the other.
"Before long the two were so inextricably joined together that the loss of
language was tantamount to the loss of faith."[42]

---

39. Ibid., p. 100.

40. Pointed out by Charles R. Foster in *Harper's Encyclopedia of Religious Education*, ed. Iris V. Cully and Kendig Brubaker Cully (San Francisco: Harper & Row,
1990), p. 227.

41. Among the many, secular and religious, that might be cited: Erik H. Erikson,
Childhood and Society, 2d ed. (New York: Norton, 1963), p. 251; V. Bailey Gillespie,
The Experience of Faith (Birmingham, Ala.: Religious Education Press, 1988) pp. 89–
109; Ernest White, "The Role of the Home in the Religious Development of Children,"
in *Review and Expositor* 53 (spring 1983): 231–43.

42. Jay P. Dolan, "The Immigrants and Their Gods: A New Perspective in American Religious History," in *The Immigrant Religious Experience*, by George Pozzetta,
American Immigration and Ethnicity, vol. 19 (New York: Garland, 1991), p. 360.

This bonding was brought home to me when I taught a ten-day seminary course at an upstate church campground. The class was a multiethnic, international group of about a dozen male and female seminary students. Members drew close to one another as they shared cabins, classes, meals, work projects, and evening worship. But before the ten days were up, a couple of class members drove the long miles back to the city for an overnight stay in their own ethnic church. Upon returning, one of the students explained, "I feel better now. I just had to speak my own language and eat our own food."

Unless churches formulate deliberate goals to promote positive attitudes toward cultural diversity among the membership, improved attitudes are unlikely to happen spontaneously. Particular groups may find diversity easy to overlook as they focus on maintaining the faith of their own people. Churches of the dominant culture may tolerate diversity ("it's the American way") but not welcome diverse voices in their midst, fearing that new perspectives may erode the unity forged from common values, beliefs, and lifestyles.

Multicultural religious education actually prizes diversity, believing that it enhances the church's life and witness. Proponents hold that the voices of diversity have a prophetic ministry within the church. Justo Gonzalez, for example, points out that marginalized groups have an important role to play in the faithfulness of the body of Christ. Gonzalez finds biblical evidence that God uses those on the margins of society to speak to the center. God spoke to Pharaoh through the exile Moses, and spoke to the Roman Empire through a message that came out of "a despised corner of a distant province." Referring to the journal *Apuntes: Reflections from the Hispanic Margin,* Gonzalez expresses hope that insights "on and from the margin" will guide the larger church to discover forgotten dimensions of the biblical message.[43]

One study of value orientations in the United States found that Americans tend to hold to a core of values that include success, achievement, work and activity, efficiency, productivity, equality, freedom, individualism, democracy, materialism, progress, morality, and humanitarianism.[44] American church members, who may be assumed to hold these same values, might benefit from exposure to values primary to some other cultures, such as cooperation, community, harmony, and wholeness.

Another gift of diversity is the educational value of learning firsthand about other people and their cultural styles. There is strong empirical support

---

43. Justo L. Gonzalez, *VOCES: Voices from the Hispanic Church* (Nashville: Abingdon, 1992), p. 3.

44. Cora Bagley Marrett, Yukko Mizuno, and Gena Collins, "Schools and Opportunities for Multicultural Contact," in *Research and Multicultural Education*, ed. Carl A. Grant (London: Falmer, 1992), pp. 208–09.

for the contention that social contact with persons of other races reduces prejudice. Studies of racial prejudice done in America in the 1940s and 1950s repeatedly showed that contact between members of different races reduces prejudice. But the contact has to be reciprocal in nature. There can be no sense in which one group or individual is giver and the other is receiver. Those same studies showed that racial understanding is optimized when people have the same social status. This phenomenon, known as the equal status contact hypothesis, holds that reduced prejudice is more likely to occur as a result of contact between, for example, fellow soldiers or fellow employees, but less likely to occur between officer and soldier, boss and employee. Similarly, studies of friendship patterns in schools found that friendships formed most readily among students in the same academic track.[45]

Church settings offer many opportunities to promote interracial respect and friendship when the contacts are mutually beneficial. Marina Herrera underscores the need for improved multicultural communication, collaboration, and celebration in the church, calling for ethnic and mainstream groups to come into close contact "to exchange gifts and to build new patterns of relating and symbolizing our common faith experience."[46]

GOALS OF MULTICULTURAL RELIGIOUS EDUCATION

The literature reviewed above suggests several goals for a religious education that is authentically multicultural. These goals supplement and harmonize with more general goals of Christian religious education, such as the goal to "help persons be aware of God's self-disclosure and seeking love in Jesus Christ and to respond in faith and love."[47] Other goals for multicultural religious education may emerge as we proceed through this and remaining chapters. At this point goals for multicultural religious education include the following:

1. An understanding of the church on earth as a multiethnic, multilingual body
2. Positive attitudes toward diversity as enriching and enabling of Christian unity rather than threatening

---

45. Gloria Ladson-Billings, "The Multicultural Mission: Unity and Diversity," *Social Education* 56:5 (1992): 311.

46. Herrera, "Theoretical Foundations," p. 9.

47. This well-known statement and other goals of religious education are discussed by D. Campbell Wyckoff in *Harper's Encyclopedia of Religious Education*, ed. Cully and Cully, pp. 268–71.

3. The ability to value and affirm one's own culture while functioning effectively in another one
4. An appreciation of the many ways faith is experienced and expressed in the religious education practice of Christians from various cultures.

To carry out these goals, churches must insist on the following:

1. Curricula and programs that reflect the diversity of the total Christian community
2. Practice that stresses participatory modes of learning and promotes leadership development within the parish
3. Close communication among ethnic and mainstream groups to affirm each others' gifts and celebrate a common faith heritage
4. Social responsibility through dialogue and action to reduce inequities and promote justice for all people.

MODELS OF MULTICULTURAL RELIGIOUS EDUCATION

A Comprehensive Multicultural Approach

It has already been observed that the appropriateness of multicultural religious education is not limited to churches with racially and culturally mixed congregations. In fact, it may be needed more by churches that are racially and culturally homogeneous. Wherever it is implemented, multicultural religious education modifies the church environment to reflect as closely as possible the ethnic composition of the community and promotes and encourages the valuing of ethnic diversity. The goal is to help learners grow as Christian disciples by developing cross-cultural sensitivity and competency. This requires a prepared learning environment and prepared religious educators.

The Learning Environment: General educators and religious educators alike have long recognized the powerful effect of the environment on learning. A nationwide study of churches in major Protestant denominations found that two of the five factors contributing to effective Christian education were environmental: the church's overall climate of emotional warmth and caring, and its intellectual climate of encouraging study and inquiry.[48] Examining classroom interaction patterns, Bowers and Flinders conclude

---

48. See Eugene C. Roehlkepartain, *The Teaching Church: Moving Christian Education to Center Stage* (Nashville: Abingdon, 1993), pp. 58–63. The three other factors that contributed to effective Christian education were quality of worship, a sense of family, and service to others.

that effectively arranging elements of the physical environment greatly enhances communication and involvement in learning.[49] James Michael Lee summarizes research on the importance of the environment in religious instruction, and describes seven distinct environments that powerfully influence any learning situation: the overall cultural environment in which the learning takes place, the local environment, the institutional (school or church) environment, the classroom or learning-group environment, the peer group environment, the home environment, and the immediate physical environment.[50]

James Banks looks at the learning environment in a similarly comprehensive way. He maintains that since multicultural education is a broad concept, it requires reform of the total educational environment. Translated into church contexts, this means that merely tinkering with one or two aspects of the program, adding a community outreach here or an ethnic board member there, will make little significant difference in religious education. A church should look at its broad policies, its communal life and values (stated and implicit), its teaching styles and materials, and all other aspects of the religious education environment. A diagram Banks uses to conceptualize multicultural education may be adapted for purposes of examining the religious education setting (fig. 1.1).[51] Many churches seek curriculum materials that reflect more diversity, but they fail to make other major changes. For example, churches may not consider whether teaching styles in their religious education programs correspond to the learning patterns of the cultural groups represented in their parish.[52] Even though one factor like curriculum may be the initial focus of change, ongoing changes in the learning environment need to take place in order to create and sustain effective multicultural religious education. What about language? Are there recent immigrants in the church who need learning materials in their own language? Are multicultural goals spelled out and assessed in evaluation procedures? Are new agencies needed to provide services to unreached groups in the parish?

---

49. See C. A. Bowers and D. J. Flinders on the use of the physical environment in their chapter, "Nonverbal Communication," in *Responsive Teaching: An Ecological Approach to Classroom Patterns of Language, Culture, and Thought* (New York: Teachers College Press, 1990), pp. 77–82.

50. James Michael Lee, *The Flow of Religious Instruction* (Birmingham, Ala.: Religious Education Press, 1973), pp. 65–73.

51. Adapted with permission from *Multiethnic Education: Theory and Practice*, by James A. Banks, 2d ed. (1988). Allyn and Bacon Inc., 7 Wells Ave., Newton, MA 02159.

52. In chap. 4 of *Multiculturalism and Learning Style* (Westport, Conn.: Praeger, 1995), Rita Dunn and Shirley Griggs summarize research findings on how culture influences the learning processes of major cultural groups in the United States. The book also includes many suggestions for adapting teaching/learning activities to learners' preferred styles.

Figure 1.1: The Total Religious Education Environment. In this figure the total church environment is conceptualized as a system that consists of major identifiable factors. In the idealized multicultural religious setting each factor reflects multicultural religious goals. Even though one factor may be the focus of initial reform, changes must take place in each factor in order to create and sustain an effective multicultural religious education environment.

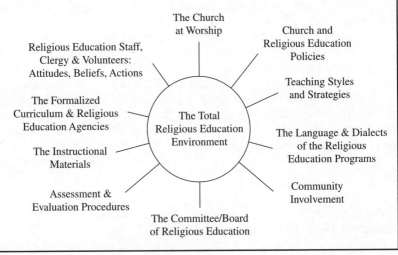

Preparing Teachers: Emphasizing the importance of preparing teachers to implement multicultural goals, Banks cites the experience of the ethnic studies movement of the 1960s, when teachers were simply given multiethnic materials to use but were not trained to use them or to develop new conceptual frameworks for viewing various cultures.[53]

Religious education directors should help teachers get in touch with their own racial and ethnic feelings so that they can deal effectively with the intercultural mandates of the gospel. How prepared do local church teachers (or religious education directors themselves) feel to understand, embrace, and minister to once-remote cultural groups, formerly the objects of evangelism overseas, but now next-door neighbors? Teaching about a group's nation of origin (possibly in a missions lesson) is not the same as teaching about ethnic features of the local community. Once again, what Banks finds true about public schools is also recognizable in churches: "Teaching about distant lands is apparently less threatening to some teachers than is teaching about ethnic cultures, problems, and conflicts within their own

53. Banks, *Multiethnic Education*, p. 41.

community."[54] Speaking of the Catholic education of African-American learners, Jacquiline Wilson advises non-African teachers to maximize interactions with learners by fostering strong cultural identity, learning from students, maintaining high expectations, creating a nurturing environment, and utilizing a multicultural curriculum designed to dissolve cultural barriers through storytelling.[55] Equipping volunteer staff to function as multicultural religious educators should occur on many levels, from planned discussions during monthly or quarterly staff meetings to attendance at seminars featuring qualified leaders and weekend retreats focusing on multicultural issues within the parish.

Writing from within the Evangelical Protestant community, James and Lillian Breckenridge stress the need for structural reorganization of churches to facilitate multicultural goals. Churches need to inform their members regarding the growing cultural diversity in society and help them identify how their own Christian traditions have been influenced by culture. They also need to identify and discourage organizational approaches and personal attitudes that are ethnocentric in nature. The Breckenridges propose several goals for religious instruction programs:

- developing cross-cultural skills in teaching to provide for various learning styles;
- assisting learners in the process of identity formation;
- teaching a Christian commitment to justice;
- fostering social relationships among children that represent cooperation, openness, an interest in others, and a willingness to include others;
- assisting parents in the task of rearing children to appreciate diversity and to live together with people of all ethnic backgrounds.[56]

Many religious educators would agree that churches of all descriptions need to help learners break out of their own cultural encapsulations and develop a true ethnic literacy that recognizes human commonalities and distinctives among all races and cultural groups. Ethnic churches would do well to help members see how they fit and function within both their own microculture and the larger society. Developing more openness to other cultures poses a dilemma for ethnic churches when the dominant American culture seems to undermine the customs, values, and even the Christian faith of the primary group. The ethnic church may seek to protect

---

54. Ibid., p. 42.

55. Jacquiline E. Wilson, "Catholic Education and African Americans," *Momentum* 25 (April/May 1994): 32–35.

56. James and Lillian Breckenridge, *What Color Is Your God? Multicultural Education in the Church* (Wheaton, Ill.: Victor, 1995), pp. 75–81.

itself from the majority influence by tightening bonds with the culture of origin.[57]

Speaking from within one ethnic community, a religious educator recently evaluated the cultural stance of many of his group's churches in America. He assessed them as being more "conservative" and more "traditional" than churches in their country of origin. He explained this tendency as growing out of a concern to avoid the negative aspects of American popular culture. He concluded that, rather than remaining isolated, these churches need to provide young people with a Christian education that authenticates their ethnic identity.[58] The ethnic church's calling is to sustain the tension between the traditional culture and the dominant culture in a way that frees members to live Christianly in both cultures.

Ethnocentric Approaches and Multicultural Religious Education

Various means of correcting educational disparities in ethnic groups have emerged since the 1970s. One approach has been to adopt an ethnocentric educational approach. The relationship between ethnocentric and multicultural education is sometimes unclear. In contrast to multicultural education's goal of developing an individual's competencies in diverse cultural situations, ethnocentrism focuses on the values and interests of one ethnic group.

While social scientists do not always agree on a definition of the term *ethnic group*, ethnicity is generally understood in terms of objective sociological markers such as race, language, religion, and national origin. However, subjective features are also involved, such as an internal sense of "belongingness" or "peoplehood." Therefore membership in an ethnic group may be voluntary or involuntary. One person may possess the objective characteristics of a particular group but not identify herself in those terms. Another person may identify closely with an ethnic group, yet have more characteristics of the dominant culture. For a variety of reasons, individuals sometimes find themselves struggling with the implications of their ethnic backgrounds as they try to relate to the larger culture.[59]

---

57. Sang Hyun Lee, "Second Generation Ministry: Models of Mission," in *Korean American Ministry*, ed. Sang Hyun Lee and John V. Moore, exp. English ed. (Louisville: Presbyterian Church (U.S.A.), 1993), pp. 239–41. Betty Lee Sung discusses cultural insulation in *Chinese Immigrant Children in New York City* (New York: Center for Migration Studies, 1987), p. 94.

58. Student paper written for course taught by the author, Christian Education in the Urban Church, Alliance Theological Seminary, 1992. The student prefers not to be identified.

59. D. John Lee and Rodger R. Rice, "Ethnic Identity and Multiculturalism: Concepts, History, Research, and Policy" in *Ethnic-Minorities and Evangelical Christian Colleges*,

Banks and other specialists in multiethnic education hold the position that the primarily Anglocentric and Eurocentric curriculum of American schools may negatively affect the minority child because he or she may find the school experience alien and defeating. The child may internalize messages she receives from a dominant culture curriculum that her own group's culture is intellectually inferior or historically insignificant.[60] Lawrence Cremin notes the charge of 1930s educator Carter Woodson that the "educated Negro" had been taught "to admire the Hebrew, the Greek, the Latin and the Teuton and to despise the African." Cremin continues, "He had been robbed of his Afro-American heritage and alienated from the deepest values of the Afro-American community. As such, he was ill equipped . . . to lead them by instilling in them the pride that would enable them to participate fully in American life."[61] Like Woodson, Banks argues that children must be able to accept their own ethnicity before they can value other groups.

I believe these ideas have special relevancy for religious education programs for several reasons:

1. Churches and their religious education endeavors are as vulnerable as the public schools to the criticism of being exclusively Anglocentric in their approach.
2. Mission-minded churches may expose learners to information about other cultures in a way that fosters comparisons rather than understandings. Churches do this when they stress superficial cultural features (national costumes, food, holidays—sometimes labeled the "Disneyworld" approach to ethnicity[62]) rather than meaningful ones like cultural worldview, values, arts, family, and community life.
3. Immigrant churches in America have increasing growth rates and at the same time experience tension concerning generational issues and problems of assimilation and cultural conflict.
4. Long-standing oppression of Native Americans, African Americans, Mexican Americans and other groups in American society has been supported by some church structures and ignored by others.

---

ed. D. John Lee (Lanham, Md.: University Press of America, 1991), pp. 68–73; and Christine I. Bennett, *Comprehensive Multicultural Education: Theory and Practice* (Boston: Allyn & Bacon, 1986), pp. 32–34.

60. Banks, *Multiethnic Education*, p. 163. Also see Sleeter and Grant, *Making Choices for Multicultural Education*, p. 130, and Janice Hale-Benson, *Black Children: Their Roots, Culture, and Learning Styles* (Baltimore: Johns Hopkins, 1982), pp. 154–55.

61. Cremin, *American Education*, p.122.

62. D. John Lee, third-generation Chinese Canadian and professor of psychology at Calvin College, used this designation in a recent communication.

Once I took students in a seminary class to visit one of the historic black churches of Brooklyn. The church's minister of education gave us a tour of the church's several buildings, offices, and ministries. She then shared with us the church's plans to open a day school that would provide an Afrocentric curriculum for the children. Later some of the seminary students questioned whether such a goal was appropriate in a Christian school and a pluralistic society.

This particular African-American church, and also some churches of the new immigration, may be addressing the concern expressed by Banks and others that traditional curricula have not served minorities well. One writer on this subject defines *centricity* as referring to "a perspective that involves locating students within the context of their own cultural references so that they can relate socially and psychologically to the other culture's perspectives."[63] Ideally, an education with these goals would seek to avoid the dangers of an extreme ethnocentricity that leads to exclusivism and isolation. It would include the goals of multicultural religious education that work to foster Christian community.

Banks believes that the goal of multiculturalism can be attained by members of minority groups only when personal issues of ethnicity and identity have been resolved. He offers a six-stage typology to guide those who work with ethnic minority youth. This typology assumes that their socialization may keep children and adults in early developmental stages. They need a clear, positive identification (stage 3) in order to attain authentic national and global identifications.[64]

A COMPLEMENTARY MOVEMENT
MULTICULTURAL MODEL

Robert Pazmiño posits a model for religious education that incorporates the seemingly opposed demands of identity and community, of diversity and unity. Writing as a multicultural religious educator of bicultural parentage, Brooklyn-born Pazmiño makes metaphorical use of the urban street game Double Dutch, which requires the player to jump adroitly between two arcing jump ropes, turned in tandem by turners at either end.

Pazmiño first describes and rejects three competing educational models: (1) the Anglo conformity model, which perpetuates racial and social exclusion in schools and churches; (2) the melting pot model, which has

63. Banks, *Multiethnic Education*, p. 41.
64. Typology used with permission from *Multiethnic Education: Theory and Practice*, by James A. Banks, 2d ed. (1988). Allyn and Bacon Inc., 7 Wells Ave., Newton, MA 02159.

Figure 1.2: The Expanding Identifications of Ethnic Youths: A Typology. This figure illustrates the author's hypotheses that students must have clear, positive ethnic identifications (stage 3) before they can attain reflective and positive national and global identifications (stages 5 and 6).

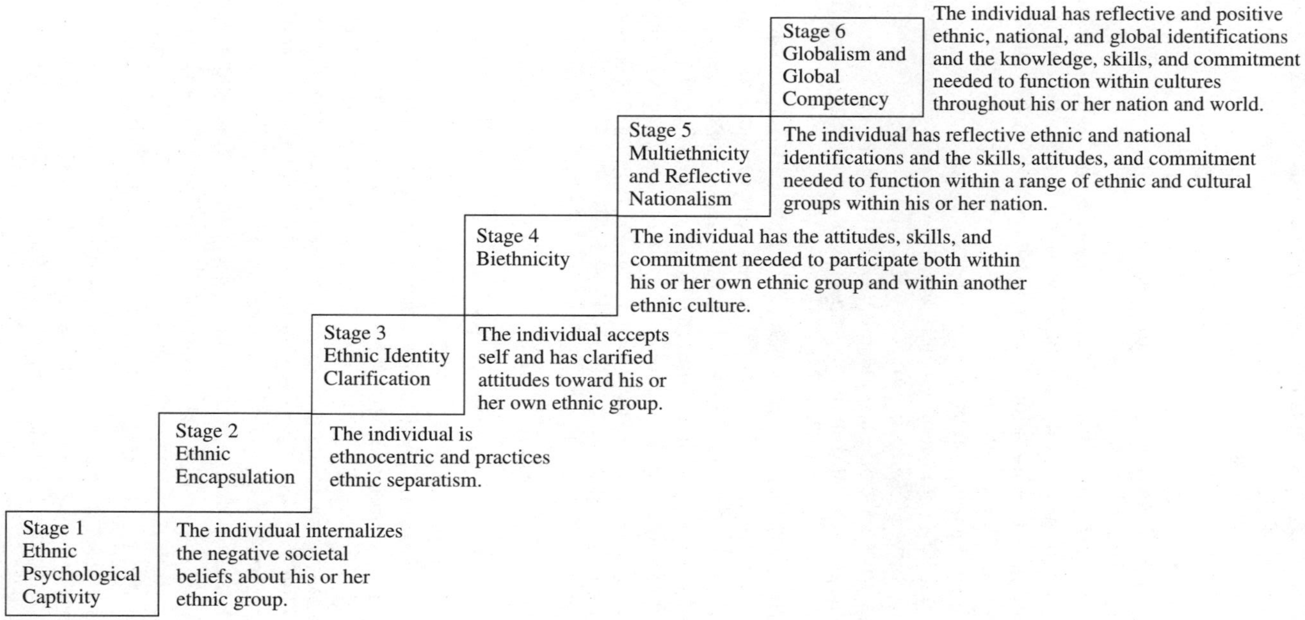

Stage 1
Ethnic Psychological Captivity

The individual internalizes the negative societal beliefs about his or her ethnic group.

Stage 2
Ethnic Encapsulation

The individual is ethnocentric and practices ethnic separatism.

Stage 3
Ethnic Identity Clarification

The individual accepts self and has clarified attitudes toward his or her own ethnic group.

Stage 4
Biethnicity

The individual has the attitudes, skills, and commitment needed to participate both within his or her own ethnic group and within another ethnic culture.

Stage 5
Multiethnicity and Reflective Nationalism

The individual has reflective ethnic and national identifications and the skills, attitudes, and commitment needed to function within a range of ethnic and cultural groups within his or her nation.

Stage 6
Globalism and Global Competency

The individual has reflective and positive ethnic, national, and global identifications and the knowledge, skills, and commitment needed to function within cultures throughout his or her nation and world.

become "intellectually outmoded but not functionally inoperative"; and (3) the cultural pluralism model, which recognizes various ethnic origins, but expects the importance of ethnic heritage to fade. Pazmiño says that all three models sacrifice diversity in the interest of unity. He suggests that religious education programs adopt a multiethnic model derived from the works of Ricardo Garcia in general education and Charles Foster in religious education.[65]

In Pazmiño's view multiethnic religious education as a specific form of multicultural education looks at ethnicity as an important and continuing part of national and personal life, not as a social problem to be overcome. It includes two educational forms, or movements. One movement includes defining and emphasizing personal ethnic identity; the complementary form seeks a common ground for community. Pazmiño sees the second movement as involving a quest for universality and unity, but not at the expense of diversity.[66] "Seeking common ground" requires that both parties be grounded in their own ethnic heritage. Pazmiño admits that in our racially divisive environment not all have the freedom to be so grounded, but argues that such grounding is needed to establish dialogue between persons of different ethnic heritage. Religious educators must pay careful attention and make an energetic commitment to the two movements, the first promoting in learners a healthy identity in relation to their ethnic heritage, and the second providing ongoing teaching and learning experiences relating them to the larger Christian and global communities. For example, in one ethnic church a Korean-American religious educator brought children together twice yearly with parents or grandparents. Older taught younger the crafts, games and songs they learned as children in Korea. Planned interactive questions kept the age groups talking together; prayer, singing, and personal faith stories in both languages provided meaningful worship. In terms of the second movement, youth and adults of the congregation supported community and international mission and relief agencies, and met regularly with a sister Anglo-American church for prayer, shared meals, and volleyball.

In the Double-Dutch jump rope game that I played as a child in our Jewish-Irish-Italian-Scandinavian neighborhood, the rope was not two strands, but one, the ends tied together in a knot. The turners stood inside the rope, which passed around their backs as they turned it with both hands. They and the jumper moved together perfectly in one rhythmic activity. Likewise, in a complementary-movement multicultural religious education the ethnic identity strand and the universal strand alternate and reciprocate, allowing each person to be an individual self as well as a contributing part of the whole.

---

65. Robert W. Pazmiño, "Double Dutch: Reflections of an Hispanic Northamerican on Multicultural Religious Education," in *VOCES*, by Justo Gonzalez, pp. 137–45.
66. Ibid., p. 144.

PHILOSOPHICAL STRANDS IN
MULTICULTURAL RELIGIOUS EDUCATION

At the outset of this chapter I declared my intention to look for the philo-sophical roots of multicultural religious education in order to identify the guiding principles that influence and direct religious educators who study, write, teach, and minister under the rubric *multicultural* and to discover how the goals they articulate fit within, or emerge from, larger theoretical frameworks for religious education.

The attempt is fraught with dangers. Not only is the notion of theory itself "a somewhat slippery concept," as Harold Burgess has observed,[67] but the broad community of scholars represented may make designations seem arbitrary. Nevertheless, I believe the work of the multicultural reli-gious educator needs to be anchored in long-standing and well-developed theoretical systems that have for many years guided religious educators in their thinking and practice. My investigation is preliminary in nature, owing to the developing state of the multicultural movement and the limits imposed by an introductory chapter. I confess to being selective. The four approaches investigated here are ones that seem to me to yield the greatest promise for nurturing multicultural religious education: (1) the liberationist approach, (2) the community-of-faith approach, (3) the public-church ap-proach, and (4) the social-science approach. Each is discussed in terms of three categories: (1) the *general principles and aims* of the approach that relate to multicultural religious education, (2) its view of the *participants* in the education process, and (3) its view of religious education *content* in both its substantive (subject matter) and structural (instructional prac-tice) aspects.[68]

---

67. Harold Burgess, *An Invitation to Religious Education* (Birmingham, Ala.: Re-ligious Education Press, 1975), p. 3. James Michael Lee brings more precision to the concept by defining theory as a statement or a group of statements that organically integrates interrelated concepts, laws, and facts. By specifying relations among variables, it issues in a systematic and comprehensive view of reality. He considers adequate and fruitful theory vital to religious instruction, since without a theory, the religious educator could neither predict whether certain procedures would work nor ascertain why they failed. Theory, says Lee, differs from speculation, which merely reflects on the nature or workings of reality, without the power to explain, predict, and verify phenomena. See James Michael Lee, "The Authentic Source of Religious Instruction," in *Religious Education and Theology*, ed. Norma H. Thompson (Birmingham, Ala.: Religious Education Press, 1982), pp. 117–21.

68. Most educational theorists agree that while subject matter and instructional practice are inseparable, they may need to be discussed separately for purposes of clarification. See John P. Miller and Wayne Seller, *Curriculum Perspectives and Practice* (New York: Longman, 1985), p. 189, and James Michael Lee, *The Content of Religious Instruction* (Birmingham, Ala.: Religious Education Press, 1985), p. 8.

The Liberationist Approach

Liberationist thought, with its emphases on critique, the perspectives of the poor, and corrective social action,[69] has provided the bedrock on which many theorists construct foundational principles of multicultural education. Liberationist themes surface at every conference or symposium on multicultural education, secular or religious. The works of theologian Gustavo Gutiérrez and the Brazilian educator Paulo Freire are frequently cited and applied to educational constructs. It is safe to say that many of the conceptual and methodological roots of the multicultural education movement lie in liberationist soil. Daniel Schipani observes that merely to couple the words *education* and *liberation* evokes immediately the work and thought of Paulo Freire.[70] Thus Sonia Nieto, writing on multicultural education and school reform, calls for a "critical and liberating education"—the opposite of what Freire calls "domesticating education." Nieto writes, "According to Freire, education for domestication is a process of 'transferring knowledge,' whereas education for liberation is one of 'transforming action.' "[71]

Chronologically, a liberationist approach to religious education emerged simultaneously with the multicultural movement. Writing in 1982, Allen Moore called for religious education to become prophetic, challenging oppressive social structures and recovering its "historic relationship to Christian social action."[72] Recognizing the contradictions inherent in such a role for the American church, Moore poses the implicit question of whether a church of the dominant culture can claim a religious education of liberation. He points to the origins of liberation theology and education in areas of Latin America where "oppression and poverty are historical realities, not ideas to be examined and debated." He recalls Freire's cautionary statement that "in the First World, liberation either would become another technique for education or it would be idealized as an optional lifestyle."[73] Daniel Schipani addresses a related danger when he warns of the attitude of *messianic paternalism* and *elitism* often expressed by would-be "conscientizers."[74] This is particularly likely to occur when the religious educator comes from outside the community.

It is not surprising to observe that when Moore was writing, and after, liberationist themes were often developed by religious educators and

---

69. Daniel Schipani, *Religious Education Encounters Liberation Theology* (Birmingham, Ala.: Religious Education Press, 1988), p. 2.

70. Ibid., p. 12.

71. Sonia Nieto, *Affirming Diversity: The Sociopolitical Context of Multicultural Education* (New York: Longman, 1992), pp. 219–20.

72. Allen Moore, "Liberation and the Future of Religious Education," in *Contemporary Approaches to Christian Education*, ed. Jack L. Seymour and Donald A. Miller (Nashville: Abingdon, 1982), p. 103.

73. Quoted by Moore, "Liberation and the Future," p. 106.

74. Schipani, *Religious Education*, p. 22.

theologians of Hispanic and African-American heritage. A prominent voice in the multicultural arena, theologian-educator Virgilio Elizondo, writes out of a Mexican-American context of a religious education that encapsulates the liberationist aim of identifying with the oppressed: "If the church is to be a faithful witness to the Master," Elizondo states, "it must be identified with the poor and the oppressed of the world. If instead it is identified with the rich, the installed, and the powerful, it betrays by its life the very gospel it proclaims in words."[75]

Similarly, writing from a Protestant liberationist perspective, Orlando Costas sees the Hispanic church as a place where a people can find meaning, can keep their language alive, and can experience solidarity. He challenges it, however, to transcend its ethnic-religious oasis, going on to confront structural oppression: "What the Hispanic church needs . . . is nothing short of an ecclesiology of liberation . . . a vision of itself and its mission beyond survival and hope. Indeed, it needs an ecclesiology which will . . . free it for mission, incarnation, and the kingdom of God. This is the enormous task that lies before the emerging generation of Hispanic pastors and theologians."[76]

From within the black Catholic community, Toinette Eugene sees "leadership for liberation" as an aim of religious education. Eugene finds an inevitable link between historical experiences of liberation and a theology of hope. Citing the words and songs of "countless black preachers, teachers, and civic leaders," she sees these as affecting the destinies of all who experience oppression in America, and also as a basis for religious education and evangelization in black churches. Eugene calls for an authentically indigenous religious education with a "serious liberation component" developed in dialogue between the church and the black Catholic community, both of whom, she insists, "share mutual responsibility for maintaining the faith."[77]

The Participants: The liberationist perspective views the participants in religious education in a relationship of reciprocity, not in the usual hierarchy of authority (teacher) and dependent (learner). Freire adopted a banking metaphor in which he rejected an education consisting of a teacher (identified by Freire with the oppressors) depositing content and the student merely receiving it, thereby becoming no more than a "container."[78] Commenting on the radical nature of Freire's educational goals, Moore writes, "Liberation means escape from a system where someone *does something* for you. The fundamental idea is that *you learn to help yourself.*"[79] The

---

75. Virgilio Elizondo, *Galilean Journey: The Mexican-American Promise* (Maryknoll, N.Y.: Orbis Books, 1983), p. 93.

76. Quoted in D. John Lee, *Ethnic Minorities*, p. 16.

77. Toinette E. Eugene, "Leadership for Liberation: Catechetical Ministry in the Black Catholic Community," in *Faith and Culture*, pp. 45–52.

78. Paulo Freire, *Pedagogy of the Oppressed* (New York: Continuum, 1982), p. 58.

79. Moore, "Liberation and the Future," p. 108.

best illustration of this fundamental idea in action may be the growth of Basic Ecclesial Communities (BECs) in regions of Latin America and the United States, similar to the Base Education Movement Freire developed in Brazil. These are grassroots gatherings of poor or common people for prayer, Bible study, and intentional social action. In both Freire's "culture circles" and the churches' basic communities, relationships of equality, respect, and mutuality are stressed, dissolving the rigid distinctions between teacher and learner. Schipani finds such communities to be a locus for religious education and vehicles for church renewal and societal transformation.[80]

Russell Butkus claims that a tradition of suffering and action for social justice exists for both Catholic and Protestant Americans, which needs to be reclaimed by Christian religious education. Butkus deplores the "social amnesia" evident among contemporary American Catholics, and sees the task of religious education in a Catholic context as cultivating "the remembrance of suffering, injustice and the quest for freedom" with the aim of promoting compassionate action and social responsibility. Identifying this tradition as one of "dangerous memory," he documents the suffering and injustice experienced by immigrant groups in both traditions and challenges religious educators to help participants recall their own dangerous memories as they grow toward social and political responsibility in public life.[81]

Elizondo points out the kind of educational assumptions that often undermine the empowerment of ethnic and other oppressed groups. Many of the oppressed, along with well-intentioned outsiders, try to help the group "improve" by ceasing to be who they are. They must forget their language, dress, customs, and religion to become "better," meaning more like the dominant group.[82] The marginalized group itself must undertake the work of liberation, thereby freeing not only themselves but the oppressor as well. Gloria Ladson-Billings cites Freire's work as suggestive of what teachers of minority students must do to "emancipate, empower, and transform *both themselves* and their students."[83] The religious educator, therefore, must be a partner in solidarity with the learner.

In is worth noting that Ladson-Billings speaks out of a public school setting that is chiefly concerned with the education of youth, while Freire and

---

80. Schipani, *Religious Education*, pp. 240–45. Also see H. M. Conn, "Liberation Theology," in *New Dictionary of Theology*, ed. S. B. Ferguson, D. F. Wright, J. I. Packer (Downers Grove, Ill.: InterVarsity Press, 1988), p. 389.

81. Russell A. Butkus, "Dangerous Memories: Toward a Pedagogy of Social Transformation," in *Religious Education as Social Transformation*, ed. Allen J. Moore (Birmingham, Ala.: Religious Education Press, 1989), pp. 206, 228.

82. Elizondo, *Galilean Journey*, p. 97.

83. Gloria Ladson-Billings, "Culturally Relevant Teaching," in Carl A. Grant, *Research and Multicultural Education: From the Margins to the Mainstream* (Washington, D.C.: Falmer, 1992), p. 109. Italics added.

his instructional procedures, both in literacy work and in religious education, have been most closely associated with adult education. This model may be uniquely appropriate to church settings where, as Wickett observes, "the experience, knowledge, and skills of all parties to the learning activity are recognized," in other words, where both parties are simultaneously teacher and learner.[84]

The Content: The liberationist approach links content, procedure, and learner. Sonia Nieto explains this linkage as providing the most successful education because it is based on the experiences and viewpoints of the learner, not on a culture imposed on the learner. The learners themselves, Nieto claims, make up the foundation for the curriculum. Nevertheless, a liberating education always takes learners beyond their own limited experience.[85]

Discussing the philosophical foundation of the black religious education experience, Grant Shockley finds the Freirean method relevant (although he believes it is necessary to move beyond it, as we will see later in the chapter). He perceives the Freirean method as being highly interactive, challenging to the church community, having an incarnational mission, being a humanizing process, and always being affirmative, never neutral. Creating a new consciousness, toward which the method moves, requires dialogue and the support of community.[86]

Educational researcher Beverly Gordon stresses the need for comprehensiveness in achieving educational goals. At the level of curriculum development and implementation Gordon sees the need for "a triumvirate of anti-racist policies"—emancipatory instruction (specifically consciousness-raising at the classroom level), cultural consciousness, and political action at both school and community level.[87] Diane Gollnick believes the preparation of teachers should include Freire's focus on *voice* in the learning process. She writes that attention to voice must be a part of multicultural instruction. By *voice* Gollnick means a dialogue between teachers and learners that starts from the learners' own descriptions of their daily life experiences, rather than from the experiences of the teacher or others who are expected to conform to the dominant school culture.[88]

The voice of those who are traditionally "the taught" will enrich and purify the church. Elizondo calls on the oppressed to actualize their capacity

84. R. E. Y. Wickett, *Models of Adult Religious Education Practice* (Birmingham, Ala.: Religious Education Press, 1991), p. 139.

85. Nieto, *Affirming Diversity*, p. 221.

86. Grant Shockley, "Christian Education and the Black Religious Experience," in Foster, *Ethnicity in Education*, pp. 36–37.

87. Beverly M. Gordon, "The Marginalized Discourse of Minority Educational Thought," in Grant, *Research*, p. 24.

88. Diane Gollnick, "Multicultural Education: Policies and Practice in Teacher Education," in Grant, *Research*, p. 24.

for loving, which, he says, is as great as has been their capacity for suffering: "What [the Mexican-American community] has been deprived of it must make possible for all. Mexican-Americans have experienced acceptance in their families, now . . . they must share it with the society which has refused it to them—this is the Christian pedagogy of the oppressed."[89]

The Community-of-Faith Approach

In proposing the Christian faith community as one guiding image for the work of religious education, Charles Foster identified what may be seen as a second philosophical foundation for multicultural religious education. Foster asserted that the Christian community, by its modeling, its instruction, and its relationships, makes available to the next generation the formative events, beliefs, values, and experiences of the faith. According to Foster, a community of faith is "a people whose corporate and personal identities are found in their relationship to some significant past event." The significant past event for the Christian community is the cross; the corporate identity is experienced through bonding relationships within the community. Foster cites Erik Erikson's thesis that trusting relationships are developed from early childhood onward, and they are essential for spiritual growth. The Christian faith community provides such relationships.[90]

For many congregations whose history and ethnic origins distinguish them from the dominant culture, the guiding image of the Christian faith community has particular salience. For these churches, it is the entire life and experience of the faith community, rather than just a narrowly defined "schooling" process, that shapes and forms the next generation. John Westerhoff, a chief proponent of the faith-community approach, advocates a religious socialization process in which the young learn, not chiefly in classroom settings, but through the multitude of interactions that take place in the life of the community.[91] For ethnic minority children and youth, interacting daily with teachers who are overwhelmingly of the majority culture,[92] the church provides perhaps their only opportunity to be taught, challenged, supported, and affirmed by a community of adults within their own culture.

---

89. Elizondo, *Galilean Journey*, p. 100.

90. Charles R. Foster, "The Faith Community as a Guiding Image for Christian Education," in *Contemporary Approaches*, ed. Seymour and Miller, pp. 53–57.

91. John H. Westerhoff III, *Will Our Children Have Faith?* (New York: Seabury, 1976), pp. 16–17.

92. Davidman and Davidman point to trends in American education suggesting that in the year 2000 nineteen out of twenty teachers in public schools will be white, while 40–50 percent of students will be people of color (*Teaching with a Multicultural Perspective*, p. 43).

In ethnic churches the history and life of the faith community includes both Christian and ethnic identities. David Ng speaks of the Pacific Asian-American faith community as a "sojourner" community whose members are marginalized by both physical characteristics and national origin. A positive affirmation of ethnic identity is a major religious educational task, not only for churches of the immigrant communities, but for all churches, including those of the ethnic majority. An affirmation of ethnic identity offers the church nothing less than recovering the inclusiveness of the gospel. In a particular way, ethnic minority persons can identify with the people of God and with Jesus Christ because they, too, know what it is to suffer. "An ethnic identity which has had to be forged on the anvil of pain can become redemptive suffering not only for one's own identity's sake, but for the sake of the whole church." When sojourner communities shape their identities, those communities become a gift to the rest of the church.[93]

In a metaphor similar to Ng's sojourner image, Sang Hyun Lee claims the biblical vision of the pilgrim life as one that provides special meaning for immigrant communities. Like Abraham, Lee explains, Korean and other Asian-American Christians live in a wilderness "as in a foreign land," not as aimless wanderers, but as a pilgrim people on a sacred journey. The pilgrimage must begin with a journey back to the community's ethnic roots in order for its people to be able to move forward through the present to an Asian-American future.[94]

The Participants: For such a pilgrim faith community, the participants in religious education include not only teachers and learners, but all the members of that community. Teaching and learning take place in formal and informal settings by means of designated and undesignated teachers who both relate and embody the events, beliefs, values, and practices of the Christian and the ethnic community. For example, after a designated teacher conducts a weekday religious education session on Christian doctrine for fourth-graders, an undesignated teacher in the person of a youth group member stops two rowdy children from that same group in the church hall, and gently but authoritatively leads them to the waiting school bus. Both members teach, the former by direct instruction, the latter by modeling behavior that this faith community expects.

William Myers describes a black church that follows the faith community model by providing both *nearness* and *directness* as means of formation. *Nearness* is expressed when adults actively live out their faith before others; *directness* involves experiences of worship, service, and open discussions

---

93. David Ng, "Sojourners Bearing Gifts: Pacific Asian American Christian Education," in *Ethnicity in the Education of the Church*, ed. Charles Foster, pp. 7, 16.

94. Sang Hyun Lee, "Asian American Theology in Immigrant Perspective 'Called to be Pilgrims,' " in *Korean American Ministry*, ed. Sang Hyun Lee and John Moore, pp. 39, 40, 49.

that enable youth to address their own questions of faith. Adults in the church are committed to their belief that faith is intimately connected with daily life and that it is conveyed through experiences, words, and traditions. Because of this commitment, youth are given leadership responsibilities that require them to learn to work with others, both peers and adults, and to do the work of ministry even as they learn. Throughout the growing years, the extended family of important adults provides what Myers describes as a kinship circle of literal and surrogate parents, aunts, and uncles, whose support provides a strong sense of identity as adolescents mature into young adults. Thus in verbal and nonverbal ways, the message is communicated that the young are expected to be participants with adults in the activities of teaching, learning, service, and worship in the church. Myers sees this kind of nurturing and facilitating religious education as one that "enables youth to publicly own their faith."[95]

David Chai comments that for the Korean immigrant church, nurturing its community of faith is a process, the second generation participating with their parents in the common body of spiritual life. It is not simply a matter of choosing curriculum materials. In the spiritual community the values and faith of immigrant life are committed to and accepted by the young, who work with their parents in the life of the church.[96]

Foster describes the interchange of teaching/learning roles in the faith community as having a dialogical character, evident in the fluid process by which teachers and learners freely exchange roles. When learners appropriate in the context of their own situation the meanings and practices introduced by the religious educator, they may in turn provide a new angle of vision for the religious educator. The perspectives of both teacher and learner are needed, Foster says, "if the community is to extend its life and mission into the future."[97] In immigrant church communities, for example, the perspective of second-generation learners may contribute to the insights and viewpoints of religion teachers who represent the first generation.

Churches of different cultures using the faith community approach may nevertheless perceive the roles of participants differently. Some may experience frequent interchange between the perspectives of teachers and

---

95. William Myers, *Black and White Styles of Youth Ministry: Two Congregations in America* (New York: Pilgrim, 1991), pp. 143–44, 158. The experience of ethnic churches that typically include close family relationships in their religious-education programs may be validated by White's research, which found that when home and church reinforce the same viewpoint, the influence of both is stronger, and by Mol's finding that a religious education provided enhanced identity and emotional anchoring for individuals and groups in society. Both are discussed in *Religion in Childhood and Adolescence*, by Kenneth E. Hyde (Birmingham, Ala.: Religious Education Press, 1990), pp. 226, 224.

96. David Hoon Jin Chai, "Second Generation Youth Education," in *Korean American Ministry*, ed. Sang Hyun Lee and John Moore, p. 145.

97. Foster, "The Faith Community," p. 61.

learners; others may resist such a sharing of roles. David Ng points out that the hierarchical relationships of the Korean-American culture (as in other Asian immigrant cultures) require that learners obey their superiors and accept their teaching and directions.[98]

The Content: For the faith-community approach, religious education content is radicated in church life. Foster stresses that the life of the community *is* the content of religious education: "The task is not to learn about, but to engage in, that life."[99] Teaching is stressed because of the community's concern to incorporate into its life "the children of an ever-new generation, through whom its corporate destiny might continue to be explored and lived out."[100] Instructional style may differ from culture to culture. In many Asian-American faith communities, in keeping with traditional hierarchical social patterns, religious instruction is likely to be transmissive in style, with little encouragement for learners to initiate discussion or other activities.[101] However, the hierarchical practices do not negate the significance of personal relationships, which remain primary. Ng highlights the priority in Asian-Pacific American churches for person-to-person interchange over the use of printed materials.[102] In Hispanic parishes, the cultural trait of *personalismo*—the preference to relate to persons rather than to organized patterns of behavior—typically requires a personal, familial style of religious education practice and devotions.[103]

As one of the chief functions of the Christian community, worship comprises both substantive and structural content. Clarence Snelling notes the centrality of worship for the faith-community approach. In worship the child is enculturated with the values of the tradition and also participates in the celebration of those values. Moreover, according to Snelling, such celebrations reaffirm the identity of the faith community.[104] William Myers quotes one young person who belongs to a church in which youth are called to participate with adults in worship, provide music, usher, read Scripture, and occasionally preach: "Grace [Church] gives us the future now. If you're *told* you're the future, but you just sit there in the pew, then—who cares?"[105]

---

98. Ng, "Sojourners Bearing Gifts," p. 15.

99. Foster, "The Faith Community," p. 64.

100. Ibid., p. 71.

101. Grace Choon Kim, *Ways to Be a Good Teacher: A Manual for Korean-American Teachers Training* (Louisville, Ky.: Presbyterian Church (USA), n.d.), p. 147.

102. Ng, "Sojourners Bearing Gifts," p. 17.

103. Joseph R. Fitzpatrick, *One Church, Many Cultures: The Challenge of Diversity* (Kansas City, Mo.: Sheed & Ward, 1987), pp. 133, 156.

104. Clarence H. Snelling, "The Proper Study and the Chief End: The Relation of Religious Education to the Social Sciences," *Religious Education* 84 (summer 1989): 432.

105. Myers, *Black and White Styles*, p. 145.

The faith-community approach strongly underscores identity issues, which are of paramount importance in churches where members bear a dual cultural identity. Ng speaks for many ethnic minority Christians when he observes that Pacific-Asian American churches need a religious education that validates the ethnic identity of the church members. As a part of Christ's community, individuals are accepted fully and are freed to be their own, full selves. Thus their personal identity is authenticated and accepted.[106]

The Public-Church Approach

The third approach to religious education that addresses multicultural goals is one frequently identified as the public church.[107] This approach sees religious education as uniquely responsible to engage and reform the whole of society. While the public-church approach shares some roots with the liberationist approach, I believe it is more firmly planted in the soil of John Dewey's educational theories, which recognized and promoted education for social change,[108] and George Albert Coe's social-transformation approach to religious education, which has been influential since it emerged in the 1920s. Citing Coe as the theorist who shaped mainline Protestant religious education in the first half of the twentieth century, Allen Moore describes Coe's understanding of religious education as both a social enterprise and a reform movement. Among the major reform movements influenced by Coe's vision of religious education, according to Moore, are "racial integration, empowerment of women, globalization of the church, peace and justice, and the rights of children."[109] The public church addresses its society prophetically (not unlike the liberationist model), but it does not speak as the voice of the oppressed. Instead, it speaks from the traditional social-reform orientation of many twentieth-century religious educators. Jack Seymour, Robert O'Gorman, and Charles Foster advance this model when they call on religious education to recognize and embrace its formative

---

106. Ng, "Sojourners Bearing Gifts," pp. 14–15.

107. Martin Marty coined this term in his book *The Public Church: Mainline-Evangelical-Catholic* (New York: Crossroad, 1981), p. 3, to describe churches that are especially sensitive to "the public order that surrounds and includes people of faith."

108. John Dewey, *Democracy and Education* (New York: Free Press, 1961), p. 99. In a related comment, Miller and Seller identify Dewey's philosophy of education as basic to the transaction position, an approach to education prevailing at the end of the twentieth century, which is characterized by efforts to use rationality to improve society. It also supports reform efforts to provide equal opportunity to minorities. The transaction position has some commonalities with the goals of the public church. See *Curriculum*, pp. 6–8.

109. Allen J. Moore, "A Social Theory of Religious Education," *Religious Education* 82 (summer 1987): 425.

role in the education of the public, insisting that simply to *be* the church is, in fact, a public posture.[110]

Seymour, O'Gorman, and Foster cite the historic commitment of religious education to create a public *paideia* that would effect justice and spiritual values in the social order and lead the nation toward the democracy of God (to use Coe's phrase). They maintain that religious educators give lip service to such public values, but in actuality seem more concerned with the internal life of the church than with its public role. Like Coe and his colleague William Clayton Bower, they recognize that the church has lost its prophetic voice partly because of its tendency to ignore significant cultural changes and accept their impact uncritically.[111] Although not specifically addressing multicultural issues, Seymour and his collaborators advance similar goals, challenging religious educators to emphasize the ethical demands for justice and mercy and to renew the church's concern "with the prophetic task of illuminating public issues and decisions with transcendent meanings."[112] There are significant points of agreement with the multicultural and social-reconstructionist approach identified earlier in the chapter.

Maureen O'Brien builds on the work of James Fowler and others to promote the public church as a valid model for religious education. O'Brien sees the task of religious education as twofold. First, the church must fulfill its primary task of educating disciple-citizens who learn that their moral identity includes both their faith traditions and a commitment to social transformation. The second task is the education of the public, which involves the cooperative efforts of disciple-citizens and other citizens in shaping principles, policies, and plans of action for the common good. In this way, O'Brien claims, the church serves society as a structure that can mediate between particular Christian values and the public consensus.[113]

Allen Richardson cites a pluralistic society's need for mediating institutions that can provide common ground for diverse elements in the population to encounter one another in public life. He sees danger to the American experience in the repeated crises of community conflicts, and says the ability to understand diversity is related to the degree to which it can be directly experienced. Acknowledging that widely divergent religious bodies encounter barriers to mutual understanding, Richardson nevertheless cites examples of interfaith councils with inclusive agendas that perform

---

110. Jack L. Seymour, Robert T. O'Gorman, and Charles R. Foster, *The Church in the Education of the Public* (Nashville: Abingdon, 1984), pp. 143–44.

111. Ibid., p. 101.

112. Seymour, *The Church*, p. 153.

113. Maureen R. O'Brien, "The Public Church as a Model for Religious Education," *Religious Education* 88 (summer 1993): 398–414. O'Brien names John Coleman as the source of the "disciple-citizen" metaphor for membership in the public church in his chapter "The Two Pedagogies: Discipleship and Citizenship," in *Education for Citizenship and Discipleship*, ed. Mary C. Boys (New York: Pilgrim: 1989).

a mediating function and are thus agents of the interrelated process of pluralism and assimilation.[114]

Seymour, O'Gorman, and Foster underscore the mediating function as one of the goals of the church's education of the public. The church must not only engage in conversations regarding the future of public life, but must also claim its place "as one of the *primary mediating structures* for making meaningful connections between personal life and public policy." To this end, religious education needs to connect with other agencies of the larger community which, in spite of differences, "share a common commitment to shape the emerging paideia or vision of the common life."[115]

In a changing New York City neighborhood one growing church sponsors an annual street fair that is organized by members of its American-black, West Indian-black, and Hispanic congregation. White and Asian groups represented in the neighborhood also participate in the event. Much interaction takes place as ethnic food, music, games, crafts, art, and history are exchanged and enjoyed. The friendly relationships begun through the fair pave the way for cooperative community efforts to solve neighborhood problems and create alliances for change.

The aim for religious education in the public-church approach extends beyond concern for the quality of Christian family life to reform and reconstruction of the whole social ethos, shaping church and society toward what Coe envisioned as the democracy of God.[116]

The Participants: The public-church approach fosters an attitude of inclusiveness toward participants, who are expected to appreciate their own culture as only one in a plurality of distinctive cultures. Discussing the impact of the new ethnicity identified by Michael Novak[117] and others as emerging in society, Charles Foster finds a new pattern of consciousness, which can be seen as defining the public-church model. This pattern emerges as a balanced awareness of other cultures and of individual cultural distinctive. The awareness is heightened by participating in cultural activities of other groups and by incorporating their music, art, and customs into another culture's own sense of personal and corporate identity.[118]

---

114. Richardson, *Strangers in This Land*, pp. 201, 219, 221.

115. Seymour, *The Church*, pp. 144, 151. Italics added.

116. Moore, "A Social Theory," p. 424.

117. See Michael Novak, "Pluralism: A Humanistic Perspective," *Harvard Encyclopedia of American Ethnic Groups*, ed. Stephan Thernstrom et al. (Cambridge: Harvard University Press, 1980), p. 774, and *The Rise of the Unmeltable Ethnics* (New York: Macmillan, 1971).

118. Charles R. Foster, "Double Messages: Ethnocentrism in Church Education," *Religious Education* 82 (summer 1987): 464. Foster has also written on the faith community approach, and he is frequently cited in the section above concerning that approach. In this later article, Foster may be reflecting on a possible hazard of that somewhat inwardly focused orientation. For his comments on the potential limitations

Foster seems to refer to a new pattern also in his reiteration of Amos Jones's call for the creation of a new religious educational framework that incorporates the religious education beliefs and experiences of the church's numerous ethnic cultures. Going beyond earlier notions of assimilating a minority culture into the majority culture, the new pattern conveys a sense of the *interplay* of cultural visions, values, and practices: participants experience a genuine cultural mutuality and come to be characterized by it.[119] Citing Janice Hale-Benson's research on the learning styles of black children, Foster sees that the learning styles of participants must be affirmed in their religious education experience.[120] Education for the public church, then, makes participants aware of their own ethnicity and history as members of one among many equal groups.

Psychologist James Fowler outlines several characteristics essential to nurture in the public church, a few of which echo O'Brien's disciple-citizen motif for participants in religious education. According to Fowler, the public church manifests a diverse membership and "fosters a clear sense of Christian identity and commitment." Further, the public church works at shaping a *paideia* for children, youth, and adults that aims to combine Christian commitment with public vocation. Fowler describes three model churches that exemplify these and other essential characteristics, all of which exhibit some racial, ethnic, and social class heterogeneity.[121]

Rather than the monocultural ethnicity of churches following the faith-community model, Robert Jones insists that religious education must be multicultural and multiracial. He believes that this is an educational, pastoral, and theological challenge called for by the gospel. He rejects churches that claim to celebrate diversity while remaining racially segregated. Only when the church's membership is multicultural and multiracial, Jones declares, will a major step toward God's kingdom be realized. "Then the church will teach by its composition as well as its verbalizations the fullness of the power of the gospel."[122]

The Content: Of paramount importance to both subject matter and instructional process for the public church is the ability of religious education to provide transcendent dimensions to public life. This is particularly true when a society's values are bankrupt. Seymour recounts the warning made by Oxford University's Edward Robinson that an acquisitive, competitive

---

of the faith community approach, see Seymour and Miller, *Contemporary Approaches*, pp. 67–70.

119. Foster, *Ethnicity*, pp. 95, 98.

120. Foster, "Double Messages," p. 465.

121. James W. Fowler, *Weaving the New Creation: Stages of Faith and the Public Church* (San Francisco: HarperSanFrancisco, 1991), pp. 155–67.

122. Robert E. Jones, "Learning to Face Diversity in Urban Churches," in *Urban Church Education*, pp. 84, 90.

society stunts the imagination and blocks the culture's spiritual potential, creating a religionless public. If churches are to shape public life, they must reconnect themselves to "the sacred dimensions of reality," infusing conversation about the public with power and possibility. To contribute to public formation, churches must recognize a dynamic religious educational ecology, fostering in learners a Christian lifestyle while supporting other community agencies that share a common vision.[123] In a similar vein, James Fowler calls for churches to provide an ecology of nurture and vocation, an inward-outward orientation that prepares people to participate both in the faith and in the life of the congregation, in its public witness and in its mission.[124]

Commenting on how religious education curricula have addressed ethnic pluralism in the past, Charles Foster notes denominational religious education curricula that move toward a truly multicultural (rather than assimilationist) selection of stories and pictures. According to Foster, the stance is "communal" rather than "missional." Cultural differences are portrayed as facts of life rather than as items of curiosity. Foster sees multicultural religious education as valuing an interplay of cultural experiences that allows people to claim their own identities and also respond to the identities of others. Learners of all groups explore different cultural heritages and develop the skills necessary to interact with people from other cultural communities.[125] Foster further sees multicultural religious educational activities as helping people to "perceive and act self-consciously out of varying cultural assumptions." He points out that most people can adapt their modes of speaking and behaving according to regional differences, as he does, for example, when he is with close friends in the city or with relatives in his rural home community.[126] Foster's goal is consistent with James Banks's principle of multiple acculturation, by which individuals learn to function well in cultural settings other than their own.

As the faith-community model may serve the goals and values of ethnic minority churches, particularly as those goals and values affect the young, the public-church model may especially serve the goals and values of integrated or multicultural churches. In a more general context, if the tension that exists between the need for continuity and the demand for social change is to be resolved in the creation of a new vessel for religious education, the approach of the public church, defined and elaborated by proponents, seasoned by practice and tested by research, may hold promise for the future.

---

123. Seymour, *The Church*, pp. 135, 128, 152.
124. Fowler, *Weaving the New Creation*, p. 189.
125. Foster, "Double Messages," p. 463.
126. Foster, *Ethnicity*, p. 100.

The Social-Science Approach

The fourth and final approach that provides generative principles for multi-cultural religious education shares the root system of multicultural education itself. The social-science approach places religious education firmly in the soil of the behavioral sciences—anthropology, education, psychology, sociology, and related disciplines—rather than under the purview of theology, where religious education is traditionally placed. Defending his point that religious instruction is a mode of social science rather than a form of theology, James Michael Lee, the major theorist of this approach,[127] insists that the content of theology is "inserted into the social science approach, not vice-versa."[128] Thus, whatever theology is represented in the teaching-learning act, learning takes place according to the way teaching and learning proceed, rather than according to the way theology proceeds. This statement is important for multicultural religious education because the social-science approach can be used by any church body of any culture as a framework for doing religious education. Because it uses contemporary data and educational methods for instructing learners in Christian living, the social-science approach effectively serves the goals of a religious education that is multicultural. Because this approach is value-free in the sense that it does not flow from a particular theological system, it can be infused with any theological content, making it especially appropriate for pluralistic contexts. And because it is informed by the social-science evidence of how learners actually learn and teachers actually teach, it provides the empirical roots necessary for effective multicultural religious education. "If religious instruction all across the board is going to be successful," says Lee, "it must have as its ultimate twin base the structure of science and the soul of religion."[129] Grant Shockley, a leading black religious educator, finds Lee's approach "quite compatible with the kind of theory which is needed to undergird a black ethnocultural pluralism paradigm," since it presents the primary purpose of religious instruction as "the fusion of one's personal experience of Christianly understanding, action, and love coequally."[130] Shockley here is responding to one of Lee's central and recurring themes—

---

127. Lee actually describes the social-science approach as a totally comprehensive macrotheory (or macroapproach), rather than simply an approach or theory. By its very nature as a macrotheory the social-science approach is capable of explaining, predicting, and verifying the validity and efficacy of any approach to religious education. See Lee, *Content*, pp. 753–56.

128. James Michael Lee, *The Shape of Religious Instruction* (Birmingham, Ala.: Religious Education Press, 1971), p. 3.

129. James Michael Lee, "The Blessing of Religious Pluralism," in *Religious Pluralism and Religious Education*, ed. Norma H. Thompson (Birmingham, Ala.: Religious Education Press, 1988), p. 82.

130. Grant Shockley, "A Black Protestant Perspective," in *Religious Pluralism*, ed. Norma Thompson, p. 65.

that religious instruction must be holistic, joining together cognitive, affective, and lifestyle learning. Only in this way can religious instruction truly be religious. This holistic view is consistent with the goals of multicultural religious education, since multiculturalism requires that the learner not just know about other cultures, but also have positive and loving attitudes toward those cultures and their members. Learners need to embody in their own lifestyle significant human and Christian values gained from those cultures.

Positing that the essential task of religious education is "delineating and designing a program for living creatively in a society that is religiously, culturally, socially, and racially highly diverse," Shockley goes on to elaborate how the social-science approach can be the theoretical means to that end.[131] Taking his outline from Lee's well-known taxonomy of the instructional process, Shockley says, "The social-science approach, an experience-directed style, a discovery strategy, and a problem-solving method all have affinity with the objective of religious education in relation to the black religious experience."[132]

The Participants: Noting the close association historically between religious education and the social sciences, Clarence Snelling explains it as resulting from religious educators' keen awareness of the persons they teach. Perhaps more than others, religious educators have seen as their proper study "not just humankind in general, but specifically the children, youth, and adults who are being taught."[133]

The social-science approach puts the learner at the heart of the instructional process. Empirical research has confirmed what earlier philosophers intuited—that all pedagogical activity is rightly based on and rightly responds to "the needs, capabilities, goals and histories of the individual learners."[134] While the learner is central, the teacher is responsible. The teacher is to so shape the conditions of the religious education environment that "a personal, living encounter between the learner and Jesus is facilitated." The encounter may take place with Jesus indwelling the learner, with Jesus abiding in other persons, and with Jesus as he is in himself.[135] Thus there is a strong relational element among the participants in the teaching-learning situation that is essential to the learning experience. Education professor Nel Noddings discusses this relational element as a matter of the teacher's *fidelity* to the learners, manifested as care for the learner as a person and as care for the quality of relations within the learning group.

---

131. Ibid., pp. 146, 148.
132. Ibid., p. 166.
133. Snelling, "The Proper Study," p. 428.
134. James Michael Lee, *The Flow of Religious Instruction* (Birmingham, Ala.: Religious Education Press, 1973), p. 210.
135. Lee, *Shape*, p. 17.

The teacher, then, is responsible both for the development of relationships and for control of the environment. Noddings sees the teacher's control of the learning environment as not being opposed to the teacher's care. "Control and caring are not opposing terms; but the form of control is transformed by the presence of care." When teachers act as models of caring, they also model other desirable qualities, such as meticulous preparation, lively presentation, critical thinking, appreciative listening, constructive evaluation, and genuine curiosity.[136]

Examining the wealth of social science research indicating a link between teacher behavior and learner achievement, Gloria Ladson-Billings cites the need among contemporary learners for culturally relevant teaching. A teacher aware of and responding to the learners' cultural styles and values uses the *learners'* culture to help them create meaning and understand the world more fully. Among eleven assertions Ladson-Billings finds important for culturally relevant teaching, three are especially tuned to religious educational settings: (1) language and communication structures should contain links to learners' home/community language and communication structures; (2) teacher effectiveness is tied to both personal warmth and rigorous knowledge of subject matter; and (3) the curriculum should be relevant to learners' lives.[137]

The Content: The social-science approach to religious education content distinguishes between structural content, which is instructional practice and therefore in the purview of teaching, and substantive content, which is religion. In other words, not only religious content but instructional procedures themselves teach. Lee maintains that how a religious educator teaches is a more powerful content than what the educator teaches.[138] This delineation has important consequences for multicultural religious education, since the teacher must include both holistic substantive content (cognitions, affects, and behavioral lifestyles) and holistic structural content, teaching in such a way that learners can gain the desired outcomes.[139] Since religion is defined as a lived experience, not just a conceptualization, the religion class or group is a "laboratory for Christian living," in which structural

136. Nel Noddings, quoted in *Responsive Teaching: An Ecological Approach to Class Patterns of Learning, Culture, and Thought,* by Charles A. Bowers and David Flinders (New York: Teachers College Press, 1990), p. 15.

137. Ladson-Billings, "Culturally Relevant Teaching," pp. 110–11.

138. See James Michael Lee, "The Teaching of Religion," in *Toward a Future for Religious Education,* ed. James Michael Lee and Patrick C. Rooney (Dayton, Ohio: Pflaum, 1970), pp. 59–60; James Michael Lee, "Compassion in Religious Instruction," in *Compassionate Ministry,* ed. Gary L. Sapp (Birmingham, Ala.: Religious Education Press, 1993), p. 203.

139. Lee, "The Blessings of Religious Pluralism," in *Religious Pluralism and Religious Education,* ed. Norma Thompson, pp. 119–24.

and substantive contents "are one reality fused together in the religious instruction act."[140]

Ladson-Billings also affirms the link between social science and instruction. She ties research inquiry to a culturally relevant pedagogy that will meet the educational, social, and cultural needs of students. She sees multicultural education as an attempt to make the curriculum more responsive to these needs. She also stresses the fusion of instructional practice and subject matter. A culturally relevant pedagogy requires religious education settings to move beyond "altering the curriculum" (which usually refers to a change in published materials) to understanding both the rationale for and the process of instruction. Ladson-Billings points to the black school settings where black children routinely perform at or above grade level. These successful schools pay attention to the curriculum *and* the teaching process: "The curriculum often stresses cultural affirmation while the teaching methods draw from the students' cultural strengths."[141]

Earlier in this chapter we noted Sleeter and Grant's concern that a failure to address both subject matter and instructional practice may thwart multicultural education, leaving it "trapped in those instructional patterns that predominate in our schools," that is, subject matter taught exclusively by textbooks and lectures.[142]

Drawing on research into learning styles can help or hinder, depending on whether the religion teacher falls into stereotyping (attributing to the learner all the characteristics associated with his or her primary cultural group) or whether the teacher sees each learner's distinctiveness.[143] Ideally, the results of such research are utilized to influence teaching/learning style, making it more responsive to the diverse needs of all learners.

Employing George Isaac Brown's concept of "confluent education,"[144] Clarence Snelling advocates a religious education that pays attention to both cognitive and affective learning styles. Each of these two powerful learning modes can take three characteristic expressions:

---

140. See Burgess, *Invitation*, pp. 134–39. In Lee's view, every religion lesson, whether taught in a formal or an informal environment, whether taught to children or adults, should strive to include the characteristics of all laboratories—firsthand experiences, the actual trying out for oneself all aspects of what is being learned.

141. Ladson-Billings, "Culturally Relevant Teaching," p. 116.

142. Sleeter and Grant, "An Analysis of Multicultural Education," p. 434.

143. See Bowers, *Responsive Teaching*, pp. 73–74.

144. Confluent education refers to the confluence of the cognitive and the affective domains in the educational process. See George Isaac Brown, *Human Teaching for Human Learning: An Introduction to Confluent Education* (New York: Viking, 1971).

Figure 1.3   Expressions of Learning Styles

Cognitive	*Affective*
Rational (logical, linear, verbal)	Feelings (emotional responses)
Iconic (visual, imaginative, spatial)	Values (ethical commitments, attitudinal stances, cultural orientations)
Kinesthetic (enactive and sensorimotor)	Structures of identity (personal sources, professional roles, symbols of identity)

Snelling says that confluent education occurs when there is a balance of cognitive and affective strategies in the teaching framework. At least at the theoretical level, "the greater the degree of inclusion of the six styles of learning, the greater the degree of incorporation of the learning and therefore of retention."[145]

In his analysis of a social science-based religious education for pluralism, Grant Shockley stresses that it must be *proactive* and *engaged*. "Its objectives, content, and methodologies should involve persons in actively shaping their present and future rather than passively reacting to the 'quiet dogmas of the past.' "[146]

The fusion of subject matter and instructional practice means that multicultural religious education must train teachers in developing or adapting curricula as well as in teaching styles. Donald Rogers states bluntly that the most effective curricula and instructional resources for ethnic or multiethnic churches are prepared locally by church religious educators. He advocates training "ordinary teachers" to engage in the writing and editing tasks of local-site production of materials.[147]

CONCLUSION

These four theoretical approaches have not been described exhaustively, and none is adequate in itself to produce a rich and mature multicultural religious education. Nevertheless, they begin to provide principles and direction. A liberationist approach stresses the empowerment and contribution of the oppressed; a community-of-faith approach fosters identity in its Christian and cultural manifestations; the public-church approach engages disciples and society in the search for social justice; the social-science approach makes available effective foundations for multiculturalism in any religious

---

145. Snelling, "The Proper Study," pp. 445–46.
146. Shockley, "A Black Protestant Perspective," p. 148.
147. Rogers, *Urban Church Education*, p. 22.

context. What must emerge is a framework for religious education in a new millennium, one in which the task of Christian religious education will be to proclaim Christ in a world different from what it has ever been—a world in which groups once distant and foreign are now near neighbors; a world of interdependent but distinct peoples, whose identities resist submersion and instinctively refuse to melt into a new culture, even while embracing aspects of it. That drive to maintain identity is God-endowed, consistent with biblical affirmations of human diversity. The calling of the church in the twenty-first century will be to unify a global Christian community without attempting to homogenize it; to preserve the gift of particularity within a context of solidarity. Only in this way, surely, will the apostle's vision be fulfilled of many tribes and tongues glorifying God on that great day.

2

SOCIOLOGICAL FOUNDATIONS OF MULTICULTURAL RELIGIOUS EDUCATION

Carol A. Jenkins
and
Dale Kratt

"Different strokes for different folks" is a slogan that describes the increasingly pluralistic culture in which we find ourselves.[1] Even though America has always been a nation of diversity, American society continues to experience great clusterings into separateness—groupings based on lifestyle, social class, national origin, race, ethnicity, politics, occupation, and religious affiliation. As a nation, the United States continues to become more multicultural, meaning multilingual, multisocial, multiracial, and multireligious. Societal organization continues to be characterized by specialization in every facet of life.

---

1. Although it is an important and complex concept that defies a simple definition, culture is usually taken for granted by most people. As anthropologist Ralph Linton says in *The Study of Man* (New York: Appleton-Century, 1936), "The last thing a fish would ever notice would be water." Similarly, James Henslin observed that people do not notice culture except in universal circumstances. *Down to Earth Sociology: Introductory Readings* (New York: Free Press, 1985). Because people are born into and begin to assimilate a particular culture early in life, the role of culture is comparable to the role of gravity. People rarely think about the presence of gravity, but if it were to disappear suddenly, life as we know it would be thrown out of balance. The influence of culture is equally pervasive. Although seldom thought about, culture provides a framework or set of guidelines for thinking and behaving with regard to other people.

56

A pluralistic society must address two questions: (1) What is the appropriate balance between people's commonality and people's differences? and
(2) To what extent does being "all things to all people" include a willingness
to communicate effectively with those unlike ourselves?

Everyone sees the world through rose-colored glasses. The lenses are
tinted by personal value systems, life experiences, and physical or sensory
limitations. Persons are socialized to become acceptable members of the
general culture and of smaller subcultural groups as well. Members of
a culture often think exclusively in terms of their own social world and
consequently develop few concepts for comparing one social world with
another. People can believe so deeply in the ways and the ideas of their
own world that they have no point of reference for discussing those of
other peoples, times, and places. North Americans can be so engrossed in
their own world that other cultures simply do not concern them. Finding
the balance between America's shared culture and its many overlapping
"microcultures" has never been easy.[2]

The concept of culture demonstrates both unifying and divisive elements.
In its unifying form, culture provides identity. In its divisive form, culture
can create barriers between people, especially if people feel their way of
life is the best way. However, insight about everyday behavior comes from
contrast. Comparing our way of thinking and behaving with other ways
teaches that human behavior is constructed, not determined; that choice
exists and people need not be prisoners of their culture. Most importantly,
learning about other cultures offers insights into the workings of American
society, helping Americans to know and understand the world beyond their
borders and enabling Christians to clarify issues they face as communities
of faith. The church that recognizes such sociocultural diversity will have a
greater chance of accomplishing its task of building bridges between groups
and reaching diverse peoples.

Viewing multicultural religious education as sociologically imperative
(considering individual experiences in their sociocultural historical context
and discovering scientific laws concerning the universal phenomenon of
religion), we will strive to understand (1) how the synergistic interaction
of religion and social systems frames our conceptual and practical understandings of humanity as well as the practice of a viable multicultural
religious education; (2) the extent to which an effective multicultural religious education paradigm and process should affirm American cultural
distinctives; and (3) that multicultural religious education aims should reflect, in a Durkheimian sense,[3] an ideologically based,[4] analytic framework

---

2. Everett Hughes, *The Sociological Eye: Selected Papers* (New Brunswick, N.J.:
Transaction, 1984), p. 474.

3. In *The Elementary Forms of Religious Life* (New York: Free Press, 1912), pp.
3–20, Emile Durkheim probes directly and systematically into the social utility of

that adequately envisions the necessary synergy between the theologies, traditions, and practices of believing communities.

The major purpose of the following discussion is to conceptualize a truly multicultural religious education paradigm as well as to envision a resocialization process that promotes the development of constructive relationships within the believer's church.

HISTORICAL REVIEW:
MULTICULTURALISM—FRAGMENTATION
OR GLOBALIZATION?

A few years after World War II David Reisman chose to present an image of a shared and stable American identity.[5] He succeeded in constructing an image of American character and national identity out of such concepts as individualism, pragmatism, optimism, idealism, and progress. Those characteristics were variously attributed to the influence of the frontier, affluence, and a classless and nonhierarchical society that celebrated an aggressive individualism nurtured by political democracy and economic prosperity. But the scholarly consensus about American identity did not last long.

In the late 1960s and 1970s efforts to bring diversity into people's intellectual lives revealed that traditional interpretations of the American character were built on silence—silence about gender, racial, and ethnic divisions in American society. The shift to a new pluralism fragmented any unified meaning of the word *American*. Ethnic and racial groups, women, poor and working class people, as well as the elite and socially prominent reformers, began to search for sources of individual and group identity.

The new research looked at the effect of cultural differences on American myths of identity. For example, African-American history (represented by Frederick Douglass, Harriet Tubman, and Martin Luther King Jr.) became

---

religion, its social origins, and the way abstract religious and sociological concepts reflect social organizations. Durkheim's general conclusion is that religion is eminently social and that religious representations are collective representations that express collective realities. Conceptual thinking turns out to be determined by social organization. The concepts of space and time, class, force, personality, and efficacy—even the principles of contradiction and identity, the basic constructs in formal logic—he finds emanating from collective representations basic in social organization.

4. The term *ideology* as used here refers mainly to a system of interdependent ideas held by a social group or society, which reflects, rationalizes, and defends its particular interests and communities.

5. David Reisman, *The Lonely Crowd* (New Haven: Yale University Press, 1950).

a contentious issue when historians like Arthur Schlesinger[6] and Peter Brimelow[7] started to ask how racism had shaped the European-American mind and the dominant economy. The history of women, hardly a threat when it spoke to the accomplishments of great women of the past such as Jane Addams, Eleanor Roosevelt, and Susan B. Anthony, created a backlash when it began to inquire whether definitions of Americanism and traits such as individualism or pragmatism were fundamentally masculine rather than universal.

Writing women and people of color into an understanding of culture required redefining the concept American to incorporate multiple definitions of identity. It made a mockery of a monolithic, predominantly Eurocentric interpretation of the American past. Was the land of *e pluribus unum* (from the many, one) disintegrating into *e pluribus plures* (from the many, many) before our very eyes, as Diane Ravitch warned?[8]

By the early 1980s criticism of what was becoming known as multiculturalism already had begun. A rethinking of the norms and values at the core of American society was needed, tracing a new narrative of American culture and deciding how to describe American culture. More specifically, there was a need for a more accurate picture of America's past, a means of coming to terms with America's even more diverse present, and preparations for all people in the United States to live in a world that is becoming increasingly interdependent. Part of an American's sense of identity is based on family roots, whether African-American, Latino, or European. Another part is rooted in input from schools, churches, and the mass media, as they try to articulate some sense of common American identity. Both of these visions—the particular and the common—interact and shape each other in a process of constant change.

Three topics appear in most literature discussing multiculturalism: (1) familiarity with other cultures, (2) receptivity to new cultures, and (3) language learning.[9] When individuals realize that there are alternative ways of thinking and interacting, they see that their own culture is not intrinsically superior, nor are others necessarily inferior. Giroux argued that multiculturalism is all about introducing language that makes it possible to recognize and contest "dominant forms of symbolic production."[10]

---

6. Arthur Schlesinger Jr. *The Disunity of America: Reflections on a Multicultural Society* (Knoxville, Tenn.: Whittle, 1991), p. 21.

7. Peter Brimelow, *Alien Nation: Common Sense about America's Immigration Disaster* (New York: Random House, 1995).

8. Diane Ravitch, "Multiculturalism: E Pluribus Plures" *American Scholar* 59:3 (1990): 337–54.

9. Centre for Educational Research and Innovation, *One School, Many Cultures* (N. Manchester, Ind.: Heckman Bindery, 1989), p. 7.

10. See Henry Giroux, *Border Crossings* (New York: Routledge, 1992), p. 3.

In the late twentieth century a sharp debate developed concerning the question, Should society encourage the growth of diverse subcultures or should it encourage common values and ways of life? This debate has been particularly intense regarding racial and ethnic cultural diversity. How can a diverse society best ensure that people from all backgrounds have the opportunity to contribute to its productivity and to benefit from its wealth? Is it better to encourage groups to preserve their cultures or encourage them to assimilate? To what extent can people from diverse backgrounds cooperate with one another? Fourth, does assimilation mean surrendering one's own values to those of a more powerful group?

These questions have taken on growing importance as the proportion of people of color from non-European backgrounds has risen in the U.S. population. Today, about one out of four Americans are from such cultural backgrounds, and this percentage will continue to grow for two reasons. First, these groups tend to have a somewhat higher birthrate than groups of European ancestry. Second, today's immigrants are coming mainly from Latin America, Asia, and the Caribbean, in contrast to earlier eras when most immigrants came from Europe.[11]

At the heart of the controversy over multiculturalism lie questions about American identity. Opponents of multiculturalism (mainly social-science functionalists and political conservatives) identify the United States with ideas about the nature of Western civilization and the particular humanistic values of individual freedom and tolerance that it is said to represent.[12]

Opponents argue that multiculturalism encourages divisiveness rather than unity by encouraging people to maintain their cultural differences. Yet the more people have in common, the argument maintains, the more they are willing to cooperate. Differences in values and outlook only lead to conflicts that divide different groups and inhibit cooperation. This view emphasizes that too much cultural diversity can be dysfunctional. Opponents also argue that multiculturalism tends to erode any claim to common truth by maintaining that all ideas should be evaluated according to the race, ethnicity, and sex of those who present them. People's common humanity becomes obscured by a plethora of African, Latin, and European experiences. Another concern is that multiculturalism may lead to precisely the kind of segregation that our

11. William P. O'Hare, "America's Minorities—The Demographics of Diversity," *Population Bulletin* 47, no. 4 (1992): 2–47.
12. See Ronald Takaki, *A Different Mirror: A History of Multicultural America* (Boston: Little, Brown, 1993), pp. 1–17. Even though issues that engage the new multiculturalism incorporate concepts of culture, cultural relativism, and interpretations of other systems of thought, *multiculturalism* often is criticized as "ethnic cheerleading" that highlights differences among Americans rather than their common heritage *or* is confined to recent economic and social trends that emphasize differences. In Herbert Kohl's words, the issues of multiculturalism are reduced to the "struggles over shifts in dominance in our society." "Social Policy," *Migration World* 19, no. 4 (1991): 3.

nation has struggled for decades to end. According to this view, differing groups in the United States should be encouraged to assimilate into one common culture. Classic Western intellectual traditions largely shaped the development of North American culture, and these traditions are the ones that should be passed on.[13]

Advocates of multiculturalism attempt to validate the wide range of cultures that coexist in the United States by arguing that the traditional canon reflects the interests and perspectives of privileged white European men while largely ignoring the contributions of women, men of color, and working people.[14] Expanding the definition of what it means to be an American does not require abandoning the idea of a national identity. It encourages us to rethink the meaning of identity as something that is fluid and susceptible to change.

There are some groups that do not want to assimilate, and indeed assimilation may not be in their interest. Many researchers have pointed out that groups brought into a society involuntarily nearly always resist giving up their own values and lifestyles in favor of those of the majority.[15] Oppressed groups resist accepting the values of the group that discriminates against them and exploits them economically. Most people of color in the United States fall into this category. African Americans, Mexican Americans, Puerto Ricans, and Native peoples all were, historically speaking, brought under American rule involuntarily and subjected to widespread discrimination and economic exploitation. Only Asian Americans originally came voluntarily, and they tend to be more culturally assimilated than

---

13. See Roger Kimball, "The Periphery vs. the Center: The MLA in Chicago," and John Searle, "The Disunity of America: Reflections on a Multicultural Society," in *Debating PC: The Controversy over Political Correctness on College Campuses*, ed. Paul Berman (New York: Dell, 1992), pp. 61–84. Well-meaning as the critics of multiculturalism may be, their misunderstanding has unfortunate consequences. They commonly confuse cultural relativism with moral relativism. They may assume that refraining from negative value judgments for the purpose of understanding cultural phenomena means that they must make universally positive judgments, implying that anything anybody does anywhere is good. Cultural relativism does not mean that all human behavior merits approval. It only means that to understand what people do, it is more useful to ask why they do it than to decide whether or not they should. The study of cultural diversity should be approached as seriously as other fields of study, many of which are far less complex and important. Richard J. Perry, "Why Do Multiculturalists Ignore Anthropologists?" *Chronicle of Higher Education*, 4 March 1992, sec. A, p. 52.

14. Henry Louis Gates, "Whose Canon Is It Anyway?" in *Debating PC*, ed. Paul Berman, p. 197.

15. Robert Blauner, *Racial Oppression in America* (New York: Harper & Row, 1972); Stanley Lieberson, *A Piece of the Pie: Black and White Immigrants since 1880* (Berkeley: University of California Press, 1980); Richard Zweignehaft and G. William Domhoff, *Blacks and Whites in the White Establishment: A Study of Race and Class in America* (New Haven: Yale University Press, 1991).

other Americans of color. Thus, whatever the theoretical merits of a society with cultural consensus, given the history of the United States, it may be unrealistic to expect many groups to ever assimilate.

The real question comes down to whether or not people can learn to respect cultural differences and cooperate despite these differences. In other words, will multiculturalism lead to fragmentation or globalization? As people become more educated and as society continues to urbanize, people tend to become more accepting of diversity.[16]

THE SYNERGISM OF THEOLOGY AND SOCIOLOGY

The conceptual and practical foundations for multicultural religious education are to be found in a handful of fundamental concepts from theology and the social sciences. We will begin this sociological inquiry by looking at multicultural religious education through a theological lens, affirming and assuming the following statements:

1. Humanity is not all that there is; what we are as persons in some respects reflects what God is.
2. Our common humanity is rooted in the original creative work of God. We all share in this equally, and our bond to all peoples is rooted in it.
3. Persons are divinely endowed to live as culturally formed beings. This is not our highest calling, yet it is a very real situation from which we cannot extricate ourselves and within which our calling is lived out. Our highest calling is to love the true and living God.
4. Every cultural form is humanly constituted and bears the imprints, in its own unique ways, of our noble likeness to God and our alienation from God. Culture is therefore a domain that stands under both divine affirmation and judgment. It may be either an instrument of good or an instrument of evil.
5. The living God, who transcends our experience of history, has chosen to be revealed in ways that we can adequately come to know in space-time history by taking on real humanity as we know it.
6. Jesus the Messiah is this revelation; this Jesus was religiously and culturally Jewish.
7. Jesus' suffering and death were for all; his resurrection was the transformation of his humanity and the transcendence of his Jewishness. In this way the Messiah embraces and affirms all of humanity in all of its uniqueness and diversity, yet he calls all humanity to transcend parochial

---

16. Steven A. Tuch, "Urbanism, Region, and Tolerance Revisited: The Case of Racial Prejudice," *American Sociological Review* 52 (1987): 504–10.

allegiances. Allegiance to Jesus brings people into the wider community of Christ's church in communion with him through his Spirit.

8. This wider community, the church, transcends time and space as we know it and encompasses all those in the past who loved this true and living God, and all those who now live on this earth who love this true and living God. Our common bond in the Messiah is therefore lived out within a very real and radical diversity of time, space, and cultural life. However, we experience only a small part of this diversity.

9. This situation forms the basis of a multicultural imperative to acknowledge and work with the truth of God and the truth of who we are; to go beyond a mere acknowledgment of human diversity by developing and fostering a genuinely multicultural orientation in thought and practice.

Theological Basis for Multicultural Religious Education

Religiously based concepts such as those cited above assume that humanity is singularly incapable of full and adequate understanding. Nevertheless, knowing the living God enables the individual to envision, understand, and practice religious truths in relation to self and others. To avoid an abstract and decontextualized understanding of humanity, the insights of religious truth must become rooted and situated not only in a supraculture (a proscriptive vision of how society could and should be) but also in the real world people live in. Thus, the synergistic interaction of religion and sociology can shape conceptual and practical understandings of humanity as well as the practice of a viable multicultural religious education.

Numerous scriptural passages emphasize that Christians are to play an active role in society. Colossians 1:28, 29, for example, provides general guidelines for action. First, Christians are to proclaim Christ. Second, although there is much empirical evidence to suggest that knowledge is not necessarily correlated with attitude and behavior, the church is to counsel and teach with wisdom, imparting knowledge about Christ. Such knowledge should help develop the attitudes and behaviors that characterized the life of Jesus. Third, by presenting "everyone perfect in Christ" bridges between people become built.[17]

The authors of this chapter assume that (1) Christian tradition provides a vision of how society could and should be and gives guidance about how to move toward that vision; (2) neither God nor most humans want society to be unjust and unpeaceful; and (3) the aims of multicultural religious education should be theoretically based, sociologically imperative, and educationally effective.

---

17. Ralph Robson and Jean Billings, *Christian Cross-Cultural Communication* (Cincinnati, Ohio: Standard, 1978), pp. 39–40.

Each person is a unique creation of God who has a special contribution to make to the Christian community. To begin to see others as God sees them, individuals must look at their potential for useful service in the kingdom, not at their differences or undesirable characteristics. How to do this is modeled by Christ Jesus numerous times in the Gospels. It is important to realize that Jesus not only spoke against unjust, discriminatory laws and traditions, but he also acted against them. He chose to relate to all people without questioning their sex, age, religious belief, or cultural pedigree and status (Jn 4:1–43). This is the example and starting point for believers: acceptance and appreciation of differences. Often human acceptance is conditional. I will accept you—if you look like me, talk like me, believe what I believe. People must learn to accept others not only in spite of differences but because of them, as long as these differences are not destructive.

The Bible clearly teaches that it is wrong for color or class to separate people. In North America more "color" and more "class" have complicated the picture. As in the larger society, division and controversy have too often characterized the church.[18] However, scriptural principles serve to unite believers in a common mission to resolve the sociocultural notions that separate them.[19] What is the basis for such a moral imperative? A

---

18. In their book *Tell It To the Church* (Wheaton, Ill.: Tyndale House 1985), pp. 18, 29, Lynn Buzzard and Lawrence Eck point out that conflict among the church's members has been the norm rather than the exception. Prophets were in conflict with kings. Greek Christians struggled with Hebrew Christians (Acts 6). The New Testament church had to deal with serious conflicts (Acts 13). Paul challenged Peter over his prejudice in Galatians 2. Yet Christians are called to live by standards that differ from the ones held by our battle-oriented society. Jesus made it plain that the world would know his disciples by their love for one another (John 13:34, 36). Disputes within the local church frequently concern opinions about implementation, methodology, times, and seasons. Standing for sound biblical doctrine is right, but allowing division over opinion is intolerable (Titus 3:9–11; Rom 16:17, 18; 1 Cor 1:10–13; 3:3–9; Jude 16–19). Finally, the church loses its credibility as a bridge builder when it fails to treat its own with love and concern. The church must therefore show the love of Christ within if it expects to influence others who are without. For church adherents to get past barriers to reconciliation, they must change their outlook on race and ethnicity. Too many view race and ethnicity as a problem to be solved rather than as a gift to be enjoyed. Second, they must hold to the conviction that viable solutions to the problems growing out of diversity are grounded in Scripture. (See Robson and Billings, *Christian Cross-Cultural Communication*, p. 42).

19. Robson and Billings argue that there are three crucial New Testament passages dealing with prejudice. Each has been written by a different author with distinct and unique purposes in mind. But all three give overwhelming evidence that God is displeased with attitudes of racial or ethnic discrimination. First, the story of the Samaritan woman recorded in chapter 4 of John's Gospel characterizes God as not receptive to worship that keeps people in their own separate camps. Second, Peter's experience with the Roman centurion described in Acts 10 suggests that to maintain a separatist attitude between people who were both recognized by God was to oppose God. And third, Ephesians 2:11–22 teaches that different heritages, cultures, customs, and habits should

God-centered view of persons. The church can take the lead in healing by recognizing that God did something wonderful in making human beings differ from each other.[20]

Sociological Basis for Multicultural Religious Education

Religion has always been an important part of life in America. In his analysis of religion, Emile Durkheim attempted to explain the universal presence of religion in human history in terms of its contributions to societal survival.[21] He argued that religion (1) provides a basis for social cohesion by uniting the members of the population in shared beliefs and values, as well as in a common set of rituals that unite people spiritually and socially; (2) promotes social stability and social control by infusing cultural norms and political rules with sacred authority, thus increasing the likelihood that people will follow them (providing what Peter Berger called a "sacred canopy"[22]) and (3) helps maintain people's allegiance to societal goals and participation in societal affairs by providing a sense of meaning and purpose.

Throughout the history of the human race people have confronted similar kinds of problems. Over thousands of years they have developed significant solutions for those problems. These historical patterns of behavior become closely integrated, forming a cultural whole that to its bearers justifies and makes reasonable their beliefs, ideas and action.

Sociologists are interested in the connection between values and concrete behavior. To study these connections, they employ the concept of norms— the written and unwritten rules that specify behavior appropriate to specific situations. However, it is not sufficient simply to say that values and norms guide behavior. We must investigate the geographical and historical circumstances that give rise to specific norms and values. To demonstrate that a particular component of culture is "useful" does not explain how it originated or why it is what it is.[23]

Sociologists assume that geographical and historical forces shape the character of culture and that culture serves as a "buffer between people and their environment."[24] Most people do not question the validity of the values

---

not be disregarded, cast aside, or simply adopted by other members. Growth within an institution cannot take place until each member is properly fitted together in relationship to God and one another. When this is accomplished, such a structure becomes a habitation of God. And where God dwells, there lives a people who are one (pp. 15–16; 28–31).

20. Dolphus Weary, "The Gift of Race," *Christianity Today* 37, no. 5 (1993): 20.

21. Durkheim, *Elementary Forms*, pp. 3–8; 10–13.

22. Peter Berger, *The Sacred Canopy* (Garden City, N.Y.: Doubleday, 1969).

23. Emile Durkheim, *The Rules of the Sociological Method* (Glencoe, Ill.: Free Press), 1938.

24. Richard Critchfield, "Science, Villagers, and Us," *Universities Field Staff International Report*, no. 3 (1985): 3.

they follow and the norms to which they conform "anymore than a baby analyzes the atmosphere before it begins to breathe it."[25] People behave as they do because they have been socialized to by the previous generation.

Failure to understand the premises that underlie these deeply rooted behavior patterns often results in arrogance and ethnocentricity.[26] Many ethnocentric attitudes stem from a belief in the commonness of experience. In other words, cultural norms and values typically are so internalized that they seem to be part of the natural order. People tend to assume that the ways they think and act are as natural as nature itself.[27] It is often difficult to accept the possibility that people may interpret experiences common to all in widely divergent ways. Sociologists are concerned with more than the number of people who believe and worship in a particular manner. They are interested in (1) how religion affects the way people behave politically, economically, and socially; (2) how the content, practice, and organization of a given religion affects people's behavior as individuals and as members of groups and institutions; and (3) how belief systems are related to social change (especially to diversification and modernization). As a catalyst for change, religion can facilitate changes in the organization of religious systems as well as lead to fundamental and sweeping changes in the larger societal system.

A clearly biblical tradition provides a supraculture as well as prescriptive guidance for the church in becoming a culturally responsive community. An informed, biblically based orientation provides the individual with a basis for viewing one's disposition as sociocultural and as an imperative for reflexive practice. A true multicultural religious education, grounded in an awareness and analysis of the realities of the human-social situation that enhance or block the vision of equity and justice, would free learners from fear of the unknown, particularly tendencies toward xenophobia.[28]

---

25. William Graham Sumner, *Folkways* (Boston: Ginn, 1902), p. 23.

26. When people from different cultures meet for the first time, they often approach the encounter with fear and anxiety. Both are wearing their cultural lenses and interpret events using their culture as a frame of reference. A major cause of the communications breakdown between members of different cultures is *ethnocentrism*—a process of judging other cultures according to the values and standards prevailing in their own culture (Sumner, *Folkways*, p. 13). Although ethnocentrism has short-term benefits of instilling a sense of pride, well-being, and security, it often inhibits understanding between peoples. There are many ways of doing things, but proponents of those various ways believe that theirs are the best. It is possible to attempt to understand others without necessarily giving up individual belief. Once a common denominator is found, there is no need to discuss whose ways are better. Instead, there is a need to recognize that people can learn from each other and make the world a better place.

27. Emory S. Bogardus, "Comparing Racial Distance in Ethiopia, South Africa, and the United States," *Sociology and Social Research* 52, no. 2 (January 1968): 149–56.

28. Harvey Seifert, from a seminar on new patterns of social education, quoted in Dieter T. Hessel, "A Whole Ministry of Social Education," *Religious Education* 78, no. 4 (fall 1983): 545.

Religious and social traditions of each group affect the pattern of relationships between and among the social structural variables that exist among other religioethnic groups.[29] Thus, the range of religious values and religious perspectives are important considerations in understanding.

The task for religious educators is, first, to focus attention on how better to combine knowledge, affect, and action in ministry, and, second, how to more adequately educate Christians for ethical responses to the crucial issues of diversity. Clarifying norms (social values, expectations, and goals) requires engaging in the task of contextual social ethics, exploring the social philosophy and values served by specific issues, and evaluating them in light of biblical realities and church tradition.[30] Thus an understanding of one's own position in the process of religious education becomes broadened and increases the potential for productive action. The greatest challenge is to bring the world of the Scriptures into contemporary thought and culture, effectively making the values of the Christian heritage relevant to societal problems, especially diversity.

Such a proscriptive vision is eschatological rather than utopian in the sense that the coming kingdom of Messiah—another coming world—is foreshadowed and given a place in our alienated world. Regardless of a tendency toward privatized and often overly politicized Christianity, the realization of anticipatory justice, equity, peace, love, power, and truth provide a basis for a spiritual vision of persistent Christian practice of equity among the diversity of classes, races, and ethnic peoples of present society.

THE RELATIONSHIP BETWEEN
THEORY AND PRACTICE

Understanding the relationship between theory and practice is fundamental to understanding how the perspectives from which people think and live are constituted.[31] All theory and practice are located within the subjective and objective roles in all social worlds. The subjective forces us to focus on the personal and social aspects of meaning, while the objective forces us to focus on the broader institutional framework within which each individual life is

---

29. Michael Homola, Dean Knudsen, and Harvey Marshall, "Religion and Socio-Economic Achievement," *Journal for the Scientific Study of Religion* 26, no. 2 (1987): 203.

30. Seifert, quoted in "A Whole Ministry of Social Education," p. 545.

31. J. M. Lee has defined theory as consisting of "a set of interrelated facts and laws which present a systematic view of phenomena by specifying relations among variables in order to explain and predict the phenomena." The significance of theory lies primarily in its fruitfulness in generating new practices, explanations, and discoveries. James Michael Lee, *The Flow of Religious Instruction* (Birmingham, Ala.: Religious Education Press, 1973), pp. 39–40.

situated. A contextual framework then provides a firm basis for assessing and understanding the different and the unfamiliar.

For example, the American church today strongly reflects the individualism of American history and culture: the me-first attitude of a success-at-all-costs way of life and the opposing need to belong to some larger community. Very different from the familiar rugged individualism of the past, the contemporary individualist orientation causes Americans to overlook the broader institutional settings of the culture and the influences exerted by those settings on the practice of Christianity. This may be one reason for the frequent inclusion of microindividualistic rather than macrocollective explanations for phenomena in church life.

Consider also that within an individualist framework, people tend to reduce cultural diversity exclusively to differences in values, perspectives, ideologies, worldviews, and the like. As important as these understandings are, to believe that in our culture our individualistic and collective experiences as a church are exempt from broader socially constitutive institutional forms is patently naive. Such naivete is one reason churches have so easily succumbed to institutionally structured, socioculturally rooted practices of evil and alienation in the forms of racism, oppressive cultural domination, and exclusion based on social class. Numerous churches are identifiably stratified enclaves of social class typified by monoculturalism and monoethnicity.

A sociological perspective on multicultural religious education helps us step back and view with detachment a topic that is often charged with emotion. Such an approach is necessary to avoid sweeping generalizations about the nature of a multicultural religious education or about how religious belief affects behavior. A sociological analysis of religion and culture helps achieve an understanding of multicultural religious education and helps explain how culture is used.

Durkheim's ideas about the nature of religion, although not without shortcomings, explicate the functions that religion performs for the individual and the group.[32] First and foremost, religion provides a rich and seemingly endless variety of responses to the problems of human existence. In a Durkheimian sense, a multicultural religious education could contribute to group unity and solidarity. Religious values supply the basic social cohesion that makes a society righteous and enduring. Because the functional requisites of religion demonstrate a multifaceted and complex phenomenon, they cannot be discussed in isolation. Rather, they must be understood within the larger social, historical, economic, and political context.

On the other hand, in a Marxian sense, religious doctrines can be used to turn people's attention away from unjust political and economic arrangements as well as to rationalize and defend the political and economic

---

32. Durkheim, *Elementary Forms*, pp. 13, 15–18, 19–20.

interests of the dominant classes. Likewise, the oppressed have used religion as a vehicle to protest and to change the existing social and economic inequities.

We can truly begin to envision the forms of evil that characterize our practice in ministry only as we begin to understand the impact of historical Christianity on the formation of the American heritage, the relationship of church in society, and broader institutional processes of inclusion, exclusion and disenfranchisement operating in so many of our churches. What is needed is a moral imperative reflecting the development of a concrete multicultural religious education strategy and a practical spirituality enabling believers to live discerningly, purely, strategically, and effectively in the midst of diversity.

INTERGROUP RELATIONS: HOW IMMIGRANT AND INDIGENOUS MINORITIES RESPOND TO THE DOMINANT CULTURE

There is more to multiculturalism than notions of theory and practice. Cross-cultural encounters require preparation to result in healthy relationships. Comprehensive descriptions and analyses of cultural groups, ways of life, and thought contribute to an adequate theory of culture on which a multicultural religious education can be based.

Immigrants to the United States

America, the land of opportunity, has welcomed immigrants from all corners of the earth. The new arrivals have brought with them a variety of languages, religions, music, dance, crafts, holidays, costumes, customs, foods, and family traditions. As the immigrants settled into their new communities, they adapted some of their customs to their new surroundings. Their neighbors adopted other aspects of their cultural heritage and thus they became a part of the local culture. At the same time, many immigrants retained their customs, traditions, and arts, pursuing them within their families, church services, and celebrations. Thus was created an American cultural mosaic of diverse peoples attempting to coexist.

All Americans share the elements of a broad national culture and also belong to other cultural groups that together constitute American society. Indeed, this marvelous "weaving of many threads of all sizes and colors" is one defining characteristic of American culture.[33] When people are exposed

---

33. Randolph Bourne, "Trans-National America," *Atlantic Monthly* 118 (July 1916): 98.

to different ways of thinking and behaving, they also gain important insights into their own ways.[34] Church members come to understand that the lives of people in North America are intertwined with those of people in other places, and that the forces affecting American life are not necessarily confined to the internal dynamics of the country. This helps to clarify issues that the church faces in global ministry.

The richness of American culture is partly the mixture of flavors we identify as "American." The greater richness, however, encompasses the separate ingredients, each one preserving its uniqueness and enduring as a distinct entity within the whole.

Some Americans are now lamenting what they call the "fragmenting of America," predicated on their perception that "shared experiences and a sense of community" are slipping away.[35] By that they mean, among other things, that "the huge influx of Latino[36] and Asian[37] immigrants has literally changed the face of America." These Americans are experiencing

---

34. Tuch, "Urbanism, Region, and Tolerance Revisited," pp. 504–10.

35. Reported by Robert Samuelson, *The Washington Post National Weekly Edition*, August 12–18, 1991.

36. The term *Latino* refers to a category of Hispanic people made up of many separate cultural and racial subgroups bound together by a common language, Spanish. In 1990, about 21 million Spanish-speaking people were officially recorded as residing in the United States, and several million others are believed to have entered the country without official documents. In 1990, the four major ethnic subdivisions within the Spanish-speaking population were Mexican Americans, Puerto Ricans, Cubans, and people from Central and South American countries, particularly the Dominican Republic, Colombia, and El Salvador. "The Hispanic Population in the U.S. March 1990," Current Population Reports: Population Characteristics, series P-20, vol. 449 (Washington, D.C.: Government Printing Office, 1991), p. 2. Differences within the Spanish-speaking minority are striking, especially in terms of education and income. Each ethnic subdivision has its own immigration history, cultural patterns, and its own internal diversity. There exists a stratification system within the Latino population, based not only on indicators of socioeconomic status but also on skin color. Race and ethnicity combine to affect the relative status of Spanish-speaking Americans, both within the stratification system of the wider society and within the hierarchy of the Latino subculture. These divisions reduce the likelihood of the development of shared interests necessary to strengthen Latino influence in society.

37. Like European Americans, Asian Americans come from different cultures and religious backgrounds and speak different languages. Yet a tendency to categorize all Asians together has dominated both immigration policy and popular attitudes. Included as dominant Asian groupings are Chinese, Japanese, and Southeast Asian peoples. The Asian-American population increased by 107.8 percent between 1980 and 1990. More than 2 million immigrants from Southeast Asia in 1980–90 brought new variety to the Asian-American population. The fastest growing ethnic groups during that time were Vietnamese (134.8 percent growth in 1980–91), Indians (125.6 percent growth), and Koreans (125.3 percent increase), Felicity Barringer, "Immigration Brings New Diversity to Asian Population in the United States," *New York Times*, 12 June 1991, p. 1. Current population surveys provide an indication of this increasing diversity. Although

confusion and pain because "our fragmented society sacrifices a large sense of belonging"—a common national heritage.[38]

This growing awareness and emphasis on differences underlies the raging debate over multiculturalism, which now means the movement toward multicultural education—revision that is designed to infuse the curriculum with information about ethnic and cultural groups other than Anglo-Europeans.

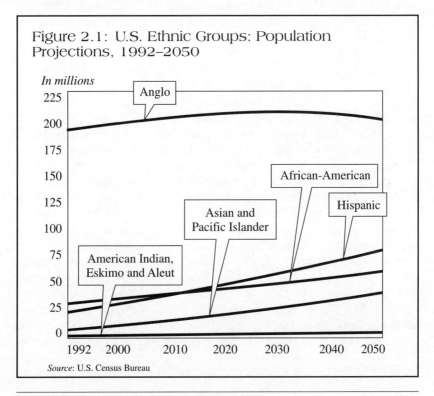

Figure 2.1: U.S. Ethnic Groups: Population Projections, 1992–2050

Source: U.S. Census Bureau

the overall educational level of Asian Americans is high, 20 percent of Asian Americans age twenty-five or over have not completed high school; although the average family income of Asian Americans ($35,900) is slightly higher than that of non-Latino whites ($35,000), the poverty of Asian Americans is nearly twice that of non-Latino whites. Census data indicate that among Asian Americans, Southeast Asians are the most disadvantaged educationally and economically, and Japanese, the most advantaged. In 1980 there were about 1.7 million people of other Asian ethnicities in the United States. Filipinos accounted for 45 percent, followed by Asian Indians and Koreans. Koreans showed the most remarkable growth, increasing from 69,999 in 1970 to 357,000 by 1980. The reception accorded to Asian Americans, like most new immigrants who are not of northern European origin, has been mixed.

38. "Multiculturalism: Fragmentation or Globalization?" *Migration World* 19, no. 4 (1991): 3.

Multiculturalism requires an adequate theory of culture that can plausibly be generated through comparative analyses.[39]

Bernard Lonergan reminds nostalgic neoconservatives in anguish over the fading of a common national heritage that the dialectic of community is to be met by the attainment of a higher viewpoint in our understanding of human beings, not by any ideas or set of ideas on the level of technology, economics, or politics.[40] It is not just a matter of socializing, belonging, communicating, and interacting; it is a matter of social responsibilities, of loyalties and solidarities, of deep commitment to other human beings, to groups, and to society within the bonds of freedom and dignity.

The immigrants' experience can be understood by examining how their distinguishing features, as well as some external factors, influence their perceptions of and responses to domination and exploitation. The collective identity system and cultural frame of reference of immigrants are different, but not necessarily oppositional. First, immigrant minorities often do not consider themselves a part of the prevailing stratification system, but as strangers outside it.[41] Second, their reference group is often located in their "homeland" or in their immigrant neighborhood, not in their host society, which creates a resistance to acculuration or assimilation. Thus emerges an alternation pattern of participating in two different but not oppositional cultures simultaneously.[42] People learn to switch back and forth between two different but not oppositional cultural frames of reference.[43]

In general, whether in the past or among the more recent immigrants, the goal of self-advancement is uppermost in the minds of the immigrant and acts as a strong incentive to exploit anticipated and unanticipated opportunities and to maintain pragmatic attitudes toward economic and other activities, even in the face of prejudice and discrimination.[44]

In the 1980s more than 10 million immigrants from Latin America, Asia, and the Middle East came to the United States, marking the largest immigration wave in the nation's history. In 1989 over one million ninety

39. George and Louise Spindler, *Interpretive Ethnography of Education: At Home and Abroad* (Hillsdale, N.J.: Lawrence Erlbaum, 1987), p. 74.

40. Bernard J. F. Lonergan, *Insight: A Study in Human Understanding* (New York: Philosophical Library, 1957).

41. J. U. Ogbu, "Stockton, California Revisited: Joining the Labor Force," in *Becoming a Worker*, ed. K. Borman (Norwood, N.J.: Ablex, 1984), p. 270.

42. M. A. Gibson, *Home-School-Community Linkages: A Study of Educational Equity for Punjabi Youth* (Washington, D.C.: National Institute of Education, 1983).

43. Ogbu, *California Revisited*, p. 274.

44. H. Cather, "History of San Francisco's Chinatown" (M.A. thesis, University of California at Berkeley, n.d.); H. B. McLendry, *The Oriental Americans* (New York: Twayne, 1972); B. L. Sung, *Mountain of Gold: The Story of the Chinese in America* (New York: Macmillan, 1967).

Table 2.2: Country of Birth of Immigrants to the United States, 1989

Place of Birth*	Total
Asia	312,139
Philippines	57,034
China	46,246
Vietnam	37,739
Korea	34,222
India	31,175
Iran	21,243
Laos	12,524
Hong Kong	9,740
Thailand	9,332
Pakistan	8,000
North America	607,398
Mexico	405,172
Dominican Republic	26,723
Jamaica	24,523
Haiti	13,658
Canada	12,151
Cuba	10,046
Central and South America	159,960
El Salvador	57,878
Guatemala	19,049
Colombia	15,214
Guyana	10,789
Peru	10,175
Nicaragua	8,830
Europe	82,891
Poland	15,101
Great Britain	14,090
Soviet Union (former)	11,128
Africa	25,166
Total	**1,090,924**

*Countries of largest immigration; the total does not match that for the continent or subcontinent.

Source: Statistical Abstract of the United States, 1991: Table 9.

thousand immigrants came from Asia, North America, Central and South America, Europe, and Africa.[45]

That these distinct entities continue to endure attests to the strength of the nation conceived by the framers of the U.S. Constitution. Newcomers to a local community, however, are not always welcomed with open arms. Human nature has a tendency to mistrust the unfamiliar, a tendency reflected in the bias, prejudice, and discrimination that further isolate new arrivals. Maintaining their uniqueness and solidarity enables newcomers to endure.

Castelike Indigenous Minorities: African Americans and Native Peoples

Immigrant minorities moved more or less voluntarily to their host society for economic, social, or political reasons,[46] whereas *indigenous* minorities originated in the Americas—Native peoples, Mexicans initially enclosed by America's expanding border, as well as those brought to the Americas involuntarily, mainly African Americans. African Americans and Native peoples learned during the course of their history as Americans that they could not easily or freely escape from their socially ascribed membership in a subordinate, disparaged group, regardless of their place of origin, their individual abilities and training, or their specific economic status. They also realized that they could not expect to be assimilated as other immigrants had been, nor could they return to their "homeland" as some non-Anglo immigrants had.[47]

For other immigrants, America represented liminality—a new world where they could pursue extravagant ambitions and do things they had thought beyond their capabilities. Like the land itself, the immigrants found themselves "betwixt and between all fixed points of classification." No longer fastened as fiercely to their old countries, they felt a stirring to become new people in a society still be defined and formed.[48]

By contrast, the indigenous groups (sometimes called castelike minorities) recognized that their experiences of being demeaned, their lack of socioeconomic advancement, and their generally unsatisfactory life situations were rooted in the dominant group's exploitation of them, not in

---

45. U.S. Bureau of the Census, *Statistical Abstracts of the United States* (Government Printing Office: Washington, D.C. 1991), table 9.

46. A. L. Mabogunje, *Regional Mobility and Resource Development in West Africa* (Montreal: McGill-Queens University Press, 1972); T. Shibutani and K. M. Kwan, *Ethnic Stratification: A Comparative Approach* (New York: Macmillan, 1965).

47. Churchill Ward, "Crimes against Humanity," *Z Magazine*, March 1993, pp. 43–47.

48. Arnold Van Gennep, *The Rites of Passage* (Chicago: University of Chicago Press, 1960); Victor Turner, *Dramas, Fields and Metaphors: Symbolic Action in Human Society* (Ithaca, N.Y.: Cornell University Press, 1974), pp. 232, 237.

anything inherently inferior about them.[49] Although some could "pass" as members of the dominant group, only a few did do so successfully, owing to the social and psychological costs of passing.[50] Under their castelike status, African Americans and Native peoples[51] responded with what DeVos and Wagatsuma called "an ethnic consolidation"[52] or with a collective sense of identity.[53] Collective oppositional identity systems serve major functions for members of minority groups. For example, an oppositional identity promotes formation of peer groups that tend to satisfy affiliative needs that are apparently not met by the family and other institutions.

Peer groups have been important historically for African Americans because they served as a survival institution at a time when African-American families were frequently broken up. According to Rawick and Fordham, African Americans adapted childrearing practices that emphasized the importance of affiliation with more enduring groups outside the family, such as peer groups and the "community," often resulting in the development of a kind of "fictive" linkage with peers and the community.[54]

Closely associated with the development of a collective oppositional identity system was the evolution of an oppositional cultural system with several mechanisms to protect and maintain the identity system. These

49. William J. Wilson, *The Truly Disadvantaged: The Inner City, the Underclass, and Public Policy* (Chicago: University of Chicago Press, 1987) and *The Declining Significance of Race: Blacks and Changing America*, 2d ed. (Chicago: University of Chicago Press, 1980).

50. J. H. Burma, "The Measurement of Negro Passing," *American Journal of Sociology* 52 (1946): 18–22; W. L. Warner, B. H. Junker, and W. A. Adams, *Color and Human Nature: Negro Personality in a Northern City* (Washington, D.C.: The American Youth Commission, 1941).

51. E. H. Spicer, "The Process of Cultural Enclavement in Middle America" (Seville: 36th Congress of Internasional de Americanistas, 1966), pp. 267–79, and "Persistent Cultural Systems: A Comparative Study of Identity Systems That Can Adapt to Contrasting Environments," *Science* 174 (1971): 795–800; G. P. Castile and G. Kushner, eds., *Persistent Peoples: Cultural Enclaves in Perspective* (Tucson: University of Arizona Press, 1981).

52. G. A. DeVos and H. Wagatsuma, eds., *Japan's Invisible Race: Caste in Culture and Personality* (Berkeley: University of California Press, 1967).

53. J. H. Apel, "American Negro and Immigrant Experience: Similarities and Differences," in *The Aliens: A History of Ethnic Minorities in America*, ed. L. Dinnerstein and F. C. Jaher (New York: Appleton-Century-Crofts, 1970); V. M. Green, "Blacks in the United States: The Creation of an Enduring People?" in *Persistent Peoples*, ed. Castile and Kushner, pp. 69–77; L. Mullings, "Ethnicity and Stratification in the Urban United States," *Annals of the New York Academy of Science* 318 (1978): 10–22.

54. G. P. Rawick, *From Sundown to Sunup: The Making of the Black Community* (Westport, Conn.: Greenwood, 1972) and S. Fordham, "Afro-Caribbean and Native Black American School Performance in Washington, D.C.: Learning to Be or Not to Be a Native" (A paper presented at the Graduate School of Education, Harvard University, April 1984).

mechanisms included collective struggles, deviant behavior (such as deviating from the point of view of the dominant group), collective hatred for the dominant group, and cultural inversion (the tendency to regard certain forms of behaviors, events, symbols, and meanings as not appropriate for them because they are characteristic of members of a different population). These developments—epistemological, instrumental, and expressive responses to their subordination and exploitation—had distinctive cultural consequences.

African Americans: What makes the culture of the African-American castelike minority truly different from mainstream culture is not its African sources or any dramatic dissimilarities with European-American cultures. Rather, African-American culture is characterized by elements of opposition and ambivalence in its relation to the European-American culture.[55]

At the ideational level one element of opposition to Eurocentrism is embodied in the belief among many African Americans that the African-American cultural frame of reference is different from the European-American cultural frame of reference. At the psychological level the ambivalence and opposition lie in the "double consciousness" of cultural dualism that DuBois noted early in the twentieth century.[56] This oppositional and ambivalent quality creates for the individual what Gordon noted as "identificational assimilation" (the loss of a distinctive group identity)[57] and what DeVos referred to as "affective dissonance" (incongruity in thought and behavior that permeates various domains of African-American culture).[58]

The affective dissonance that characterizes castelike minority cultures distinguishes them from the cultures of immigrant minorities. Significantly, it is this aspect of castelike minority culture that is most relevant to learning achievement because of the tendency of castelike minorities to equate the culture of the schools with the culture of the dominant group and to equate schooling with acculturation. It is this "affective dissonance" coupled with an "identificational assimilation" that differentiates African-American culture from the culture of the dominant group.

Native Americans: The collective oppositional cultural identity strategies used by Native American tribes in response to the European invasion[59]

---

55. Gunner Myrdal, Richard Steiner, Arnold Rose, *An American Dilemma: The Negro Problem and Modern Democracy* (New York: Harper, 1944).

56. W. E. B. DuBois, *The Souls of Black Folk* (Chicago: Clurg, 1903).

57. Milton Gordon, *Assimilation in American Life* (New York: Oxford University Press, 1964).

58. G. A. DeVos, "Ethnic Persistence and Role Degradation: An Illustration from Japan" (Paper prepared for the American-Soviet Symposium on Contemporary Ethnic Processes in the U.S.A. and the U.S.S.R., New Orleans, April 1984).

59. Duane Champagne, *American Indian Societies: Strategies and Conditions of Political and Cultural Survival* (Cambridge: Cultural Survival, 1989).

have been characterized historically by armed resistance, religious movements, and centralization of tribal organizations. Native Americans were
reduced to a racial and ethnic group and were categorized as "Indians."
Their cultural diversity and various histories ultimately were subjugated to
the U.S. government.[60]

Because Native Americans were not entitled to equal status with other
Americans, the government ignored its treaties with them. During the
nineteenth century, whole tribes were resettled forcibly onto reservations
distant from centers of population and business. There the tribes were
transformed from self-reliant harvesters of nature's bounty to dependent
wards of the government who relied on food shipments for sustenance. The
social structure of these indigenous peoples, once built on an active role for
all within the tribe, collapsed under their imposed passivity. The complex
interaction of relocation, war, and forced culture change combined with
disease to reduce the Native American population from 600,000 in 1776 to
its low point of roughly 237,000 people at the start of the twentieth century.[61]

By the beginning of the twentieth century an unknown number of Native
Americans had joined the industrial labor force, intermarried, and disap-
peared into the multicultural urban population. In the 1950s and 1960s, many
more left the reservations to live and work in the cities. Rather than melting
into the urban masses, however, these newcomers often found cohesive
communities in which Native American traditions were maintained.[62]

There are about two million Native Americans today, most heavily
concentrated in Oklahoma, Alaska, the Southwest, and the Rocky Mountain
states.[63] However, the diversity among tribes is great. There is no typical
Native American, no one Indian culture, language, religion, or physical
type. Although increases in the Native American population are hard to
measure, their population is growing faster than the general U.S. population,
having increased 38 percent between 1980 and 1990, compared to a roughly
10 percent increase in the total U.S. population.[64] It seems likely that
many people who identified themselves as belonging to some other race or
ethnicity in earlier censuses now identify themselves as Native Americans.

Native Americans remain among the most disadvantaged of all race
and ethnic groups in the United States. They have less higher education

60. Russell Thornton, *American Indian Holocaust and Survival: A Population History since 1492* (Norman: University of Oklahoma Press, 1987).

61. U.S. Bureau of the Census, *American Indian, Eskimo and Aleut Population in
the United States*, prepared by the Racial Statistics Branch, Population Division (n.d.);
Thornton, *American Indian Holocaust*.

62. Joan Weibel-Orlando, *Indian Country, L.A.: Maintaining Ethnic Community in a
Complex Society* (Urbana: University of Illinois Press, 1991).

63. Felicity Barringer, "Census Shows Profound Change in Racial Makeup of the
Nation," *New York Times*, 11 March 1991, sec. 1B, p. 8.

64. C. Matthew Snipp, *American Indians: The First of This Land* (New York: Russell
Sage, 1989).

than European Americans or African Americans and are more likely to be unemployed. Native Americans' income is far lower than European Americans', but now slightly above that of African Americans. Ironically, Native Americans living in urban areas are not much better off economically than those on the reservation.[65]

Although reservations have been notorious for their lack of economic opportunities, by the early 1980s about 53 million acres, or 2.4 percent of U.S. land, was managed in trust by the Bureau of Indian Affairs. Self-determination and economic self-sufficiency cannot be achieved easily when the most basic needs, such as adequate education, housing and health care have not yet been met.[66]

The few tribes possessing natural resources such as mineral and energy resources have encountered a high social cost in attempting to develop productive, sustainable, safe industry for the future.

Although the survival strategies of involuntary minorities reduce to some extent the burden of minority exploitation and subordination, these strategies also encourage attitudes, competencies, and behaviors that are not necessarily compatible with performing well in formalized learning environments. As suggested earlier, such cultural discontinuities tend to arise from secondary cultural differences emerging from responses of subordinate minorities to their treatment by the dominant group.[67] As a result, the survival strategies are part of boundary-maintaining mechanisms that do not readily change through contact between minority and majority group members.

Secondary cultural differences among castelike minorities, particularly attributes of style rather than content, do differ from the primary cultural differences accompanying immigrant minorities from outside their host society. For example, most writers on the problem of cultural discontinuities in castelike minority learning generally stress the problem of style: Shade on cognitive style, Gumperz on communication style, Erikson and Mohatt on interaction style, and Boykin and Philips on learning style.[68] For immigrant

---

65. Ibid.

66. Demonstrations and lawsuits have called attention to the three hundred treaties broken by the U.S. government and the unmet needs of Native Americans. However, during the 1980s, court cases asking for compliance with treaties have resulted in favorable judgments, including three hundred thousand acres of prime land in Maine returned to the Penobscot and Passamaquoody, and fishing rights restored to the Great Lakes tribes. See William Richardson, "More Power to the Tribes," *New York Times*, 7 July 1993, A:15.

67. J. U. Ogbu, "Cultural Discontinuities and Schooling, *Anthropology and Education Quarterly* 13, no. 4 (1982): 290–307.

68. Significant sources on these styles are J. J. Gumpers, "Conversational Inferences and Classroom Learning," in *Ethnographic Approaches to Face Interaction*, ed. J. Green and C. Wallet (Norwood, N.J.: Ablex, 1982); F. Erikson and G. Mohatt, "Cultural

minorities, on the other hand, the primary cultural differences are not associated with boundary-maintaining mechanisms and are less resistant to change in contact situations, thus suggesting differences in nature.[69] The epistemology or group logic that sustains the oppositional cultural frame of reference is learned more or less unconsciously by castelike minority children as they grow up.

Not all African-American or Native-American members of castelike minorities are caught in the web of content and style differences. Middle-class young people who are not engulfed in peer group pressures do quite well in formal learning environments, as do minority young people who "escape" from peer group engulfment and group logic. In general, the evidence suggests that certain characteristics distinguish castelike minority young people who do well: (1) they adopt pragmatic attitudes and apply themselves more seriously than others; (2) they escape from or remain more or less outside peer-group engulfment and oppositional group logic; and (3) they invest more effort in their formalized learning.[70]

Intergroup Relations: Explaining and Accounting for Differences

Of particular importance in explaining and accounting for differences in perceptions, interpretations, and responses between immigrants and caste-like minorities are the twin phenomena of identity and cultural frame of reference. Initially successful minorities do not necessarily share the same cultural attributes with the dominant group. Among castelike minorities, both the identity system and the cultural frame of reference are often in opposition to those of the dominant group. Of importance to religious educators is the tendency of castelike minorities to often equate the culture

---

Organization of Participant Structures in Two Classrooms of Indian Students," in *Doing the Ethnography of Schooling: Educational Anthropology in Action*, by G. D. Spindler (New York: Holt, 1982), pp. 132–75; A. W. Boykin, "Reading Achievement and the Socio-Cultural Frame of Reference of Afro-American Children" (paper presented at NIE roundtable discussion on issues in urban reading, Washington, D.C., November 1980); and S. U. Philips, "Commentary: Access to Power and Maintenance of Ethnic Identity," in "Anthropological Perspectives on Multicultural Education," *Anthropology and Education Quarterly* 7, no. 4 (1976): 30–32.

69. Gibson, *Home-School-Community Linkages*; G. P. Guthrie, "An Ethnography of Bilingual Education in a Chinese Community" (Ph.D. diss., College of Education, University of Illinois, Champaign-Urbana, 1983).

70. R. Clark, *Family Life and School Achievement: Why Poor Black Children Succeed or Fail* (Chicago: University of Chicago Press, 1983); J. U. Ogbu, "Understanding Community Forces Affecting Minority Students' Academic Efforts" (manuscript prepared for the Achievement Council of California, Oakland, Calif., 1984); Lois Weis, *Between Two Worlds: Black Students in an Urban Community College* (London: Routledge & Kegan Paul, 1985).

of the mainstream churches with the culture of the dominant group, and to equate religious education curriculum with lessons in acculturation.[71] The result appears to be a model of religious education in which the minority groupings view religious education as a one-way acculturation or assimilation process of adopting the host culture. That is, castelike minorities like African Americans and Native Americans often view religious education as learning European-American culture and identity. Because African Americans and Native Americans have a collective identity and cultural frames of reference that tend to be in opposition to those of European-Americans, the acculturation model is problematic. There is, therefore, the possibility of conscious and/or unconscious opposition and an affective dissonance[72] toward learning what is taught in church, or "acting Anglo." For example, the dilemma for an individual African American or other castelike minority is having to choose between cultural distinctiveness or Anglo conformity.

The immigrant minorities, on the other hand, do not tend to equate schooling with acculturation or assimilation and are more free to adopt behaviors that enhance learning success. Unlike the nonimmigrants who see schooling as one-way acculturation, the immigrants adopt what may be called an "alternation model" that permits them to behave one way in the school setting and another way when they are at home or in the community.[73]

One conclusion that may be drawn from the variability in the school performance of minorities in the United States and elsewhere is that the minorities who are doing relatively well in school appear to be immigrants or those who regard themselves as immigrants. The minorities who are not doing well in school appear to be indigenous minorities or, in some cases, subjects of former colonial territories.

Dominant-group members usually rationalize their exploitation of castelike minorities by what DeVos and Wagatsuma called "caste thinking," which they state always involves the belief that there is some unalterable biological, religious, or social inferiority that distinguishes members of the minority group from those of the dominant group. The exploitation by the dominant group is both instrumental (economic exploitation through job ceilings for minorities) and expressive (immigrants frequently scapegoated for taking jobs away from local citizens).[74]

71. P. N. Williams, "Contextualizing the Faith: The African American Tradition and Martin Luther King Jr.," in *One Faith, Many Cultures*, ed. R. Costa (Maryknoll, N.Y.: Orbis Books, 1988); D. F. Wells, "An American Evangelical Theology: The Painful Transition from Theoria to Praxis," in *Evangelicalism and Modern America*, ed. G. Marsden (Grand Rapids, Mich.: Eerdmans, 1984), pp. 83–93.
72. Adapted from G. A. DeVos, "Adaptive Conflicts and Adjustment Coping: Psychocultural Approaches to Ethnic Identity," in *Studies in Social Identity*, ed. T. Sarbin and K. E. Sheibe (New York: Praeger, 1982).
73. Ogbu, "Cultural Discontinuities," p. 258.
74. G. A. DeVos and H. Wagatsuma, eds., *Japan's Invisible Race: Caste in Culture and Personality* (Berkeley: University of California Press, 1967); G. A. DeVos, "Ethnic

Description and analysis of the historic differences between immigrant and indigenous cultural experience yields a contextual framework for assessing and understanding that which is different and unfamiliar[75]—a necessary beginning point for a multicultural religious education.

MULTICULTURAL RELIGIOUS EDUCATION—INSTRUCTIONAL PROCESSES

The demand for educational resources that address the needs of diverse populations is increasing, but such materials and approaches have not been readily accessible. Instruction that is developmentally, racially, culturally, and gender responsive is not only effective but moral.[76] Getting to know people of diversity is a necessary prelude to understanding and respecting them, but such knowledge does not resolve differences or ensure liking people whose ways are alien.

Communication: A Process

Effective communication among diverse peoples can be viewed as a process whereby one person deliberately attempts to convey meaning to another with the intention of modifying behavior.[77] This process takes place whenever meaning is attached to messages[78] or meanings are attributed to behavior and culture-related past experiences.[79] Regardless of how communication is defined, it is important to note that this process is critical to understanding human existence and recognizing that people from different cultures communicate differently.[80]

Persistence and Role Degradation: An Illustration from Japan" (paper prepared for the American-Soviet Symposium on Contemporary Ethnic Process in the U.S.A. and the U.S.S.R., New Orleans, April 1984).

75. Spindler and Spindler, *Interpretive Ethnography*, p. 62.

76. Carol Jenkins and Deborah Bainer, "Common Instructional Problems in the Multicultural Classroom," in *Ethnic Minorities and Evangelical Christian Colleges*, ed. D. J. Lee, A. Nieves, and H. Allen (Lanham, Md.: University Press of America, 1991), p. 39.

77. Gerald R. Miller and Mark Steinberg, *Between People: A New Analysis of Interpersonal Communication* (Chicago: Science Research, 1975).

78. Jurgen Ruesch, "Value, Communication, and Culture," in *Communication: The Social Matrix of Psychiatry*, ed. Jurgen Ruesch and Gregory Bateson (New York: Norton, 1951), pp. 6–7.

79. Larry A. Samovar and Richard E. Porter, *Intercultural Communication: A Reader* (Belmont, Calif.: Wadsworth, 1991), p. 28.

80. Language is a symbolic system that uses certain verbal and written forms to express meaning. Culture is a symbolic system that encompasses all of life, including the language one speaks. Items that identify activities and values are all expressions of

When people communicate with one another, they bring to the situation their whole state of being, including sentiments, values, emotions, attitudes, and physical dispositions. It is therefore important that communicators know as much as they can about the person with whom they are interacting in order to avoid a misinterpretation of information. Research has found age, race, and gender to be key variables in influencing communication across cultures.[81] For example, there is virtue in Americans' emphasizing the future rather than the past. Such a viewpoint is optimistic, allowing a person to make a fresh start despite past mistakes. This viewpoint can be destructive, however, if the past is considered irrelevant or is misunderstood, with the result that: (1) mistakes may be repeated, (2) older people may feel useless because most of their major accomplishments took place in the past, and (3) a feeling of continuity between generations may be lacking because each generation perceives itself as starting from scratch.

A Korean-style emphasis on the past and on tradition has its virtues: (1) perhaps fewer mistakes from the past tend to be repeated, (2) older persons tend to feel useful, and (3) the generations feel a common bond. Yet this Korean-style viewpoint can also be destructive if (1) the ways of the past do not allow change, (2) the old do not learn from the young, and (3) an individual is trapped in the mistakes of the past.

---

some deeper meaning that lies within the culture and is expressed in social interaction. See Marvin Mayars, *Christianity Confronts Culture* (Grand Rapids, Mich.: Zondervan, 1987), p. 205. For a discussion of language and culture as symbolic see Edward T. Hall, *The Silent Language* (New York: Doubleday, 1966) and *The Hidden Dimension* (1969). There are remarkable differences between communication patterns of people from different cultures. Edward Stewart, in *American Cultural Patterns: a Cross-cultural Perspective* (Yarmouth, Me.: Intercultural Press, 1985), argued that because American people emphasize rationality, they tend to assume that events can be explained and reasons for their occurrence can be determined. They see the world as explained by facts from which ideas can be generated, thus the emphasis on explicit meaning. Arabs and Asians, on the other hand, look for the implicit level and metaphoric association in messages. In Arab culture, poetry, plays, and storytelling are regarded as inspired language because they portray an image of a well-educated speaker, capable of rendering judgment and advice. A high value is placed on the persuasive power, rhythm, and sound of words because these qualities heighten the impact of the message. See Samuel H. Hammond, "Arab and Moslem Rhetorical Theory," in *Central State Speech Journal* (1963), pp. 97–102. This is unlike the dominant American style of speech in which communication is individualistic, whereby each communicater is a separate individual engaging in diverse communicative activities to maximize self-interest, usually by persuasion. Robert Bellah et al., *Habits of the Heart: Individualism and Commitment in American Life* (New York: Harper & Row 1985), p. 12.

81. N. Sussman and H. M. Rosenfeld, "Influence of Culture, Language, and Sex on Conversational Distance," *Journal of Personality and Social Psychology* 42 (1982): 66–74.

Language: A Symbol of Experience

Also critical to cross-cultural communication is the understanding that all humans symbolize their experience in language.[82] Are language groups to be understood as distinct culture groups? If so, what levels of linguistic differentiation will be employed?[83]

Sapir observed that human beings do not live in the objective world alone.[84] They are heavily affected by the particular language that is the medium of linguistic expression for their society. It is through language that people conceptualize the world around them.

Acknowledging the interdependent relationship between speech and silence, we can learn a great deal about a culture from the way it treats silence. The role of silence in the communication process is interpreted differently in every culture. Whereas the Western tradition views silence and ambiguity negatively, Far Eastern cultures are biased toward it.[85] Bruneau sees a general misconception in the West regarding silence. American culture, for example, interprets silence to mean sorrow, critique, obligation, regret, or embarrassment. The Japanese, on the other hand, mistrust verbal skills, associating them with superficiality in contrast to less articulate innuendo.[86] In this, as in other Eastern cultures, anticipatory communication is common, whereby the listener has to guess and accommodate the speaker's needs. Sensitivity and "catching on" quickly to the unsaid meaning are very valuable skills that show intelligence.

While different languages use culturally variant written symbols (specific words to convey certain meanings), many messages are transmitted nonverbally. It is therefore not enough to learn other languages in order to understand how other people live. It is equally necessary to place particular words in their proper contexts and to recognize the importance of nonverbal cues or gestures in fostering human understanding. For example, a single idea often "feels" different if spoken in Spanish rather than in English or Chinese.[87] When people who speak different languages encounter one another, much of their communication tends to involve gestures, simple hand movements, or body language.

Culture and language can adversely affect immigrant learning in the American culture. Early in the twentieth century, Chinese immigrants

---

82. Spindler and Spindler, *Interpretive Ethnography*, p. 67.

83. M. Stubbs and H. Hillier, eds., *Readings on Language, Schools and Classrooms* (London: Methuen, 1983).

84. Edward Sapir, "The Status of Linguistics as a Science," in *The Selected Writings of Edward Sapir in Language, Culture and Personality*, ed. David Mandelbaum (Berkeley: University of California Press, 1949), pp. 160–66.

85. T. J. Bruneau, "Communicative Silences: Forms and Functions," *Journal of Communication* 56 (1973): 17–46.

86. E. Reischauer, *The Japanese* (Cambridge: Harvard University Press, 1977).

87. Gerhard Falk, personal communication with author, 1987.

brought to America a learning style that emphasized external forms and rote memorization rather than observation, analysis, and comprehension. They also brought a language that is very different from English and an authority structure of the family that discouraged training children in independence and autonomy. In spite of these factors the learning success of many Chinese immigrants has been exceptional, which is due in part to the traditionally high value Chinese culture places on learning.[88] Despite strong pressures to abandon native language and culture, many immigrant groups actively strove to maintain their cultural roots and aggressively supported church and synagogue-related schools, the majority of which offered bilingual education.[89]

Early in the twentieth century, American public policy makers, eager to absorb newcomers into the melting pot, hungered to believe that an individual could shed one culture and acquire another, like the changing of a pair of shoes, if he or she just learned English. English monolingualism became closely tied to Americanism. English monolingualism, democracy, and capitalism became the visible means by which our relatively new country forged a national identity.[90]

Yet it is evident that many immigrants, consciously or unconsciously recognizing acculturation as a process, did not share the prevailing point of view. They persisted in finding ways (like establishing parochial schools) to preserve their old culture and language while they were adapting to the new. Despite the successes of public education in socializing the children of immigrants to a common language and culture, ethnic and religious differences were never completely erased. Supporters of the melting pot ideal had overlooked the crucial importance of religion and ethnicity as sources of identity and community.[91]

Bilingualism: Maturity and Tolerance in Intergroup Relations

Immigrants have always had to adapt to the host country, and there is no question that every American child, immigrant or not, should gain full mastery of the English language. Immigrant groups differ in their grasp and use of both English and their first language. Hispanic migration, however, was affected by three often overlooked factors. First, fully one-third of the

---

88. Andrew Sanchirico, "The Importance of Small Business Ownership in Chinese-American Educational Achievement," *Sociology of Education* 64 (October 1991): 293–304.

89. Joane Nagel, "Constructing Ethnicity: Creating and Recreating Ethnic Identity and Culture," *Social Problems* 41 (February 1994): 152–76.

90. Vincent N. Parrillo, *Diversity in America* (Newbury Park, Calif.: Pine Forge Press, 1996), pp. 58–61; 71–73.

91. Nagel, "Constructing Ethnicity," pp. 152–76.

contemporary Hispanic residents of the United States are neither immigrants nor the descendants of immigrants. Hispanics settled the Southwest and Puerto Rico before the Pilgrims landed on Plymouth Rock. They were incorporated into the country, with their culture and language, by treaty or conquest, along with Native Americans, African slaves, Virgin Islanders, and residents of Samoa, Guam, and Hawaii. In a very real sense, they are involuntary Americans. Second, substantial numbers of Mexicans and Puerto Ricans do not come to the United States to establish permanent residence. They come for economic gain and then return to their places of origin, traveling back and forth many times over a lifetime. Third, substantial numbers of Hispanics who come to the United States have little formal education. They tend to lack mastery of Spanish as well as English. An ability to express oneself clearly, richly, and fully in the spoken word as well as in the written word is essential to upward mobility and intellectual development. These people have only an impoverished command of two languages, neither of which seems to be a first language.

These cyclical migrants, who move between monolingual societies, tend to cluster together when they are in the continental United States. Even putting aside philosophical questions of how conquered peoples should be treated or what a nation's responsibility should be to cyclical migrants, the fact is that substantial numbers of Hispanics in the United States have to function bilingually on a daily basis. The need for bilingual capability is a reality that cannot be ignored.

Many churches provide alternative meeting schedules for members who cannot meet for fellowship with the others do because of job schedules. Is it not similarly reasonable for churches to provide religious education activities and worship in the language of members who speak a different language? Such accommodating actions are consistent with Paul's statement that he became all things to all people in order to win some (1 Cor 9:22).

Thus Americans today find themselves in the understandable but curious position of being a nation that glorifies its immigrant heritage but feels threatened by the cultural diversity that this heritage implies. The country has existed for more than two hundred years and is one of the world's richest and most powerful nations. Perhaps the time has come when the United States can dare to be multilingual and truly multicultural.

A MULTICULTURAL RELIGIOUS EDUCATION MODEL: MULTICULTURAL ORIENTATION

How and to what extent should a multicultural religious education affirm American cultural distinctives? How should a multicultural religious education symbolize cultural diversity? What analytic framework adequately envisions the necessary synergy between our theology, traditions, and practices?

Lack of shared meanings requires the development of conceptual frameworks that may challenge existing categories and ways of thinking, especially in the areas of race, ethnicity, social class, and culture. The truth value of information is best measured by criteria of usefulness (a priori assumptions) in predicting and explaining people's experience in the natural world.[92]

Developing an appreciation of other cultures is a difficult process, understanding that the past has been rooted in politicized demographic divisions. Individuals need to look at the world from a perspective that does not equate differentness with inferiority. In considering the uniqueness and diversity of lives, settings, and perspectives, a genuinely multicultural orientation positions Christian leaders to critically view their own thought and practice, and to engage the process of understanding and engaging in religious education with others whose cultural worlds are very different from their own.

Sustained experience with the cultural worlds of others enhances the development of a multicultural orientation toward unfamiliar social worlds. Such experiences also enable the development of different strategies and competencies needed in social interaction. Interactions in which people encounter dominating cultural differences position them to genuinely understand the imperatives of a multicultural religious education. Doing religious education with people of different cultures can be very pleasant or very painful. It is painful when the religious educator is not adequately prepared for the experience, and so is prone to misconceptions and confusion. Interacting with people from other cultures demands a great deal of personal flexibility—an ability to change behavior and course of action according to the situation. Flexibility also requires adjusting to how other cultures make use of time and space.

There are principles that can help in establishing a proper perspective of others, which is so important in religious education: a posture of value neutrality, appreciation of inner beauty, respect for diversity, and tolerance of differences.

Being able to remain neutral about culture-bound values when dealing with people from other cultures can help avoid many misunderstandings. Although cultural influences are so strong that they often get in the way of objectivity, intentional efforts to be open-minded can help. Steps to developing a value-neutral posture include recognizing and confronting biases instead of suppressing them; seeing beauty in things that appear

---

92. P. J. Pelto and G. H. Pelto, "Anthropological Research," in *The Structure of Inquiry*, 2d ed. (Cambridge: Cambridge University Press, 1978).

unfamiliar; and developing a high sense of self-esteem.[93] Understanding is the product of habit and tradition, which in turn reflects the beliefs of a given culture.

Before religious education can build bridges between cultural groups, it must understand the environment in which religious education takes place and have a concern with the structures and patterns by which people interact on a daily basis. It is helpful in dealing with all people, whether they are alike or different, to have a feel for and a knowledge of factors that shape people's lives and influence their associations.[94]

Although diversity can sometimes be a threat to unity, it also has the potential to create greater harmony. The inclusion of different voices and perspectives in our understandings is a morally, religiously, and (yes!) politically correct goal. If diversity is seen as a source of strength because it offers variety, then qualities that are unique to particular groups can be used for the benefit of the larger group. Tolerating differences is based on an ability to respect diversity.[95]

The goal is not to replace Eurocentric culture models with Afrocentric or any other model, but to find models of a broader, more democratic nature while at the same time demanding religious education curriculum that provides an accurate account of what our society has been and a vision of what it may become if its democratic ideals are taken seriously.[96]

Multicultural Religious Education Model: Curriculum as a Window and a Mirror

Sociologist Emile Durkheim believed that the function of education is to serve the needs of society (whether the needs be to transmit values, to train a labor force, to take care of children while parents work, or to strip away identities of ethnicity or social origin in order to implant a common national identity). In particular, formal learning environments function to teach children the skills they need to adapt to their environment. It is the task of education to achieve a sufficient community of ideas and of sentiments, without which any society is impossible.[97] In a Durkheimian sense, a multicultural religious education could contribute to group unity and solidarity because religious values supply the basic social cohesion that makes a society righteous and enduring.

A second Durkheimian conception views education as a liberating experience that releases learners from the blinders imposed by the accident of

---

93. Daisy Kabagarama, *Breaking the Ice: A Guide to Understanding People from Other Cultures* (Needham Heights, Mass.: Allyn & Bacon, 1993), p. 49.

94. Robson and Billings, *Christian Cross-cultural Communication*, p. 35.

95. Kabagarama, *Breaking the Ice*, p. 50.

96. Kohl, "Social Policy," p. 3.

97. Emile Durkheim, *Education and Sociology* (New York: Free Press, 1956).

birth into a particular family, culture, religion, society, and time in history.[98] Formal learning settings therefore should be designed to broaden learners' horizons so they will become aware of the socializing influences around them and will learn to think independently. Religious education learning environments, when designed to achieve these goals, can function as agents of change and progress.

As a democratic, pluralistic society, America draws its strength from educating all its citizens to achieve their full potential. It is therefore imperative that the formal religious education curriculum, which conveys the central messages of religious education, provide students with "mirrors" reflecting their own experiences as well as with "windows" revealing those of others. Learners should see the realities of their own lives and perspectives reflected in the curriculum they experience. One of the contributors to this chapter remembers serving as a Sunday school teacher in Peru many years ago. The curriculum materials used with the children ("windows") were produced in the United States. The materials included no illustrations of children who looked like them. The pictures were all of middle-class European-American children (no "mirrors"). Unfortunately, particularly for historically underrepresented groups, current curricular materials also seem to provide many windows and few mirrors. Equity in education, including a representative multicultural religious curriculum (one offering both "windows" and "mirrors"), remains an elusive goal.

Once educators begin to recognize the complexity of cultural identity, the problem of how culture relates to religious education curriculum becomes more acute.[99] In a pluralistic society, the question must be asked, How does the curriculum balance our commonality and our differences? How do we develop an ability to communicate and function effectively with diverse groups and within multiple cultures?

If religious educators can see that they stand at a historical turning point, they can move deliberately and consciously to choose their direction.[100] Global vision can emerge from a willingness to learn about the elements of common culture that bind different groups together as a community of believers. Such global vision enables everyone not only to participate in church life, but also to analyze and critique it. Members of "other" cultures also deserve to experience the enabling that comes to people from studying their own culture and learning in their own style. By exploring the many varieties of American experience, we can construct a representative

---

98. Ibid.

99. A. J. Cropley, *The Education of Immigrant Children: A Social Psychological Introduction* (London: Croom Helm, 1983).

100. Robert E. Freeman, *Promising Practices in Global Education* (New York: National Council on Foreign Languages and International Studies, 1986); R. Muller, *New Genesis* (New York: Doubleday, 1982).

and equitable multicultural religious education that conveys the common culture we share while respecting the complexities of American cultural pluralism. By being culturally open or by communicating cross-culturally (assuming that both our own culture and the culture we are exploring are valued and that members of each live responsibly within the cultural context), members are enabled to communicate with as full an understanding as possible.[101]

Most American educators today believe that a curriculum reflecting the variety of cultures and races that have forged American society is defensible and laudable.[102] A religious education curriculum that focuses exclusively on the experiences and perspectives of a single cultural group is viewed as monocultural and ethnocentric (tending to judge other cultures by the standards that prevail in one's own culture[103]), the exact opposite of multicultural. A truly multicultural religious education requires rethinking curriculum from a global rather than from an exclusively Western European perspective.

The term *multicultural religious education curriculum* is used in this book in its broadest sense, to encompass both *what* is taught and *how* it is taught. This includes both formal classroom environments and informal environments such as a home Bible study or a youth retreat. A multicultural religious education must define concisely the nature and origins of the problems that need to be resolved. If religious educators agree that the design of a curriculum, as well as how it is delivered, can be a major cause of disunity, passivity, or intolerance, then they need to examine how the curriculum is designed and delivered in other religious education contexts. If educators decide that an unfamiliar teaching technique might be useful in resolving problems between divergent cultures, they also have to ask what it is about the other setting (its history, family structure, economic incentives, cultural values) that supports the technique and permits it to work well. Clear insights are the first step toward meaningful change.

If, as many educational theorists agree,[104] an equitable and just mul-ticulturally based curriculum should in some way reflect the cultures of its participants, then why not so in a multicultural religious education curriculum? Many churches with ethnically homogeneous populations tend to follow a standardized ethnocentric religious education curriculum. In

101. Mayars, *Christianity Confronts Culture*, p. 242.

102. Michael Marriott, editorial, *New York Times*, 11 August 1991.

103. Sumner, *Folkways*, p. 13.

104. See Cohen and Manion, "The Shaping of Men's Minds: Adaptations to the Imperatives of Culture," in *Anthropological Perspectives on Education*, ed. K. I. Wax, S. Diamond, and F. E. Gearing (New York: Basic, 1983), pp. 19–50; D. W. Hicks, *Minorities: A Teacher's Resource Book for the Multi-Ethnic Curriculum* (London: Heinemeann Educational Books, 1981); H. James and R. Jeffcoate, eds., *The School in the Multicultural Society* (New York: Harper & Row, 1981).

practice, Sunday schools and CCD programs often follow a highly uniform curriculum that has been shaped by tradition—essentially European (English) cultural patterns.[105] Few dispute that monocultural churches share a common cultural heritage that should be taught, but disagreement arises over what should be included in that shared body of knowledge. Regardless of the church's cultural heritage, it is imperative that content standards become multiculturally representative.

Although the culture transmitted by the traditional public school curriculum is often viewed as Eurocentric,[106] some critics contend that the traditional curriculum's emphasis on the Western European roots of American institutions serves two functions: (1) promoting cultural unity and (2) enabling learners by immersing them in the mainstream culture that dominates the American social and political system. Emphasizing our differences, they contend, will only exacerbate cultural isolation and social tension.[107] For example, an emphasis on Afrocentrism (the dominance of African cultural patterns in peoples' lives), although valued as a corrective for centuries of minimizing or ignoring the cultural achievements of African societies and African Americans, may be divisive rather than unifying.[108]

On the other hand, offering learners an uncritical, mythical image of a monocultural religious community does not necessarily create unity. As learners mature, they discover that the realities of history and society belie this myth. Their disillusionment may lead to far more cultural isolation and alienation than would have been the case if they had had opportunity to explore the complexities of cultural pluralism.

The American church and culture are much more diverse, complex, and rich than the traditional religious education curriculum teaches. Research continues to demonstrate that people who have been exposed to other cultures have an advantage in handling conflict and problem solving.[109] Religious education today needs a culturally representative curriculum that prepares coming generations to live and work peacefully in a pluralistic church and society.

In attending to diversification, local churches must be willing to be innovative and flexible. Rigid thought and behavior often get in the way of building trust. For example, although Americans may find it easy to be spontaneous because of the value placed on informality, their strict attitude toward the management of time and their adherence to schedules may cause

---

105. Molefi Kebe Asante, *The Afrocentric Idea* (Philadelphia: Temple University Press, 1987), p. 7.

106. J. Twitchen, *Multicultural Education: Views from the Classroom* (London: BBC Publications, 1981).

107. Takaki, *A Different Mirror*, pp. 1–17.

108. John J. Macionis, *Sociology* (Englewood Cliffs, N.J.: Prentice-Hall, 1995), p. 80.

109. Philip S. Gang, *Rethinking Education* (Atlanta: Dagaz, 1989).

conflict in intercultural situations.[110] To improve relationships, Americans may have to develop a more flexible attitude and be willing to sacrifice some time and privacy.

In planning curriculum, churches need a willingness to provide programs and religious education activities that meet the specific and diverse needs of the people and the community. New forms and structures for meeting the multicultural religious education needs of people should be sought and utilized. This does not mean that old and traditional forms of religious education are to be discarded, nor does it mean changing for the sake of change. Innovation does mean, however, improving on what is currently used and looking at alternative ways to evangelize, nurture, worship, and fellowship. A traditional teaching style based on memorization and competition often proves unproductive for learners whose style is more relational. Emphasizing group activities and a cooperative learning approach provides a helpful alternative more suited to learners' needs (see chap. 9).

Reforming religious education always has the potential for controversy. When cultures collide, the "sacred canopy" of each tradition is forced to compete in a cultural marketplace. The church that plans with others in mind will be innovative by necessity. Churches must be viewed as gateways to life's opportunities and choices. The key to success is including everyone who has a stake in the curriculum in an effective, productive process.

CONCLUSION

One of the challenges of pluralism is the nurture of mutual respect and acceptance. Thus religious education activities need to be developed that free people from ignorance, prejudice, fear, and economic bondage while developing maturity of judgment, a thirst for knowledge, strength of conviction, and direction for life. Christian believers need to recognize the diversity that exists in North America and view that diversity as a source of strength. All of humanity's accouterments are expressions of basic human needs. The expressions themselves vary from one culture to another, but the basic needs do not. As persons come to know and understand each other's language, religion, and music, they discover a common humanity.

Religious education should be used as a vehicle to empower people in their struggles to resist the influence of socioeconomic structures on religious institutions—what Weber called the "iron cage"[111] of the modern

---

110. Robson and Billings, *Christian Cross-cultural Communication*, p. 44.

111. Max Weber, *The Protestant Ethic and the Spirit of Capitalism* (New York: Scribner, 1904/1958), p. 181. Weber was concerned with the disenchantment he believed would inevitably result from secularization. With the death of religion, he believed, life

socioeconomic order—and also the growth of what Simmel called "objective culture," a culture lacking in unifying ideals.[112] A commitment to diversity in religious education offers an unprecedented opportunity for growth. Christians should look forward to the day when the church, an institution for the people of God, moves out onto the cutting edge in the struggle for equity among all of its people.

---

would lose its magical, meaningful qualities. Modern society would then become an "iron cage" imprisoning people in unsatisfying and ultimately pointless work and a life bereft of spirituality. He argued that a spirit of religious asceticism would help people escape the iron cage.

112. "Objective culture" is associated with a growing rationalization of society as social relations lose their traditional and religious content and become mediated by impersonal standards—law, intellect, logic, and money. See Georg Simmel, *The Philosophy of Money* (Boston: Routledge and Kegan Paul, 1978), p. 393.

3

PSYCHOLOGICAL FOUNDATIONS OF MULTICULTURAL RELIGIOUS EDUCATION

Donald Ratcliff

Religious educators know that an understanding of culture is essential to working effectively across cultures and with subcultural groups. Culture has traditionally been relegated to social science, specifically the disciplines of sociology and anthropology, Much of the research and theory produced by these disciplines can be of help to religious educators (see chap. 2). Past study of culture rarely incorporated insights from psychology, principally because the discipline emphasizes the individual rather than the social, and thus sociological, nature of culture. However, psychology and sociology achieve a degree of rapprochement in the subdiscipline of social psychology, and most sociology textbooks include the psychological theories of Erik Erikson, Jean Piaget, and even Sigmund Freud under the topic of socialization. In addition, a multicultural approach to psychology is included in an increasing number of general psychology textbooks, and cross-cultural counseling has developed as a subfield within psychotherapy. These innovations indicate an interest by some in relating the sociological concept of culture to the discipline of psychology. Perhaps there is an emerging realization that the social cannot be separated from the individual, and that indeed culture is the product of collective interchange between psyches (selves).

In this chapter the discipline of psychology will be examined to discover research and theories that have implications for multicultural relationships and thus for multicultural religious education. By no means will a comprehensive survey of psychology be attempted, as even a brief survey

93

of psychology requires several hundred pages *without* cross-cultural or religious education applications.[1]

BASIC PROCESSES OF THOUGHT AND EXPERIENCE

Sensation and Perception

Vision, hearing, touch, and all the other senses are channeled through the lower part of the brain, the brain stem, and the information is either passed on to other areas of the brain or discarded.[2] The person gives attention to the stimulus or the stimulus is ignored. The vast majority of the information that comes to the brain stem is ignored.

What causes this part of the brain to give conscious attention to some things and not to others? This capability is learned in one way or another. Researchers have found that unusual stimuli are more likely to be given attention. Stimuli that are more constant and expected are more likely to be ignored.[3]

The tendency to give greater attention to unusual stimuli may help explain why differences in culture stand out so strongly; they are different from that to which one is accustomed. Differences in values are manifested in variations in behavior across cultures. Many of the author's students, on returning from overseas internships, describe how differently time is valued in non-Western cultures. Extended church services, unexpected delays, and the like are especially acute to the students because the devaluing of time and the corollary valuing of *event* radically depart from what Americans commonly assume. Differences in dress, language, and daily activities also stand out because they are different.

Subliminal Communication: Some stimuli received by the brain are not given conscious attention, yet they can affect the individual's reactions in a cultural context. Psychologists describe these as "subliminal" because they are below (*sub*) the level of awareness. Early reports of people being subliminally influenced to eat foods and drink beverages were not well

---

1. For an overview of psychology that includes numerous explicit applications to religious education, see Paul D. Meier, Frank B. Minirth, Frank B. Wichern, and Donald E. Ratcliff, *Introduction to Psychology and Counseling*, 2d ed. (Grand Rapids, Mich.: Baker, 1991). I am also impressed with the high-quality applications of psychology to religious education by two Christian educators who have doctoral degrees in educational psychology: Klaus Issler and Perry Downs. See Perry G. Downs, *Teaching for Spiritual Growth* (Grand Rapids, Mich.: Zondervan, 1994); Ronald Habermas and Klaus Issler, *Teaching for Reconciliation* (Grand Rapids, Mich.: Baker, 1992); and Klaus Issler and Ronald Habermas, *How We Learn* (Grand Rapids, Mich.: Baker, 1994).

2. Ibid., p. 86.

3. David Myers, *Psychology*, 2d ed. (New York: Worth, 1987), pp. 143–44.

substantiated.[4] Likewise, later claims that hidden messages in music can drastically change behavior have been shown to be doubtful.[5] There is evidence that people can be influenced to a minor degree by stimuli of which they are not aware.[6] Such influence is most likely to occur in relation to behavior already being considered; it is highly unlikely that the person would compromise strongly held convictions because of subliminal influence. Individuals are most likely to be influenced subliminally when the situation is ambiguous, when hunches are likely to be used in decision making, and when guessing involves little or no cost.[7]

Multicultural exchanges can sometimes meet the criteria of ambiguity, hunch making, and guessing without cost as suggested above. From these criteria it follows that if little is known about a cultural group, it is likely that reactions will be due to unconscious influences as much or more than to conscious influences. Nonverbal communication (such as body language) may be the hidden stimulus that produces a reaction.[8] Nonverbals learned within a culture, such as the amount of space appropriate between people or gestures, tend to be culturally specific. For example, a Hispanic religious educator will probably maintain a closer space with learners than a European-American religious educator. But when a European-American teaches a Hispanic learner, the larger space may communicate an unintended interpersonal distance. The unintended communication is due to a divergence in normative behavior that is not processed consciously; nonverbal communication is often unconsciously, or subliminally, processed.

How can unintended communication be overcome? Giving overt attention to nonverbal activities can make the subliminal more obvious. For example, the differences in eye-gaze norms across ethnic groups can be underscored, emphasizing that what is a normal length of gaze in one group may be excessive in another cultural group (denoting intrusion and rudeness) or too short in another (possibly denoting deceit). Ignoring genuine differences between cultural groups will not make mutual acceptance and cooperation more likely. Denying or overlooking cultural divergences will

---

4. These early reports are summarized by Eleanor Mead, "How to Keep from Being Manipulated," *Christian Life*, May 1976, pp. 16–17. These are also summarized in many older general psychology textbooks.

5. J. Vokey and J. Read, "Subliminal Messages: Between the Devil and the Media," *American Psychologist* 40 (1985): 1231–39.

6. R. Bornstein, D. Leon, and D. Galley, "The Generalizability of Subliminal Mere Exposure Effects," *Journal of Personality and Social Psychology* 53 (December 1987): 1070–79.

7. Ronald Philipchalk, *Psychology and Christianity* (Lanham, Md.: University Press of America, 1988), pp. 52–53.

8. Erving Goffman, *Interaction Ritual* (Garden City, N.Y.: Anchor, 1967). Also see James M. Lee, *The Content of Religious Education* (Birmingham, Ala.: Religious Education Press, 1985), pp. 378–474.

more likely produce discomfort and distrust, although the persons involved may not realize *why* they are uncomfortable. Ignorance of cultural differences is a breeding ground for interpersonal misunderstanding. Religious education should avoid both exaggerating cultural and subcultural differences, which can easily become prejudice, and ignoring genuine differences. One major goal of multicultural religious education is to understand and accept differences, value people who are culturally different, and, especially, affirm differences that are adaptive and helpful.

Perception: Once a sensation is transmitted to the rest of the brain by the brain stem, it is then processed. This processing of sense data is termed *perception*. Perception is not passive, as was suggested by the old cliché "soaking up knowledge." Rather, the brain creatively acts on sensations, constructing meaning from them as much as possible.[9] Sometimes sensory data are sufficiently different from past experiences that basically new understandings are required, a process Jean Piaget termed *accommodation*.[10] A mental category can be extended or modified as well, which is also considered to be accommodation. For example, an initial observation of baptism may result in a child's understanding it as a purely physical action, but with maturity a later observation may result in the child's understanding baptism as a spiritually significant act as well. Much of the time, though, the brain simply subsumes new sensations into existing mental categories, which is termed *assimilation*.

In multicultural religious education it is crucial that assimilation and accommodation be facilitated when appropriate. Racial and ethnic stereotyping can be considered inappropriate assimilation; the existing mental understanding is that members of a group are inferior in some way, and all people within that classification are assimilated into that stereotype. Piaget emphasized that the only way people can move from assimilation to accommodation is if the discrepancy between stimulus and mental representation is sufficiently large to produce psychological discomfort, or *disequilibrium*. One of the tasks of religious educators is to help learners realize and appreciate the limitations of prejudicial categories and to encourage more flexible categories that allow for greater diversity. In other words, religious educators should create an openness to differences.

How can such an openness be created? One possibility is to use biblical materials that call into question the judgmental values behind prejudicial categories. For some individuals, disequilibrium comes by regular, egalitarian association with those of different ethnic backgrounds, perhaps by overseas experience or by volunteer service with minorities. Words alone

---

9. Paul Meier, *Introduction to Psychology and Counseling*, pp. 66–70.
10. Jean Piaget, *The Construction of Reality in the Child* (New York: Basic, 1954).

often fail to produce changed perspectives. In contrast, acting differently is likely to change opinions and attitudes.[11]

Perceptual psychologists have emphasized at least four influences on people's perceptions.[12] First, past experience influences one's perception of the present situation. If individuals have had pleasant, positive experiences with other cultures and subcultures, a likely result is positive perceptions of them in the present and future. The author lived on an island in the British West Indies for a year and had a number of very positive experiences there. Today he finds himself especially likely to be acutely aware of a West Indian accent in others, and usually initiates a conversation with a stranger who has such an accent.

Second, situations also influence perceptions. The immediate situation in which religious educators interact with people of differing ethnicity may influence how that experience is perceived. Someone who is unduly fearful of an unfamiliar context may be more likely to perceive threat from those who reside there. For example, an Asian newly arrived in the United States might experience considerable anxiety and suspect the possibility of threat when attending a European-American church for the first time, perhaps because of the architecture or perhaps because of the many non-Asians in that context. Conversely, a religious educator who initially enters an Asian community for the purpose of evangelism may feel anxiousness at the unfamiliar surroundings and may sense threat when approached by a friendly Asian in that context.

Third, personal values affect perceptions of intercultural exchange. Values are very important influences on perception. Common values can attract individuals to relationships with those who are culturally different. Contradictory values may unconsciously influence people toward interpersonal distance. For example, if culturally different people share a common concern for environmental issues, this may encourage mutual exchange. In contrast, two people who are culturally different and share little in common will probably not interact a great deal about religion or any other subject.

Finally, perhaps the most important influence on perception is expectation, which actually incorporates the other three influences. People tend to find aspects of another person that validate what is expected; they search for confirmation of latent biases and stereotypes.[13] In the process individuals can distort what they see or they can overlook evidence to the contrary.

The very act of perceiving involves a wide array of factors: unconscious influences, past experiences, situations, values, and expectations. Sense data

---

11. R. Held and A. Hein, "Movement-Produced Stimulation," *Journal of Comparative and Physiological Psychology* 56 (1963): 872–76.

12. James Geiwitz, *Looking at Ourselves* (Boston: Little, Brown, 1976), p. 89.

13. Paul Meier, *Introduction to Psychology and Counseling*, p. 70.

are carefully sorted by these aspects of perception *before* people have the opportunity to reflect consciously on and react to those experiences.

The Brain

As emphasized in the last section, sensations are transmitted to the brain, where perceptual processing occurs. The brain, without question the most important organ in the body, is likewise a vital component in multicultural religious education endeavors.

The differences that exist in various cultures can be traced, ultimately, to differences in brain function. There is no evidence that the brains of various cultural groups are different from birth, but the learning that takes place after birth significantly changes the structure and functioning of the brain. The microscopic neurons of the brain are literally connected or disconnected during the learning process. While different sections of the brain can be separated conceptually for the sake of discussion, to do so is a bit misleading. The brain functions as a whole, and every part of the brain is interrelated and physically connected to every other part. The vast majority of brain tissue consists of neurons that connect one section to another. An important foundation for a holistic view of human behavior is the organically interrelated nature of the brain itself.

Perhaps the most widely disseminated understanding of the brain is the division between right and left cerebral hemispheres, a dichotomy drawn from the work of Roger Sperry.[14] While much has been made of the distinctions in functioning between the two halves of the brain,[15] some of the conclusions by popularizers are misleading and exaggerated.[16] For example, the highly artistic and creative right hemisphere is capable of limited linguistic abilities, although language is predominantly a left hemisphere function in most individuals. Keeping in mind that brain functions are not entirely lateralized to separate hemispheres, perhaps it is still possible to gain some understanding of multicultural variations by examining the differences that exist.

Different cultures and subcultures emphasize some of the attributes of one hemisphere over the other. Do so-called right hemisphere cultures emphasize creativity, art, and more intuitive aspects of life? Might these cultures therefore be more receptive to the symbolic and experiential aspects of religion?[17] If a culture emphasizes left hemisphere tasks, might

---

14. Roger Sperry, *Perception and Its Disorders* (New York: Association for Research in Nervous and Mental Disease, 1970).

15. See, for example, Julian Jaynes, *The Origin of Consciousness in the Breakdown of the Bicameral Mind* (Boston: Houghton Mifflin, 1976).

16. M. Gazzaniga, "One Brain—Two Minds?" *American Scientist* 60 (1971): 311–17.

17. This point is made by several different writers, each working from within a different framework but arriving at very similar conclusions. See James M. Lee, *The*

it encourage verbal abstractions and therefore a theology that is separated from lifestyle in the religious domain? To take the argument further, could a culture elevate the emotional above the intellectual, thus giving priority to limbic system functions?[18] Conversely, could the intellect be elevated over the emotional to an unhealthy extent so that the cerebral overwhelms feeling and experience? Would these imbalances in a culture be reflected in the religion of that culture? Could the specific emphasis of the culture provide important clues as to what multicultural religious education approaches might be most effective?

Again, these distinctions should not be overemphasized. The brain is a single unit and, at least in nonpathological individuals, it functions as a unit. Yet cultures can overemphasize or deemphasize one or more of these aspects of brain functioning. Likewise, subgroups of people can overvalue and undervalue such functions, which is one of the reasons people are attracted to different kinds of churches. The goal of balance between the cognitive, intuitive/artistic, and emotional domains is a worthy goal for religious endeavors, so that the verbal, creatively symbolic, and affective content are all included. Another valuable goal is to understand and appreciate the different emphasis that different cultures afford to these functions. The differences in cultures, subcultures, and other subgroups within society require that religious educators appeal to all those distinctives to be maximally effective in their endeavors. They should start where people are in order to understand and reach them, even though the multicultural religious education goal might be a healthy balance between various characteristics.

MOTIVATION

Multicultural relationships are likely to be affected by the degree to which those involved are motivated toward productive interchange, as is needed in religious education efforts. Someone who is not motivated to make multicultural interactions probably will not take the time and effort to do so. People are more or less motivated to engage in relationships across cultures. Motivation is a crucial element in multicultural religious education, both for those receiving the instruction and for those giving it. What motivates people?

Content of Religious Education (Birmingham, Ala: Religious Education Press, 1985), pp. 502–3, 585; Virginia Owens, "Seeing Christianity in Red and Green," *Christianity Today*, fall 1983, pp. 281–89; S. Meyer, "Neuropsychological Worship," *Journal of Psychology and Theology* 3 (fall 1975): 281–89.

18. The limbic system of the brain is the region most associated with emotional expression.

Maslow's Hierarchy

Perhaps the best-known theory of psychological motivation is the one by Abraham Maslow, who suggested that there are different levels of motivation for different people.[19] His five levels of human needs assert that an adequate degree of satisfaction must be obtained at the first level before second-level needs emerge. After the second level is adequately fulfilled, the third level becomes more prominent. It is important to note that each level of the hierarchy need not be absolutely satisfied before the subsequent level becomes salient. Thus a person can have needs at several different levels simultaneously.

The first area of need, the most primary of all needs on Maslow's hierarchy of human motivation, is physical desire. Requirements such as food, water, and air are fundamental to existence, and thus serve as powerful motivators among those who are lacking in these areas. For multicultural religious education this suggests that the satisfaction of the learner's physical needs should be the top priority in interchange with those lacking in these necessities. A gnawing hunger is a significant impediment to any effective multicultural religious education, particularly for someone who faces the extra obstacle of cultural difference. Conversely, the satisfaction of physical needs is not only a motivator for learners to participate in religious education, but serves as a model of Christian love and compassion.[20] While certainly less urgent, the case can also be made that religion teachers, especially volunteer religious educators, may also be positively influenced by refreshments such as donuts and coffee.[21]

The second level of motivation involves safety needs. Protection from the elements is highlighted in increased concern for the homeless and those who are unemployed or underemployed. As with physical needs, multicultural religious education that helps provide for these needs is providing a context that enhances receptivity to instruction. Even though ethnic differences exist, those who are needy in this area are more likely to participate in religious education when these needs are provided for, as exemplified in classic inner-city mission work.

Love needs are the third level of Maslow's hierarchy. Love and acceptance are crucial to multicultural religious education. The love conveyed during the act of religious education teaches as much or more than the

---

19. Abraham Maslow, *Motivation and Personality*, 2d ed. (New York: Harper & Row, 1970).

20. One of few books, and probably the most complete book on the topic of religious compassion, is Gary L. Sapp's *Compassionate Ministry* (Birmingham, Ala.: Religious Education Press, 1993).

21. For more on motivating religious education volunteers, see Donald Ratcliff and Blake J. Neff, *The Complete Guide to Religious Education Volunteers* (Birmingham, Ala.: Religious Education Press, 1993).

verbal content. The way teaching is done is an important structural religious education content in its own right.[22] The acceptance that is part of love can be communicated by learning about the culture or subculture to be reached and trying to perceive reality from within that culture, taking an insider's or participant's perspective. Cross-cultural love and acceptance also involves valuing the different culture and incorporating the components of that culture, such as speaking the language and adopting the norms to the degree possible. The effective, loving religious educator can also work within the framework of the culture by living in the community and seeking to understand and help meet pressing needs.

Esteem needs, Maslow's fourth level of human motivation, are also crucial to multicultural endeavors. Often religious educators unintentionally mirror society's message to minorities that the dominant culture is intrinsically superior and that the ethnic group is entirely inferior. Many members of minority groups, especially those who are impoverished and powerless, feel a pervasive low self-esteem as a result. Christian religious education can address feelings of inferiority and build self-esteem by providing experiences of success, both in everyday life and in religious instruction. Religious educators can also emphasize the productive and perhaps even superior aspects of the ethnic group. The multicultural religious educator can also introduce values distinctive to religious faith that are in opposition to the dominant culture. Self-esteem is derived from one's reference for values,[23] and a change of that reference is implicit in affirming religious faith; the reference becomes religious faith rather than society or one's peers.[24] For example, some individuals have wealth or possessions as their source of self-esteem, and consequently self-esteem might change if their values were revised to concur with the Sermon on the Mount.

The fifth and highest level is self-actualization, which involves harmony with self, individuality, and peak experiences. Maslow considers peak experiences, or moments of ecstasy, an aspect of the fifth stage.[25] The author of this chapter disagrees with Maslow that these are characteristic only of the highest level of need, having observed moments of ecstasy and mystical experiences among people at all levels of the hierarchy, even among the hungry and homeless. Moments of mystical awareness and transcendence

---

22. James M. Lee, *The Content of Religious Instruction*, p. 8.

23. Paul D. Meier, Donald E. Ratcliff, and Frederick L. Rowe, *Child-Rearing and Personality Development*, 2d ed. (Grand Rapids, Mich.: Baker, 1993).

24. Perhaps the finest book on teaching moral values from a Christian perspective is Bonnidell Clouse's *Teaching for Moral Growth* (Wheaton, Illinois: Bridgepoint, 1993). Also see chapters by Jerry Aldridge in Donald Ratcliff's *Handbook of Children's Religious Education* (Birmingham, Ala.: Religious Education Press, 1992) and *Handbook of Youth Ministry* (Birmingham, Ala.: Religious Education Press, 1991).

25. Abraham Maslow, *Religions, Values, and Peak Experiences* (New York: Penguin, 1964).

are affirmed by followers of many religious faiths, and can be facilitated through religious education (Jerome Berryman even advocates this for children[26]). Peak experiences within worship can be a unifying factor across cultural and subcultural groups, a phenomenon the author of this chapter has seen in ethnic churches and gatherings in the United States and in his experience overseas.

Maslow's theory of human motivation has much to offer multicultural religious education. It is very important for religious educators to accurately assess the most important area of need for the ethnic group they wish to reach, as well as for the specific learners to be reached, and focus attention at that level while not excluding needs at other relevant levels.

Maslow's theory of motivation is only one of several theories of human motivation. A second theory that has considerable merit for multicultural religious education is behaviorism, which will be considered in the next section.

LEARNING

Three major theories of learning predominate in this area of psychology: classical conditioning, which emphasizes learning by association; operant conditioning, with its focus on rewards and punishments; and modeling, or learning by imitation. Each of these can contribute significantly to understanding others in a multicultural context and thus to effective religious education within that context.

Classical Conditioning

Classical conditioning was made famous by Russian psychologist Ivan Pavlov[27] and in the United States by John Watson.[28] Essentially, classical conditioning theory suggests that people (and animals) learn by making associations between some physical response that already exists (dogs salivating when eating) and a new stimulus (a bell being rung) so that one produces the other (a ringing bell produces salivation). Watson showed that the same sort of association could account for the development of fear reactions in humans.

An illustration of how classical conditioning theory explains reactions to multicultural experience may help. The author was a high school student when he first met an African American. Like many middle-class whites in

---

26. Jerome Berryman, *Godly Play* (San Francisco: HarperCollins, 1991).

27. Ivan Pavlov, *Conditioned Reflexes* (New York: Dover, 1927).

28. John Watson and R. Rayer, "Conditioned Emotional Reactions," *Journal of Experimental Psychology* 3 (1920): 1–14.

the 1960s, the author had been reared in complete isolation from African Americans in school, church, and community. Because of curiosity about different faiths, the author decided to visit an African-American church in a nearby city. The experience was very interesting because of the highly emotional nature of the singing and preaching in that church. Afterward, as the author made his way toward the door, several young African-American males walked toward him with hands outstretched. Immediately, without any reflection or thought about what was happening, adrenaline surged throughout the author's nervous system. His heart began to race, his breathing quickened, and he began a frantic search for the fastest way out of the church, oblivious to the warm, friendly faces of those young men who were doing their best to welcome him. Finally the author was able to compose his emotions to some extent and return their greeting, albeit with sweaty palms!

Where did this fear come from? Classical conditioning learning theory suggests that somehow the stimulus of seeing African-American teenagers was paired with something that produced fear, thus the two became powerfully associated. While the author does not recall ever before talking with an African-American teenager or even meeting an African-American child or adult, the author had observed African-American youths many times on television newscasts. At that time, during the 1960s, African-American teenagers were repeatedly shown on television looting and burning buildings in inner-city riots. Apparently the pictures aroused fear. The most prominent stimuli were young African-American men, and the stimuli and fear were strongly associated. Therefore the author experienced fear and desire to escape in his first actual encounter with African-American male youths, in spite of their warm welcome.

Fortunately classical conditioning theory also describes how classically conditioned fears can be overcome. Learned fears tend to subside when people are repeatedly exposed to the conditioned stimulus without any fear-producing associations, a process termed *extinction*. For example, this process involved the author's being with young African-American men without the associated violence he observed on television. The author decided to overcome those initial fears of young African-American males by returning to the same African-American church and eventually developing a friendship with one of the young men. The enjoyable service and the personal friendship resulted in decreased and eventual absence of the fear.[29]

The natural human reaction to a feared object is to avoid it, a tendency verified by classical conditioning research. But avoiding the feared object does not allow extinction to occur, and so some fears can last a lifetime. Can the interethnic avoidance, tension, and fear that exist today be partly

---

29. This experience is analyzed in detail using conditioning theory in Donald Ratcliff, "Basic Concepts of Behavioral Counselling," *The Christian Counsellor's Journal* 3:2 (1981): 11–15.

explained by early classical conditioning, the associating of fear or pain with a particular ethnic group, either from the media or from personal experience?

Classical conditioning theory emphasizes that learned responses can easily be generalized from one stimulus to a similar stimulus. In other words, objects or situations similar to the original learned stimulus tend to produce the same reaction in the individual. The writer once had a very negative experience involving a violation of trust with a college student of his from India. A few days later the writer was served in a restaurant by another young person from India. He found himself beginning to feel the same negative feelings he had felt with the student. By mentally fighting the unpleasant and unwelcome reaction, as well as by acting pleasantly to the waitress, he eventually overcame those feelings. Had the author not actively reacted to the generalized response, would he have developed the beginnings of an unwarranted prejudice against people from India?

Multicultural religious educators may occasionally have negative experiences with learners and others from different cultures and subcultures. The classically conditioned fears, or other unpleasant learned reactions, may need to be confronted or at least ignored until the emotive association decreases. Of course ignoring or confronting fears is also a possibility for learners as well, if they have associated fear or other unpleasant reactions with teachers or other learners of a culture different from their own. For example, the author visited an African-American friend whose oldest child had just completed his first day in a public school of all white children. During the day the youngster had met with ridicule and laughter because of his race. Had this been the boy's only encounter with white children, the experience might well have instilled fear and even hostility toward all white children in general. Fortunately, the author's oldest child, who was the same age, played happily with the African-American child without comment about his race, as he had done several times in the past. Their friendship, as well as positive experiences with other white children, helped avoid unfortunate emotive associations and a desire to avoid white children. Any child who has been conditioned with fear or hatred of children of another race needs repeated exposure to the other race in the absence of ridicule or injury to decrease the inclination to avoid the other-race children.[30]

---

30. Some of the dilemmas in working with children's racial prejudice and differences in children's ethnicity within the context of counseling are considered by Christiane Brems, *A Comprehensive Guide to Child Psychotherapy* (Boston: Allyn & Bacon, 1993), pp. 68–93; and Charles Thompson and Linda Rudolph, *Counseling Children*, 3d ed. (Pacific Grove, Calif.: Brooks/Cole, 1992), pp. 379–87.

Operant Conditioning

The second major theory of learning is operant conditioning, which emphasizes the importance of rewards in learning. Learning is most likely to occur when the atmosphere is positive and the consequences are desirable to the learner. However, what is rewarding to one person is not necessarily rewarding to another, so it is important to determine what is most likely to motivate the learner. Advocates of operant conditioning learning theory might suggest that multicultural religious education should be pleasant to be effective; learners need to experience success and positive consequences for what they learn. Yet there is a cultural component to what is rewarding (and nonrewarding). Knowledge of a specific culture or subculture can help multicultural religious educators identify what is most likely to be effective as a reward. Religious educators should never assume that something most people find rewarding will be perceived as rewarding by a member of another ethnic group. For example, a reward of a bright floral scarf may appeal to some subcultures but not others. Similarly, individual rewards might not be acceptable in a group where everyone shares what they have equally.

Research indicates that rewards are most likely to be effective when short-term influence is desired or if learners perceive the desired action as boring.[31] The most effective reward is a task that is intrinsically rewarding, yet intrinsic interest may actually be decreased when an external reward is added.[32] External rewards may also communicate that personal gain is a prominent value (which may oppose religious values) and that the action being rewarded is not inherently worthwhile. The researchers conclude that it may be good to use rewards occasionally, but they should be unexpected and should be used to provide feedback to learners, not to control them. Operant conditioning emphasizes that the general atmosphere should be positive and stimulating and that the religious education task should be pleasant and interesting, perhaps functioning as a means to the person's own nonmaterial goals in life. All of these factors have a part to play in multicultural religious education endeavors.

People do not learn every task all at once. Operant conditioning theory emphasizes the need to break down a complex task into its individual components or into manageable steps that can be learned one at a time. This process, called chaining or shaping, is an important aspect of religious education. Crucial to this process is clearly articulating the ultimate goals—the end products or objectives to be attained.[33]

---

31. This research is summarized by Martin Bolt and David Myers, *The Human Connection* (Downers Grove, Ill.: InterVarsity Press, 1984), p. 75.

32. D. Green and M. Lepper, "How to Turn Play into Work," *Psychology Today* 8 (September 1974): 49–53.

33. Several goals of multicultural religious education are suggested by James and Lillian Breckenridge in *What Color Is Your God?* (Wheaton, Ill.: Bridgepoint, 1995),

While specific religious education activities do well to use this step-by-step process as part of their structures, the adjustment to a different culture also takes a stagelike progression. Initial positive encounters with individuals belonging to a particular ethnic group lead to further encounters, perhaps for a longer period of time and at a deeper level of involvement. Intercultural contact is thus shaped, potentially for both learner and religious educator. Multicultural skills can likewise be shaped as long as perfection is not required upon the first encounter. This calls for patience and tolerance on the part of both religious educators and learners, as well as a personal desire to learn from mistakes.

Is there a standard progression that people go through in adjusting to a new culture? Can shaping help change that progression? Serving as a missionary overseas, this writer found that Peter Wagner's stage theory of cultural adjustment was the most helpful resource in understanding his own experience.[34] Wagner posits four stages of culture shock: (1) the tourist, (2) rejecting new values, (3) craving the values of the former culture, and (4) becoming depressed.

1. The tourist. A person who initially comes into contact with a new culture finds it exotic aspects appealing and exciting. This stage predominates among people who serve on short-term mission work teams: they take lots of pictures and enjoy exploring the new environment. Likewise, religious educators in their own countries may find themselves intrigued by cultural distinctives and excited by the challenge of multicultural instruction in their local context for the first weeks as they begin their work.

2. Rejecting new values. The individual who is not just a visitor to the new culture or subculture soon assumes a critical, judgmental stance toward it. Members of the different culture are perceived as breaking the rules when they do things differently. Sometimes the newcomer to the culture feels, unconsciously if not consciously, that people should be punished or changed because they do not fit into the newcomer's norms. Similarly, after the first few weeks of working in multicultural endeavors, the religious educator may become more critical of learners from different cultural or subcultural backgrounds. Even the religious educator who attempts to suppress this critical attitude can require learners to demonstrate greater conformity to the

---

pp. 75–83. While these goals are worthy ideals, and the book as a whole is insightful, their goals fall short of the specificity required to qualify as behavioral objectives. See Donald Ratcliff and Blake Neff, *The Complete Guide to Religious Education Volunteers* (Birmingham, Ala.: Religious Education Press, 1993), pp. 60–63. Developing objectives is also considered in detail by a number of writers who contributed to the three developmental religious education books edited by Donald Ratcliff and published by Religious Education Press (see fn. 64).

34. Peter Wagner, *Frontiers in Missionary Strategy* (Chicago: Moody Press, 1974), pp. 90–94.

dominant cultural norms than is actually needed to accomplish the religious education task at hand.

3. Craving the values of the former culture. At this stage the familiar values of one's home culture are desired. People at this stage often daydream and experience homesickness. Craving for the familiar occurs commonly in any cross-cultural adjustment. It can be a harmless means of progressing to something better or it can lead to loss of vision and withdrawal from the new culture. If they constantly criticize the norms of the new culture and begin to associate only with each other, this step has taken an unhealthy turn. The multicultural religious educator, working within her own country, may seriously consider giving up the challenges of cross-cultural instruction and think of escaping to an easier, safer religious education task involving only her own culture or subculture.

4. Becoming depressed. Unless stage three is resolved in a healthy manner, severe depression can occur, including a delusional component or physiological symptoms such as pain. Those who reach this stage need psychotherapy, whether they stay in the new culture or return to the old culture.

These steps chart adjustment and maladjustment to cross-cultural work, either in a foreign culture or in multicultural endeavors. A multicultural religious educator can profit from examining the stages and perhaps accepting some of his personal reactions as a temporary means of adjustment. Similarly, religious education learners who are not enculturated to the dominant culture may find themselves going through similar stages as they have increasing contact with the dominant culture. A sensitive religious educator realizes that those he is attempting to reach will go through stages of adjustment, and that those stages may be a temporary means of eventually gaining more from intercultural contact.

Wagner suggests six ways of avoiding the fourth stage of depression and adjusting productively to the new culture.[35] The six steps may be conceptualized as a shaping sequence, but *each* step may also require a series of steps for complete acquisition.

Step 1. Learn more about the differences between the new culture through discussions with those who have made the adjustment previously, as well as through readings.

Step 2. Attempt to mentally distance or bracket yourself from your culture of origin by realizing that no culture is inherently superior to other in all respects.[36]

---

35. Ibid., pp. 94–96.

36. It may be helpful to assess the advantages and disadvantages of both the culture of one's background, as well as the advantages and disadvantages of the other culture or subculture, an idea not specifically addressed by Wagner.

Step 3. Learn to communicate effectively within the culture by learning the different kinds of verbal and nonverbal languages used: the formal, the regular, the casual, and the intimate modes of speech.

Step 4. Spend time away from people of your culture of origin.

Step 5. Attempt to understand the reasons for the norms and rules of the new culture, seeing them from the perspective of members of the culture.

Step 6. As much as is feasible, begin practicing the norms of the culture.

Wagner suggests that making a positive adjustment to a new culture includes a broadened understanding of humanity and a loss of ethnocentrism—the belief that all aspects of one's own culture is superior to or more natural than others.[37] The second culture becomes a vantage point from which to critique the culture of origin more objectively. There is also the potential for spiritual development, since one gains a broader perspective of God's work from another cultural vantage point. One elderly missionary told the writer that his cross-cultural experience changed his view of God dramatically. He came to understand that God was far more than what his white, middle-class, American experience had encouraged him to think. Intensive experience in a different culture or subculture can potentially be enriching to any Christian; multicultural experience can be a religious education in itself!

Behavioral psychologists have identified the phenomenon of *learned helplessness*, which has important implications for multicultural relationships.[38] Seligman restrained dogs and gave them shocks that they could not avoid. A second group consisted of dogs that were allowed to jump out and avoid further shock. The researcher found that when dogs in the first group were placed in a box from which they could easily escape the shock, they did not. They had learned helplessness: even though they could avoid punishment, they continued to suffer needlessly.

People too can learn to be helpless. A person who has encountered many punishments and hurts comes to believe that she has no control over what happens, and tends to become passive and does not recognize the possibility of change for the better, even when it exists. Ethnic minority groups that get caught in the "cycle of poverty" can come to believe that it is all inevitable and ignore possible exits from that cycle. They may blame fate or their ethnicity for their helplessness, when actually they have learned it through personal experience or what they have been told. Breaking this learned helplessness requires a change of belief structure. Such individuals need to learn that they are not helpless through positive examples and

---

37. Wagner, *Frontiers*, pp. 98–99.

38. M. Seligman, *Learned Helplessness and Depression in Animals and Humans* (Morristown, N.J.: General Learning, 1975).

through the hope engendered by positive religion. Multicultural religious education should help instill new belief structures that will counteract learned helplessness. New belief structures may be needed by both religious educators and learners.

Learning by Imitation

A third learning theory, articulated by Albert Bandura, suggests that people learn by observing others and then imitating what they see.[39] This suggests that multicultural religious education is more likely to occur when there are good examples or models available that can be imitated. The religious educator who is able to adapt to cultural differences can serve as a model for learners to imitate by adapting to some extent to the culture of the religious educator. Observing the religious educator's acceptance and appreciation for cultural differences can be an important source of multicultural understanding.

Bandura suggests that four factors maximize the likelihood of learning by imitation. First, the learner's attention should be drawn to the activity and specifically to the crucial aspects of the observed behavior. The model must be attractive or must be perceived as similar to the person observing, and it must be readily available for observation. Second, the learner needs to be able to recall the action observed. Third, the learner should have the potential to perform the behavior. Fourth, the learner needs to be motivated to imitate. All of these factors are essential in multicultural religious education, but it is again important to keep cultural distinctives in mind when evaluating what is attractive or similar (guideline 1) and what motivates the person (guideline 4).

For example, a multicultural religious educator can exemplify the appreciation of a second culture to learners who share the dominant culture. The educator can encourage a person from another culture to share interesting aspects of the second culture to exemplify this appreciation. The religious educator may outline specific aspects of the second culture using an overhead projector, modeling to the learners a method of deriving greater understanding of the second culture. In the process of talking about the outline and the understandings gained, the educator can make positive comments about the other culture, modeling appreciation and respect for the second culture. If the religious educator draws the attention of learners to the outlining and is sufficiently attractive or is perceived as being like the learners, repeatedly engages in such appreciative behavior, and motivates the learners, imitation of that appreciation becomes more likely.

---

39. Albert Bandura, *Principles of Behavior Modification* (New York: Rinehart & Winston, 1969).

COGNITIVE PSYCHOLOGY

Many aspects of cognitive psychology have an important bearing on all religious education, especially in the area of concept acquisition and facilitating memory and recall. Multicultural religious education can make particular use of the prototype theory of concepts.

Prototype theory states that people identify objects as belonging to a conceptual category because those objects are similar to their mental prototype of that concept. The person's prototype is what the individual believes is the best example of the concept.[40] The physical resemblance between the person's mental prototype and the specific object encountered results in identifying the object with the concept. Mental prototypes often develop from the first experiences an individual has with a given concept; the initial examples of the concept significantly shape the mental prototype used in subsequent identification of objects with the conceptual category.[41]

The whole idea of multiculturalism is misunderstood by some because their first encounters with the idea produce distortions of it. Some religious conservatives, for example, have associated multiculturalism with anti-European, antimale sentiment.[42] Some advocates of multiculturalism have undervalued or devalued the predominant Western culture because it has tended to ignore or minimize the accomplishments of women and ethnic minorities. But this is a misunderstanding of healthy multiculturalism. Genuine, balanced multiculturalism underscores accomplishments by both men and women, and elevates accomplishments of all races and ethnic groups, including the majority group. To put down or belittle any cultural group, including a group that has been overly dominant in the past, is *not* healthy multiculturalism; it is a cultural elitism of the minority. Exchanging one form of elitism for another is simply asking for another kind of oppression and ignorance.

Multicultural religious education seeks to foster the understanding of, valuing of, and effective education of people within a society comprising many cultural influences. Prototype theory underscores the importance of initial experiences of a concept. These initial experiences with multiculturalism should be positive, affirming all cultural groups and demeaning none.

------

40. Eleanor Rosch, "Cognitive Representations of Semantic Categories," *Journal of Experimental Psychology* 104 (1975): 192–233.

41. E. Smith and D. Medin, *Categories and Concepts* (Cambridge, Mass.: Harvard University Press, 1981).

42. S. D. Gaede provides several examples of these reactions to multiculturalism in *When Tolerance Is No Virtue* (Downers Grove, Ill.: InterVarsity Press, 1993). This book describes both advantages and pitfalls of multiculturalism in a very evenhanded manner and is worthy of careful study. James and Lillian Breckenridge cite similar examples of extremist reactions to multiculturalism in *What Color Is Your God?*

Healthy multiculturalism needs to be taught early to children in a positive manner, and initial experiences in religious education settings should also be balanced and positive. People do not respond positively to threats and criticism. The first examples should be positive, desirable, nonthreatening examples so the reference point for later experiences in multiculturalism will be adequate.

In local churches that place a high priority on missionary work, religious educators can introduce multiculturalism as an extension of what missionaries do. Missionaries meet cultural differences daily, and those who have been trained well have learned to value differences and work within the framework of the new culture's values. Some missionaries even incorporate some of those cultural values into their own personal value system, blending them with values from the culture of origin. Of course, some missionaries are not good examples of multiculturalism, such as missionaries who emphasize what they consider to be the peculiarities of a new culture and ignore commonalities, or missionaries who manifest a condescending attitude toward the second culture. But religious educators can include good missionary speakers or materials from missionary preparation as a first step for introducing multicultural religious education.

INTELLIGENCE AND LEARNING STYLES

Some proponents of intelligence testing have, unfortunately, given ammunition to those who foster racism and cultural elitism. A storm of protest resulted when in 1969 respected researcher Arthur Jensen suggested that the difference in IQ between African Americans and white Americans was due to genetic deficiency in African Americans.[43] His argument was misleading because of the wide discrepancies that exist in income, social status, and other social factors between African Americans and whites as groups. Later studies that controlled for these social differences showed far less difference in IQ between African Americans and Americans of European descent.[44] Jensen's argument was later restated and elaborated by researchers Richard Herrnstein and Charles Murray,[45] who also met with strong but less volatile reactions from the public.

The issues raised by these researchers are too elaborate to consider in detail in this chapter, but a fundamental question that can be raised is whether

---

43. Arthur R. Jensen, "How Much Can We Boost IQ and Scholastic Achievement?" *Harvard Educational Review* 39 (summer 1969): 1–123.

44. S. Scarr and R. Weinberg, "IQ Test Performance of Black Children," *American Psychologist* 31 (October 1976): 726–91.

45. Richard J. Herrnstein and Charles Murray, *The Bell Curve* (New York: Free Press, 1994).

standardized intelligence tests actually assess all that is meant by the concept of intelligence. This is clearly not the case; Guilford posits 120 different components of intelligence, all of which could never be measured on any test of intelligence.[46] Both the cultural bias of IQ tests and the oversimplified concept of intelligence underlying them call into question their value for measuring intelligence.

Rather than developing a single number to measure intelligence, it is more accurate to reflect the diversity of areas of intelligence through a recognition of differences that exist across cultures. For example, Howard Gardner states that there are seven kinds of intelligence, each of which may be considered a different aspect of intelligence: (1) *linguistic* intelligence, which includes speaking and writing abilities; (2) *logical/mathematical* intelligence, involved in problem solving and reasoning; (3) *spatial* intelligence, involved in creating, visualizing, building, drawing, and so on; (4) *musical* intelligence, playing an instrument, singing, and enjoying or appreciating music; (5) *kinesthetic* intelligence involved in dance, sports, and other physical activities; (6) *interpersonal* intelligence in which group activities, friendships, leading and following, and other interactions are crucial; and (7) *intrapersonal*, marked by personal reflection and thought.[47]

These seven "intelligences" are by no means exhaustive of all possibilities. Guilford calculated that at least 120 different kinds of intelligence are possible. The point is that intelligence is reflected in different ways in different cultural and ethnic groups. To underscore a few of these kinds of intelligence to the exclusion of the rest, as an IQ test does, is to be culturally biased in supposedly measuring intelligence. IQ tests are currently most likely to be used as a predictor of school achievement for perhaps two or three years following the test, but even that limited use is potentially biased culturally. The test predicts probable achievement in classrooms developed by and for the dominant American culture, the same culture reflected in the test. It does not suggest what might be accomplished by ethnic minorities in a learning environment that is more oriented toward the specific learning styles of that minority.

Multicultural religious educators should affirm the diversity that exists in learning styles and intelligence. This affirmation requires a flexibility in methodology that incorporates different ways of learning. The seven aspects of intelligence suggested by Gardner are a good start, and truly effective religious education will include several of these in every session. Every aspect should be reflected at least occasionally. Incorporating multiple

---

46. J. Guilford, "Theories of Intelligence," in *Handbook of General Psychology*, ed. B. Wolman (Englewood Cliffs, N.J.: Prentice-Hall, 1973).

47. Howard Gardner, *Frames of Mind* (New York: Basic Books, 1983). Also see his more recent book, *Multiple Intelligences: The Theory in Practice* (New York: Basic, 1993).

intelligences makes it more likely that all learners will be exposed to some aspect of learning that is optimal for them. It may also expose learners to new, unfamiliar styles of learning. The religious educator who adapts instruction to various learning styles affirms the variety of intelligences. As a result, this adaptation makes the religious education process an important model even as it provides a valuable means of learning.[48]

While Gardner's list of learning styles is a good start, religious educators should remain open to other conceptualizations of learning styles that may more specifically reflect the characteristics of specific ethnic groups. For example, James Anderson contrasts the learning styles of Eurocentric college students (predominantly middle- and upper-class persons, mostly white) with people of color (many African Americans, Hispanics, Native Americans, and high risk students regardless of race) and found these differences:

Figure 3.1 Learning Style Differences

Eurocentric	People of Color
Distant	Closer/Relational
Fact centered (depersonalized)	Story centered (social)
Critical thinking	Rote learning (needs applications)
Internal standards	Needs praise and support
Field independent	Field dependent
Dichotomous	Holistic
Extracts key ideas	Does not extract key ideas
Theory oriented	Imagery oriented
Time-centered	"Elastic" time
Conjunctive concepts	Disjunctive concepts

Anderson considers these differences crucial distinctives not only between majority and minority individuals, but between Western and non-Western people in general, although individuals from the Far East were a major exception to many of the characteristics in the people-of-color column.[49]

Shirley Heath has also identified a specific learning-style difference between many African-American and white children.[50] African-American youngsters tend to be taught by parents through direct statements, whereas white youngsters often are taught via questions. As a result, white children

---

48. Also see Timothy Lines, *Functional Images of the Religious Educator* (Birmingham, Ala.: Religious Education Press, 1992).

49. James Anderson, "Cognitive Styles and Multicultural Populations," *Journal of Teacher Education* 39 (1988): 2–9.

50. Shirley Heath, *Ways with Words* (Cambridge: Cambridge University Press, 1983).

are better prepared for the question-answer format of many learning contexts. Religious educators should be aware of these differences and adapt
teaching styles accordingly, rather than insist on the question-and-answer
format that often occurs in schools. Folktales, enactment, and dance may
be particularly effective teaching procedures for some cultural and subcultural groups.[51] These may also prove beneficial to learning for everyone, regardless of ethnic background, as they involve additional sensory
modalities and alternative learning styles and perhaps a wider variety of
intelligences.

Learning styles vary considerably, and the empirical research cited is only
a beginning point for multicultural religious education. Additional differences in learning styles probably exist between ethnic groups. Religious education needs to pave the way for culturally sensitive educational endeavors
and not relegate large numbers of people to the "learning disabled" category,
as public schools once did, simply because they learn differently from the
majority. Differences in learning styles require innovative adaptations in
religious education endeavors.[52]

SOCIAL PSYCHOLOGY

One of the most fruitful areas for exploring multicultural differences is
social psychology. Social psychology, overlapping with both psychology
and sociology, deals with the way people relate to one another, how they
influence each other, and in general how they think about each other.[53] Each
of these topics is loaded with implications for multicultural relationships of
any kind, including those involving religious education. Only a few of the
best-known studies in the area are surveyed here; a thorough analysis for
multicultural use would require a separate chapter, if not an entire book.

Attitudes

Attitudes are more than opinions. Attitudes involve thinking (cognition),
feelings (affect), and a predisposition to act in a given way.[54] A change in
attitude is often an aspect of religious education in general and multicultural
religious education in particular.[55]

---

51. M. McCarron, "Folktales as Transmitters of Values," *Religious Education* 82:1
(1987): 20–29; E. Mitchell, "Oral Tradition," *Religious Education* 81:1 (1986): 93–112.
52. For example, see Tom A. Steffen's "A Narrative Approach to Communicating
the Bible," *Christian Education Journal* 14:3 (1994): 86–109.
53. Myers, *Social Psychology*, p. 3.
54. Ibid., p. 36.
55. Lee, *The Content of Religious Instruction*, pp. 216–29.

Leon Festinger discovered that sometimes different aspects of an attitude are not consistent.[56] For example, when people hold an opinion that is inconsistent with the way they act, an inward tension develops that they seek to reduce. Individuals seek to reduce that tension by changing their opinions, changing their actions, or justifying their inconsistency.

Perhaps the most cogent multicultural application of Festinger's research is that prejudiced people who claim to lack prejudice have three options when they are confronted with that inconsistency.[57] First, they may decide they are prejudiced and affirm prejudicial attitudes; second, they may change their prejudicial behavior to fit nonprejudicial attitudes; or, finally, they may attempt to convince themselves that racist behavior is not actually racist. Festinger maintained that people are driven to achieve consistency, even if it requires dishonesty!

Cognitive dissonance theory can be used to influence people in positive directions. For example, a person who distrusts and dislikes all persons of a particular race may be exposed to exemplary individuals of that race or at least to stories of such exemplary persons. Such exposure can foster the tension Festinger described, and a small change of attitude is likely. Broad, dramatic changes are not likely to occur at any one time. Gradual, successive changes can eventually result in a much less prejudiced person, particularly if the person doing the influencing is credible and personal. Demanding a great change, however, is likely to result only in self-justification and rejection of the religious educator.

Another aspect of attitudes is the "self-fulfilling prophecy."[58] Rosenthal found that teachers' expectations of children, apart from children's actual ability, can significantly affect children's performance in the classroom; children who are expected to excel tend to improve more than youngsters not expected to excel. Everyone has a natural inclination to act as others expect. It takes a strong will for minority group members to work against society's expectations of them, even if those expectations are prejudicial. The same is also true of the expectations that minority groups have of those in the majority. Self-fulfilling prophecy is also possible among different

---

56. Leon Festinger, *A Theory of Cognitive Dissonance* (Stanford, Calif.: Stanford University Press, 1957).

57. This brief application of Festinger's research does not consider the extensive research of prejudice as it relates to religion, as this is beyond the scope of this chapter. Gordon Allport, C. D. Batson, and many others have contributed to the research on prejudice. The topic of prejudice and religion is important for religious education in general, not just multicultural religious education. For a thorough survey of some of the literature on prejudice, see David Myers, *Social Psychology*. Paul Meier, Frank Minirth, Frank Wichern, and Donald Ratcliff offer a brief overview in *Introduction to Psychology and Counseling*, p. 247.

58. Robert Rosenthal and L. Jacobson, *Pygmalion in the Classroom* (New York: Holt, Rinehart and Winston, 1968).

ethnic groups and even within a specific ethnic group. The topic of self-fulfilling prophecy has an extensive literature that is beyond the scope of this chapter.[59]

Influence

Three methods of influence have been suggested by social psychologists: compliance, identification, and internalization. Each can have a place in multicultural religious education. Understanding and appreciating a different cultural group may result from engaging in discussion and interaction with or about persons in that group, a form of compliance considered earlier in this chapter. This can at least encourage people to enter the multicultural arena, the first step in dialogue and understanding. Identification occurs when an individual considered interesting and attractive by the learners creates further interest in the topic and ideas involved. Identification has its parallels in modeling, described earlier. The third and most powerful form of influence is internalization, in which people adopt another's perspectives as their own, rather than simply responding to rewards or examples. Internalization is most likely to occur when the influential person is credible, is perceived as an expert, and can apply the ideas in a practical manner.[60] An important goal of multicultural religious education is for learners to internalize the importance of understanding people from a different cultural or subcultural context, which is most likely when the religious educator can demonstrate the practicality of doing so and is seen as a trustworthy and knowledgeable person. The personal characteristics of the teacher, as well as good training in the area of multiculturalism, are extremely important in a successful religious education program.

Relationships

A classic study in social psychology drew on the parable of the good Samaritan from the Bible (Lk 10:30–35).[61] Students at Princeton Theological Seminary were asked to walk to another building and speak briefly on this parable. As the students walked to the building, they confronted a person lying on the ground, coughing, and groaning. Only 10 percent of the theological students stopped to help the man, in spite of the fact they were on their way to deliver a message on the good Samaritan! The researchers

---

59. See David Myers, *Social Psychology*. Also see James M. Lee's consideration of the topic in *The Content of Religious Instruction*.

60. Myers, *Social Psychology*, pp. 278–82.

61. J. Darley and C. Batson, "From Jerusalem to Jericho," *Journal of Personality and Social Psychology* 27 (1973): 100–108.

discovered that time was a major factor; if students were given plenty of time to get to the building, many more stopped to help the man.

While this psychological experiment clearly demonstrated that there is a difference between what people say and what they do, it may also suggest why some religious people are less concerned than others about disadvantaged ethnic groups.[62] Perhaps they are unconcerned because they are in too great a hurry. Perhaps religious individuals do not see the unfortunate because they never go near the needy. Finally, as noted earlier, it may be that the costs of time, money, and effort outweigh the potential benefits (or perhaps the person has never perceived any possible benefits) of involvement. The same could be said about multicultural contact. Many religious people feel they are too busy to really understand members of another cultural group, or they may isolate themselves so they do not contact, or at least not in a meaningful way, other ethnic groups frequently. Perhaps they calculate the costs in time and effort without considering the possible benefits to themelves.

It is interesting that the good Samaritan parable was used as the springboard for the previous study, as Jesus used that parable to show that a despised minority (Samaritans) could be more willing to help than those of the religious and cultural majority (those who passed by the injured man). Sometimes members of cultural and ethnic minorities are more willing to reach out, learn, and help others in multicultural contexts. Religious educators, especially those representing the majority ethnic group, need to make a special effort not only to follow the example of the good Samaritan but also to point out the positive qualities of subcultural groups, as Christ did by telling the parable.

This section on social psychology is but a brief survey of many potential areas of interface between social psychology and multicultural religious education.[63] Attitudes, influence, and relationships are vital to effective religious education of any kind.

HUMAN DEVELOPMENT

Once dominated by the topic of child psychology, developmental psychology has expanded to include the entire life span of human development.

---

62. See I. Deutscher, *What We Say/What We Do* (Glenview, Ill.: Scott, Foresman, 1972) for more on inconsistencies commonly maintained by people.

63. For a more complete survey of social psychology written by a Christian, though not reflecting an overtly Christian perspective, see David Myers, *Social Psychology*. Also see an early brief work he coauthored with Martin Bolt that more explicitly includes Christian perspectives and applications: *The Human Connection* (Downers Grove, Illinois: InterVarsity Press, 1984).

Multicultural religious education can be particularly helpful in preparing children for intercultural relationships. These efforts should be carefully adapted to the child's cognitive, psychomotor, affective, and social levels of development, as should all religious education efforts. (For details, see the author's three handbooks.[64]) However, the distinctive aspects of adult development are also important for effective multicultural religious education after the childhood and adolescent years.

Piaget's Theory

While Freudian psychology once dominated child development, and neo-Freudian Erik Erikson's[65] theory is still quite popular, the cognitive development theory of Jean Piaget[66] achieved prominence during the 1970s. Some aspects of Piaget's theory are still being revised in regard to specific conclusions,[67] but his picture of the child's mind is still one of the most powerful influences in the field of human development. Earlier in this chapter his outline of *how* children learn was considered (assimilation, accommodation, and disequilibrium); here the constraints of culture on that learning will be the focus of attention.

Piaget maintained that the child goes through a succession of stages in cognitive development. Some researchers believe that the last stage, *formal operations*, does not occur in some cultures.[68] Is it fair then to say that some cultures fail to encourage, perhaps even impede, cognitive development? Even if that were found to be so, is that not a very ethnocentric criticism of cultural groups—just the opposite of the intent of multiculturalism?

The problem with much of the cross-cultural research into formal operations thinking is the inadequacy of the measuring tools used. For example, some researchers' conclusion is based on tests of abstract thinking that require formal schooling. Cultures that lack formal classroom experiences and make use of informal education may not encourage this aspect of formal

64. Donald Ratcliff, *Handbook of Preschool Religious Education* (Birmingham, Ala.: Religious Education Press, 1988), *Handbook of Children's Religious Education* (Birmingham, Ala.: Religious Education Press, 1992), and *Handbook of Youth Ministry* (Birmingham, Ala.: Religious Education Press, 1991).

65. Erik Erikson, *Childhood and Society*, 2d rev. ed. (New York: Norton, 1963).

66. Jean Piaget, *The Construction of Reality in the Child* (New York: Basic, 1954).

67. Most child-development textbooks consider some of the adjustments that have been made to Piaget's theory. One of the better ones, although it is already a bit dated, is Elizabeth Hall, Michael Lamb, and M. Perlmutter, *Child Psychology Today*, 2d ed. (New York: Random, 1986). The writer also considers some of the changes made in Piaget's theory, specifically in relation to preschooler developmental characteristics, in his first chapter of *The Handbook of Preschool Religious Education*.

68. P. Dansen, "Cross-Cultural Piagetian Research," *Journal of Cross-Cultural Psychology* 3 (1972): 23–39.

operational thinking, but encourage other aspects of that form of thinking, such as allegory and symbolism.[69] It is fair to say that Western culture does not have a monopoly on the highest level of mental development, if a variety of measures are used.

The implication of research on the formal operations stage for multicultural religious education is that it is very unwise to judge a cultural or subcultural group as being less cognitively advanced on the basis of a single attribute. Difference does not necessarily imply inferiority. In addition, there is the implication that differences in how a cognitive level (e.g., formal operations) is demonstrated should be taken into account in religious education endeavors. Multicultural religious education should not only be adapted to a presumed cognitive level, such as presenting biblical materials to school-aged children at a concrete operations level, but also it is important to assess how the cognitive level of an individual of any age is demonstrated (i.e., learning styles).

Multicultural Religious Education with Children

A long-standing area of intercultural contact between children is the experience of missionary kids (MKs). These children and young people are generally reared in a culture different from that of the parents. They are exposed to the parents' culture for only one out of four or five years, when the family returns to the culture of origin for deputation. The exception is the MK who spends a great deal of time in a boarding school, which often reflects American education and American culture to a greater extent.

What effect does extensive exposure to different cultures have for these children? While these children may have more identity and adjustment problems because of their cross-cultural experience,[70] such as difficulty adjusting to the "home" culture and feeling like an outsider in both the "home" and "host" cultures, there are also distinct personal advantages. These cross-cultural experiences tend to broaden their personal outlook, yet they are more influenced by their parents than other children are. MKs schooled within the host culture and outside the boarding school tended to be more open-minded about cultural values.[71] They are far more likely than children and young people reared in the United States to become "world Christians" sensitive to culture. The multicultural environment can also facilitate multiple language skills and other positive

---

69. E. Mitchell, "Oral Tradition," *Religious Education* 81 (1986): 93–112; M. McCarron, "Folktales as Transmitters of Values," *Religious Education* 82 (1987): 20–29.

70. S. Werkman, "Hazards of Rearing Children in Foreign Countries," *American Journal of Psychiatry* 128 (1972): 992–97.

71. L. Sharp, "How Missionary Children Become World Christians," *Journal of Psychology and Theology* 18 (1990): 66–74.

qualities.[72] In contrast, the boarding school experience by MKs, which is far more monocultural, can be very problematic, at least for those who attend as children.[73]

MKs provide an example of multicultural religious education already in place, but what about multicultural religious education of children in their own culture? Accomplishing multicultural religious education with children in general is no easy task. One helpful resource, *Helping Kids Learn Multi-Cultural Concepts*, details many instructional strategies that might be adapted for religious education contexts and topics.[74] The author of this book describes how teachers can develop a multicultural climate in the school, and he stresses the importance of in-service preparation of teachers as well.

Multicultural religious education requires careful planning and preparation. Merely dumping various ethnic groups into a common learning environment is asking for trouble. Interethnic contact and exchange are worthy goals, but this requires preparation of both teachers and learners. It is crucial for learners and teachers not only to be prepared but also to have positive first experiences in cross-cultural religious education. It is interesting that many megachurches today have separate church services, and sometimes even different pastors, for various minority groups. Separate, distinctive programs to reach ethnic groups need to be balanced with multicultural gatherings that reflect the diversity of the body of Christ, but, at least in children's groups, careful planning and preparation is a must.

How is childhood different in various cultures and subcultures? This important issue is far too involved to be considered in detail here, but it is worthy of extensive study. A number of excellent resources, keyed to specific characteristics of children and families of various cultural groups, are available.[75]

---

72. Idem, "Toward a Greater Understanding of the Real MK," *Journal of Psychology and Christianity* 5 (1985): 73–78.

73. Donald Ratcliff, "Social Contexts of Children's Ministry," in *Handbook of Children's Religious Education*, pp. 119–42.

74. Michael G. Pasternak, *Helping Kids Learn Multi-Cultural Concepts* (Champaign, Ill.: Research Press, 1979).

75. Children of a number of racial and ethnic groups are considered in detail in *Education and Cultural Process*, ed. George Spindler, (Prospect Heights, Ill.: Waveland, 1987). The family interface with children of various cultural and subcultural groups is considered in *Cultural Diversity and Families*, by K. Arms, J. Davidson, and N. Moore, (Dubuque, Iowa: Brown, 1992); and *Family Ethnicity*, ed. Harriette McAdoo, (Newbury Park, Calif.: Sage, 1993). For specific characteristics of African-American children, see *Black Children*, by J. Hale-Benson, rev. ed. (Baltimore: John Hopkins University Press, 1986); and *Black Children*, by Harriette and J. McAdoo, (Beverly Hills, Calif.: Sage, 1985. A doctoral dissertation by B. Villarreal considers some culturally distinctive aspects of learning among Hispanic children: *An Investigation of the Effects of Types*

Multicultural Religious Education in Adolescence

As teenagers move from childhood to adulthood, personal identity becomes an important quest.[76] This quest often involves questioning some of the basic components of society and sometimes religious faith. Thus identity is formed by adolescent questioning and eventual resolving of questions, and by adopting or rejecting the values of the parental home.[77]

Multicultural religious education can be a particularly important component of youth ministry because it relates to both religious values and cultural values. Experience with the perspectives of another culture or subculture can help youths gain a broader perspective of the world; indeed, it can help them become somewhat like the world Christians mentioned in the previous section on MKs. Triangulating faith to the variety of cultural contexts can further enhance both mental and spiritual development of youths.

For example, the writer of this chapter recalls visiting a number of different ethnic churches at the age of seventeen. These visits powerfully influenced the author's multicultural awareness, but they could have been more influential if an experienced guide and/or group of peers had also participated in the visits and later discussed the experiences. Youths from African-American churches could have reciprocated by visiting white churches. Then both groups could have met together to talk about the differences in worship, feelings of acceptance and rejection, and other issues. In college the author was introduced to the distinction between a vital religious faith that had been enculturated, and a syncretistic faith that blended pagan and Christian beliefs. While this distinction was introduced in an anthropology class at a Christian college, many of the same issues could have been introduced in an adolescent-level religious education context. Concern for adapting religious education for age appropriateness should not lead to underestimating the abilities of young people. Teenagers, with their formal operational abilities, need to be challenged with the possibilities and ambiguities of multicultural religion.

Developing personal identity may be particularly difficult for youths who have not learned about their ethnic heritage. A vivid case study of one young woman who encountered this difficulty and its implications for

---

of Play (Ph.D. diss. Pennsylvania State University, 1982). B. Sung studied Chinese immigrant children in New York in her chapter "Bicultural Conflict," in *Chinese Immigrant Children in New York* (New York: Center for Migration Studies, 1987). Hmong children attempting to adapt to the American culture are considered in detail in a fine book by H. Trueba, L. Jacobs, and E. Kirton, *Cultural Conflict and Adaptation* (New York: Falmer, 1990).

76. Erik Erikson, *Childhood and Society*; idem, *Identity, Youth, and Crisis* (New York: Norton, 1968).

77. Gary Sapp, *Handbook of Moral Development* (Birmingham, Ala.: Religious Education Press, 1986). Also see his "Adolescent Thinking and Understanding," in the writer's *Handbook of Youth Ministry*.

child welfare policies are presented by B. E. Williams.[78] Linda, an African-American teenager, had been reared in communities where she was the only African-American child. Her strongest role model was a white social worker who became involved when her parents neglected her. As a teenager, she became a ward of the court and was admitted to a public care facility. Her ethnic background and family did not shape her life, yet she did not feel that she belonged to the predominant white culture either. The difficulty manifested itself in depression, crying, and nightmares. As Williams states, "She was a creature of both worlds and a citizen of neither."

Sung notes that peer group identity among cultural minorities can require a negation of previously existing beliefs and values.[79] But identity cannot be accomplished by negation alone. These young people suffer from intense cultural conflict because they are forced to participate in two cultures simultaneously, while remaining on the margins of both and not identifying fully with either.[80]

Piaget also emphasized the idealism of adolescents,[81] who believe that simple solutions can solve the world's problems. While religious educators should encourage realism among youths, such realism must not involve the abandonment of ideals. Rather, the ideals of multicultural understanding, in contrast to the uniformity of a single dominant culture, should be affirmed by religious educators. In addition, the more practical steps involved in moving toward that ideal need to be delineated. These steps, as well as how they can be accomplished, should be detailed through dialogue between the youth leader, teenagers, and other interested persons.

Selman has formulated a theory of how adolescents mentally represent relationships, and how they distinguish the views of others from their own ideas.[82] He notes that in early adolescence young people can adopt a more objective "outsider" framework of social relationships. Later in the adolescent and adult years they become able to take an even more abstract perspective, viewing their actions from the perspective of society at large. Young people also become aware that unconscious feelings and thoughts can affect their behavior in ways beyond their immediate understanding.

---

78. B. E. Williams, "Looking for Linda," *Child Welfare* 66 (1987): 207–16.

79. Sung, "Bicultural Conflict."

80. For other aspects of adolescent ethnicity and identity, see the work of L. Steinberg et al., "Ethnic Difference in Adolescent Achievement," *American Psychologist* June 1992, pp. 723–29; K. Majorbanks, "Relationship of Children's Ethnicity, Gender, and Social Status to Their Family Environments and School Related Outcomes," *Social Psychology Quarterly*, February 1991, pp. 83–91; and J. Streitmatter, "Ethnicity as a Mediating Variable of Early Adolescent Identity Development," *Journal of Adolescence*, December 1988, pp. 335–46.

81. Jean Piaget, *Six Psychological Studies* (New York: Random, 1967), p. 64.

82. R. Selman, *The Growth of Interpersonal Relationships* (New York: Academic, 1980).

These two stages of Selman's four-stage theory are crucial in the development of multicultural religious education efforts.[83] Selman's theory indicates that adolescents can adopt a third-person perspective on their own relationships with members of another culture as early as the early teen years. A more general and abstract societal view of multiculturalism is more likely to come later, when they become more aware of the possibilities of latent racism and ethnocentrism.

Multicultural Religious Education in Adulthood

Young adults between the ages of twenty and thirty are concerned with intimate relationships, often marriage, and career development.[84] While beginning a family is important to many, others defer having children until their thirties.[85] Multicultural religious education in early adulthood might emphasize the importance of cross-cultural relationships, including those with the opposite sex. Young adults might be interested in talking about positive and negative aspects of interracial dating and marriage. Perhaps even more important would be contrasting how different cultural and subcultural groups understand male and female roles, how those understandings vary within those groups, and the effect that has in multicultural contexts. A parish religious education class might have a simulation game involving different ways Christian love can be demonstrated at work by understanding and respecting cultural and gender differences and similarities. Learners might also discuss how society, and churches, often make interracial couples feel unwelcome.

The developmental changes of middle and late adulthood may not especially resonate with multicultural religious education per se, but neither do they rule out multicultural religious education. In fact, retired individuals may have more time for multicultural experiences such as working in an inner city or joining a work team traveling overseas. These kinds of experiences can be an effective form of religious education for other adults and teenagers as well. Multicultural religious education is possible for adults of every age.[86]

---

83. Selman describes two other stages prior to adolescence. While the preschooler is egocentric, school-aged children consider only one perspective to be accurate, while preadolescents begin to consider how others might view their actions differently.

84. Diane Papalia and S. Olds, *Human Development* (New York: McGraw-Hill, 1986).

85. S. Olds, *The Working Parents' Survival Guide* (New York: Bantam, 1983).

86. Several recent adult religious education books may be consulted for age characteristics that may suggest appropriate topics in multicultural endeavors. These include Douglas Fagerstrom, ed., *Single Adult Ministries* (Wheaton, Ill.: Victor, 1993); Jerry Stubblefield, ed., *A Church Ministering to Adults* (Nashville: Broadman, 1986); Charles Sell, *Transitions through Adult Life* (Grand Rapids, Mich.: Zondervan, 1991); Nancy

COUNSELING AND PSYCHOTHERAPY

Cross-cultural counseling has become an important area of psychology. Counselors need to understand that good counseling is more than helping members of cultural minorities adjust to the dominant cultural norms. Effective counseling among ethnic groups and in cross-cultural contexts requires an understanding and a respect for the distinctives of the person being counseled.

In the 1980s and 1990s Christian counseling began to affirm the importance of cross-cultural counseling, first by a pioneering text in the area, David Hesselgrave's *Counseling Cross-Culturally*,[87] and later by an issue of *Journal of Psychology and Christianity*.[88] Understanding subcultural distinctives is also important in reaching different ethnic groups, as underscored in the Christian book *Healing for the City: Counseling in the Urban Setting*.[89] It includes separate chapters on counseling Hispanics, African Americans, and Asians in urban areas, thus emphasizing the unique characteristics of each subculture rather than the myth of a homogeneous "urban culture."

Multicultural religious education can benefit greatly from an appreciation of cultural and subcultural distinctives in counseling. While counseling is education[90] because learning, understanding, and behavior change are its goals, ideas from counseling are also beneficial for the more typical religious educator, including the distinctive aspects of cross-cultural counseling. Learners will be likely to seek informal counseling from the religious educator who has taken the time to establish good rapport. While religious educators should not attempt counseling that requires professional expertise, they need some skills in lay-level counseling in order to meet the personal and spiritual needs of their learners. If learners are not members of the dominant culture, and the religious education reflects that dominant culture, a knowledge of cross-cultural counseling can be invaluable in helping religious educators reach across the cultural chasm.

Foltz, ed., *Handbook of Adult Religious Education* (Birmingham, Ala.: Religious Education Press, 1986); Linda Vogel, *The Religious Education of Older Adults* (Birmingham, Ala.: Religious Education Press, 1984).

87. David Hesselgrave, *Counseling Cross-Culturally* (Grand Rapids, Mich.: Baker, 1984).

88. Winter 1992.

89. Craig Ellison and E. Maynard, *Healing for the City* (Grand Rapids, Mich.: Zondervan, 1992).

90. James M. Lee and Nathaniel J. Pallone, *Guidance and Counseling in Schools* (New York: McGrawHill, 1966).

FROM SEPARATION AND ASSIMILATION
TO TRANSCULTURAL APPRECIATION

Members of all cultures have much in common, but they all have their distinctive components as well. An overemphasis on the importance of commonalities leads to the assimilation of ethnic groups into a dominant culture, while an overemphasis on the importance of cultural distinctives leads to separation and exclusion from the common culture.

Perhaps a commonalities/distinctives dialectic is instructive in terms of the direction of multicultural religious education. Is the goal of religious education solely to emphasize and encourage the distinctives of a culture or subculture or to erase all cultural differences in one huge melting pot? Many find the blending idea repugnant,[91] (although intermarriage between ethnic groups is at an all time high[92]) and thus tend to focus solely on the importance of distinctives. In the 1960s it was fashionable to minimize all ethnic differences because of the emphasis on equality.[93] In the 1970s and 1980s the opposite became fashionable as ethnic pride and cultural roots were emphasized.

Yet these extremes are rarely acted out in real life. For example, Jewish minorities have retained aspects of their culture of origin by clustering in certain urban areas, keeping alive many of its customs and distinctives. Yiddish can still be heard in some metropolitan areas. Yet a degree of acculturation has come through acquisition of the English language and other adaptations to the dominant culture.[94] Such acculturation may have been easier in the past because many immigrant groups came with Eurocentric values. These adaptations are to some degree necessary to achieving a successful interface with the dominant culture. The same trend can be seen among Chinese, Vietnamese, Middle-Eastern, and even Italian populations in the United States. Each group to some degree adapts to the dominant culture, most notably in the use of the English language, while some group members retain some of their distinctives, at least in early generations. Many Appalachian people have retained elements of their Scotch-Irish ancestry of long ago.

---

91. See Harriette McAdoo's first chapter in *Family Ethnicity*.

92. Tim Bovee, "Mixed Marriages Double," Associated Press News Release, 12 February 1993.

93. K. Arms, J. Davidson, and N. Moore, *Cultural Diversity and Families*, p. viii; Janice Hale-Benson, *Black Children*, p. 2.

94. The distinction between *acculturate* and *enculturate*, as used here, is that the former involves adjusting to cultural norms different from one's culture of origin, while the latter refers to initial learning of one's culture of origin during childhood.

If the above commonalities/distinctives dialectic is considered to have worked well in the past, perhaps it can inform future efforts in multicultural religious education. It is important to understand, appreciate, affirm, and make use of cultural and subcultural distinctives of various groups, but also to recognize that some degree of acculturation into the dominant culture may be of benefit to ethnic minorities. For example, African Americans are more likely to succeed in the United States when they develop some of the norms of the dominant culture, including the dialect of the majority. Thus it is sometimes recommended that African-American children learn standard English as a second language.[95] Why can't this be done while valuing African-American heritage? Why can't the values of the Hispanic subculture, such as a strong family orientation, be maintained as standard English is acquired? Gibson indicates that Punjabi immigrants from India who settled in the United States maintained a strong ethnic identity and resisted assimilation to the dominant culture while accommodating to the American culture in some respects.[96] Chandler notes many megachurches that hold separate services for ethnic minorities, but also hold combined services once a month.[97]

The choice of approaches to education, and to religious education in particular, can profitably move from an either/or mentality—either complete adaptation or complete separation—to a both/and orientation: both the subculture's values and norms *and* the dominant culture's ways of doing things can be honorable and worthwhile. The creative juxtaposition of those values and norms is the goal suggested for minorities within a culture, and specifically in multicultural religious education. This juxtaposition involves accepting the dominant culture's ways, when acceptance expedites effective participation in society, and affirming of the subculture's ways for personal and subcultural identity.

The twin goals of affirming both commonalities and distinctives, applied within a religious education context, give the creative juxtaposition more direction. Rather than merely looking at the utilitarian aspects of blending with the dominant culture and the identity aspects of remaining distinct from the dominant culture, religious faith suggests that there are limits to the blending and subcultural distinctives. Christian values are higher than either utilitarian expediency or the complete and unreflective affirmation of subcultural identity. While not denying a place for expediency and identity, and thus commonality and distinctiveness, the affirmation of religious faith requires us to determine if commonality with the dominant culture produces greater Christlikeness or if distinctiveness is closer to the biblical ideal, or

---

95. See, for example, Janice Hale-Benson, *Black Children*, p. 165.

96. M. Gibson, "Playing by the Rules," in *Education and Cultural Process*, ed. George Spinder (Prospect Heights, Ill.: Waveland, 1987), pp. 274–81.

97. R. Chandler, *Racing toward 2001* (San Francisco: HarperCollins, 1992).

if neither of these is consistent with religious values. For example, if we take the Sermon on the Mount seriously, we will probably call into question some of the values of any dominant culture *and* any subculture. A genuine and thoroughly Christian individual in any society will stand apart in some respects from both subculture and culture.[98]

Thus for multicultural religious education an important goal can be to produce a transcultural people, creatively interfacing with both culture and subculture, yet remaining in some ways distinct and separate from both. As the old gospel song proclaims, "This world (cosmos, which includes culture) is not my home, I'm just a' passin' through." This transcultural attribute involves distinctiveness from *any* culture or subculture. This is the case whether we currently identify more closely with the dominant culture or with a specific subculture.

CONCLUSION

Addressing the 1991 annual conference of the North American Professors of Christian Education, Ted Ward made a strong plea for Christian involvement in intercultural relationships and in helping to resolve conflicts that occur in relationships across cultures. The urgency of this clarion call is underscored by the increasing global interdependence of cultures around the world, as well as the rapidly expanding cultural diversity of the United States. Demographers assert that people of color will soon make up a majority of the U.S. population. Members of "minority" groups already constitute a majority in some cities.[99] Ward affirmed that Christians should have greater skill in cultural interfacing than non-Christians because the New Testament church was multicultural.[100] The early leaders of the church were directly involved in the joys and struggles of intercultural relationships. Consider the resolution of cultural conflict in Acts 6 and 7, Jesus' many positive relationships and illustrations using a despised minority of that day, the Samaritans, and the apostle Paul's religious education work with various cultural groups. Furthermore, an understanding of cultural differences between biblical contexts and contemporary situations is required for adequate biblical interpretation—a multicultural task.[101] The emphasis

---

98. Robert Clark, "Thinking about Culture," in *The Sociological Perspective*, ed. Michael Leming, Raymond DeVries, and Brenda Furnish (Grand Rapids, Mich.: Zondervan, 1989), pp. 61–80.

99. R. Chandler, *Racing toward 2001*, pp. 27–34.

100. Peter Tze Ming Ng similarly makes a strong case for the Old Testament, Jesus Christ, and the early Christians affirming multicultural faith. See Ng's "Toward a New Agenda for Religious Education in a Multicultural Society," *Religious Education* 88:4 (1993): 585–94.

101. R. Sproul, "Controversy at the Culture Gap," *Eternity*, May 1976, pp. 13–15, 40.

on multicultural understanding has also been underscored by the Religious Education Association, which has published a number of valuable articles over the years in its journal *Religious Education*. Roehlkepartain affirms a future strong role for multicultural religious education, even though only a minority of churches (17 percent) participated in this endeavor in the early 1990s.[102]

The multicultural dimension of psychology began to emerge only in the late twentieth century, and the process of making multicultural applications of psychological constructs is definitely in its infancy. As a result, the ideas in this chapter are exploratory, not definitive. Psychology has much to offer as one of several foundations for effective multicultural religious education.

---

102. Eugene Roehlkepartain, *The Teaching Church* (Nashville: Abingdon, 1993), pp. 132–34.

4

BIBLE, THEOLOGY, AND MULTICULTURAL RELIGIOUS EDUCATION

Randolph Crump Miller

Human beings are born into families. Thus they are born into a particular culture and a small ethnic community. They inherit a social context with role models, rituals and rites, and language. When their social horizon is expanded, they are exposed to other social institutions, schools, religious communities, and political structures. The larger the context, the more pluralistic it tends to become, although the individual remains in a small subgroup or family and participates in the conventional wisdom of the group.[1]

Societies generally do not remain monocultural. People live in multicultural communities, and although some seek ethnic isolation, they cannot escape the influences of surrounding cultures. Thus multicultural education, including in its religious form, becomes inevitable because there is an infusion of many cultures into the educational process. Such a multicultural perspective is a particular challenge to those who hold their religious beliefs and actions as divinely revealed, for they develop what might be

---

1. Robert W. Steffer, "Multicultural Education," in *Encyclopedia of Religious Education*, ed. Iris and Kendig Cully (San Francisco: HarperSanFrancisco, 1990), pp. 431–34; see also John H. Westerhoff, "Enculturation," in *Encyclopedia of Religious Education*, pp. 217–18; Franklin F. Wise, "Culture," in *Encyclopedia of Religious Education*, pp. 172–74; Norma H. Thompson, ed. *Religious Pluralism and Religious Education* (Birmingham, Ala: Religious Education Press, 1988), pp. 131–32.

called "fixed bliks,"[2] an outlook that cannot be challenged by evidence. For multicultural religious education in such settings there are biblical and theological resources. To the biblical resources we now turn.

A MULTICULTURAL BIBLICAL THEOLOGY

In 1956 I wrote a book called *Biblical Theology and Christian Education.*[3] In writing this book I did not foresee Bible study developing in a pluralistic vein. I spoke of five acts in the drama of redemption: Creation, Covenant, Christ, Church, and Consummation. What was valid in the book was its making relationship theology the background for educational theory and practice.

The emphasis on the drama of redemption was central to much biblical theology at that time. The key books for me were G. Ernest Wright's *God Who Acts: Biblical Theology as Recital,*[4] and in religious education, Bernhard Anderson's *The Unfolding Drama of the Bible.*[5] Both books provide an overall view of the biblical story, but they do not do justice to the Jewishness, pluralism, and integrity of the Hebrew Scriptures.[6]

Biblical studies have moved away from seeing the Bible as a single story. The view of most scholars is that the biblical narratives are more often pluralistic and in many cases, multicultural.[7] The stories are not located in Palestine only, but extend from Egypt to Babylon, Africa to Asia, and only finally to Europe (Greece and Rome). The people of the Bible represent a mixture of the races in these diverse areas. Until recently, however, most biblical studies have been directed by white men of European and North

---

2. See Randolph C. Miller, *The Language Gap and God* (Philadelphia: Pilgrim, 1970), p. 29: a fixed blik is "a basic conviction, probably grounded in the unconscious, that cannot be falsified."

3. Randolph C. Miller, *Biblical Theology and Christian Education* (New York: Scribners, 1956).

4. G. Ernest Wright, *God Who Acts: Biblical Theology as Recital* (Chicago: Henry Regnery, 1951). See also Millar Burrows, *An Outline of Biblical Theology* (Philadelphia: Westminster, 1946); B. Davie Napier, *From Faith to Faith* (New York: Harper, 1955); Emil Brunner, *The Christian Doctrine of Creation and Redemption* (Philadelphia: Westminster, 1952).

5. Bernhard Anderson, *The Unfolding Drama of the Bible* (New York: Association Press/Haddam House, 1953); idem, *Rediscovering the Bible* (New York: Association, 1951).

6. Joseph F. Lukinsky, "Jewish Theological Concepts," in *Encyclopedia of Religious Education*, pp. 342–44; Emil L. Fackenheim, *God's Presence in History* (New York: Harper, 1970).

7. Cain Hope Felder, "Recovering Multiculturalism in Scripture," in *The Original African Heritage Study Bible*, ed. Cain Hope Felder (Nashville: James C. Winston, 1993), p. 99, quoted in *Coming Together: The Bible's Message in an Age of Diversity*, by Curtiss Paul DeYoung (Valley Forge, Pa.: Judson, 1995), p. 8.

American cultures. The same is true of theological studies. Because of this monocultural perspective, multicultural religious educators have difficulty finding biblical and theological resources for their tasks.

Curtiss Paul DeYoung has provided new understandings of the plurality and diversity of the Bible in his book, *Coming Together: The Bible's Message in an Age of Diversity.*[8] The earliest biblical stories, DeYoung points out, are located in the world known to the Hebrews. Isaiah writes: "On that day will Israel be the third with Egypt and Assyria, a blessing in the midst of the earth, whom the LORD of hosts has blessed, saying, 'Blessed be Egypt my people, and Assyria the work of my hands, and Israel, my heritage' " (Isa 19:24–25). God's love, therefore, is extended to all people.[9] The Bible records many interracial marriages. Abraham was not only married to Sarah in Ur of the Chaldees but to Hagar, an Egyptian. Moses married a woman from Cush (Num 12:1), certainly a black African. Solomon was married to the daughter of an Egyptian pharaoh (1 Kings 3:1). DeYoung concludes: "It seems very reasonable to assume that the ancient Hebrews, as well as the Jews of the New Testament, were an Afro-Asiatic people who would today be considered people of color."[10] He cites the presence of Africans throughout the story of the Hebrew Bible. That presence continued to be evident in the New Testament as well.[11]

The Asian presence in the Bible, although not as dramatic as the African, is constantly in the picture. Abraham and Sarah, as well as Isaac and Rebekah, came from Babylon, and Jacob was sent back to Paddan-aram to find his wives, Rachel and Leah. Esther was a queen of Ahasuerus of Persia, who ruled over a vast expanse from India to Nubia. Jews spent many years in Babylon.[12] The apostle Thomas is reputed to have ministered in southern India.

A European presence is scant but not unknown in the Old Testament. The Cherethites who served in King David's army (2 Sam 8:18) are considered to be Cretans,[13] and the books of Joel (3:6), Zechariah (9:13), and Daniel mention Greece (8:21; 10:20; 11:2). There are many more references to

---

8. DeYoung, *Coming Together,* chap. 1, "One Human Family, Many Cultural Expressions," pp. 1–30, and chap. 2, "Jesus Christ: Culturally Human, Inclusively Divine," pp. 31–62. See also Virgilio Elizondo, *Galilean Journey: The Mexican-American Promise* (Maryknoll, N.Y.: Orbis, 1983), pp. 107, 124; Jung Young Lee, *Marginality: The Key to Multicultural Theology* (Minneapolis: Fortress, 1995), pp. 110–19; and Michael Omri and Howard Winant, *Racial Formation in the United States: From the 1960s to the 1990s* (New York: Routledge & Kegan Paul, 1986).

9. DeYoung, *Coming Together*, p. 4.

10. Ibid., pp. 10–11.

11. Ibid., pp. 11–16.

12. Ibid., pp. 17–19.

13. See *The Interpreter's Dictionary of the Bible*, vol. 1 (Nashville: Abingdon, 1962), p. 557, and *The Westminster Dictionary of the Bible*, rev. Henry S. Gehman (Philadelphia: Westminster, 1944), p. 99.

Europe in the New Testament as early Christians enlarged the world of the early church as far as Rome. The Greek and Roman cultures became part of the later New Testament and the early church. The inclusiveness and the compassion of God became so evident that Paul could write: "There is no longer Jew or Greek, there is no longer slave or free, there is no longer male or female; for all of you are one in Christ Jesus" (Gal 3:28).

Today the Bible is available in many translations, and people in most cultures can read it in their own language. However, since most of these translations are the product of Western scholars, the influence of Western culture cannot be escaped. Stanley Samartha, who has taught in and headed seminaries in India as well as serving the World Council of Churches, suggests that Asian scholars should begin with the texts in their original languages (Hebrew, Aramaic, and Greek) and translate directly into their native language. The theology that then emerges must also take into account the rich background of Asian religions that predate Christianity by many centuries. We cannot expect people in these cultures to assume that Christianity is the only way to salvation. An Asian understanding of the Bible must be seen through Asian eyes. A similar approach is essential for various African, Native American, and Latin American cultures, as well as others. Traditional Western scholars can begin to accomplish this with openness to particular cultures and the use of creative imagination to view Scripture from a different perspective.[14]

The Exodus story is significant for any oppressed people, especially for those who have been enslaved. It has been central to much of African-American Christianity. It is also the focus of liberation theology, as it provides hope for the oppressed.[15] The story also carried a strong warning, for those who were freed from slavery in Egypt became the oppressors of the Canaanites. Native Americans identify with the Canaanites in the Exodus story.[16]

The Eighth-Century Prophets

The eighth-century prophets—Hosea, Amos, and Micah—are significant for multicultural religious education because of their concern for the poor, the alien and the outcast from society. *Hosea* has a wife, Gomer, who is a harlot as well as the mother of their three children. Hosea takes her back because his love for her is constant. From this experience he discovers that Israel has been unfaithful to Yahweh, and yet Yahweh remains faithful to

---

14. DeYoung, *Coming Together*, pp. 71–73.

15. See Daniel S. Schipani, "Liberation Theology and Religious Education," in *Theologies of Religious Education*, ed. Randolph C. Miller (Birmingham, Ala.: Religious Education Press, 1995), p. 293.

16. DeYoung, *Coming Together*, p. 23.

her. The point is clear that those who are separated from Yahweh are not without hope, for as Hosea took back Gomer, so will Yahweh take back Israel. The story is cross-cultural on both the human and the divine level.[17]

Amos, the earliest of the eighth-century prophets, was a sheepherder who had visions of a God of righteousness. He prophesied the doom of Israel, although he prayed that it would not happen. The sins of greed and wealth, uncontrolled lust, oppression of the poor, and corruption of temple worship were not recognized by the people as offenses against Yahweh. God, for Amos, was the Lord of both nature and history. "Therefore because you trample on the poor and take from them levies of grain, you have built houses of hewn stone, but you shall not live in them; you have planted pleasant vineyards, but you shall not drink their wine" (Amos 5:11). "I hate, I despise your festivals, and I take no delight in your solemn assemblies" (Amos 5:21). "But let justice roll down like waters, and righteousness like an everflowing stream" (Amos 5:24).

Amos promises devastation by locusts, fire, and the plumb line. Israel will be destroyed. But Amos (or probably another writer) softened the message in the final chapter, in which all is restored (Amos 9:11–15).[18]

Micah was a contemporary of Amos, and their messages were much the same. Micah warned of the danger of the invading Assyrians and condemned the people, especially the upper classes, of sinful living. To leaders he spoke roughly: "Should you not know justice?—you who hate the good and love the evil, who tear the skin off my people, and the flesh off their bones; who eat the flesh of my people, and flay their skin off them, and break their bones in pieces, and chop them up like meats in a kettle, like flesh in a caldron" (Mic 3:1–3).

Using the image of the slaughter and disposal of meat, Micah likened the elite to a heartless butcher. He criticized the false prophets, seers, diviners, and priests who had the spirit of falsehood. Only he, Micah, was filled with the spirit of power and of the Lord. The climax of Micah's prophesying and perhaps the high point of the Hebrew Scriptures comes at 6:6–8:

With what shall I come before the LORD,
and bow myself before God on high?

---

17. *Interpreter's Bible*, vol. 6 (Nashville: Abingdon, 1956), pp. 566–725; James Limburg, *Hosea—Micah*, Interpretation: A Bible Commentary for Teaching and Preaching (Atlanta: John Knox, 1988), pp. 3–4, 51–54. See also Fritz A. Rothschild, ed., *Between God and Man: From the Writings of Abraham J. Heschel* (New York: Free Press, 1959); Abraham J. Heschel, *The Prophets* (New York: Harper & Row, 1961).

18. *Interpreter's Bible*, vol. 6, pp. 777–853; Limburg, *Hosea—Micah*, pp. 79–81; Francis I. Anderson and David Noel Freedman, *Amos: A New Translation with Introduction and Commentary*, The Anchor Bible (New York: Doubleday, 1989), pp. 3–73.

Shall I come before him with burnt offerings,
with calves a year old?
Will the LORD be pleased with thousands of rams,
with ten thousands of rivers of oil?
Shall I give my firstborn for my transgression,
the fruit of my body for the sin of my soul?
He has told you, O mortal, what is good;
and what does the LORD require of you
but to do justice, and to love kindness,
and to walk humbly with your God? (Mic 6:6–8)[19]

The treatment of the alien is an important theme of some prophets: "And do no wrong or violence to the alien, the orphan, and the widow" (Jer 22:3; 7:5, 6). "So you shall divide this land among you according to the tribes of Israel. You shall allot it as an inheritance for yourselves and for the aliens who reside among you and have begotten children among you. They shall be to you as citizens of Israel; with you they shall be allotted an inheritance among the tribes of Israel. In whatever tribe aliens reside, there you shall assign them their inheritance, says the Lord GOD" (Ezek 47:21–23).

These prophets hit at the problems of modern life in virtually every culture. All over the globe we find elites with political power or great wealth or economic control. By contrast, others are insecure and have no power. Among them we find the alien, the oppressed, the politically isolated, the racially downtrodden, the widow, the orphan, the female, the homeless, and the landless. In between those with power and those who lack it are those of the middle class, the size of which varies from culture to culture. Some of them aspire to more economic and political power; many are content with their position. There are also reformers who reflect the need for justice and moral sensitivity.

All, however, can find themselves in the unfaithfulness of Gomer or those who sold the poor for a pair of sandals or those rejoicing in the rituals of worship. It is so much easier to ignore the conditions in the sweatshops, the ravaged neighborhoods, the suffering of the alien, the poor, and the orphan. We need the prophets of Israel to disturb our consciences. Multicultural religious education needs these prophets to assess the human condition and religious demands of today.

A multicultural religious educational approach to the prophets could entail a research project. Begin with a recognition that the prophets are addressing a culture different from the cultures of today. There is a monarchy ruling an agrarian people in which there is a dominant, privileged, upper

---

19. *Interpreter's Bible*, vol. 6, pp. 901–49; Limburg, *Hosea—Micah*, pp. 159–62; 189–93; Hans Walter Wolff, *Micah the Prophet* (Philadelphia: Fortress, 1981), pp. 8–16; 187–98.

class, which is not morally sound. The problem is to find in the ancient prophets' writings what applies to the current culture. The discussion at this point should bring out a variety of views, but should aim at the idea of God as just and compassionate and at our responsibilities in responding to the insights of prophetic religion.

Jesus of Nazareth

The "new" search for Jesus of Nazareth, popularized by the Jesus Seminar in the 1990s, goes as far back as 1935, when Charles Guignebert's *Jesus* broke new ground. In *The Review of Religion* for March 1939 I reviewed four books dealing with the historical Jesus: Guignebert's *Jesus; The Mission and Message of Jesus,* by H. D. A. Major, T. W. Manson, and C. J. Wright; *Christian Beginnings,* by Morton Scott Enslin; and *The Peril of Modernizing Jesus,* by Henry J. Cadbury.[20]

All except Major concluded that Jesus was a typical (though superior) Jewish prophet, who saw himself within the prophetic tradition and taught repentance in light of the coming kingdom. "He was surrounded by a small band of disciples, and went his way, teaching and doing good. The essence of his teaching was repentance in the light of the coming kingdom. Finally, he met with opposition from the Roman authorities, and was crucified. As a result of later experiences, especially of Peter, the little band of disciples was energized and enlarged," and in time broke away from the synagogues. "The center of the movement was the recollected person of Jesus, conceived as an apocalyptic Messiah. They lived in expectation of the great consummation. Only as the generation of disciples passed away did there come to be any writing about Jesus. The gospels were written in the light of these later thoughts."[21]

Whatever one's view of the search for the historical Jesus, it is clear that the European art and literature that have dominated in North America deem Jesus to be white. But in a multicultural society a white Jesus is not representative. He is associated with the dominant race, with Europeans, perhaps slaveholders and oppressors, and as such is hardly one who can serve as a model for nonwhites.[22]

---

20. Charles Guignebert, *Jesus* (New York: Knopf, 1935); H. D. A. Major, T. W. Manson, C. D. Wright, *The Mission and Message of Jesus* (New York: Dutton, 1938); Morton Scott Enslin, *Christian Beginnings* (New York: Harper, 1938); Henry J. Cadbury, *The Peril of Modernizing Jesus* (New York: Macmillan, 1937); Ray O. Miller, *Modernist Studies in the Life of Jesus* (Boston: Sherman, French, 1917) pp. 12–52. See also Burton Scott Easton, *What Jesus Taught* (Nashville: Abingdon, 1938).

21. *The Review of Religion* 3 (March 1939): 333; see pp. 321–35. Also see Randolph C. Miller, *What We Can Believe* (New York: Scribners, 1941), p. 87, and *This We Can Believe* (New York: Hawthorn, 1976), p. 85.

22. DeYoung, *Coming Together*, pp. 38–45.

The Jesus presented to much of the world as one in whom they must believe was a "European" Jesus, stripped of his historical and cultural context. Yet the historical Jesus was Jewish, a product of a culture that was Asian and African. His people had lived in Egypt and Babylon. His background as a Galilean was multicultural and multiracial. It is this historical Jesus who is ideally placed at the center of an approach to multicultural religious education. This suggests that much cultural baggage and theological support for such baggage needs to be jettisoned. Historical study can accomplish this. A return to the historical Jesus assists us greatly in this effort.[23]

Jesus was born of peasant parents who lived in Nazareth. Even his Galilean accent was strange to the people of Jerusalem. Baptized by John and deeply moved by John's summary execution, he began his own ministry, gathering a band of men and women and becoming an itinerant teacher.[24] He was driven by a sense of the holy. He was a man of deep visions and deep prayer. He had authoritative power that was reflected in stories of healing, and he attracted disciples as well as hearers. Those who search for the historical Jesus have sketched many portraits of him. Marcus Borg summarizes six, which we will consider briefly.

E. P. Sanders claims that Jesus was *an eschatological prophet* who expected a restoration of Israel in the near future. The cleansing of the temple and the prophecy of its restoration in three days suggests this. Thus Jesus is understood as firmly otherworldly or next-worldly.[25]

For Burton Mack, Jesus is *a more or less Hellenized Cynic sage or teacher*. There were many early Jesus groups. Mack seeks to go behind them to find Jesus who "was a striking teacher, a gadfly or mocker, who dined in private homes with small groups of people."[26] This view separates Jesus from his Jewish world. Only a core of wisdom teaching remains.

Elisabeth Schüssler-Fiorenza uses her feminist perspective as well as specialist tools to portray Jesus as *a prophet in the wisdom tradition* whose renewal movement within Judaism was based on a socially radical vision. Jesus' concentration on a society of equals challenged the power of the priests and the temple. The table fellowship practiced by Jesus and his friends brought in the outcasts of all kinds. Thus a new lifestyle for both individuals and community became a reality. Traces of women in the stories

---

23. DeYoung asserts that Christians need to resolve the dichotomy between the Jesus of faith and the Jesus of history. See *Coming Together*, pp. 42–47.

24. Marcus J. Borg; *Jesus: A New Vision* (San Francisco: HarperSanFrancisco, 1987), pp. 3, 39–51; also see n. 25 p. 20.

25. Marcus Borg, *Jesus in Contemporary Scholarship* (Valley Forge, Pa.: Trinity International, 1994), pp. 19–21. See E. P. Sanders, *Jesus and Judaism* (Philadelphia: Fortress, 1985); idem, *Paul and Palestinian Judaism* (Philadelphia: Fortress, 1977).

26. Borg, *Jesus in Contemporary Scholarship*, pp. 21–23. See Burton L. Mack, *A Myth of Innocence: Mark and Christian Origins* (Philadelphia: Fortress, 1988).

give evidence of a much larger role for women in the movement than tradition has recognized.[27]

Schüssler-Fiorenza alerts us to the use of *sophia* (wisdom) in some of Jesus' sayings. "The earliest Jesus traditions perceive this God of gracious goodness in a woman's *Gestalt* as divine *Sophia* (wisdom)."[28] Jesus was a prophet of *sophia*, concerned with a "this-worldly" transformation of Jewish life. For Schüssler-Fiorenza, Jesus' eschatology was in the here and now.[29]

Richard Horsley sees Jesus as *a social prophet*. Jewish Palestine was a colony dominated by Rome that consisted of a small elite and a majority of oppressed peasants and farmers. Jesus, a peasant himself, sided with the poor and was prophetic in his condemnation of the system. He did not seek a political revolution, but the transformation of village life. He was not speaking to the Romans or to the Jewish elite. Most of Jesus' teachings served to make village life more humane. In the villages we can forgive debts, give up possessions, and forgive our enemies. The local communities can do away with hierarchical structures and patriarchal dominations and become egalitarian societies. Horsley is not opposed to eschatology and makes use of such texts to help remember "past deliverances," look forward to a more meaningful life, and expose the ruling class and its demonic character. The kingdom is already under way in this world, and God will bring down the political structure. The kingdom is this-worldly.[30]

Borg added to his original essay the portrait of Jesus by John Dominic Crossan, who has been cochair of the Jesus Seminar. Borg considers Crossan's method and results a significant contribution to the search for the historical Jesus. Crossan holds that Jesus was *a peasant Jewish Cynic* with an alternative social vision. As a peasant, he had a simple education and could communicate easily with other peasants. Like a Hellenistic Cynic, Jesus taught what was subversive. But the Hellenes were urban and he was rural. Jesus was a healer; Crossan calls him a magician: "Magic is subversive, unofficial, unapproved, and often lower-class

---

27. Ibid., pp. 24–25. See Elisabeth Schüssler-Fiorenza, *In Memory of Her: A Feminist Theological Reconstruction of Christian Origins* (New York: Crossroad, 1983), pp. 75–159.

28. Ibid., p. 132. See Charles Melchert, "Wisdom Is Vindicated by Her Deeds," *Religious Education* 87 (winter 1992): 127–51.

29. Borg, *Jesus in Contemporary Scholarship*, pp. 25–26.

30. Ibid., pp. 28–30. See Richard Horsley and John S. Hanson, *Bandits, Prophets, and Messiahs: Popular Movements in the Time of Jesus* (Minneapolis: Winston, 1985); Richard Horsley, *Jesus and the Spiral of Violence* (San Francisco: HarperSanFrancisco, 1987); idem, *The Liberation of Christmas: The Infancy Narratives in Social Context* (New York: Crossroad, 1989); Jane Schaberg, *The Illegitimacy of Jesus* (New York: Harper & Row, 1987; New York: Crossroad, 1990).

religion."[31] Nevertheless, Crossan emphasizes Jesus as a healer more than do most scholars. Often, in gratitude, Jesus and the disciples were given a meal. What stood out was that they ate with others regardless of social standing, thus contradicting the social mores of both Jews and Romans. Crossan explains Jesus' strategy as "the combination of *free healing* and *common eating*, a religious and economic egalitarianism that negated alike and at once the hierarchical and patronal normalcies of Jewish religion and Roman power."[32] Crossan ignores the "son of man" sayings and eschatology.[33]

Marcus Borg presents a portrait of Jesus similar to that of Schüssler-Fiorenza and Crossan. He sees Jesus as *a "Spirit person,"* sensitive to the mystical or numinous element in life.[34] This implies a worldview that includes a nonmaterial reality that we can experience. Jesus taught in parables and short sayings (known as aphorisms) as a teacher of wisdom. He was subversive of the current culture and operated as a social prophet. Finally, he was the founder of a movement that grew during his lifetime and continued after his death as a basis for the early Christian church.[35] Borg supplies a careful analysis of compassion as a key to Jesus' central message: "Be compassionate in the way your Father is compassionate" (Lk 6:36).[36] Jesus contrasted the purity system with compassion. Compassion is demonstrated in the parable of the good Samaritan, in Jesus' healings of the "unclean," in his table fellowship which included outcasts, and in his relationships with women. Paul caught this sense of inclusiveness in his statement that "in Christ there is no longer Jew or Gentile . . . slave or free . . . male and female" (Gal 3:28).

Borg writes that those in our culture who would be faithful to Jesus need to think and speak of a "politics of compassion," both in the church and in shaping the political order. "A politics of compassion as the paradigm for

---

31. Borg, *Jesus in Contemporary Scholarship*, p. 34; see pp. 28–36; 191–92; John Dominic Crossan, *The Historical Jesus: The Life of a Mediterranean Jewish Peasant* (San Francisco: HarperSanFrancisco, 1991), p. 305.

32. Crossan, *The Historical Jesus*, pp. 521–22, italics in the original.

33. Ibid., p. 424, and Borg, *Jesus in Contemporary Scholarship*, pp. 160–61. See also John Dominic Crossan, *In Parables: The Challenge of The Historical Jesus* (New York: Harper & Row, 1973); idem, *In Fragments: The Aphorisms of Jesus* (San Francisco: HarperSanFrancisco, 1983). Also see *The Five Gospels*, new translation and commentary by Robert W. Funk, Roy W. Hoover, and the Jesus Seminar (New York: Macmillan, 1993). For a critique of the Jesus Seminar, see Luke Timothy Johnson, "The Jesus Seminar's Misguided Quest for the Historical Jesus," *Christian Century*, 3–10 January 1996, pp. 16–22, and *The Real Jesus: The Misguided Quest for the Historical Jesus and the Truth of the Traditional Gospels* (New York: Harper Collins, 1996).

34. Marcus Borg, *Meeting Jesus Again for the First Time* (San Francisco: Harper-SanFrancisco, 1994), pp. 31–36.

35. Ibid., p. 30.

36. Ibid., pp. 46–48.

shaping our national life would produce a social system different in many ways from that generated by our recent history."[37]

For his day, Jesus' relationships with women were radical. Men did not speak to strange women, especially those outside the Jewish community. Yet Jesus did. He attracted women to him, and they became his disciples. Those who followed him probably included wives of his male apostles, widows, and single women willing to face the risk of scandal. Mary and Martha, Mary of Magdala, and others were close to him. It is difficult to determine whether Jesus was married, although the custom in ancient Israel was for early marriage.[38] One suggestion is that Mary Magdalene was Jesus' wife: certainly she acted like a grieving widow at his death and burial.[39]

Borg divides the story between the pre-Easter Jesus and the post-Easter Jesus.[40] The resurrection appearances cannot easily be described. They were not the resurrection of a corpse, yet they affected those who knew Jesus in the flesh. Paul in his writings centers on Peter's experience of the resurrection and aligns his interpretation of the resurrection with his own experience on the Damascus road. The Gospel's focus is on the women at the tomb, especially Mary Magdalene. The women inform Peter. No one will believe them.

Gerald Sloyan writes that Paul's model for personal conduct is himself, not Jesus. According to Sloyan, Paul avoids adopting as a standard Jesus as he was before the resurrection, "lest, in Jesus' voluntary association with sinful humanity, he get in the way of 'Christ our righteousness' who succeeded him."[41]

Christology

Jesus of Nazareth stands at the center of Christianity and is the basis for any multicultural dialogue. It is at this point that cultural, religious, and personal differences are most critical to deal with. Almost all people start with Christological and theological assumptions about Jesus. The attempt to get back to the human figure of the historical Jesus is fraught with

---

37. Ibid., p. 60.

38. William E. Phipps, *Was Jesus Married?* (New York: Harper & Row, 1970), pp. 63–70; 99–102; Anthony T. Padovano, "Is It Possible That Jesus Was Married?" *National Catholic Reporter* 12 April 1996, pp. 12–15.

39. Phipps, *Was Jesus Married?* pp. 104–10; 135–38. See Gerard S. Sloyan, *Jesus in Focus* (Mystic, Conn.: Twenty-Third, 1983), pp. 132–36.

40. Borg, *Meeting Jesus*, pp. 15–17. See Peter Hamilton, *The Living God and the Modern World* (London: Hodder & Stoughton, 1967), pp. 180–249; Norman Pittenger, ed., *Christ for Us Today* (London: SCM Press, 1967); Millar Burrows, *Jesus in the First Three Gospels* (Nashville: Abingdon, 1977), pp. 270–95.

41. Sloyan, *Jesus in Focus*, p. 163; see Gerard S. Sloyan, "Toward a Christology for Our Times," in *The Jesus Tradition* (Mystic, Conn.: Twenty-Third, 1986), pp. 106–7.

difficulties, for the historical records are hidden even in the primary sources of the Synoptic Gospels, which are already overladen with Christological assumptions and are written from a post-Easter perspective.

Because all Christologies are culturally conditioned, my pedagogical preference in a learning situation is to start with Jesus as pictured in this chapter, as the pre-Easter Jesus, and then let the learners struggle with this portrait. This is contrary to the approach of the creeds and to most educational efforts in the Western churches, and to their missionary approaches in foreign cultures, but it avoids the danger of placing Westernizing ahead of Christianizing and lets Jesus have meaning free from cultural domination. Such a portrait of Jesus could be a starting point for multicultural religious education, to which learners could add or subtract their own insights.

After a basis of starting with the historical Jesus is agreed upon, learners could then consider their approach to the post-Easter Jesus and construct a biblical Christology that reflects their own culture. In this way religious education achieves an Asian, African-American, Native-American, or European-American picture of Jesus as the Christ. The post-Easter picture of Jesus begins with Christology. Paul had inserted a non-Jewish concept of a human mediator between God and human beings. According to Paul, Jesus was the intermediary for both Jews and Gentiles.[42] "For no one can lay any foundation other than the one that has been laid: that foundation is Jesus Christ" (1 Cor 3:11). "For you know the generous act of our Lord Jesus Christ, that though he was rich, yet for your sakes he became poor, so that by his poverty you might become rich" (2 Cor 8:9). "And those who belong to Christ Jesus have crucified the flesh with its passions and desires. If we live by the Spirit, let us also be guided by the Spirit" (Gal 5:24–25). Paul stayed within his Jewish heritage as a Christian, but he was already moving toward Greek culture. Thus, the post-Easter Christology was increasingly interpreted by Greek, and later by Roman, terms.

Christology has been developed in many different ways, but often has been the creature of a specific culture and thus unavailable on a multicultural basis. But it is possible to develop Christologies for different cultures. Steve Charleston writes, "In the Pauline sense, I can assert that while as a man Jesus was a Jew, as the risen Christ he is a Navajo. Or a Kiowa. Or a Choctaw. Or any other tribe."[43]

DeYoung proposes five images of Christ to illustrate how Christ can be thought of in different cultural situations. First, for DeYoung, is "the

42. See Sloyan, *Jesus in Focus*, pp. 168–69. Sloyan says Paul undermined the Jewish concept of Israel as a people whose race and religion were identical. See also Sloyan, *The Jesus Tradition*, pp. 14–15, 18.

43. Steve Charleston, "The Old Testament of Native America," in *Lift Every Voice: Constructing Christian Theologies from the Underside*, ed. Susan Brooks Thistlethwaite and Mary Potter Engel (San Francisco: HarperSanFrancisco, 1990), p. 59, quoted by DeYoung, *Coming Together*, p. 47.

gold-crowned Christ." In his play by that name, the Korean poet Kim Chi Ha shows both the irrelevance and the relevance of Jesus. In the play, a stone statue of Jesus has a gold crown on its head. The statue does not respond to the suffering and needy or to the successful in their frustrations. Finally, a leper removes the gold crown and immediately the statue speaks:

> I have been closed up in this statue for a long, long, time . . . entombed in this dark, lonely, suffocating prison. I have longed to talk with you, the kind and poor people like yourself, and share your sufferings. I can't begin to tell you how long I have waited for this day . . . when I would be freed from my prison, this day of liberation when I would live and burn again as the flame inside you, inside the very depths of your misery.[44]

Some of the listeners who are privileged are affronted by Jesus' conversation with the leper, the beggar, and other people on the margins, and they grab the golden crown. A priest places it back on the statue's head. Instantly Jesus returns to being a cold, silent stone statue. The point is that the real Jesus can be released only by the common people, not the concrete dogma of a cold church.[45]

In a continuation of the story, after Jesus is freed by the peasants, he joins the Puerto Rican poor as a Galilean *jibaro* (peasant). As one who had experienced rejection and marginalization as a Galilean, he understood the condition of many people throughout the world. Jesus stood in solidarity with the common people.[46]

DeYoung then suggests an image of Jesus held by the Burakim, the indigenous people of Japan, who view Jesus as the One crowned with thorns, one who suffered the mockery of those who called for his death. For the Burakim, the crown of thorns also points to resurrection as a symbol of Jesus' overcoming suffering, and thus promises a new world of justice and compassion. Significantly, the Burakim, before they became church attenders, simply read the Bible and related their own experiences to the message of freedom.[47]

In parts of Africa, Jesus is named "the great Healer." This title is sometimes misunderstood in places of great suffering because many people are

---

44. Kim Chi Ha, *The Gold Crowned Jesus and Other Writings* (Maryknoll, N.Y.: Orbis, 1978), pp. 121–23, quoted in DeYoung, *Coming Together*, pp. 49–50.

45. Ibid., p. 50.

46. Ibid., pp. 51–52. See also Orlando E. Costas, "Liberation Theologies in the Americas: Common Journeys and Mutual Challenges," in *Yearning to Breathe Free: Liberation Theologies in the United States* ed. Mar Peter-Raoul, Linda Rennie Forcey, and Robert Frederick Hunter Jr. (Maryknoll, N.Y.: Orbis, 1990), pp. 42–43; Elizondo, *Galilean Journey*, pp. 11–12, 54, 56.

47. DeYoung, *Coming Together*, pp. 52–53; Kuribayasha Teruo, "Recovering Jesus for Outcasts in Japan," in *Frontiers in Asian Christian Theology: Emerging Trends*, ed. R. S. Sugirtharajah (Maryknoll, N.Y.: Orbis), pp. 11–26.

not healed and continue in their misery. But Jesus is proclaimed holistically as a therapeutic force working on people at all levels of the social and political scale. The crucified Messiah is a scandal, foolishness, sickness to various cultures, but the image of Jesus as a healer of both individual and social misery becomes good news.[48]

Finally, DeYoung suggests the image of a Jim-Crowed Jesus. In this image Jesus is a black in today's world and is expected to act as a segregated person. He is in the suburbs and in the segregated ghettos of the inner city. The Jesus of the Gospels did not play by the rules of the power elite, but joyfully joined various "sinners" and outcasts at meals, and such were the objects of his ministry. Today he would be a person who ignores practices of segregation and customs that separate the races.[49]

The white Jesus is well and powerful today. The most segregated hour of the week is still the Sunday-morning worship service. Colonizers, slave-holders, and segregationists have found support in a white Jesus. The pre-Easter Jesus, possibly of mixed Asiatic-African stock, needs to be understood by white Christians who can then interpret the post-Easter Jesus in terms of their own culture, as other cultures do. Paul interpreted Jesus in terms of both his own Jewishness and his Hellenic upbringing. The church councils saw Jesus as the Christ, and they formulated the creeds according to Greek and Roman cultures. Thus a white Jesus emerged. If he is not submerged in such a culture, a white Jesus can serve within the culture as critic and prophet, as teacher of compassion and token of freedom, as the hope of all persons for a better world. This image could be the center of Western Christianity.

Muslim Views of Jesus

Muslims consider Christians as a people of the Book. While Christians know little about Judaism, even though they share the Jewish Scriptures, they know even less about Islam. The Religious Education Association has sponsored interreligious dialogue among Jews, Muslims, and Christians, but this has been limited to scholars in the field. We can hope that more knowledge will become available in the future to enrich multicultural dialogue.

Mohammed wrote of Jesus in the Koran.[50] From Jesus' birth, Allah intended for Jesus to glorify Allah. Jesus was a slave of Allah, and Jesus was a prophet. He was a wisdom teacher and a messenger of Allah. The Koran always praises Jesus, but never claims that Jesus is a son of God.

---

48. DeYoung, *Coming Together*, pp. 53–55.

49. Ibid., pp. 55–57.

50. E. van Donzel, B. Lewis, and C. Pellat, eds., *The Encyclopedia of Islam*, new ed., vol. 4 (Leiden, The Netherlands: E. J. Brill, 1978), pp. 81–84.

Allah is one—not three. "It is far removed from his transcendent majesty that he should have a son."[51]

Although Muslims number Jesus among the prophets, it is clear that the single-minded worship of Allah is considered the supreme religion. Jews and Christians make similar claims. The three monotheistic religions are very much on the same level in their claims, and they worship the same deity. The leaders or founders did not ask for or expect to be worshiped, but they could not control the future thoughts of their adherents.[52]

Muslims are indigenous to Middle Eastern culture and demand significant attention from any global assessment of religious faith. They have much to contribute to a multicultural religious education dialogue, with claims that are at odds with Christianity. In teaching about Islam and Christianity, dialogue might begin with such questions as, Are *Yahweh* and *Allah* different names for the same deity?

Multicultural Religious Education and Teaching about Jesus

The role of Christianity in a multicultural world is to place Jesus of Nazareth at the center. As we have seen, Jesus was a provincial peasant of the Jewish culture, but with an appeal that stretches beyond his narrow sphere to the outside world. He was interested primarily in his own people and taught a message of compassion, both God's compassion and compassion between people, with a strong sense of justice. Stripped of many cultural accretions, the pre-Easter Jesus can be an appealing religious figure to persons of all cultures, as clearly he is to Muslims. This Jesus can be presented in any multicultural dialogue.

Christology grew even before Jesus' death, but it was obviously the resurrection appearances that provided the primary stimulus. We find the resurrection Christology in all the Gospels, but especially in the fourth, as well as in the letters of Paul.[53] It took hold in the Greek and Roman cultures and reached a momentary peak in the Nicene formula. In these theories the pre-Easter Jesus was practically ignored. Christianity spread widely throughout Europe, based primarily on a post-Easter Christ. There is no doubt that Christianity can grow without consideration of who Jesus was

---

51. Koran, Surah 4, *Women*, pp. 172–73, quoted in Gerard S. Sloyan, *Jesus in Focus*, pp. 191, 192. See also John Hick and Edmund S. Meltzer, eds., *Three Faiths—One God* (Albany, N.Y.: SUNY Press, 1989); H. A. Alexander, "Religion and Multiculturalism in Education," 90 (summer/fall 1995): 377–87; Terence J. Lovat, "Multifaith Religious and Values Education: Apparent or Real?" *Religious Education* 90 (summer/fall 1995): 412–26; Eugene B. Borowitz, *Contemporary Christologies* (New York: Paulist, 1980).

52. Christians disagree on this issue. See Sloyan, *Jesus in Focus*, pp. 165; 171–72.

53. Marianne Sawicki, *The Gospel in History: Portrait of a Teaching Church, The Origins of Christian Education* (New York: Paulist, 1988), pp. 103–5.

historically, and much scholarship has been successful without concern for the historical Jesus. Teaching about Jesus has been influenced by views of the post-Easter Jesus, mixing the Synoptic Gospels with the Fourth Gospel and the Christology of the Pauline letters. The opposite approach is more satisfactory, that is, using our best knowledge of the pre-Easter Jesus to correct our Christologies.[54]

In a multicultural religious education event, as suggested above, we could start with the historical Jesus and let learners formulate their own answer to the question, What do you think of Jesus as the Christ? Learners could then answer in terms of their own cultures, struggling first with questions about the post-Easter Christ in such a way as to build on their own religious and cultural heritage.

THEOLOGICAL RESOURCES FOR
MULTICULTURAL RELIGIOUS EDUCATION

We turn now to the ways in which selected theologies may serve multicultural religious education. We will look at mainstream, evangelical, process, feminist, and liberation theologies.

Mainstream Theology

In his classic volume, *A Faith for the Nations,* Charles Forman makes a case for a Christ-centered approach to theology. No one, no matter how isolated, can escape the impact of the whole world. The world makes an impact on individuals either personally or technologically. Forman mentions the Arab town of Dharan where large international planes landed on a regular basis, and the passengers were inspected by men in full Arabic dress. The world came to Dharan every day. He also writes of Missoula, Montana, where people travel from all over the world to study forestry. The world is at the doorstep for all of us.[55]

People in today's society have new neighbors who were once aliens, as well as immediate neighbors who are becoming strangers. The urban lifestyle of those who live close together, especially in large housing units,

---

54. A helpful discussion of this process is found in Virginia Fabella, "Christology from An Asian Women's Perspective," in *Asian Faces of Jesus,* ed. R. S. Sugirtharajah (Maryknoll, N.Y.: Orbis, 1993), pp. 211–22. See also John Knox, *Christ the Lord* (New York: Harper, 1945); idem, *On the Meaning of Christ* (New York: Scribner's, 1947); H. Richard Niebuhr, *Christ and Culture* (New York: Harper, 1956); Dorothee Soelle, *Christ the Representative* (Philadelphia: Fortress, 1967); Howard Thurman, *Jesus and the Disinherited* (New York: Abingdon-Cokesbury, 1949); Kelly Brown Douglas, *The Black Christ* (Maryknoll, N.Y.: Orbis, 1994).

55. Charles W. Forman, *A Faith for the Nations* (Philadelphia: Westminster, 1957), p. 9.

often leads to neighbors not knowing each other, while those in isolated suburbs are also cut off from close communication with their neighbors. On the other hand, people in rural communities often feel close to others who are miles away.

People are involved with each other, whether they like it or not. Armies include diverse mixtures of people drawn together to seek a common goal. Our economic welfare depends on various levels of international cooperation. Raw materials are shipped from nation to nation. Even when walls are set up, whether they are solid, like the Berlin wall, or economic, like high import taxes, fears escalate on both sides. In time people on both sides are drawn together despite the wall.[56] For example, Forman carries the interpretation of exchanges from goods and technologies to the hidden factors accompanying such exchanges. Hidden factors emerge more slowly, but their influence may be profound. He believes that only philosophies claiming to be universal have a chance of surviving in such a world.[57] The U.S. relationship with other nations and cultures has been uneven, but is improving, in spite of the isolationism that continues to surface occasionally. Christian missionaries, Forman observes, may have been among the first Americans to work in alien cultures.[58]

Forman rejects proximity, information, common interests, and similarity as bases for global unity. Ultimately, unity must be *willed*. People must want it enough to make the changes and sacrifices required to achieve it. The command for Christians to love God and neighbor is impossible. Only as we are loved can we love others. We are assured of God's love through the death and resurrection of Jesus Christ.[59] In this atoning event, early Christians saw the love of God at work in the suffering of Jesus.

There is a theological basis for unity in this approach. All human beings are sinners: "All have sinned and fall short" (Rom 3:23). The impact of the cross is double: it eliminates human pride and leads to unity of sinners. The gift of that unity comes from God, not other people. In discovering that God loves all people, we are enabled to receive and give love. "We love because he first loved us" wrote the elder in 1 John 4:19.

In multicultural religious education, a theological approach based in God's gift of love promises much in achieving mutual understanding and even a degree of genuine unity. It does not say that God loves good people only, or that God loves people because they go to church or synagogue or mosque. We are taught that God loves the world. That includes all people.[60] Forman cites Satis Pravad of India, Norman Cousins, and Arnold Toynbee as among those who have suggested ways of making diversity of religion

---

56. Ibid., pp. 12–13.
57. Ibid., p. 13.
58. Ibid., pp. 15–18.
59. Ibid., p. 42.
60. Ibid., p. 48.

acceptable to all people in all cultures, including a world parliament of religions. But that would only include those who are already religious. Another approach would be to consider what all religions have in common. The recognition that the mystery of God is so profound that no one road can reach its depths points to a plurality of approaches and a need for tolerance as we seek a multicultural basis for religious education.[61]

Seeking a multicultural basis does not require a simplistic tolerance that reduces truth claims to their lowest common denominator. Such an attempt is finally oppressive, says David Tracy, since "all is allowed because nothing is taken seriously." On the contrary, each group is concerned to speak truths that can be heard by all.[62] Theologian C. S. Song calls for speaking and hearing those truths through a multicultural religious education approach that recaptures the ancient human love of storytelling because "doctrines alienate, while stories unite." As adherents of different faith and cultural traditions listen to one another's traditional narratives, they each find that the narratives reveal ultimate concerns.[63]

However, even with such respectful tolerance, people may come together without coming together with God. This is the crux of Forman's thesis, and it is the crux of Christian multicultural religious education. People are separated from God, and if they are to get together with God, "something has got to give."[64] That "something" comes from God's side, not humanity's. "In Christ God was reconciling the world to himself, not counting their trespasses against them, and entrusting the message of reconciliation to us" (2 Cor 5:19). We can rejoice in this good news, for it is a once-for-all-time act.[65] This is the missionary thrust that Christians bring with them into a multicultural dialogue. This is the source of unity for Christians.

The unity that comes from reconciliation with God and others tends to bring about greater diversity. The white, Western culture that was imitated by many other cultures is giving way to a recapturing of the original cultures, with or without the acceptance of Christianity. Christianity seeks a unity of love and concern for all people, and it does not require uniformity in any cultural sense. Cultures keep changing, and the influence of Christians may lead them to change in ways others do not understand. For example, a positive change would be the base communities of Latin America with

---

61. Ibid., pp. 51–56.

62. David Tracy, *The Analogical Imagination: Christian Theology and the Culture of Pluralism* (New York: Crossroad, 1986), pp. xii, 81.

63. Choan-Seng Song, "Christian Education in a World of Religious Pluralism," quoted by Sara Little in *Theologies of Religious Education*, ed. Randolph Miller, p. 33.

64. Forman, *A Faith for the Nations*, p. 58.

65. Ibid., pp. 59–60; also see the familiar Protestant hymn, "In Christ There Is No East or West."

their liberation theology; an example of a negative change would be the destruction of Native American cultures by overzealous missionaries.

Forman has made his case within the framework of the Christian missionary movement. Today there are Christians in almost every nation and culture. Forman's approach may play a significant role in multicultural religious education by providing a theological framework for recognizing and embracing diversity among Christians and in the wider world, thus keeping alive the dialogue between diverse groups.

Evangelical Protestant Theology

Evangelical Protestants believe that the one they worship is shrouded in mystery, for the finite mind cannot understand the infinite. There are revelations, however, in the natural world, so that we can see God's work in the cosmos. The psalmist writes that "the heavens are telling the glory of God; and the firmament proclaims his handiwork" (Ps 19:1). God, as creator of all that is, is also a mystery beyond comprehension. God is more than we can think. God transcends human thought.[66]

Kenneth Gangel presents a deity of righteousness and compassion. God is three in one. The secret is found in the Incarnation, meaning that God visited humanity in human flesh. This teaching is found in Scripture and was developed in the early church at the council of Nicaea (A.D. 325). God is a loving presence in human life. Humanity cannot share in God's omniscience or omnipresence, but does share in "a measure of love, a desire to see justice done, a compassion for the weak, and wrath for those who oppress the downtrodden."[67]

The story of the fall in Genesis 3 explains why humanity is separated from God. But there is hope. George Peters writes of his conviction that the Fall, although horrible in its consequences, did not accomplish all that Satan intended. Human beings remained salvable creatures, since the effect of the Fall did not reach the core of the human being or obliterate the image of God.[68]

God acted to save humankind by sending his Son, the Messiah, to die for our sins. This ransom is the atonement, summed up in the Gospel of John: "For God so loved the world that he gave his only Son, so that every one who believes in him may not perish but have eternal life" (Jn 3:16).

---

66. Kenneth O. Gangel and Christy Sullivan, "Evangelical Theology and Religious Education," in *Theologies of Religious Education*, ed. Randolph Miller, pp. 59–60.

67. Gangel, "Evangelical Theology," pp. 60–62; see also Donald G. Bloesch, *Christian Foundations: A Theology of Word and Spirit* (Downers Grove, Ill.: InterVarsity Press, 1992); Millard J. Erickson, *Christian Theology* (Grand Rapids, Mich.: Baker, 1985); George W. Peters, *A Biblical Theology of Missions* (Chicago: Moody Press, 1984).

68. Peters, *A Biblical Theology of Missions*, p. 78.

Scripture, for evangelicals, is the inspired and authoritative word of God, and evangelical theology is built on this foundation. The use of scriptural inerrancy is a highly sophisticated understanding of the process, and includes careful distinctions. The Bible is God's revelation, and in its original autographs, fully inspired by God. It is authoritative when properly understood, which means that the critical tools of interpretation are needed for gaining this understanding.[69]

The God thus revealed is transcendent and lies outside human experience. Human beings do not investigate God; rather, they receive God's revelation of himself. The normative conclusion is that Jesus is the all-sufficient revealer, and no further revelation is necessary.[70]

Evangelical Protestants fit into the multicultural dialogue primarily by their missionary outlook. They believe that the gospel should be heard everywhere, and they are behind many efforts to translate the Bible into native languages. In many cases, this means living with indigenous peoples to learn their oral language and then formulating a written language into which the Bible may be translated. Theological assumptions have accompanied the spreading of the gospel in this way, but more often today the local culture determines the interpretation. By following this approach, the American Bible Society has produced Bible translations for many nations and cultures.

Evangelicals should be distinguished from fundamentalists, many of whom refuse to meet with other Christian bodies or non-Christian groups and thus participate in no multicultural dialogue. Some denominations on the fringes of Christianity do not seek dialogue; others, such as Mormons and Jehovah's Witnesses, stand outside mainline groups.

Evangelicals provide a traditional, biblical approach to Christianity. This is both a strength and a weakness in multicultural religious education. They do not expect to be swayed by other positions, but they expect to be heard. This is consistent with their expectation that Christianity should be the world religion, which is an underlying assumption of historic Christianity. By contrast, modern non-Evangelical Christianity participates in mission without claiming universal acceptance. In terms of multicultural religious education, we must hope that evangelicals can resolve the conflict between universal truth claims and openness to pluralism.

Evangelical religious educators Ronald Habermas and Klaus Issler acknowledge the need to confront "the question of God's gracious work through other religions." They affirm Norman Anderson's statement that

---

69. Gangel, "Evangelical Theology," pp. 67–70. Concerning the evangelical understanding of inerrancy, Gangel states that " 'inerrancy' simply affirms the full reliability, dependability, and truthfulness of Scripture," p. 69.

70. See Erickson, *A Biblical Theology*, p. 178.

through God's general revelation and all people's common humanity "the Spirit of God, or the 'cosmic Christ' brings home to men and women something of their need."[71]

Speaking from an evangelical Protestant viewpoint in *What Color Is Your God: Multicultural Education in the Church,* James and Lillian Breckenridge describe the "splendid multiplicity" of a diverse church based on one unified faith. They offer this definition: "Christian multiculturalism is the personal application of Christian life and thought to all social groups which seek their spiritual identity in the church. In its broadest sense, a multicultural approach for the church would be viewed as a process that affects the structural organization of the church, pastoral/instructional strategies, and personal values of members of the congregation."[72]

Process Theology

As current thinking draws more on developments in science and in assumptions about nature and human life, process theology is gaining acceptance. Because the dominant theologies do not deal with the interpretation of nature, process theology is being taken up seriously by both theologians and other Christians concerned with the environment. Larry Rasmussen writes that process theology has moved "from the minor leagues to the majors, largely because nature abhors a theological vacuum, too."[73] Originating in the West, it nevertheless has much to contribute to multicultural religious education.

Process theology sees all reality as a process of becoming and perishing, with new beginnings building on what is past. It is a philosophy of organism in which interrelationships are central. The starting point for process theology is an understanding of the relationships between human beings and a superhuman reality we call *God.* The method is based on the radical empiricism of William James, which includes the experience of

---

71. Ronald Habermas and Klaus Issler, *Teaching for Reconciliation: Foundations and Practice of Christian Educational Ministry* (Grand Rapids, Mich.: Baker, 1992), p. 401 n. 4. See also Norman Anderson, "A Christian Approach to Comparative Religion," in *The World's Religions,* ed. Norman Anderson, 4th ed. (London: Inter-Varsity Press, 1975).

72. James and Lillian Breckenridge, *What Color Is Your God: Multicultural Education in the Church* (Wheaton, Ill.: Victor, 1995). p. 75.

73. Miller, *Theologies of Religious Education,* pp. 6, 342; Larry Rasmussen, "Ecocrisis and Theology's Quest," *Christianity and Crisis* 16 (March 1992): 85; Helen Goggin, "Process Theology and Religious Education," in Miller, *Theologies,* pp. 123–47; Randolph C. Miller, *Theory of Christian Education Practice* (Birmingham, Ala.: Religious Education Press, 1980), pp. 13–14. Also see William Temple, *Nature, Man, and God* (New York: Macmillan, 1933).

relationships as well as that of objects.[74] Process theology is a pragmatic and pluralist approach. In the thought of Alfred North Whitehead, this leads to a God who is an active entity within the process working toward value. God is also a transcending and abstract factor who is everlasting.[75]

When radical empiricism is used to interpret the data of experience, we begin by assuming that God *is* what God *does.* William Temple, in *Nature, Man, and God,* writes that there is unceasing revelation in the whole world process, and also in special occurrences. In both cases *"the principle of revelation is the same–the coincidence of event and appreciation. . . . There is no such thing as revealed truth. There are truths of revelation, that is to say, propositions which express the results of correct thinking concerning revelation; but they are not themselves directly revealed. . . .* Revelation is chiefly given in objective fact, yet it becomes effectively revelatory only when that fact is apprehended by a mind qualified to appreciate it. Like Beauty, Revelation exists or occurs objectively but is subjectively conditioned. Some direct self-communication no doubt there also is from God to the soul."[76]

God is identified with the creating order of the world, a process that transforms human beings, brings values from a potential to an actual state, and works to overcome evil with good. God is that very process by which we are made new, strengthened, directed, comforted, forgiven, saved, and by which we are lured into feelings of wonder, awe, and reverence.[77]

If reality were solely process, it could easily turn into chaos. God provides or is the principle of limitation. God is also the concrete process that works through nature and humanity. Here the persuasive love of God is at work. This is God's free gift of God's love. It is God's grace. God shares in our suffering and our enjoyment, and changes as circumstances change.

This theology is both incarnational and sacramental. It provides a basis for understanding how God worked through Jesus as the Christ and how the spirit of Christ may be present in the sacraments of the church. God draws us into community, an action that forms the basis for the church, that has worship for its focal point. As Whitehead said, "The power of God is the worship [God] inspires."[78] God is "the lure for feeling, the eternal urge of

---

74. William James, *Essays in Radical Empiricism* (New York: Longmans, Green, 1912), pp. iii–xiii; 1–91; also *The Meaning of Truth* (New York: Longmans, Green, 1909), pp. xii–xiii.

75. Miller, *Theory of Christian Education Practice*, pp. 13–14.

76. William Temple, *Nature, Man, and God* (New York: Macmillan, 1934), pp. 314, 315, 317, 318. Italics in original.

77. Helen Goggin, "Process Theology and Religious Education," in *Theologies of Religious Education*, ed. Randolph Miller, p. 129. See also Randolph C. Miller, "Theology in the Background," in *Religious Education and Theology,* ed. Norma H. Thompson (Birmingham. Ala.: Religious Education Press, 1982), p. 35.

78. Alfred North Whitehead, *Science and the Modern World* (New York: Macmillan, 1925), p. 276.

desire." One worshiper becomes aware of other worshipers, and the lure of feeling draws worshipers together.[79]

If chance, human freedom, and the emergence of novelty operate in our world, then the future is not known even to God, and both we and God may be surprised. Helen Goggin reminds religious educators of what it means to be cocreators with God. Process theology, according to Goggin, offers a vision for understanding reality, providing an approach to religious education that is "relational, creative, and redemptive, moving with the church into the future."[80] There is hope for the oppressed, power to achieve God's aims, comfort when we meet insurmountable obstacles, and wisdom to distinguish among them.

The emerging novelty that arouses our curiosity is the source of a process view of the atonement. It is agreed that Jesus died on the cross, but his death was neither a deal with the devil nor the price of sin. God did not choose to have his Son crucified. Jesus died because he was considered subversive by the political and religious powers. He was pronounced "the king of the Jews" by the Roman colonizers. His death, therefore, stands as a moral example to those who are his disciples.

Peter Abelard, although hardly a prototype of a process theologian, wrote a hymn that illustrates this approach:

Alone thou goest forth, O Lord
in sacrifice to die;
is this thy sorrow naught to us
who pass unheeding by?

Our sins, not thine, thou bearest, Lord;
make us thy sorrow feel,
till through our pity and our shame
love answers love's appeal.

This is the earth's darkest hour, but thou
does light and life restore;
then let all praise be given thee
who lives forever more.

Grant us with thee to suffer pain that,
as we share this hour,
thy cross may bring us to thy joy
and resurrection power.[81]

---

79. Alfred North Whitehead, *Process and Reality*, corrected ed. (1929; reprint, New York: Macmillan, 1978), p. 344.

80. Goggin, "Process Theology and Religious Education," in *Theologies of Religious Education*, ed. Randolph Miller, pp. 132, 147.

81. Peter Abelard [1079–1142], *The Hymnal 1982* trans. F. Bland Tucker (New York: The Church Pension Fund, 1985), p. 164.

Multicultural religious education is congenial to process thought. Religion, for Whitehead, is based on a concurrence of three related concepts in one self-conscious moment. Their separate relationships and mutual relations are settled only by a "direct intuition into the ultimate character of the universe." The three concepts are (1) the value of an individual for itself; (2) the value of the diverse individuals of the world for each other; and (3) the value of the objective world, which is a community derived from the interrelations of its component individuals, and also necessary for the existence of each of these individuals.[82]

Whitehead's theory of education is also congenial to multicultural education. He speaks of the rhythm of education, always beginning with romance, moving to precision, and then moving to generality. He never reverses this order.[83] Whitehead warns against premature closure. He advises us both to seek simplicity and to distrust it. Rigidity of belief is deadly. Exactness is a fake. All knowledge is tentative, and theological knowledge especially so.[84]

Process theology is open to the claims of other religions and cultures, and its leaders are often in conversation with Buddhists, seeking to discover connecting beliefs. This openness provides opportunity to maneuver in multicultural dialogue and to add to the understanding of process thinking as a source for other religions and cultures. At present, process thinking appears to be a minority effort among theologians and religious educators, but its promise is great because of its alliance with scientific thinking. Its educational theory and practice are suitable in any culture affected by modern physics, including religious education in a multicultural context.

Feminist Theology

There is a mosaic on the wall of a church in Rome picturing four women, one of whom is identified as Theodora Episcopa, meaning that she was a bishop of the early church.[85] In Romans 16:7 Paul refers to a woman named Junia as one of the apostles. John Chrysostom, in common with most early commentators, including one as late as Peter Abelard, identifies Junia as "outstanding among the apostles." But her name was changed to Junias in some translations because only a male could be an apostle.[86] Women

---

82. Alfred North Whitehead, *Religion in the Making* (New York: Macmillan, 1926), p. 59.

83. Alfred North Whitehead, *The Aims of Education* (New York: Macmillan, 1929), pp. 17–22.

84. See Miller, *Theory of Christian Education Practice*, p. 19.

85. Karen Jo Torjesen, *When Women Were Priests* (San Francisco: HarperSanFrancisco, 1993), pp. 9–10; see also Leonard and Arlene Swidler, eds., *Women Priests* (New York: Paulist, 1977); Stanley J. Grenz with Denise Muir Kjesbo, *Women in the Church* (Downers Grove, Ill.: InterVarsity Press, 1995), p. 40.

86. Elizabeth Dodson Gray, "Feminist Theology and Religious Education," in *Theologies of Religious Education*, ed. Randolph Miller, pp. 212–14; see also Bernadette

worked with men in spreading the good news in the early church. They combined this with their domestic responsibilities. In time, as the church became institutionalized, it adopted the practices of the dominant culture and began to restrict women from holding offices.[87] By the fourth century, however, a new option was available: a career of celibacy and virginity. Women could be freed from domesticity and motherhood. As convents developed, women gained more power within their monastic communities, and sometimes beyond.[88] The rise of romantic love and the cult of Mary were further steps in defining a female presence in Christianity. Since the Revelation of John, the church had been called "the bride of Christ" (Rev 21:2). The next step was to describe Christ in female terms. Julian of Norwich, a key thinker and woman of real influence in the fourteenth century, saw God as Mother as well as Father.[89] But Thomas Aquinas had already agreed with Aristotle's description of females as "misbegotten males," the result of nature's "second intention," rather than its first and perfect intention—males (*Summa Theologica* 1.52.1–2).[90] This perception of women prevailed.

Martin Luther's high view of marriage and vocation gave married women a new status. Soon after, the Quakers gave leadership roles to women. Schleiermacher thought that all people had both male and female characteristics, a shocking view both for his time and from the standpoint of Karl Barth, who held the traditional view of man as the head of the woman.[91]

Changes continued. American women sought more formal education and the right to vote. Married women won the right to own property. With the discovery of contraceptives they gained freedom to choose when to have children. Women today have almost equal rights, although they face opposition in fields where men remain dominant.[92]

Elizabeth Dodson Gray begins her chapter on feminist theology with a survey of "Adam's world," in which Adam named everything. Today we have male-constructed philosophy, psychology, and theology. Women are simply left out of the picture, or they are fundamentally misunderstood and libeled. Although it was agreed at the Second Synod of Mâcon in A.D. 585

Brooten, "Junia, Outstanding among the Apostles," in *Women Priests*, by Swidler and Swidler, pp. 141–44.

87. Grenz, *Women in the Church*, p. 40.

88. Ibid., p. 41.

89. Julian of Norwich, *Revelations of Divine Love*, trans. Clifton Wolters (London: Penguin, 1968), p. 121. See Sloyan, *The Jesus Tradition* (Mystic, Conn.: Twenty-Third, 1986), pp. 42–44.

90. Gray, "Feminist Theology and Religious Education," in *Theologies of Religious Education*, ed. Randolph Miller, p. 203.

91. Elizabeth Clark and Herbert Richardson, eds., *Women and Religion* (New York: Harper & Row, 1977), pp. 131–48; 173–90; 239–58.

92. Clark and Richardson, *Women and Religion*, pp. 6–13.

that women are human, it was also declared that they are the source of evil. Women were considered grotesque in their sexuality, their sexual organs, and reproductive functions. Pregnancy and birth were considered unclean.[93]

Traditional Christianity's understanding of women as inferior, subordinate, and prone to evil is based on a theological violence to women. Certainly this was not the way Jesus treated women, as I have shown earlier in the chapter. Women were the first to experience the resurrection and were leaders in the early church. Jesus compared God to a mother hen (Mt 23:37) and to a woman who found her lost coin (Lk 15:8).

Gray is clear in stating that the "blood of the cross" message is a distortion of the atonement. This proclamation of "divine child abuse," she believes, leads to human child abuse and violence toward women.[94] The glorification of suffering as redemptive, while inspiring to some men, is for women a call to submit to all the indecencies of the past.

Some women turn to a new image of God with a female face, such as Sophia, and incorporate similar images into their worship. Gray, however, does not agree that putting female images in competition with male images is the answer. She cannot perceive of "the Mystery of creative energy which brought into being 193 billion galaxies" has a male or female form, even as image or metaphor. Our problem now, she holds, is to *"strip the male language/image/metaphor from our references to deity* in worship and church life."[95] This includes reinterpreting male statements to include females or asking for repentance for the patriarchy behind such statements. Gray has many suggestions for improving church life and religious education. She asks how it is that "women's experience of giving birth has *never* been honored as sacred (even though it brings new life and the only ongoing life our species knows in time)? Instead, women's natural bodily functions of menstruation and giving birth were declared 'unclean' and 'defiling' to the religious sanctuary."[96]

Gray calls for a religious education "which focuses on the historical Jesus and his startling message of liberation and diversity and inclusion, because that message and example would be relevant in a positive way to our

---

93. Gray, "Feminist Theology," pp. 201–7.
94. Ibid., pp. 216–19.
95. Ibid., p. 220. See also Schüssler-Fiorenza, *In Memory of Her*; Fern M. Giltner, ed., *Women's Issues in Religious Education* (Birmingham. Ala.: Religious Education Press, 1985); Letty M. Russell, ed., *Feminist Interpretation of the Bible* (Philadelphia: Westminster, 1985); idem, *The Future of Partnership* (Philadelphia: Westminster, 1979); idem, *Human Liberation in a Feminist Perspective* (Philadelphia: Westminster, 1974); Ellen Carol Debois, ed., *The Elizabeth Cady Stanton—Susan B. Anthony Reader* (Boston: Northeastern University Press, 1992); Rosemary Radford Ruether, *Sexism and God Talk* (Boston: Beacon, 1983); Phyllis Trible, *Texts of Terror* (Philadelphia: Fortress, 1984).
96. Gray, "Feminist Theology," p. 223.

contemporary struggles with racism, sexism, classism, and specificism."[97] Seeing church life as a "latent curriculum," Gray wants women of the local church, women of the Bible, and women in church history, to be as visible as men. At the same time religious education must function to empower and heal all learners. "That is what the Jesus who called the children to him certainly had in mind."[98]

Feminist Christian theology, seen in this light, contributes to multicultural religious education a recognition of the diversity and wonder of the created life system. It speaks to the universal experience of most women in all cultures, stressing the specifics of the female gift of life to male and females alike. It sees God in images that are neither feminine nor masculine, and it finds in Jesus a historical figure to whom women can relate.

Liberation Theology

As Daniel Schipani observes, liberation theology began as an interpretation of oppressed people. It rejects traditional theological models and focuses on the radical model of solidarity with the oppressed. It leads to a costly discipleship for followers of Jesus Christ. It deals with the social contexts of human suffering. For the liberation model, theological reflection issues in social and political action. Thus it is theology from below. It has two fundamental assumptions: that God is compassionate and liberating, and that the gospel announces the reign of God in the here and now. The human longing for justice, freedom, and peace can be realized, which is the basis for hope. Reflection and action come together in the practice of the ethics and politics of God.[99]

Liberation theology is a new development in theology and offers "a preferential option for the poor and oppressed" as a challenge to the church. For liberation theology, "the optimum locus of revelation and faith is also the optimum locus for the liberating salvific praxis and theological praxis."[100] This has led to the rise of "base communities," in which the work of the church is really done. These base communities challenge both Catholic and

---

97. Ibid., p. 225.
98. Ibid., p. 229.
99. Daniel S. Schipani, "Liberation Theology and Religious Education," in *Theologies of Religious Education*, ed. Randolph Miller, pp. 287–89. Also see Schipani, *Religious Education Encounters Liberation Theology* (Birmingham, Ala.: Religious Education Press, 1988); for bibliography, see pp. 5–8; Gustavo Gutiérrez, *A Theology of Liberation* (Maryknoll, N.Y.: Orbis, 1988); Leonardo Boff, *Church, Charisma, and Power* (New York: Crossroad, 1985); José Miguez Bonino, "Who Is Jesus Christ in America Latina?" in *Faces of Jesus: Latin American Christologies*, ed. José Miguez Bonino (Maryknoll, N.Y.: Orbis, 1984); Paulo Freire, *Pedagogy of the Oppressed* (New York: Herder, 1970).
100. Schipani, *Religious Education*, p. 293.

Protestant churches to let go of their traditional and safe ways and to face the problems of social justice. They are a grassroots challenge to institutional rigidity and lack of vision. They question the culture-bound missionary activity of both Protestant and Catholic institutions.[101]

We have already seen how Jesus was socially and politically subversive.[102] Liberationists view Jesus, like the God of the Hebrew Scriptures, as a liberator. "The praxis of Jesus actually liberates, and his resurrection confirms the truth of the life of Jesus and the ultimate truth of his person."[103] The model of Christ liberating culture brings together striving for justice and solidarity with the poor. The affirmation of Jesus as liberator leads to the denunciation of traditional Christologies and the seeking of a new lifestyle based on discipleship and loyalty to Jesus. The only way to know Jesus is to know him in real life. This means to get rid of private piety and to serve in social and ecclesial ways.

One benefit of liberation theology is its contribution to the education of the nonpoor.[104] This serves the goals of multicultural religious education. Robert Evans provides a summary and interpretation of the eight case studies on which his book is based. In these case studies, learners are led to significant change through encounters with the poor and oppressed: immersion that challenges assumptions; openness to vulnerability; community of support and accountability; vision and values; socioeconomic analysis; commitment, involvement and leadership; symbol, ritual, and liturgy.[105]

Although particularly meaningful in Latin America, where it originated, liberation theology can be a significant element in religious education in other cultures. In middle-class areas, however, liberation theology is often ignored. For example, in 1983 the Religious Education Association featured Paulo Freire at its annual conference, with the expectation that he would draw a large attendance in the southern California area. In spite of the publicity preceding the conference, the number attending actually decreased from previous conferences of the Religious Education Association. In countries with large numbers of poor and oppressed, liberation theology has great appeal. The World Council of Churches headquarters in Geneva employed Paulo Freire as a staff member for a number of years. Books by other liberationist leaders concerned with the oppressed, mostly Latin

---

101. Ibid., p. 291. See Bernard J. Lee, "The Nature of the Church," in *Empirical Theology: A Handbook*, ed. Randolph C. Miller (Birmingham, Ala.: Religious Education Press, 1992), pp. 194–202.

102. Borg, *Meeting Jesus Again*, pp. 53–61.

103. Daniel S. Schipani, "Liberation Theology and Religious Education," in *Theologies of Religious Education*, ed. Randolph Miller, p. 293.

104. Ibid., p. 294.

105. Alice Frazer Evans, Robert A. Evans, and William Bean Kennedy, *Pedagogies of the Non-Poor* (Maryknoll, N.Y.: Orbis, 1987), pp. 257–84.

American, remain available and are widely read. Because of its praxis-oriented view of faith, its attention both to the importance of the Bible in the life of the people and to understanding those elements of the sociocultural context which lead to injustice and oppression,[106] liberation theology can make a strong contribution to multicultural dialogue in religious education.

CONCLUSION

Besides the ones we have selected, other theologies can serve as a resource for multicultural religious education, including Thomistic theology, Orthodox theology, narrative theology, black theology, ecological theology, and others.[107] In this chapter we have dealt with important theologies that exemplify how the pluralistic nature of theologies can face an equally pluralistic world. The problem for religious educators is to establish a basis for unity and tolerance in multicultural dialogue. This means a willingness to listen with open minds and to respect other positions. There are wide discrepancies in the ways those in the same culture interpret the Bible and theology. The differences are even more difficult to understand when other religions have a place in a culture, as they do in North America. This is especially true of Buddhism and Islam, religions that have their own integrity and application to the whole world. In addition, there are those who claim no religious allegiance, and making a place for them within the multicultural dialogue is another challenge. The presence of these realities in our culture should inspire humility and openness, and enable discussion on a more profound level.[108]

---

106. Schipani, *Religious Education*, pp. 296–99.
107. See chapters on each of the theologies named in *Theologies of Religious Education*, ed. Randolph Miller.
108. See Thompson, *Religious Pluralism and Religious Education*, pp. 211–314.

PART II

RELIGIOUS EDUCATION AND CULTURAL GROUPS

5

AFRICAN-AMERICAN
RELIGIOUS EDUCATION

Harold Dean Trulear

The history, development, and ministry of the African-American church must be understood within the context of historic racial conventions in America. Put simply, the systems of racism, slavery, discrimination, and segregation have defined the social stage on which the drama of black life in America has been enacted. The church, as the central institution in the African-American community, has carried forth its religious education mission ever—and painfully—aware that the community in which it ministered was wrestling daily with problems directly related to their strained status as "minorities" in power and influence in American society.

RELATIONAL IDENTITY AND SOCIAL
CONTEXT IN RELIGIOUS EDUCATION

This chapter puts forth the viewpoint that such a mission, to the extent that it has been undertaken as a matter of the nurturing of a Christian personhood, has involved three signal dimensions, namely, identity, relationship, and social context. Through identity formation, the church provides alternative constructs for self and group location in the midst of the American world's unfriendliness. Through relationships, the church provides role models, teachers, and mentors—what J. Deotis Roberts and Wallace Charles Smith have called respectively an extended and a surrogate family—through which the new identity is nurtured.[1] Lastly, these churches provide men, women, boys, and girls with a hermeneutical scheme for interpreting the social context, most particularly the persistence of racism in the society around them.

Religious education in African-American churches has never been concerned solely with the development of Christian identity as a "spiritual," disembodied phenomenon. Neither is its function primarily cognitive. Rather, it has carried on its broad shoulders the heavy responsibility of helping African Americans find answers to the following question: What does it mean to be black and Christian in a society where many people are hostile to the former while claiming allegiance to the latter? In such a reality the question of one's relationship to God and humanity exists in clear contradistinction to the prevailing ideology of a society which embraces both Christianity and racism. One's self-definition as Christian is constantly rehearsed against the backdrop of racist pronouncements that question the humanity of African Americans, whether explicitly through overt denial or implicitly through practices of discrimination, segregation, and stereotypes. In this environment, religious education is called to teach members of the African-American community that God does love and care for them, and has entered into covenant with them as his children. Ultimately their status as his children is the ground whereon they find their humanity.

This move to establish black Christian humanity is called "the black Christian tradition" by Peter Paris in his book *The Social Teaching of the Black Churches*. It is a fundamentally nonracist formulation of Christian faith that affirms the parenthood of God and the kinship of all people. Paris avers that this formulation "represented the capacity of the human spirit to transcend the conditions of racism in both thought and practice," drawing its authority from a biblical anthropology that the black churches believe "strongly affirms the equality of all persons under God regardless of race or any other natural quality."[2] Interestingly, Paris's commitment to inclusive language to express an ideal that the churches themselves would have expressed in the masculine gender (as in the African Methodist Episcopal motto: "God Our Father, Christ Our Redeemer, Man Our Brother") gives us the opportunity to note that the gender politics of religious education in the black churches of this era is still underexplored. That women were central in the religious education of the African-American community is undeniable. Scholars such as Cheryl Townsend Gilkes, Jualynne Dodson, and Evelyn Brooks Higginbotham are helping all Christians see black

---

1. J. Deotis Roberts, *Roots of a Black Future: Family and Church* (Philadelphia: Westminster, 1980), pp. 10, 11, 132. Wallace Charles Smith, *The Church in the Life of the Black Family* (Valley Forge, Pa.: Judson, 1988), pp. 29–42; 73–83.

2. Peter Paris, *The Social Teaching of the Black Churches* (Philadelphia: Fortress, 1985), pp. 10, 11.

women's leadership with critical eyes that both celebrate their contributions and challenge the oppression that they faced.[3]

Three Central Dimensions of Christian Faith among African Americans

Paris's definition points to each of the three central dimensions of Christian faith in the African-American tradition. First, as suggested above, the definition points to identity formation. God's parenthood implies human participation in an identity called the "children of God." To be God's child is to be "somebody." It is a radical declaration of one's humanity. While the world may attach some stereotypical notion of "being" to one's identity, God exclaims, "You are my child." Chattel slavery taught men and women to *be* slaves, that is, to derive their sense of selfhood (or "thinghood") from the commodification of their labor. Segregation assigned "being" to inferior spaces in the society—inferior neighborhoods, inferior schools, inferior jobs. Stereotypes denied individuality and made physical characteristics of race the determining factors in judgments about the identification and attendant worth of blacks. But Christian conversion invited African Americans to participate in identities that affirmed their humanity. They were God's children, just like the Israelites of the Old Testament. In the biblical stories of the children of God, they saw their own situation, struggles, and hopes.[4]

Second, the definition points to relationship: parenthood/kinship language is relational. God is defined in relational terms in this metaphor, and so are God's people. This relational aspect, so crucial to the learning of faith, has been a strength of African-American church life. The religious education of the early black historical era reflected the intense relationalism of the tradition. Community elders and church leaders were expected to disciple those coming behind them, much as their ancestors in Africa were charged with the mentoring of succeeding generations. Black Christian communities of the eighteenth and nineteenth centuries in America were tight-knit groups with strong social ties that provided the context for religious education and development. With the large majority of African Americans of that time period living in the rural South, such a style of social organization in

---

3. Jualynne Dodson and Cheryl Townsend Gilkes, "Something Within: Social Change and Collective Endurance in the Sacred World of Black Christian Women," in *Women and Religion in America*, vol. 3, 1900–1968 (San Francisco: Harper & Row, 1986), pp. 84–85; Evelyn Brooks Higginbotham, *Righteous Discontent: The Women's Movement in the Black Baptist Church, 1880–1920* (Cambridge: Harvard University Press, 1993).

4. For a theological critique of discrimination, segregation, and stereotyping, see *The Racial Problem in Christian Perspective*, by Kyle Haselden (New York: Harper, 1964), pp. 90–152, and *Racism and the Christian Understanding of Man*, by George Kelsey (New York: Scribner's, 1965), pp. 43–48; 96–116.

the churches is not surprising. Smaller communities provided networks of support for identity formation that were important countervailing forces for wholeness in an unfriendly world.[5]

Third, Paris's formulation refers to social context with the word *all*. The kinship of all people, what the African Methodist Episcopal Church called in its motto, Man Our Brother, is a direct critique of the social order that sought to separate the races through label and space, legislation and place, even on Sunday morning. The word *all* cuts across these boundaries to affirm the connectedness of humanity under God, and forces the devotee and the worshiping community to wrestle with the contradiction between such a lofty pronouncement and the existing social order. Simply put, religious education must face the question, If it is the will of God that all people be kin, how do we explain the dividedness of society, and how can the church be faithful in such a world? While much attention has been given to the extent to which the Black church, especially its preaching and worship, has functioned to maintain spiritual wholeness for the communities who pose these questions, less has been offered concerning the role of religious education as a distinct enterprise in the Black churches of the historic period.

RELIGIOUS EDUCATION IN AFRICAN-AMERICAN HISTORY

The latter half of the nineteenth century saw the rapid growth and expansion of black churches and denominations, as thousands of black Christians withdrew from white churches and the historic black denominations were born. The development of religious education efforts quickly took the form of Sunday schools, a familiar institution known among blacks in the South through the efforts of Baptist and Methodist missionaries,[6] and significant in free black communities of the north.[7] Later, paralleling the youth movement emerging in white churches, black denominations formed

-----

5. Roberts, *Roots of a Black Future*, pp. 57–79. Also see E. Franklin Frazier's *The Negro Church in America* (New York: Schocken, 1974), pp. 37–40.

6. Lawrence A. Cremin, *American Education: The National Experience, 1783–1876* (New York: Harper & Row, 1980), pp. 222–24. For insight into the paucity and politics of religious education among African Americans before the Civil War, see *The Religious Instruction of the Negroes in the United States*, by Charles C. Jones (New York: Negro Universities Press, 1969); originally published in 1842 by Thomas Purse, Savannah.

7. Katherine Ferguson, a free woman born in slavery, established the first Sunday school in New York in 1793. See *Women and Religion in America*, vol. 2, *The Colonial and Revolutionary Periods: A Documentary History*, ed. Rosemary Radford Ruether and Rosemary Skinner Keller (San Francisco: Harper & Row, 1983), pp. 254–55.

youth organizations like Christian Endeavor, Epworth League, and the Baptist Young People's Union.[8] More specific information on the role of religious education in black identity formation becomes available to the social historian with the dawn of the twentieth century, such as the analysis of black Sunday school material that is an important part of Benjamin Mays's landmark study, *The Negro's God as Reflected in His Literature.*[9] Mays's study raised the question of the extent to which the images of God contained in Sunday school literature reflected a theology of challenge to prevailing social conditions or offered a compensatory perspective toward social reality. In both cases, the point of departure for Mays was the ability of Christian faith to help African Americans interpret their faith in light of their experience of American racism.

That religious education played a significant role in the lives of black children and families is without question. Mary Love's study of the contribution of the black Sunday school details the significance of that institution, from the eighteenth century to the present, in developing the talents and abilities of children and youth. Moreover, according to Love, the caring relationships of teacher and learner fostered in the young "a sensitivity to care in a station of life where the masses of blacks witness some sort of oppression and need to find avenues of hope and liberation."[10] What is open to question is the extent to which religious education, most often experienced in the Sunday school class, addressed the core dimensions of identity, relationships, and social context. On the contrary, Grant Shockley has documented the extent to which religious education among blacks before the Civil War accommodated the interests of slaveholders, and later in the nineteenth century seldom related itself to the experience of racism that dominated the lives of African Americans.[11]

Growing Tensions in Religious Education
The literature of the twentieth century period reveals some growing tensions in religious education in the black community. Much of this tension reflected

---

8. According to Grant Shockley, these tended to be patterned after white organizations and generally failed to help black youth meet the changes they increasingly faced in society. Grant Shockley, "Historical Perspectives," in *Working with Black Youth: Opportunities for Christian Ministry*, ed. Charles R. Foster and Grant S. Shockley (Nashville: Abingdon, 1989), pp. 11–13.

9. Benjamin Mays, *The Negro's God as Reflected in His Literature* (New York: Athenaeum, 1969).

10. Mary Love, "Musings on Sunday School in the Black Community," in *Renewing the Sunday School and the CCD* (Birmingham, Ala.: Religious Education Press, 1986), p. 156.

11. Grant S. Shockley, "Christian Education and the Black Experience," in *Ethnicity in the Education of the Church*, ed. Charles R. Foster (Nashville: Scarritt, 1987), pp. 32–33.

the change in social organization in the black community in particular, but also in America as a whole. Between the World Wars African Americans began an intense period of migration from the small rural communities of the South to the cities of both North and South.[12] This process of increasing urbanization led many blacks to seek better jobs in the cities; not surprisingly, their churches went with them. Sociologist Charles Johnson noted that the better educated preachers followed the migratory pattern, leaving the rural areas with pastors whose educational levels quickly fell behind even the rural youth who were being given increased, albeit inadequate, opportunities for schooling denied their predecessors.[13]

Another problem noted by Johnson and others was the growth of Sunday schools and other religious education programs in areas either minimally influenced or even unaffected by trained leadership because of the well-known "preaching circuit." In many southern communities, pastors of Baptist and Methodist churches operated on a circuit whereby they would pastor two to four churches, rotating between them from Sunday to Sunday. On the Sundays that the pastor was not present, the church sustained a Sunday school program operated solely by the laity of the congregation. This pattern offered both the strength of the historical relational model of black Christian identity formation and also the weakness of the missing informed pastoral voice that could interpret well the changing times and their impact on the black community. Leadership skills were developed and recognized through this model as lay persons alternated roles as learners and teachers. However, a consistent voice could have brought some changes in black religious education in these areas that would have offered youth a stronger context for integrating their faith with the changes in American society in general, and could have provided them with tools for development as well-rounded individuals.[14]

A structural corollary to this development is the relative local autonomy with which the Sunday school and other religious education activities have developed in African-American churches. With most pastors not present for leadership in these religious education endeavors, the Sunday school and its superintendent function almost as "churches within the churches," raising questions of accountability and direction in the total church program. Even as black churches move away from the circuit pastor form of governance, the territorial battle set up by this historic form looms

---

12. See Frazier, *The Negro Church*, pp. 52–71. Also Max Lerner, *America as a Civilization*, vol. 2, *Culture and Personality* (New York: Simon and Schuster, 1957), p. 516, and Lawrence A. Cremin, *American Education: The Metropolitan Experience 1876–1980* (New York: Harper & Row, 1988), pp. 123–24.

13. Charles S. Johnson, *Growing Up in the Black Belt: Negro Youth in the South* (New York: Schocken, 1967), pp. 162–64.

14. Ibid., pp. 164–69.

large in the structure and maintenance of religious education departments in contemporary churches.

This is not to negate the heroic efforts of black religious educators. They have been particularly effective where the pastor works in concert with the church's religious education structure. Two of the few studies done on religious education in black churches have stressed the centrality of the pastor to the work of religious education. Both studies point to the pastor as the main agent of instruction, and both find a high rate of religious education activities in the churches studied, 100 percent of which had Sunday schools. Most also sponsored vacation Bible schools and youth training programs. The percentage of black churches having boards of Christian education (61.3 percent) was similar to that of white churches (65.3 percent).[15]

Indeed, the contributions of religious education have included the work of the publishing houses of the educational departments of such denominations as the National Baptists, the African Methodist Episcopal and African Methodist Episcopal Zion (A.M.E. Zion) churches, and the Christian Methodist Episcopal Church. These denominational publishing houses regularly produced literature for their constituencies. Black Pentecostal denominations such as the Church of God in Christ developed literature from their theological perspective. All of the traditions sponsored workshops, founded religious education departments, and held conventions that took seriously the need for quality religious education in black churches.

In addition to the traditional literature provided by denominations for religious education at the local-church level, the last decades of the twentieth century witnessed the development of specialized professional religious education literature as well. It is no coincidence that one of the first public articulations of the need for a recontextualizing of religious education in the African-American community appeared in this specialized, professional form of communication. Looking with care at the shifting social arrangements of modern society, and especially the post-Civil Rights era, the National Baptist Publishing Board produced a document in 1972 that attempted to set what was then a contemporary agenda for African-American religious education. Edited with an introduction by Riggins Earl Jr., then director of black literature publications for the board, the volume was entitled *To You Who Teach in the Black Church: Essays on Christian Education in the Black Church*. In the introduction, Earl called the book part of the

---

15. Cited by Colleen Birchett, "A History of Religious Education in the Black Church," in *Urban Church Education*, ed. Donald B. Rogers (Birmingham, Ala.: Religious Education Press, 1989), p. 80. One study, "Report on Christians in Black Churches," was done by the Scripture Press Foundation of Chicago in 1970. The other was a dissertation by Thomas Elgon Leland, "Developing a Model of Religious Education for Black Southern Baptist Churches" (Louisville, Ky.: Southern Baptist Theological Seminary, 1981).

denomination's ongoing attempt "to publish religious literature to meet the specific needs of black churches of its denomination." Earl also recognized the need for a curricular reformation to meet the times. He cited the results of a consultation held as part of the 1970 meeting of the Congress of African People in Atlanta, Georgia, which made the following observations about religious education in the black church of that period.

1. Few religious educational programs were geared toward the struggle of liberation.
2. Religious materials were prepared by people with white orientation.
3. Teachers were not trained adequately.
4. Few materials promoted concepts of (black) nationhood.
5. Religious materials reached very few black people.
6. Religious education consumed only a small part (one day at most) of total education.
7. Religious education did not speak to learners' social development.
8. Religious education was private (individualistic) as opposed to communal.
9. Religious education did not provide formal training for lay people involved at the local church level.[16]

Earl allowed for the overstatements contained in these judgments, even as present readers can also identify them as a product of an earlier era. Yet religious educators such as Earl are careful to hear the truth contained in friendly, informed criticism and to offer response. Careful perusal of the above litany reveals that its contents reflect black religious education's concern with the three central dimensions of identity, relationship, and social context.

As they point to issues of race and oppression, the congress's statements reflect a concern for *identity formation*. Phrases such as *the struggle for liberation*, combined with the critique of the narrow white framework of religious education materials, indicate the desire of the congress that the religious education curriculum ought to nurture the alter identity of black Christian humanity in the face of American racism.

The concern of the congress for the *relational dimension* of Christian education is seen in its statements on lay ministry and the communal ethos. Strong lay ministry and teacher training would focus on discipleship as a primary mode of religious education, while a shift from privatistic to communal modes of religious education would similarly stress the relational nature of Christian identity.

---

16. Riggins Earl, ed., *To You Who Teach in the Black Church* (Nashville: National Baptist Sunday School Board, 1972), p. 7.

Finally, the analysis of *social context* is found both in the call for a sense of black nationhood and in the critique of racism and oppression. In this regard the congress broadened the parameters of black religious education from a singular focus on the pastoral mode to one that is prophetic as well. In all, the responses of Earl and his collaborators constituted an important chapter in the reformulation of religious education in the African-American church.

While the studies described thus far concern the Protestant denominations that represent the overwhelming majority of black churches, similar situations have existed in the religious education of African-American Catholics. The small numbers of black Catholics grew in the twentieth century from about three hundred thousand early in the century to about one million by 1990.[17] Religious education programs, largely in the form of CCD (Confraternity of Christian Doctrine) classes and parochial schools, have experienced many of the same shortcomings common among Protestants churches. Educator Nathan Jones has called for a black Catholic religious education that moves beyond yesterday's limitations and provides for African-American learners what Jones sees as imperatives: a sense of self, a sense of the African-American heritage and community, a sense of the possibilities of disciplined growth, and a sense of freedom to experience and express the sacred.[18] These goals illustrate the universality of the challenge to African-American religious education—Protestant or Catholic.

The Loss of an Historic Function
for African-American Churches

The black church addressed by Riggins Earl and his associates later emerged as a significantly diverse institution, reflecting the increased participation of African Americans in a variety of social venues in the post-civil rights era. Political, educational, and economic gains following that period were reflected in new social class divisions in black communities. While class divisions in black churches have been noted at least since W. E. B. DuBois's landmark study, *The Philadelphia Negro*, in 1898,[19] the impact of these divisions became particularly pronounced in the last three decades of the twentieth century. New forms of social relationships and patterns of interaction emerged in response to increased urbanization and integration. On the one hand, this means that more blacks have moved into the middle class, its

---

17. Grant S. Shockley, "Historical Perspectives," in *Working with Black Youth*, ed. Charles R. Foster and Grant S. Shockley (Nashville: Abingdon, 1989), p. 11.

18. Nathan Jones, "An Afro-American Perspective," in *Faith and Culture: A Multicultural Catechetical Resource* (Washington, D.C.: Department of Education, United States Catholic Conference, 1987), pp. 77–80.

19. W. E. B. Du Bois, *The Philadelphia Negro* (New York: Schocken, 1967).

professions, and its neighborhoods. Even more important, developments in technology, coupled with integration, have made the mind-set of middle-class America available, even desirable, to a greater segment of the black community and its churches.[20] To that extent, I believe, the church has experienced some loss of memory with respect to its historic function in nurturing an alternative black identity, and has become increasingly captive to the middle-class ethos of consumerism, careerism, and materialism. Historic forms—the style of preaching and worship, church polity, even pastoral theology—have been preserved. However, the creative genius that formed them out of the synthesis of Christian life and thought, extant cultural artifacts and reflection on social location, has waned. This is a special concern of religious education.

As a result of the loss of that creative synthesis, the tares of American individualism, vested interest, and self-centeredness are growing amid the wheat of black prosperity and affluence. As these realities confront the black church and its religious educational mission, the question becomes, How do church leaders define the role of religious education in the black church in contemporary society, in light of this church's relationship (or lack of relationship) with the black underclass, with middle-class America as a whole, and with the world community? Or, to use the terms we have selected to describe the heart of black religious education, how does the African-American church redefine its religious educational mission in light of (1) the nihilation[21] of black Christian identity and the need for identity formation, (2) black alienation and the need for the restoration of holistic relationships, and (3) black oppression and the need for spiritual and social empowerment in the present social context?

FOUR HISTORICAL MOMENTS
AND BLACK CHRISTIAN IDENTITY

The remainder of this chapter will examine the black church as it wrestles with contemporary consciousness, asserting that it does so in light of four historical moments that account for the bulk of black middle-class alienation

---

20. See *The New Black Middle Class*, by Bart Laundry (Berkeley: University of California Press, 1987), p. 27–52; also see *The Fruits of Integration: Black Middle-Class Ideology and Culture, 1960–1990*, by Charles Banner-Haley (Jackson: University of Mississippi Press, 1994), pp. 27–52; 157–75.

21. Cornel West speaks of "the nihilistic threat" to black America's very existence. Defining *nihilism* as "the lived experience of coping with a life of horrifying meaninglessness, hopelessness, and (most important) lovelessness," he claims that contemporary American society has failed to grapple with this threat. See *Race Matters* (Boston: Beacon, 1993), pp. 12–14.

from the common black heritage and which, therefore, strain current efforts in religious education in black churches. These historical moments include (1) an uncritical integration into the American mainstream; (2) the lack of a clear, socially defined mandate based on racist structural arrangements; (3) the stratification of the black community, which depicts the underclass as "other"; and (4) an unfortunate acceptance of a definition that ties human "being" to certain forms of accomplishment rather than to quality of life.

The creation of black Christian identity as, in fact, the dominant central enterprise of African-American religious education, must therefore address all of these moments and their attendant forms of consciousness. In this vein, the chapter will conclude by suggesting several possible and complementary religious education strategies for reversing the trend in black middle-class alienation. These strategies mirror the historic dimensions of identity, relationship, and social context. They will be represented here as new thinking in the areas of black churches' self-identity, their relationship to the underclasses, and their understanding of their place in the world community. These suggestions take the form of (1) a radical rethinking of the biblical record in light of the reality of biblical anthropology and the social structure of the biblical world; (2) intentional partnerships between middle-class and underclass congregations; (3) a deliberate networking with Third World churches, which places black American Christians in the posture of learner, thus bringing full circle the pan-African Christian vision of such early twentieth-century Christians as Henry McNeal Turner and Marcus Garvey.[22] Each of these strategies carries with it practical suggestions for religious education.

Uncritical Integration

W. E. B. Du Bois prophesied that the primary problem of the twentieth century would be the color line.[23] Events in the 1980s and 1990s showed that the racial problem did not go away in spite of the gains of the civil rights movement and integration. The politics of race in Philadelphia and New York, the projection of criminality onto young black male faces in Boston, Massachusetts, and Camden, New Jersey, during the 1992 presidential election, as well as events of and responses to the Rodney King affair and

---

22. See Henry J. Young, *Major Black Religious Leaders, 1755–1940* (Nashville: Abingdon, 1977), pp. 127–51. Young writes, "True manhood for Turner meant the realization of one's authentic identity with himself and God, and one's capacity for full participation in societal institutional structures" (p. 147). "Garvey realized that if blacks were to be truly free they must take the initiative in the process. All Garvey's theological motifs were geared toward the actualization of the freedom and liberation of blacks throughout the world" (p. 162).

23. Du Bois, *Philadelphia Negro*, p. xi.

the O. J. Simpson trial demonstrated the persistent presence of America's racial malaise.

The problems of a black underclass persist: unemployment, poor schools, drug trafficking, crime, and similar social ills. Yet these problems stand in stark contrast to a newfound affluence in the black community made possible by the gains of the civil rights movement. African Americans hold positions of major responsibility in the world of finance, business, and industry; they are among the movers and shakers in the realm of politics, are marked contributors to the academy, participate in the world military leadership, excel in athletic competition, and have expanded their rich tradition of excellence in human service professions, as doctors, teachers and social workers.

Yet African Americans still struggle with drug misuse, miseducation, and homelessness. An often quoted comment serves as an interpretive lens through which to view African-American complicity in the development of this seeming paradox. "Black people have argued for a seat at the front of the bus for so long that they've forgotten to ask where the bus is going."[24]

It is interesting that both black conservatives such as Walter Williams and Thomas Sowell and African-American progressives such as Manning Marable and Cornel West find fundamental agreement on the issue that the civil rights movement in many ways benefited an already upwardly mobile, but legally constrained class of blacks, without providing for the proper care and supportive services needed to enable those now in the underclass to have meaningful participation in American society.[25] In his biography on Alexander Crummell, a nineteenth-century black educator and missionary, Wilson Moses notes that such participation is possible because the black nationalist movement late in that century spawned both the industrious spirit of black conservatives and the radical commitment to social justice of progressives.[26]

Conservatives complain that the primary beneficiaries of poverty programs have been low- to middle-level employees and administrators. They claim that many strategies of intervention have created undue dependency on the government (which thanks to integration is increasingly black), while socialists claim that nothing less than a full-orbed restructuring of society represents the true manifestation of justice in our time.[27] And while particular strategies for change in both camps have their weaknesses, they certainly challenge the black middle class to rethink what the civil rights movement was all about.

---

24. The remark is usually attributed to W. E. B. Du Bois, but may be apocryphal.

25. For example, see Cornel West, *Race Matters*, pp. 36–37.

26. Wilson J. Moses, *Alexander Crummell: A Study of Civilization and Discontent* (New York: Oxford University Press, 1989).

27. For example, see Thomas Sowell's *Civil Rights: Rhetoric or Reality?* (New York: Morrow, 1984), especially pp. 13–60.

The issue, simply put, is this: Was the goal of the civil rights movement placing black faces in high places, or was it the intention of men like Martin Luther King Jr. and women like Fannie Lou Hamer[28] that African Americans would bring to an integrated society positive social and cultural values that had been forged in the crucible of slavery and segregation, and still had a lot to teach white America? If integration is merely the opportunity for blacks to get good jobs and live where they want to live, then what has really been gained? If a company's business practices are unjust, does it really matter that it has significant black presence in senior and middle management? If a university offers a curriculum that writes off the black experience, does it really matter that it has significant black presence among faculty and administration (or for that matter, on the basketball team)? Is the mere inclusion of the faces of black folk (without the souls of black folk) sufficient to render a religious education curriculum relevant to African-American constituencies? The questions are rhetorical. It is the transformation of society, not mere participation in society, that is at the root of African-American spirituality and its interpretation of social context. It is therefore a task of black religious education to help learners embrace such a spirituality of transformation.

Martin Luther King's vision for humanity was not confined to Negro prosperity and position, nor was it confined to removing barriers that denied individuals an opportunity to "succeed." Rather, his movement consisted of incremental steps that ultimately would lead to a "beloved community," in which all human beings had value in and of themselves and were subjects worthy of love. King challenged African Americans—and all people—to lay full claim to their *identity as relational beings*. He said that people live in an inescapable network of mutuality, noting that even when one sits down to the breakfast table a host of persons in the international community have participated in bringing together the necessary elements for early morning preparations for the day.[29] King understood that the network of mutuality was there, but that people failed to recognize it. It was this failure to recognize human interrelatedness, he believed, that was the primary impediment to wholesome living.

King pushes people to understand the connections between all human beings in the grand tradition of the black church, which has historically

---

28. Fannie Lou Hamer, a cofounder of the Mississippi Freedom Democratic Party, was a sharecropper whose agitation and activism on behalf of voting rights has become legendary. See *When and Where I Enter: The Impact of Black Women on Race and Sex in America*, by Paula Giddings (New York: Bantam, 1984), pp. 287–90, and *Black Feminist Thought*, by Patricia Hill Collins (New York: Routledge, 1991), p. 38.

29. Martin Luther King Jr., "A Christmas Sermon on Peace," in *A Testament of Hope: The Essential Writings of Martin Luther King, Jr.*, ed. James M. Washington (San Francisco: Harper & Row, 1986), p. 254.

offered love as the badge of fidelity. ("You've got to love everybody if you want to see Jesus.") Love is the expression of the theological concept of related "being" and is the context for all relationships of Christian nurture. Religious education apart from the context of loving relationships is not only unfair to the church's history, it is patently unbiblical. Addressing his denomination in 1970, Joseph Johnson said that hatred and oppression have forced African Americans to draw upon the spiritual and moral resources imbedded in the black tradition and the black religious experience, both of which teach them that "racism is an extreme departure from Christ's mandate."[30] It was love for one another, Jesus said, that identified his disciples to the world.[31]

It is often difficult to see clearly the relational agenda in the struggle of African Americans against post-civil rights alienation. At times, our failure to recontextualize old forms and values such as those mentioned above betrays us. Our churches, including their forms of religious education, have adopted power structures that "lord it over" people "just like the Gentiles." African-American Christians must consider what they really mean when they celebrate the black church's religious education role in identity formation, deeming it a place where "the world's nobodies" become "God's somebodies." The need to reconsider this role was brought home forcefully to me as I listened to Mayor Wilson Goode of Philadelphia preach in 1987, not as presiding officer of the city but as chairman of the deacon board at First Baptist Church, Paschall, a position he had held a dozen years prior to his election as the municipality's chief executive officer. Said Goode, "I trained to be mayor of this city by being chairman of our deacon board. If you can run a black Baptist church, you can manage a city." Deacon Goode went on to extol the genius of the black Baptist church, where "you can be a janitor all week, but on Sunday you're chairman of the board. You can be a maid all week, but on Sunday you're president of the ladies auxiliary."

Goode's perception of black church culture is instructive. He noted that the church became the place for identity formation, but also declared that in his tenure as mayor, he brought his sense of "somebodiness" to bear on the practice of municipal governance. However, the issue is not Sunday status, but the implications of religious conversion for each day of life, even when I am a janitor or a maid. It is not for people merely to find their somebodiness in church, but to discover it in such a way that all of life changes. Religious education needs to challenge learners to question whether life is, in fact, found in one's position or in somebodiness in a church office.

---

30. Quoted by Olivia Pearl Stokes, "Black Theology," in *Religious Education and Theology*, ed. Norma H. Thompson (Birmingham, Ala.: Religious Education Press, 1982), p. 88. Joseph Johnson spoke as a bishop of the Christian Methodist Episcopal Church to that denomination's twenty-seventh conference in 1970.

31. John 13:35.

Martin Luther King's life and ministry moved persons in the other direction, toward humanity defined by relationships rather than accomplishments. King called for new attitudes as well as new achievements. King called for new partnerships as well as new prosperity. King saw the need for interracial, intercultural, and interclass cooperation that reflected a healthy respect for persons and a commitment to work on their behalf.[32] These goals cannot be achieved merely by pointing to those exceptional individuals who have made noble achievements in society. To do so is to uncritically adopt the individualistic values of the majoritarian American culture. There is no need to create a hall of fame of individual black success stories. There is no need to celebrate more black "firsts." (Chuck Stone, former aide to Adam Clayton Powell, reports his mentor to have remarked upon hearing of another black first, "I'm tired of firsts; give me some seconds and thirds."[33])

To concentrate on black firsts and black individuals in religious instruction is to fail to recognize the strength inherent in historic black values, which place a premium on the good of the community rather than the good of the individual. Those values also stress character over achievement and a strong sense of bonding, especially centered around the roles of women in the community. It is particularly frightening to see the devastation that radical individualism wreaks on black families so that person, privilege, and preference gain the upper hand over laboring together and mutual submission.

Religious educators must recapture the whole notion of bonding and mutuality and make a concerted effort to help learners resist Western tendencies toward overt individualism, which leads to alienation and depersonalization. The individual who concentrates primarily on his or her own personal subjectivity is likely to objectify others. A concerted effort would include cognitive, affective, and behavioral goals—Bible study of Old and New Testament passages that stress God's regard for beings created in God's image, reflection on and critique of contemporary society's narcissistic focus on the self, and active service on behalf of others.

Eugene Roehlkepartain says that contemporary teenagers encounter people of so many races that they need to hear the apostle Paul's message to the Galatians, "You are all one in Christ Jesus."[34] He recommends face-to-face

---

32. King stated that the struggle for civil rights was not a racial one. "In the end, it is not a struggle between people at all, but a tension between justice and injustice. Nonviolent resistance is not aimed against oppressors but against oppression. Under its banner consciences, not racial groups, are enlisted." Martin Luther King Jr., "Stride toward Freedom," in Washington, *A Testament of Hope*, ed. James Washington, p. 483.

33. Quoted in an address given to the Youth Department of Mt. Zion Baptist Church of Germantown, Pa., February 1990. Stone, then senior editor of the *Philadelphia Daily News*, is now professor of journalism at the University of North Carolina at Chapel Hill.

34. Galatians 3:26–29.

encounters where people from different racial or ethnic groups work, study, and pray together. Small groups focusing on a shared mission help people break down stereotypes and establish relationships across racial, ethnic, and gender lines.[35]

Lack of a Clear Social Mandate

In her insightful and undervalued book, *The Black Church in Urban America: A Case Study in Political Economy,* Ida Rousseau Mukenge argues that part of the current dilemma concerning the black church and social awareness stems from the fact that it is no longer clear what the problems are.[36] Simply put, slavery, segregation, and discrimination were visible forms of racist arrangements. The eradication of these ills was a visible goal to aim for, whether from the pulpit or from the picket line, in prayer or in politics. As each structure was dismantled, as each law was repealed or passed, as each accommodation was made truly open, the African-American church and community could celebrate a tangible victory and look for the next social ill.

The problems now, however, are more complex. How do you solve problems of drug misuse and homelessness by marching? Can teen pregnancy be addressed by the existing structures of church and society? Will forming another church auxiliary address the problems of black male unemployment? How can the religious education program of the church address these issues squarely and firmly? The fact is that religious educators really do not know what to do about any of these problems. They really do not know what to do about domestic violence, child abuse, and incest. They really do not know what to do about HIV/AIDS in the community. They really do not know how to solve family crises. They are not sure about their responsibility in addressing the needs of the elderly on fixed incomes. And in areas such as public education, where religious educators may think they do know some things, there is often disagreement within the African-American community on how best to train up children in the way they should go.[37]

These problems require a level of analysis that exceeds previous efforts in the area of racial discrimination. Increasingly, black middle-class churches will have to demand that the professionals in their ranks be held accountable to the community for their labors in the marketplace as well as in the church. It will no longer be enough to celebrate the doctors and the lawyers in the

---

35. Eugene C. Roehlkepartain, *Youth Ministry in City Churches* (Loveland, Colo.: Group, 1989), pp. 170, 184.

36. Ida Rousseau Mukenge, *The Black Church in Urban America: A Case Study in Political Economy* (Lanham, Md.: University Press of America, 1983).

37. George and Yvonne Abatso discuss some of these tensions in their book, *How to Equip the African American Family* (Chicago: Urban Ministries, 1991), pp. 13–30.

congregation. Religious educators will have to ask the MDs and the JDs in what ways their Christian commitment has affected their professional identity so that their work has a demonstrable, positive effect on the quality of life of African Americans and others. It will no longer be enough to celebrate Student Recognition Day without a corresponding challenge to youth to redefine the American maxim "A good education means a good job." The black church once said, "Good education develops a good person and a good person will be a blessing to the community in whatever position she or he holds." There must be less concern with how many young people in the church are sent to Ivy League schools and their black counterparts, and more concern for how they are making a conscious contribution to bringing justice to the human order. Religious education must be aimed toward helping black professionals, as well as young aspirants to professional ranks, to recontextualize their own identity in terms of God's concern for the commonwealth, not merely in terms of individual stories of career success.

Concerned especially with the religious education of young black adults, Walter McCray has a fivefold aim: helping them grow past adolescence and into young adulthood, helping them grow into full assurance by reevaluating their faith, helping them mature holistically in God's will, helping them depend on the Holy Spirit in appropriating God's Word, and helping them settle into adulthood by serving Christ and his people. Assuming a full-time pastor and an equipped and dedicated volunteer staff, a church committed to reaching unchurched young black men and women can offer what McCray calls "interest centers"—support groups for the unemployed, tutoring preparation for G.E.D. exams, single-parent groups, community-service groups—to attract and integrate young adults into the religious education program and the church fellowship.[38] What is being said here is that religious education in black churches has a social mandate as well as a mandate for identity formation. While it can be argued that these play a role in religious education in all churches, for the African-American church they are imperative.

As Christian identity becomes a priority for black professionals, they will see better the need for their gifts and talents in the service of the church. These teachers, doctors, and lawyers, along with a host of other professionals, hold insights into the world of human service that must be considered in developing a critical perspective for social ministry and workable solutions toward social problems. More churches need to incorporate support programs into the work of religious education, connecting people to mentors and other persons who can share their skills, knowledge, and experience. At Shiloh Baptist Church in Trenton, New Jersey, for example, fifty church members serve as mentors to young people with particular

---

38. Walter Arthur McCray, *Black Young Adults: How to Reach Them, What to Teach Them*, rev. ed. (Chicago: Black Light Fellowship, 1992), pp. 72–95.

career interests or needs in a specific subject area. A teenager having trouble with chemistry may be paired with a chemical engineer for tutoring and relationship building.[39] John Kinney likens this process to God's call to Moses to bring God the water of the Nile, which God then turns to blood. "Bring Me the world's water of finance, social science, medicine, psychology, educational theory, natural and physical science, and I shall turn it into blood, the stuff and substance of redemptive purposes."[40]

Black professionals have access to analytic techniques with regard to the workings of the American social system that need to be employed in a critical assessment of society's contemporary malaise, as well as in the process of developing workable solutions to such complex problems. The social mandate may not be clear, but images of devastation are. The results are evident, but not the process. Because of the professionals in their midst, black middle-class churches are uniquely poised to take on the job of social analysis and transformation. By pooling the resources of their congregations and looking for ways to employ the competencies of their professionals in the service of Christ, black religious educators can make visible and clear the problems and their attendant strategies with true detail and nuance. They can develop religious education materials that help learners of all ages to reflect on Christian identity and practice in the contemporary era.

Stratification of the Black Community

The black church has historically offered a holistic vision of pastoral and religious educational ministry. Religion has been viewed as a way of life, not a formula or a specific set of behaviors. The historic black church made no distinction between sacred and secular. Building on West African epistemological sensibilities, where daily events were integrated around a goal of spiritual transformation, the black church has posited that all aspects of life are within the realm of the religious.[41] As a result, black churches have developed ministries that address various dimensions of life, education, economic development, social justice, and so forth. The organization of mutual aid societies, such as the Free African Society founded by Richard Allen and Absalom Jones in Philadelphia in 1787,[42]

---

39. Roehlkepartain, *Youth Ministry in City Churches*, p. 190.

40. John Kinney, "To Fulfill My Ministry" (address given at the Pulpit and Pew Consultation, Interdenominational Theological Center, 1994). Kinney spoke as dean of Virginia Union University's school of theology.

41. For example, see Roberts, *Roots of a Black Future*, pp. 39–43, and Abatso, *How to Equip the African American Family*. The Abatsos identify four components of traditional African culture that they believe religious education needs to reclaim: (1) A harmony of the sacred and secular, (2) harmony between male and female roles, (3) a sense of community, and (4) next life preparation (pp. 18–22).

42. See Young, *Major Black Religious Leaders*, pp. 25–40.

the development of black denominational colleges such as Wilberforce University and Livingstone College,[43] strong and stable soup kitchens such as those started by Abyssinian Baptist Church in Harlem and Tindley Temple Methodist Church in Philadelphia, and strong black participation in social justice organizations from antislavery to civil rights all point to the black church worldview captured in a statement by DuBois and still vital to African-American religious education, that the church is "the world in which the [African American] moves and acts."[44]

However, the integration of African Americans into the mainstream of American society has led many into a radical structural differentiation and a social stratification that reflects the larger American society. The price to be paid for middle-class advancement is found in its alienation from the poor. The right to live in the suburbs lures many away from proximity to those with whom God would have Christians be in relation. Simply put, there has been an exodus of role models from the inner cities and impoverished rural areas. While that exodus has often been chronicled for the toll it takes on those left behind, it has also been instrumental in truncating the holistic vision of the black church and limiting the opportunities for relationship building and mentoring. In the past the consequence of such holism was the general betterment of the community. Of course, the church community itself was the community of need. As the needs of black churchpersons have been met, and as they have achieved middle-class status, they are no longer the persons who stand to benefit from a ministry to the poor. The poor is not "us," it is "them." The ones in need of jobs, housing, and social services are not "us," but "them." Persons who are isolated and alienated from others begin to lose the desire to help them.

At a screening of the documentary video *Ministry in the Hood*,[45] a group of black pastors and theologians discussed methods and strategies of engaging and reaching black at-risk youth in their communities. The video's depiction of the successful programs of Boston's Ten Point Coalition of churches and Baltimore's Bethel A. M. E. Church stood in stark contrast to the attendees' stories of the ongoing struggle of black churches to reach this population. Jeremiah Wright, pastor of Trinity United Church of Christ in Chicago, noted that many black congregations had become so captive to middle-class cultural forms that they were virtually incapable of meaningful communication with poor urban black teenagers. In response to this widening gap, his congregation voted to amend its constitution to include reconciliation between social classes within the African-American

---

43. Several such institutions are listed in Cremin, *American Education*, pp. 118–19.
44. W. E. B. Du Bois, *The Philadelphia Negro* (New York: Schocken, 1967), p. 201.
45. The documentary *Ministry in the Hood* was sponsored by the Ford Foundation and produced by Black Entertainment Television. For information, contact BET at 202-608-2000.

community. The church's new mission statement declares the church to be officially "classless," a place where intentional work is done to reconcile members of what society has designed and deemed to be distinct social classes. Others present noted some past and contemporary examples of churches trying to bridge the gap, but it was clear that there was a long way to go.

The helping ministry of black churches has been historically grounded in West African holism and existential need. Uncritical integration into prevailing American values has cost black churches the former and their imprisonment by affluence and suburban captivity has rendered the latter irrelevant. There is no longer a vested interest in social ministry in most black middle-class churches. Now that the church is middle class, all of these social efforts will benefit someone other than the church's own members. Beyond this, those "someones" are horrid reminders of a past whose very appearance puts middle-class African Americans in touch with everything they are trying not to be. Their poverty and hopelessness are present emblems of one's own frailty. And because the black middle class buys into the radical individualism of the culture, many wonder why "those people don't get their acts together" or "get off the corner and get a good job."

This kind of attitude represents a clear assault on relational identity and the right interpretation of social context. Religious education in black churches must take a new look at the holistic vision and face up to the fact that to help others is to help oneself. Religious education in both urban and suburban churches needs to devise means to restore relatedness and bring the alienation to an end. Religious educators must accept responsibility to help the growing number of black middle-class church adherents understand that they are fully connected with those they have left behind, who live in the neighborhoods into which they drive for church and who curiously watch them ape the indifference of white churches that have already fled the scene.

Definitions of the Human: A Biblical Anthropology for Religious Education

The black middle class can best be reconciled to itself by reconceptualizing its current definition of human being. This represents a basic recovery of historic African-Christian identity, albeit framed in a new social context. Having been allowed to capitulate to a worldly Western understanding of the human, with its attendant emphasis on success, materialism, and social status, African-American churches must recapture a biblical anthropology faithful to historical cultural norms like community, kinship, and the sacred. They must hold up this new humanity as the object of the goal of conversion.

Such a biblical anthropology argues that to be fully human is to participate in quality relationships with God and other human beings. This is the intention of God in the creation narrative when he said, "It is not good for man to be alone" (Gen 2:18). Having shown Adam that the animal kingdom was inadequate for meaningful partnership with humanity, God formed Eve to be bone of his bone and flesh of his flesh. It therefore is impossible for the man to experience wholeness apart from his relationship with his partner, the woman. Original sin leads to a breach in this relationship as Adam, rather than taking full responsibility for his own actions, blames the two upon whom he is dependent for his wholeness.[46]

Jesus Christ, as the second Adam, came to repair the breach not only between earth and heaven but also between earth's inhabitants. The standard by which his followers are to be judged—indeed the mark of their fidelity to him—will be the quality of their relationships. It is to this love ethic that black Christians have consistently appealed in their attempts to assess the goodness of the individual and ultimately what it means to be human. Their integration into the mainstream of American society has undercut this definition of the human as being in loving relationship, offering in its place accomplishment, achievement, and status as standards for wholeness. For many in the black as well as the white middle classes, bonding has been replaced by business, mutuality takes a backseat to marketing, altruism is crushed by accomplishment, and it is better to be successful than to be in love.

Whereas the black church-related colleges once extolled the values of human character and service, the ethos of these institutions is now littered with the achievement of individual graduates of status and prestige whose work in their various fields may or may not be socially redemptive. The black communal definition of self, the definition of the human rooted in West African philosophy that says the "I" can only be known within the "we," found strong support in the biblical record of human mutuality. A deep sense of the kinship of all persons emerged as the controlling ethic for the treatment of persons and for shalom in the community. As this sense of the self comes under attack, the African-American church must reappropriate the biblical witness in an intentional way that clearly presents God's intention for human life and living. That means, as black educator Joseph Crockett has shown, teaching the Bible in a way that gives voice to the black historical and cultural experience, "listening to the voice of our ancestors, and living a language we feel, think, and act upon."[47]

---

46. Genesis 2:21–3:24. Old Testament scholar H. L. Ellison points out that human beings, made in God's trinitarian image, were created as social beings; the temptation was to choose independence. H. L. Ellison, "Genesis," in *The International Bible Commentary*, ed. F. F. Bruce (Carmel, N.Y.: Guideposts), pp. 117–18.

47. Jack L. Seymour, Margaret Ann Crain, and Joseph V. Crockett, *Educating Christians: The Intersection of Meaning, Learning, and Vocation* (Nashville: Abingdon, 1993), p. 15.

It is not too much to consider how religious education literature, for example, might work to address such issues. Stories, examples, and illustrations that point plainly to the contrasting models of wholeness offered by biblical and worldly paradigms can supplement or supplant mere moralisms. Small-group work and assignments to service in the community or beyond offer potential for enabling black Christians to act out the biblical anthropology proffered in a new literature that is true both to Scripture and to African-American religious experience, rather than a superficial adaptation of mainstream curriculum. This leads to consideration of the three preliminary suggestions stressing identity, relationships, and social context for reforming religious education in the contemporary African-American church. Much of what is discussed here is being developed in a variety of places, and some examples will people the vision we put forth.

Rethinking Scripture for Religious Education

There are numerous biblical resources waiting to be mined for their fullest hermeneutical riches for the ministry of religious education in black churches. The problem is that certain appropriations of Scripture consistent with the slave status of two hundred years ago have come to be reified in the public consciousness. The texts are not the problem. The fault lies in our failure to do what our foreparents did—see current events, situations, and trends in light of the biblical narrative. Such was the case when enslaved Africans appropriated the exodus narrative as definitive of God's activity in history as well as representative of their own oppressed plight. Liberation from Pharaoh's cruelty and Egyptian bondage became the paradigm for understanding the need for freedom from American chattel slavery. The exodus event provided the hope for deliverance that fueled slave aspirations even to the point of resistance and revolt.[48]

While we will always appropriate the exodus paradigm, we need to offer, with Joseph Crockett, the Babylonian exile as a more accurate representation of contemporary social arrangements between African Americans and the United States as a whole.[49] It is in the exile, Crockett argues, that the people of Israel struggle with the Babylonian oppressor, but also acknowledge the complicity of the oppressed in their own oppression. Many of those whose heroism is celebrated in the exilic texts were members of the middle class, well educated, politically connected and resourceful, and grappling with

---

48. Richard Allen, David Walker, and Nat Turner were among the nineteenth-century black leaders who used this imagery. See Young, *Major Black Religious Leaders*, pp. 34–59. Martin Luther King often cited the exodus as well. See Washington, *A Testament of Hope*, pp. 482, 495, 619.

49. Joseph V. Crockett, *Teaching Scripture from an African American Perspective* (Nashville: Discipleship Resources, 1990), pp. 15–26.

the issue of maintaining the Hebraic tradition of ethical monotheism within the context of Babylonian culture. Daniel, the vice president, Shadrach, Meshach and Abednego, the provincial senators, Queen Esther, who found it no longer convenient to "pass," and Nehemiah, who was at least a civil servant of advanced rank, all wrestled with their connectedness to the whole of the Hebrew community. While participating in a certain form of structural integration, they consistently challenged (and in Esther's case were challenged by) the prevailing ethos of materialism and political domination.

These events call a roll of men and women who embodied the characteristics of identity, relationality, and interpretation of social context consistent with contemporary black Christian concerns. To the extent that the historic black church could interpret their stories for communal identity and social interpretation in the eighteenth and nineteenth centuries, the contemporary church can do so in the current era. Religious educators instructing children, working with youth, training mentors, and engaging adults in Bible study need to explore these biblical narratives for personal and social meaning and application.

The development of the monarchy in Israel is another subject for study in contemporary black religious education contexts. In 1 Samuel 8 the tradition reminds us that there are dangers associated with the transition from a theocracy with human leadership (the Hebrew judges) mediating the will of Yahweh to a structured monarchy whose system energy will be greatly consumed in maintaining the prerogatives of human power. The ways in which some in the black community leaped headfirst into American militarism and structural domination (uncritical integration) in order to be like the rest of the nation comes dangerously close to ancient Isreal's development of a monarchical military-industrial complex in the name of "being like the other nations." The egalitarian ethic that is called for in the covenant community is in tension with a hierarchically defined social order. This conflict calls for an evaluation of the decision-making processes of, for example, such privileged members of the Hebrew people as David and Ahab, who both (to different extents) at times confused their own pursuit of power with that of the reign of God. Religious education resources using the insights of these texts can be coupled with service projects that reflect their redemptive emphases and help the contemporary church understand its role in contemporary society.

The New Testament introduces us to a host of individuals who show Christians both how not to be captured by the *nomos* of culture and how to resist the tendencies to replicate structural domination in religious institutions. Jesus and his band may not have been the Rockefellers of Palestine, but they certainly were not the lowest of the low. Theirs was a life lived in dramatic tension with Rome and the synagogue, yet still in relation to the realities of both. Peter, Andrew, James, and John were fishermen of some means. Matthew's job with the Roman equivalent of the Internal Revenue Service was no small thing. Women were significant contributors to the economic maintenance of the community as well, financing much of the movement out of their own resources. Kelly Brown Douglas reminds us that to be a carpenter in first-century Palestine was not to occupy the lowest rung of society.[50] Jesus was not the champion of the poor because he was existentially poor. His poverty was of his own choosing. His homelessness was of his own volition, his itinerancy was solely the consequence of a lifetime of obedience he chose. The apostle Paul was well educated, a productive tradesman whose resources were recontextualized for the gospel's sake.

It is not solely as individual exemplars of the faith that religious educators should help learners consider these saints, but as exemplars who modeled and understood community. The possibilities for revisioning Scripture in light of the actual social arrangements represented therein, rather than solely through our natural bias as members of a historically oppressed race, create opportunities for pronouncements that can collectively remake the mind of the black churches. Contemporary black youth and adults would do well to examine the Pauline texts on the body of Christ (Rom 12; 1 Cor 12; and Eph 4, for example) in light of the history of African-American churches as institutions that develop community. This would help them form a better understanding of the New Testament Scriptures as well as provide a historic context and a memory for developing relevant outreach and service ministries to others.

Some religious education programs are noted for their effective appropriations of the biblical narrative in their instructional programming. The religious education program at Second Baptist Church in Perth Amboy, New Jersey, for example, includes a drama ministry in which the biblical narratives are reenacted in contemporary contexts that challenge learners similarly to live out their lives in the present society. At Hartford Memorial Baptist Church in Detroit, black theology is part of the religious education curriculum. St. Thomas Episcopal Church in Philadelphia includes in its curriculum the teaching of the history of the two-hundred-year-old congregation and its role in the community as a continuation of the African presence in Scripture and in church history.

Religious educators must lead the present generation of African-American Christians to reflect critically on both the Scriptures and their own culture, and to consummate that reflection in action that talks and walks the gospel—that seeks to free individuals from materialism and self-absorption, and also from poverty, oppression, and injustice. Writing on religious education among young black adults, Anthony Headley finds such activity

---

50. Kelly Brown Douglas made this statement in an Open Forum presentation at Drew University, March 1986.

especially needed by middle- and upper-class African Americans "who may have lost touch with the inner-city impoverished."[51]

Partnership between Middle-Class and Underclass Congregations

For churches that are both characterized by middle-class consciousness and clearly located in the socioeconomic spaces of middle-class America, there is a need to seek ongoing opportunities for religious education activity in impoverished areas. They must do so in a spirit of mutuality, not paternalism.

Structurally, partnerships with congregations whose memberships are drawn primarily or exclusively from areas of economic decay can be an even greater opportunity for the development of community-based religious education, an important increment toward recapturing a sense of relationality and egalitarianism. This means eschewing an attitude of helping the poor in favor of entering into loving relations with "them" who are really "us." While pastoring a church struggling with this issue, I heard our own trustee board chairman, Charles Branch, rightly observe that often in our work with the poor we think of ourselves as "doing them a favor" instead of "being a blessing." In a loving relationship the blessing goes two ways, for in relationships of mutuality, the middle-class church must be willing to learn from the underclass. Religious education contexts can provide for dialogue among equals, celebration of commonality, and appreciation for all the resources brought to the table. A Saturday gathering where the host inner-city church leads worship and Bible study and the visiting suburban church offers teacher training or parent education (or vice versa), and both provide lunch, would be such an occasion. Churches that are for the poor and of the poor have much to teach us about love and bonding, about sacrifice and sympathy.

Such partnering also represents a sharing of resources, not unlike the circuit churches of an earlier era. Joint Sunday schools, like those proposed by United Methodist educator Walter McKelvey,[52] or Saturday church schools, such as that of New Shiloh Baptist Church of Baltimore, which draw upon the resources of a number of churches, are also possible.[53]

---

51. Harley Atkinson, Elizabeth Conde-Frazier, Anthony J. Headley, and David Wu, "Young Adult Religious Education of Major Cultural Groups," in *Handbook of Young Adult Religious Education*, ed. Harley Atkinson (Birmingham: Ala.: Religious Education Press, 1995), pp. 313–39.

52. Walter McKelvey, "A Study of the Developing Cooperative Curriculum Education Project in a Cluster of Black Churches in the Triad Region of the Western North Carolina Conference of United Methodist Churches" (Ph.D. diss., Drew University, 1983).

53. See *10 Super Sunday Schools in the Black Community*, by Sid Smith (Nashville: Broadman, 1986), pp. 152–71.

Joint youth and other religious education and service projects, which model the commitment of the congregations to each other, would flow out of the relationships developed by the congregations. A youth-led vacation Bible school held in a local park, a paint-and-polish workday in the apartments of elderly members, a joint task force working to improve the local school system—in such activities congregations are yoked together. The yoke cannot, however, be forged through joint activities themselves. Worship and fellowship and essential, for without such activity we lapse into that false anthropology that defines our humanity by our accomplishments rather than by our relationships. By worshiping together, by playing and praying together, by having fellowship together, we can really develop relationships whereby we can feel each other's pain and thus minister to one another. This is religious education of a holistic type, not confined to classrooms or formal settings but experienced in a multitude of settings.

For some suburban Christians, these religious-education efforts may eventuate in relocation. For one of John Perkins's primary principles in the Voice of Calvary Ministries of Mississippi, it necessitated moving back to the old neighborhood or hometown.[54] Others may find new friends in old places. Still others will be reminded that steel doors with four or five locks cannot dehumanize some persons. Black members of the middle class must know the poor intimately, as brothers and sisters, and the poor must know the black middle class as people whose true humanity is hidden behind the outward evidences of a capitulation to consumerism, whose troubling addictions may be cognac, not crack, whose music is Anita Baker and Wynton Marsalis, not Ton Loc or 2 Live Crew, and whose gold chains are always 100 percent worsted. A religious education that is concerned with black Christian identity, relationships, and social context will provide opportunity for such intimacy.

Churches located in urban areas can be encouraged to "adopt" local schools in providing volunteers and other resources for everything from tutoring to athletics to in-class grandparenting, as retired citizens lend the presence of wisdom and experience to students in elementary through high school. This means not just showing up on Career Day or Just Say No assembly, but an ongoing partnership with regular presence and involvement in the life of the learners. Diamond Street Mennonite Church, a predominantly black congregation in North Philadelphia, has done just this with children in Duckrey Elementary School. One little-known fact concerning the success of movie subject (*Lean on Me*) Joe Clark at Eastside High School in Paterson, New Jersey, was his insistence on religious education on campus, which was provided in a myriad of ways, including counseling, chaplaincy programs, a chapter of Youth for Christ/Campus Life, and an annual citywide

---

54. John Perkins, *With Justice for All* (Ventura, Calif.: Regal, 1982).

youth revival. Karen Daughtry, minister of House of the Lord Pentecostal Church in Brooklyn, New York, began one of many mentoring programs in black churches, the distinguishing characteristic of that program being that her target population is young girls and adolescent women.[55] The key is that religious education happens in relationships, not programs. If we enter into relationships with the underclass, religious education ministry will flow as the natural response to the need of a friend, rather than as a charitable but perhaps unloving act.

Networks with Third World Churches

Finally, there is a significant need for religious education in black churches to develop networks that cast African-American Christians as part of the global church. The historic church stood against slavery, racism, and segregation because it had some understanding of how Christian faith interfaced with the larger world. It engaged its social context. Today's larger world is global, and much of what learners in contemporary black churches need to reflect upon is contained in an understanding of global social context. Bahamian evangelist Myles Monroe once told a predominantly black audience, "You need someone like me from outside your country to help you expand your horizons. You Americans are the only people in the world who play the World Series all by yourselves." (Thank goodness for the Toronto Blue Jays!)

James Cone once expressed concern that black churches in America are growing complacent due to a false barometer, one calibrated to signs of life in comparison to white churches.[56] Put simply, many black Christians have deluded themselves into thinking that because they have growing memberships, lively worship, new buildings (or even old buildings brought from white churches that are dying, dead, or on the run), successful fund-raising and preaching, and many of their white counterparts do not, they are doing all right. They find that the white churches are the ones losing members, meeting the church budget off endowment, moving and selling buildings, watching their preachers reel with scandal, sing boring music, and offer ten-minute homilies. Because black church members feel so much better off, they easily assume a self-congratulatory posture. Cone's antidote for such complacency is a tonic for African-American religious education: to observe and network with churches of the Third and Second World, where, reminiscent of African-American Christians of the nineteenth

---

55. Karen Daughtry, "A Mentoring Program for Young Women" (M.Div. thesis, New York Theological Seminary, 1996). See also *And Your Daughters Shall Preach: Developing a Female Mentoring Program in African American Churches*, by Ann Farrar Lightner (St. Louis, Mo.: Hodale, 1995).

56. James Cone, personal conversation with the author, October 1988.

century, people are galvanized in their commitment to Christian instruction through discipleship, zealously devoted to each other in ministry, and tireless in their efforts for social change and the betterment of human conditions for all.

African-American Christians are probably far more American than African, committed to charity rather than sacrifice and preoccupied with maintaining institutions rather than investing in religious education and other ministry. One reason for the petty conflicts in many churches is a lack of vision for the global happenings and causes that face all Christians, but particularly contemporary black Christians. Third World churches are far more aware, experiencing the fallout of international economic injustice, global economic imperialism, and severe political repression. An effective religious-education enterprise would be to arrange and finance study tours for clergy and laity that enable them to see these churches firsthand—not to see how African Americans can help but to see who they should be. When they come to understand their connectedness with the Christians in South Africa and their role in the changes being wrought in their country and when they come to understand the need for black Americans to face both their complicity in these global events and their ability to be about meaningful change in the world, then they will spend less time fighting to maintain the prerogatives of office, arguing over what color the choir will wear on their anniversary, and standing as accomplices to the slaughter of millions of chickens to meet the annual church budget. When black church members have heroic models of commitment, community, and sacrifice standing before their eyes, they will feel accountable to God for developing the same ethic in themselves.

It is interesting to note some shift in the representation of the global church in Christian education literature. During the 1994 Lenten season Episcopal churches used a curriculum that focused on the Anglican Church in the Caribbean and its ministry. No doubt the Afro-Anglican movement, led by theologians such as Kortright Davis, and other important developments in that tradition's understanding of its constituency in the African diaspora helped to bring this change about.[57]

The good news is that there is much to be hopeful about. Many churches are developing and maintaining authentic religious education ministries that place a premium on new humanity in Christ, mutuality, and social change. In New York City and Chicago, black churches have committed themselves to focus on black Christian identity formation. The Living Consortium in New York and Project Image (for young men) and Project

---

57. See Kortright Davis's article, "Where Do We Go from Here?" in *The Journal of Religious Thought* 44, no. 1 (summer/fall 1987): 78–83. This entire edition was dedicated to publishing the papers given at the 1985 conference on Afro-Anglicanism held at Codrington College, Barbados.

Pride (for young women) provide relational programs with these goals. Shiloh Baptist Church in Washington, D.C., with its Family Life Center, and Concord Baptist Church in Brooklyn, New York, are among the many that have mounted systematic efforts to preserve the integrity of the black family.[58] The Congress of National Black Churches, representing five historic black denominations, has a significant program to assist black youth. Called Project SPIRIT (strength, perseverance, imagination, responsibility, integrity and talent), the project aims to nurture personal, moral, spiritual, and educational formation among African-American youth.[59] In Chicago, Urban Outreach's Christian Education Enrichment Center offers weekly teacher and leadership development classes, as well as an annual National Christian Education Conference.[60]

CONCLUSION

As the world sits poised on the brink of a new era, in this time of "in-betweenness," there also sits a church that is uniquely qualified to assert world leadership in Christian religious education—qualified by spiritual, financial, educational, and technological resources, along with a keen memory (and sometimes contemporary experience) of how it feels to be oppressed. However, if the black church's collective voice does not arise, if the moment of opportunity for prophetic witness is lost, God has many Russian Baptists, Korean Presbyterians, Ukrainian Catholics, Caribbean Methodists, African Anglicans and Latin American evangelicals who will be faithful. "Think not with thyself that thou shalt escape in the king's house, more than all the Jews. For if thou altogether holdest thy peace at this time, then shall there enlargement and deliverance arise to the Jews from another place; but thou and thy father's house shall be destroyed; and who knoweth whether thou art come to the kingdom for such a time as this?" (Esther 4:13–14 KJV).

---

58. Foster and Shockley, *Working with Black Youth*, p. 81.
59. Ibid., pp. 80–81; 98. The CNBC includes five denominations: African Methodist Episcopal (AME), Christian Methodist Episcopal (CME), Church of God in Christ (COGIC), the National Baptist Convention of America, and the Progressive National Baptist Convention.
60. The address of the Christian Education Enrichment Center is 1350 W. 103rd St., Chicago, IL 60643.

6

PACIFIC-ASIAN NORTH AMERICAN RELIGIOUS EDUCATION

Greer Anne Wenh-In Ng

As a contribution toward theory and practice in multicultural religious education in North America, this chapter addresses two distinct audiences—those whose ethnicity and cultures originated in Asia and other non-European nations, and those whose ethnicity and cultures originated in Europe. Readers of different ethnocultural identities will probably perceive the ideas, analyses and suggestions offered here somewhat differently. Keeping this in mind, readers are invited to enter into dialogue with what challenges them or feels unfamiliar to them as well as what they can affirm. Wherever circumstances allow, readers are encouraged to seek out a person or a group in the other category of readership with whom to converse and compare impressions, thus practicing multicultural religious education on a concrete and personal as well as a theoretical and professional level.

At the same time, it must be borne in mind that no single individual, however wide the person's experience and however deep her engagement in the field, can begin to represent all the viewpoints and experiences possible within the multiform and complex Asian communities of North America. What is offered here is but an invitation to start or to continue addressing the religious education needs of this particular segment of the body of Christ. In many ways, therefore, this chapter is another step on a long journey, a journey begun when Asian faith communities were first formed in North America, often as mission fields or stations as a gesture of outreach to those "strangers from a different shore"[1] who came to better their fortunes in the

---

1. The phrase is taken from Ronald Takaki's history of Asian Americans, *Strangers from a Distant Shore: A History of Asian Americans* (New York: Penguin, 1989).

land across the seas known as *Mei Guo* ("Beautiful Kingdom") and *Gum San* ("Gold Mountain"), and in the sugarcane fields of Hawaii.

This chapter will explore the historical and cultural contexts for Pacific-Asian North American religious education, selected issues in the religious life and development of Pacific-Asian North American Christians, the "doing" of religious education in such churches, and projections for the future of religious education in Pacific-Asian North American churches.

HISTORICAL AND CULTURAL CONTEXTS FOR PACIFIC-ASIAN NORTH AMERICAN RELIGIOUS EDUCATION

The term *Asian American* gained usage during the consciousness forming years of the civil rights movement in the United States among Americans of Japanese, Chinese, Korean, and Filipino/a origin. This emerging Asian American identity includes four distinct ethnocultural groups.

1. *Far East Asian* groups strongly influenced by Confucianism, that is, Chinese, Korean, Japanese, Taiwanese, as well as ethnic Chinese elements from Vietnam, Singapore, Malaysia, and other locations. These groups come from ancient civilizations with sophisticated artistic, literary, scientific, and religious histories. They each possess a distinct Sino-Tibetan language very different from English and other Indo-European languages.

2. *South and Southeast Asian* groups such as Filipinos/as and Asian Indians/Pakistanis/Sri Lankans, each with their own "world religion" and a very small percentage of Christians (except in the Philippines, where the majority are Roman Catholic), with their own indigenous language or dialect but with a good percentage of the population being able to use the English language.

3. *Laotians/Cambodian/Hmongs* from the former Indochina, a fair number of whom come from rural/agricultural backgrounds. They share significant aboriginal cultural characteristics emphasizing, for example, the oral over the written, the communal over the individual, cooperation over competition, to mention just a few.

4. *Pacific Islanders*, including native Hawaiians, Samoans, and others, with aboriginal cultures and spiritualities.[2]

---

2. See Eleanor W. Lynch and Marci J. Hanson, *Developing Cross-Cultural Competence: A Guide for Working with Young Children and Their Families* (Baltimore: Brookes, 1992); chap. 8: "Families with Asian Roots," Chinese Americans—pp. 181–91; Korean Americans—pp. 192–97; Southeast Asian Americans—pp. 198–231; chap. 9: "Families with Philipino Roots," pp. 259–300; and chap. 10, "Families with Native Hawaiian and Pacific Island Roots," pp. 301–18.

The term *Pacific-Asian North American* has been coined to refer to the first (Far Eastern plus Chinese elements in the Southeast Asian) group and the Pacific Islander group. Owing to some very real cultural differences between the first group and the others, the present chapter will deal primarily with the former. The second group, the Filipino/a and South Asians, stands somewhat in between, and where appropriate will be included in the present discussion. Where situations and characteristics are common among all four groups, principles may be appropriated by readers for their religious education work—always with the understanding, however, that significant differences might make some things in the chapter less applicable.

North American Immigration
History among Asian Groups

In addition to the ethnic distinctiveness of Asian peoples who now reside in the United States and Canada, there is a clear distinction between pre-1965 and post-1965 immigrants within the same ethnocultural group because of differences in immigration history. Take the Chinese population, for instance. Takaki points out that by 1985 a "bipolar Chinese American community" had come into existence, comprising a "colonized working class" mainly in service and operator sectors of the labor force, and an "entrepreneurial professional middle class" in professional and manage-rial positions.[3] By 1993 a Vancouver, British Columbia, newspaper head-line read: "Yuppies Challenge Old Guard in Chinese Community: 'Five Solitudes' Have Trouble Finding Common Ground in Rapidly Changing Community."[4] The complexity of issues for religious education within these communities can easily be imagined. Yet the majority population remains largely unaware of this "great divide." Many European-North Americans stereotype every Asian as a Chinese launderer or assume that every new Asian resident is a wealthy entrepreneur from Hong Kong or Taiwan, thus forgetting about exploited Asian garment workers in major North American cities. A fuller understanding can only be achieved by learning about all three phases of Asian immigration to North America.

The First Wave of Asian Immigration: Laborers Who Crossed the Pacific: The first wave of Asian presence in North America came as a response to the need for cheap labor in the mid-1880s, occasioned by the discovery of gold along the northwest coast of the continent and by the construction of transcontinental railroads in both the United States and Canada. Owing to legislated prohibition against property ownership and citizenship, discriminatory practices in educational opportunities, and bar-riers to the professions, early Chinese laborers who survived accidents and

---

3. Takaki, *Strangers from a Distant Shore*, p. 425–26.
4. Frances Bula, *The Vancouver Sun*, 24 March 1993, n.p.

harsh working conditions subsequently had to make their living as laundry and restaurant operators. Bachelor communities grew up in the various Chinatowns because family members were discouraged or prevented by legislation in North America from joining their male "heads" of families.[5]

Japanese presence in the late nineteenth and early twentieth centuries took the form of sugarcane workers and farmers in Hawaii and California, and fisherfolk in British Columbia. Unlike the earlier Chinese immigrants, they were able to form families, usually through the "picture bride" system. By the time Japanese were relocated to internment camps in the early 1940s, children and teens had become viable parts of Japanese North American communities.

The first Koreans came to Hawaii as sugarcane workers in 1903. They, too, established families via the picture bride system. A similar phenomenon happened with Filipino and East Indian imported laborers of the period. There was often rivalry and competition among these groups.[6]

These early Asian laborers shared several characteristics. First, they shared a "sojourner" mentality.[7] This was especially true of the Chinese, most of whom worked long hours to send money home to support their families in China, all the while longing for the day when they could return with glory to *Tong Shan* (Tang Mountain) to build a big house in their home village. Such was their dream of bringing honor to their ancestors and living out their last days in comfort and peace, reunited at last with their wives and children. The same was true, but not to the same extent, for Japanese and Korean laborers because they were allowed to start families while in America.

Church work among Asian immigrants during this first period concentrated mainly on providing a stable and relatively safe place for these populations. Most churches served as community centers as well as places

---

5. The United States passed exclusion acts with varying degrees of harshness in 1882, 1892, and 1902. They remained in effect until 1943. See Harry H. L. Kitano and Roger Daniels, *Asian Americans: Emerging Minorities* (Englewood Cliffs, N.Y.: Prentice-Hall, 1988), p. 23. Canada imposed an exorbitant head tax of $500 in 1885. Canada's form of legislated exclusion, the Chinese Immigration Act, lasted from 1923 to 1947. See Peter S. Li, *The Chinese in Canada* (Toronto: Oxford University Press, 1988), pp. 29–30.

6. Ronald Takaki, "Pacific Crossings: Seeking the Land of Money Trees," in *A Different Mirror: A History of Multicultural America* (Boston: Little, Brown, 1993), pp. 246–76, and idem, "Strangers at the Gate Again: Post-1965," in *Strangers from a Distant Shore*, pp. 406–71. See also Stephen S. Kim, "Seeking Home in North America: Colonialism in Asia, Confrontation in North America," in *People on the Way: Asian North Americans Discovering Christ, Culture, and Community*, ed. David Ng (Valley Forge, Pa.: Judson, 1996), pp. 15–23.

7. David Ng entitled his chapter "Sojourners Bearing Gifts: Asian American Christian Education," in *Ethnicity in the Education of the Church*, ed. Charles R. Foster (Nashville: Scarritt, 1988), pp. 7–23.

of worship, evangelism, and religious instruction. By organizing English language classes for the adults and heritage language classes for the children, the church was at once an agent of acculturation or assimilation and an agent of cultural retention. English classes were operated as mission projects by Roman Catholic and major Protestant denominations, often under the supervision of returned missionaries. Heritage language classes were the work of volunteers from the congregation and from the ethnic communities. Roman Catholic churches sometimes sponsored parochial schools in Asian enclaves, such as the Transfiguration School in New York City's Chinatown. Another form of social action was ministry to women and girls. In San Francisco, Presbyterian deaconess Donalda Cameron pioneered the rescue of prostitutes. In Victoria, British Columbia, Methodists (one of the three major denominations that joined together in 1925 to form the United Church of Canada) operated an orphanage for abandoned girl babies. After Korea was annexed by Japan in 1910, Korean-American congregations in Hawaii and California led in generating overseas support for the independence movement—involving, incidentally, a high degree of participation by women members of churches and communities.[8]

When Japanese Americans and Canadians were confined to internment camps (1942–45), ministry was carried out in the relocation centers by both Caucasian and Japanese-American/Canadian pastors, and by deaconesses/educators of the mainline denominations, thus ensuring a minimum amount of education and Christian education for the children and teens interned.[9] At the end of World War II, Japanese Canadians were relocated east of the Rockies, spurring the formation of a series of new congregations in the urban centers of central Canada (Montreal, Hamilton, Toronto). By this time many were entirely English-speaking Nisei (North-American-born second generation) or Sansei (third generation), fairly well assimilated into the dominant culture. The repeal of the Exclusion Act for the Chinese population in 1947 also meant that wives and children and sometimes parents could join male wage earners in North America. A number of university students also gained residence and eventually citizenship on the strength of their refugee status after the outbreak of the 1949 revolution in China and of the Korean War in the early 1950s.[10]

---

8. See Ronyoung Kim, *Clay Walls* (Sag Harbor, N.Y.: Permanent Press, 1986), and Diana Yu, *Winds of Change: Korean Women in America* (Washington, D.C.: Women's Institute Press, 1991).

9. See *A Centennial Legacy: History of the Japanese Christian Missions in North America, 1877–1977*, vol. 1, comp. Sumio Koga (Chicago: Nobart, 1977); Koga was chairperson of the Centennial Celebration Coordinating Council; "The Churches and Relocation Center Experience," by Lester E. Suzuki, pp. 40–42; "A Brief History of Japanese United Church of Canada," by Kenneth Matsugu, pp. 354–69.

10. For brief accounts of the churches' work among the Chinese in Canada, see Edgar Wickbert, ed., *From China to Canada: A History of the Chinese Communities in Canada*

In California during this period Asian churches with a sizable number of second-generation members began seeking English-speaking pastors and emphasizing integration into mainstream society. First-language ministries continued to be important where parents, wives, and children had recently arrived, and where university students stayed on after graduation. From being "missioned to," they were becoming members of the body of Christ in their own right. Catholic parishes in urban centers continued to provide language schools that also acted as social gathering places for parents and other community members.[11]

The Second Wave of Asian Immigration, 1965–85: Sojourners No Longer: In 1965 both the U.S. and Canadian governments passed legislation making modifications in immigration policy, abolishing hitherto rigidly held quotas according to national and ethnic origin. The new legislation also permitted nonquota entry of immediate family members. The official Canadian statement on immigration was based on a universal point system applicable to all national and ethnic groups. The combination of the new legislation and unstable political situations occurring in Asia from the mid-1960s to the mid-1980s (for example, riots in Hong Kong following the start of the Chinese Cultural Revolution in 1966, the autocratic regime of President Chung Hee Park in South Korea, and the dictatorship of Ferdinand Marcos in the Philippines) resulted in an influx of large numbers of urbanized, better-educated, middle-class Chinese, Korean, Filipino/a, and South Asian immigrants. These second-phase immigrants brought their families with them, thus increasing the proportion of women to men. The arrival of considerable numbers of young Korean immigrants gave rise to what became known in those communities as the "1.5" generation—the cohort that came to North America as children or young teens, being neither first nor second, but a "1.5" generation.

Second-wave Asian immigrants characteristically intended to be permanent residents and eventually citizens, not sojourners, in their adopted countries. Large numbers chose California and New York as home in the United States, and the metropolitan areas of Toronto and Vancouver in Canada. In the 1970s they were joined by Vietnamese refugees of Chinese descent, followed by Cambodian, Laotian, and Hmong refugees bringing comparatively prolific, extended families with them.[12]

A significant reality facing many second-wave immigrants once they settled in North America was (and remains) underemployment and "the

---

(Toronto: McClelland and Stewart, 1982), pp. 172; 236–37. For the role of women in Japanese-American churches, see Mei T. Nakano, *Japanese American Women: Three Generations, 1890–1990* (Berkeley, Calif.: Mina, 1990) pp. 51–53; 115–17.

11. See Wickberg, *From China to Canada*, pp. 236–37.

12. For more details about the second wave of Asian immigrants to North America, see Takaki, *Strangers from a Distant Shore*, pp. 406–71; also see Peter S. Li, *The Chinese in Canada* (Toronto: Oxford University Press, 1988), pp. 85–125.

glass ceiling." Many college graduates from Manila ended up as school janitors, and Korean engineers and pharmacists ended up as grocers.[13] Speaking of a representative Asian group, sociologist Peter Li comments that there is a "cost of being Chinese in the Canadian labour market."[14]

Many new Asian Protestant congregations and large influxes into existing Roman Catholic parishes in the urban centers of North America resulted from this second wave of significant Asian immigration. This was especially true of the Korean immigrant population which, unlike the Chinese or earlier Japanese immigrant populations, is "church centered," since most of the Korean immigrant population has at least nominal ties with a local Korean church.[15] In previously established Chinese congregations, the second wave resulted in a sharp revival of first-generation and immigrant ministries. Generational issues (of which more will be said) came to the fore as young children quickly assimilated, much to the consternation of their elders.

It was also during this period that an Asian-American movement of identity and struggle was birthed, "not with the initial campaign for civil rights," according to one contemporary assessment, "but with the later demand for black liberation," the leading influence not being Martin Luther King Jr., but Malcolm X.[16] As part of the spirit of the times, religious education within these churches began to focus on the learners' Asian identity. In the following decade second-generation Asian Christians, faced with their children's questions about roots, began to pay attention to cultural recovery and cultural specificity in their religious education programs.[17]

It was in response to such felt needs, and with the realization of a common Asian-American identity, that a core group of Pacific Asian-American church leaders began in the 1970s to form ecumenical coalitions such as the Pacific Asian American Center for Theology and Strategies (PACTS, based at the Pacific School of Religion and later at the Graduate Theological Union in Berkeley, California) and also the Pacific Asian American Christian Education (PAACE, later expanded into PAACCE with the participation of two Canadian denominations). The latter, started as a movement by a group of concerned Asian-American pastors and educators

---

13. Takaki, *Strangers from a Distant Shore*, pp. 432–36.

14. Li, *The Chinese in Canada*, p. 119.

15. Sang Hyun Lee and John Moore, eds., *Korean American Ministry: A Resource Book* (Louisville, Ky.: General Assembly, Presbyterian Church [U.S.A.], 1987, 1993), p. 241. Also see chap. 3 of the same volume, "Korean Immigrant Churches and the PC (U.S.A.)," by Joseph H. Ryu, pp. 25–36.

16. Glenn Omatsu, "The 'Four Prisons' and the Movements of Liberation: Asian American Activism from the 1960s to the 1990s," in *The State of Asian America: Activism and Resistance in the 1990s*, ed. K. Aguilar-San Juan (Boston: South End, 1994), pp. 20–21.

17. David Ng, "Sojourners Bearing Gifts," p. 13.

in the San Francisco Bay Area in 1978, worked with the relevant unit of the National Council of Churches of Christ to sponsor groundbreaking projects targeted for Asian-American/Canadian leaders. These projects included national writers' workshops to recruit and train Asian-American writers and editors, local and regional leadership training events, and specifically Asian-American curriculum resources.[18]

The author's own observation and experience in Canada indicates that for the Roman Catholic community, matters of inculturation in religious symbols have held more attention from religious educators. The use of incense and visual symbols, devotion to Mary, and intercession by the saints are practices that easily find parallels in more than one Asian culture. The use of the vernacular, made possible by the liturgical reforms of the Second Vatican Council, has meant that immigrant Chinese Catholics, for example, are able to attend Mass in their native dialect. Filipino priests and acolytes now serve in many local parishes.

The Third Wave of Asian Immigration: Globalized Settlers: Since 1985 there has been another distinct wave of Asian immigrants—entrepreneurs and investors who gained entry into Canada and the United States by bringing in required minimum amounts of investment capital. The majority of those from Hong Kong in this group were motivated by apprehension about the political future of their territory, which will revert to the government of China after 1997. Immigrants from Taiwan, South Korea, and Singapore/Malaysia may have similar political misgivings, or they may simply want a better future for their children. The economic status of this wave of immigrants is the highest ever, numbering retired professionals and their parents, and midcareer professionals (who sometimes end up returning to work in their homelands) and their families. This latest career trend has given rise to the so-called astronauts, with their particular brand of single-parent or sans-parent families. Often a spouse, sometimes with inadequate English-language skills, is left for long periods alone with the children to cope in an unfamiliar situation. In extreme cases, teenage children are left to live on their parents' newly purchased property, under only indirect supervision from a relative or a parental friend living at a distance. Such "globalized settlers" present special challenges for the churches in terms of both religious education and pastoral care.

The increasing numbers of Asian North American Christians, especially in the Korean community (as high as 70 percent of Korean im-

---

18. Among resources developed through PAACCE are *Asian Pacific American Youth Ministry*, ed. Donald Ng (Valley Forge, Pa.: Judson, 1988), and a volume resulting from a Lilly Endowment-funded research project directed by David Ng, *People on the Way: Asian North Americans Discovering Christ, Culture, and Community* (Valley Forge, Pa.: Judson, 1996).

migrants, by some counts),[19] has meant the establishment of yet more immigrant or original-language congregations and parishes. As tensions between first and second and subsequent generations demanded greater attention, it became clear that religious education programs and resources designed for mainstream white congregations could not meet these needs. Some mainline denominations responded by establishing Asian-American or ethnic minority ministries and multicultural staff portfolios. A major denomination in Canada, the United Church of Canada, voted at its general council in 1994 to establish an ethnic ministries council to enable and facilitate non-Anglo ministries, including strategies for educational ministry.

A Multifaith Context: Large percentages of the Asian populations of North America, it must be remembered, do not belong to Christian churches. Adherents of Buddhism, Islam, Hinduism, Sikhism, and Janism, not to mention cultural-religious heritages such as Confucianism, Taoism, and shamanism, form viable religious communities with their own places of worship. Some have adopted structures from Christianity, such as Sunday schools, without giving up more traditional forms, such as public lectures by masters or individual master/guru discipleship relationships. Others, primarily traditional Confucianist families, have simply continued with their practice of noninstitutional, family-centered ancestral veneration. Learning to relate to and support one another across faith lines in religious education endeavors is fast becoming one of the most urgent and challenging tasks facing Christian religious educators concerned with the Pacific Asian communities of North America.[20]

SELECTED ISSUES IN THE RELIGIOUS LIFE AND DEVELOPMENT OF PACIFIC-ASIAN NORTH AMERICAN CHRISTIANS

The history of Pacific-Asian existence in the United States and Canada cannot but exercise significant impact on religious life. This section examines issues from Asian immigration experience and from Asian ethnocultures that affect both the development of individuals in Christian faith communities, and the religious education goals of those communities.

---

19. See Eui-Young Yu, "Korean American Community Issues and Prospects," in *Korean American Ministry*, ed. Sang Hyun Lee and John Moore, p. 178.

20. For a fuller discussion, see "Asian Ways of Spiritual Pluralism," in "The Central Issue of Community," by Heup Young Kim and David Ng, in *People on the Way*, ed. David Ng, pp. 26–38.

The Centrality of the Immigrant Experience

Unlike their white counterparts, who answer to the appellations *American* and *Canadian* without second thought, Pacific-Asian North Americans remain hyphenated Americans or Canadians most of their lives. Because their visibly different appearance often triggers questions such as, When did you come to America (Canada)? even third- and fourth-generation Pacific-Asian Americans or Canadians are prevented from merging fully into mainstream society and gradually forgetting their immigrant origins, as most white immigrants eventually do. Thus both recent arrivals and longtime residents require a religious education that takes their particular identity and context into account. While special support and services needed by recent arrivals are usually provided by an ecology of social and government agencies, the focused religious education, pastoral care, and other forms of faith nurturing needed by all immigrant groups fall more naturally to the purview of the churches.

Religious educators and denominational personnel seeking to be effective in their ministry to Pacific-Asian North American Christians and congregations will find a helpful conceptual model, which gives basic understanding of the immigrant response, in the four modes of immigrant experience described below.[21]

Traditionalist immigrants reject Western values and avoid associating with the dominant white society of North America. They tend to shop and utilize services offered in their own ethnic community, attend ethnic churches, and continue using their heritage language. Some of this behavior is constrained by necessity—a lack of fluency with the language and customs of the host society or the kind of racial discrimination that led to the establishment of the first Chinatowns and Japantowns in North America's urban areas. The initial need of new immigrants to operate at a level of comfort is understandable. As author Roland Kawano pointed out to this writer,[22] such behavior could even function as a tool of survival in a hostile climate.

Assimilating immigrants, at the other extreme, take on uncritically the lifestyle and values of the host society and tend to associate primarily with mainstream colleagues or schoolmates. They avoid involvement with their own community and prefer to live in a neighborhood that is predominantly white. They attend mainstream churches and often become active members there.

Biculturally integrated immigrants maintain active contact with both their original and their host cultures, moving from one to the other with

---

21. The schema is adapted from Kitano and Daniels, *Asian Americans: Emerging Minorities*, pp. 190–94.

22. Roland Kawano is author of *The Global City: Multicultural Ministry in Urban Canada* (Winfield, B.C.: Wood Lake, 1992).

the skill of the "socially amphibian."[23] Over time they develop a bicultural competence and perspective that respects and integrates the specific values of both their own culture and the host culture.

Marginal immigrants tend to withdraw from both their own ethnocultural communities and from the white, Western society of their host culture, living an isolated, alienated existence "at the margin." Such persons may not show up in either kind of church, even if they were nominally Christian, or they might worship in congregations that require minimal personal contact. It must be noted, however, that the concept and experience of marginality need not be interpreted only in a negative manner, as Korean-American theologian Jung Young Lee makes clear in his work on marginality.[24]

Knowing where members of a particular congregation belong on this continuum can help determine appropriate educational programs that address the needs of specific groups of learners in their various immigrant modes, and thus help to mitigate the particular degree of resistance to them. Persons in the assimilationist mode are not likely to think much of suggestions to incorporate Asian art motifs into banners or bulletin covers, while traditionalists might expect total "importing" or "transplanting" of original Asian language liturgies and prayers from their countries of origin. Some may be entirely Western, but are familiar. (Singing golden-oldie hymns straight from the hymnbooks of Scotland is a good example.) Their styles and structures of ecclesial organization may be at variance with the polity of their denomination in the host country. For Asian Christians whose Christianity has been formed in a Western mode in their homeland by overzealous white missionaries, the matter is complicated by a tendency to adhere rigidly to faith stances and expressions received as orthodox from those external authorities. Any suggestion of stepping outside such perceived orthodoxy, even in the simple invitation to sing a "globalized" hymn rather than a traditional Western hymn, will be felt as a threat. First-generation members need to be affirmed, and at the same time gently encouraged, to move toward greater integration of their cultural and Christian heritages. An important skill to emphasize in professional and leadership development, therefore, is the ability to discern when and with whom to try what kind of innovations in congregational worship and religious educational programming.

---

23. This term was created by Roy Sano, Japanese-American United Methodist bishop of Los Angeles and Hawaii. Sano was the founder and first director of PACTS (Pacific Asian American Center for Theology and Strategies), mentioned earlier in this chapter.

24. Lee finds a "contemporary self-affirming" form of marginality that exists in addition to the negative form. He calls this an "in-both" rather than an "in-between" experience: "A marginal person is in-both worlds without giving up either one. I am more than an Asian because I am an American, and I am more than an American because I am an Asian." See Jung Young Lee, *Marginality: The Key to Multicultural Theology* (Minneapolis: Fortress, 1995), pp. 57–58.

Ethnocultural Identity Issues
for Subsequent Generations

First-generation Pacific-Asian peoples are not the only ones who have to adapt to living in the predominantly white, Western society of the United States and Canada. So must their offspring, both those who entered North America with their parents or guardians and those who are born here. Identity issues, especially issues of ethnocultural identity for minority groups, are of particular concern to the children, youth, and young adults of Pacific-Asian North American communities, owing to the often contradictory nature of their socialization. On the one hand, in the Asian ethos at home they are taught to be modest and reserved in public (including the classroom), to be obedient to elders and people in authority, and to value family (immediate and extended) and community over the individual. On the other hand, in the predominantly Western cultural ethos at school, they are expected to assert themselves, to speak their mind, to claim autonomy even if it contradicts the voice of authority, and to value the individual as much as, if not over, family and community. How do they cope with such conflicting demands?

One alternative is to operate in two worlds, one at home and ethnic church and community and the other at school or work. Another alternative is to trace the stages of racial/cultural identity development so as to understand personal reactions. Derald Wing Sue and David Sue in their highly acclaimed work *Counseling the Culturally Different* offer a model of such development, a model with which anyone committed to religious education with racial-ethnic minority groups would do well to become acquainted.[25] The five stages of this model imply a progression toward bicultural identity.

In the *conformity stage* children and teens desire to be like their white peers at school or in the media. Like their assimilating immigrant counterparts, they prefer mainstream white culture, values, and friends. They tend to harbor negative feelings and beliefs about their own heritage and culture. Their experience in the general atmosphere of white superiority, aggravated by personal encounters with racist attitudes and behavior from peers and strangers, often leads to racial self-hatred. To make matters worse, "made in America" or "made in Canada" Pacific-Asian young people whose thinking and value system conform to the majority society's norms are often given derogatory labels by their own Asian community, labels such as *banana* (yellow outside, white inside) or *jook sing* (bamboo stalk which does not reach either end).

In the *dissonance stage*, a crisis such as a confrontation with racism brings about confusion, leading the person to question accepted values and

---

25. Derald Wing Sue and David Sue, *Counseling the Culturally Different: Theory and Practice* (New York: Wiley, 1981). See chapter 5, "Racial/Cultural Identity Development," pp. 93–117.

current experience. An older teen or young adult, for example, might start paying attention to questions about ethnic identity while dating a non-Asian or trying to establish a career or profession in the face of discrimination.

In the *immersion and resistance stage*, persons begin to react against or even reject Western culture and Western values, somersaulting into uncritical endorsement of their heritage culture and values. Cultural and ethnic recovery become prime concerns—heritage language and history, customs, social values, non-Western spiritual practices.

In the *introspection stage*, the person struggles between independence/ autonomy and loyalty/responsibility to one's family, ethnic group, and eth- nic church. Young adults begin to notice desirable elements in mainstream culture, but they are not sure how to integrate such elements into their own functioning and still retain their ethnocultural authenticity. There is at the same time a dawning consciousness of the problematic nature of some elements in one's own culture. The search for a viable racial-cultural identity continues.

In the *integrative and awareness stage*, the ability to encompass "both/ and" is satisfactorily developed, and there is an owning of both cultures in a workable way. Cultural values (including religious values) of the dominant society, the cultures of origin, and other minorities, are more objectively examined and evaluated. In time, the person attains a bicultural stance that is realistic and workable.

This neat progression of stages can be upset by certain immigration patterns of the late twentieth century. One is the phenomenon of the 1.5 gen- eration in the Korean community, those large numbers of persons who came from Korea as preteens or young teens with their middle-class families. Their Korean formation separates them from more assimilated second- and third-generation peers; their traumatic catapulting into dominant English- speaking society alienates them from older siblings, parents, and grandpar- ents, who accuse them of becoming too Western too fast. Theirs is therefore a historically unique struggle. Their needs are not only educational but also formational. They need support in achieving an identity that takes into account both the Asian and the Euro-Anglo dimensions of their existence, an identity that allows them to function as bicultural and indeed multicultural members of North American society.[26] The church can work with specific ethnocultural and linguistic communities to strengthen their Asian aspects, as well as to provide a safe space for questioning, searching, and struggling.

Although described here in personal terms, these stages of minority racial-ethnic identity development are not purely psychological. They are also societal in the sense that societal factors such as racist incidents can

---

26. For a poignant first-person account of a 1.5 generation young adult, see "Power to Name Ourselves," by Richard Chung-sik Choe, in *Generations Trying to Live Together*, ed. Greer Anne Wenh-In Ng (Toronto: United Church of Canada, 1995), pp. 16–17.

trigger some of the transitions from one stage or phase to another. As with the immigrant modes described earlier in this section, they provide an added and essential dimension to faith development theories in the religious life of Asian-Pacific Christians in North America.[27] With all three schemas (faith development, immigrant modes, and ethnocultural minority identity development), the effectiveness of a given educational endeavor also depends on the correlation of the stage or mode of the learner with that of the religious educator or teacher as they interact in the learning situation.

Generational and Gender Issues in Family and Church

Generational Issues: I have chosen the term *generational* rather than the more frequently used *intergenerational* to highlight the difference between the issues represented by the two terms. In mainstream religious education theory and practice of the 1980s and 1990s, intergenerational concerns focused on including children and youth in worship and advocating their active participation in the life of the congregation in such areas as access to the table, full membership via baptism, empowerment through sitting on committees, and the possibility of mutual learning at educational events where adults and children are both present.[28] Such issues are not uppermost in the minds of Pacific-Asian Christians. Their cultures have always included children as a matter of course in all community and church gatherings. Here the "faith community" or "enculturation" approach in religious education works well.[29] On the other hand, their traditions have

---

27. James W. Fowler, in *Stages of Faith: The Psychology of Human Development and the Quest for Meaning* (San Francisco: Harper & Row, 1980), proposed a six-stage theory prefaced by a pre-stage, or Stage 0 of undifferentiated faith. The six stages are stage 1, intuitive-projective faith (usually early childhood); stage 2, mythic-literal faith (elementary school years); stage 3, synthetic-conventional faith (mainly adolescent, but also many adults); stage 4, individuative-reflective faith, (young adulthood and adulthood); stage 5, conjunctive faith (mid-adulthood and older adult); and stage 6, universalizing faith. For another model, see V. Bailey Gillespie, *The Experience of Faith* (Birmingham, Ala.: Religious Education Press, 1988). Gillespie describes the growth of faith in seven life situations: the borrowed faith of early childhood, the reflected faith of middle childhood, the personalized faith of early adolescence, the established faith of later youth, the reordered faith of young adulthood, the reflective faith of middle adulthood, and the resolute faith of older adulthood (pp. 66–88).

28. For inclusion of children at worship, see *Children in the Worshipping Community*, by David Ng and Virginia Thomas (Philadelphia: John Knox, 1981). For empowering children to be full members of the congregation, see the United Church of Canada's task force report, *A Place for You* (Toronto: United Church of Canada, 1988). For a resource on generations learning together, see *Intergenerational Religious Education*, by James W. White (Birmingham, Ala.: Religious Education Press, 1988).

29. The "faith-community" or "enculturation" approach is one of five approaches to Christian education delineated by Jack Seymour and Donald Miller in their text,

always held that older persons are wiser: it would be unthinkable to suggest that adults could learn from youth or children. In addition, difference in heritage-language proficiency between first-generation adults and younger, English-speaking members will often render common religious educational events impracticable or even irrelevant or impossible.

Instead, in Pacific-Asian North American communities, generational issues tend to focus on tensions between immigrant first-generation parents/grandparents and their offspring, and between first-generation church leaders/members and younger, 1.5 or second and subsequent generation leaders and members. These tensions occur in addition to the usual generation gap, the testing of limits and assertion of independence and autonomy on the part of the young people, peer pressure, teen culture versus adult culture, and the like. Traditional values like respecting older and more senior adults often make it difficult for younger members to be heard, let alone be allowed to make suggestions and decisions on an equal footing. In such circumstances, a kind of reverse ageism takes place, with discrimination not against the old, but against the young. Generational tensions in these communities, therefore, are overlaid with a complex of meaning-making endeavors. There is obvious need for educating the older, as well as the younger, about these dynamics and realities. Given the strong bias of wisdom belonging more (or solely!) to older persons, however, the difficulty of making headway in this particular educational need will be one of the stiffest challenges of introducing adult religious education in Pacific-Asian North American churches. The fact that most volunteer religious educators and the rare trained religious educator tend to be years younger than the seniors among the target learners does not make matters any easier.[30]

Within the family, tensions around issues of authority and autonomy are aggravated in the extreme case of a traditionalist parent confronted by the autonomy needs of a teen son or daughter in the conforming stage. This is especially true of cultures heavily influenced by Confucian values, characterized by social requirements of hierarchically achieved harmony, i.e., Chinese, Korean, and Japanese cultures. Sometimes this plays out in the way a grandparent and a parent argue about how to bring up or discipline a grandchild. Another area of contention is the often unrealistic educational and career expectations of parents and grandparents.[31] A somewhat less

---

Contemporary Approaches to Christian Education (Nashville: Abingdon, 1981). See especially pp. 53–71. The other four approaches are the religious-instruction (or schooling) approach, the developmental approach, the liberation approach, and the interpretation approach.

30. Sang Hyun Lee discusses leadership relations in "Models of Ministry," chap. 5 of *Korean American Ministry*. See pp. 242–50.

31. For a first-person account, see "What's Bred in the Bone," by Una Chih-Hua Ng, in *Generations Trying to Live Together*, ed. Greer Anne Wenh-In-Ng, pp. 11–12. For

serious, but no less irritating, expectation is that teens and young adult children will as a matter of course accompany elders to dinners and gatherings of the extended family.[32] These tensions exist because opposing family members often stand at opposite or at least different places on the continuum between "high context" cultures and "low context" cultures whose members respond to realities about family belonging, individual-collective preferences, and even time perceptions, very differently.[33]

Depending on the particular immigrant mode and where individuals in a family stand in the continuum of minority racial-ethnic identity development, some tensions may not get resolved until the stages or modes of those concerned come closer together. Some tensions may never get resolved at all. A traditionalist grandfather may never accept his grandson's casual clothing styles, misuse of respectful forms of address to elders, and lack of interest in his ethnic heritage. Religious educators and pastors can do much to help alleviate self-blame and feelings of guilt or failure by raising the awareness of both senior and junior members engaged in a tug-of-war over the complications surrounding their relationship due to the added ethnocultural dimension. Cross-generational workshops in both English and the Asian language may help to educate both generations; mediation by 1.5 generation members, who understand both viewpoints, and role-play and similar opportunities for youth to explore their own feelings are also helpful. Religious education programs that work with families to deepen their understanding of these aspects can do much to promote harmonious coexistence.[34]

---

another discussion of the tensions between immigrant parents and their offspring, see Grace Sangok Kim's "Asian North American Youth and Their Immigrant Parents," in *People on the Way*, ed. David Ng, pp. 129–45.

32. For a screen presentation of the parental-authority versus daughter-autonomy theme, see the film *Double Happiness*, directed by Mina Shum (1994). For an example of differences in disciplining children, see the first session of David Ng, *Generations Trying to Live Together*, pp. 3–6. For a narrative-cum-analytical treatment of expectations in regard to family togetherness, see chapter 4, "Asian Sociocultural Values: Oppressive and Liberative Aspects from a Woman's Perspective," by Greer Anne Wenh-In Ng, in *People on the Way*, ed. David Ng, pp. 63–103.

33. See Dorothy Chave Herberg's excellent exposition of high and low context cultures as applied to North American groups in *Frameworks for Cultural and Racial Diversity: Teaching and Learning for Practitioners* (Toronto: Canadian Scholars Press, 1993), pp. 29–68.

34. Examples of programs dealing with these tensions can be found in Ellen Tanouye, *Learning Parenting Skills Together in an Asian American Context*, vols. 1-2 (Japanese Presbyterian Conference, 1991). Volume 1 includes sessions ranging from "Communicating with our Children," to "Celebrating Family Histories." Volume 2 includes a session on "Conflict Management." *Generations Trying to Live Together*, ed. Greer Anne Wenh-In Ng, contains four sessions ranging from disciplining young children in a three-generation household to one on the struggle between a 1.5-generation Korean

Within the faith community, tensions sometimes get expressed as conflict between the Asian-speaking first generation part of the congregation and the English-speaking, younger part. For Koreans, there is the added factor of the 1.5 generation. Conflict often arises from matters of church life. How legitimate are some 1.5 activities? To what extent should they use which part of the church building? How often should they employ their worship style rather than the traditional style? To what extent should they be involved in decision making that affects the whole congregation, not just themselves? Situations are often exacerbated by the differing approach and style of conflict management employed by the two camps. First generations prefer an Asian, i.e., behind-the-scenes, nonconfrontational, approach. They usually want to keep things "in the family." More Westernized younger generations tend to employ a more direct, face-to-face approach; they would also accept the mediation of a third party in the form of a consultant.[35] Learning about these different approaches is a crucial part of the religious education curriculum for Pacific-Asian North American churches and for anyone who works with them. A focus on religious education ministry with youth and young adults of 1.5 and subsequent generations, as a distinct but by no means second-rate ministry is urgently necessary, as Korean-American Presbyterians and others have realized.[36]

Gender Issues: Within the Pacific-Asian North American churches, gender issues are aggravated by the highly patriarchal nature of Asian society. Upon being transplanted to North American soil, such social norms can hardly remain untouched. For one thing, the host culture's greater degree of female participation in society, however far from ideal by Western standards, still appears far too "liberated" to Asian male eyes. Exposure to attitudes at school, the workplace, and in the media render it impossible

---

Canadian and his church community. Eric Law's *The Wolf Shall Dwell with the Lamb: A Spirituality for Leadership in a Multicultural Community* (St. Louis, Mo.: Chalice, 1993) may be applied to intergenerational situations, since older and younger generations virtually belong to different cultures.

35. For an introductory understanding of Asian ways of dealing with conflict and what it implies for conflict management in Pacific-Asian congregations in North America, see "Asian American Conflict Management," by Virstan B. Y. Choy, in *Yearbook of American and Canadian Churches, 1995* (Nashville: Abingdon, 1995), pp. 17–19. Also see the same author's excellent exposition based on case studies in chapter 12, "Conflict and Decision-Making in Congregations," in *People on the Way*, ed. David Ng.

36. The following chapters from *Korean American Ministry*, ed. Lee and Moore, speak pertinently to this concern: "Korean Youth Ministry: Second Generation," by David Hoon Jin Chai (pp. 138–51); "The 1.5 Generation," by Won Moo Hurh (pp. 215–32); and "Second Generation Ministry: Models of Mission," by Sang Hyun Lee with Ron Chu and Marion Park (pp. 233–55). Another helpful discussion is Grace Sangok Kim's chapter, "Asian North American Youth: a Ministry of Self-Identity and Pastoral Care," in *People on the Way*, ed. David Ng, pp. 201–27.

to keep Pacific-Asian women and girls secluded and obedient, as before. Combined with the generational factor, this issue provides fertile ground for struggle. By assisting members to acknowledge tensions and by providing a more neutral space away from the volatile atmosphere of the home to address contentious issues, the church can play a significant mediating and educative role.

One educational strategy is to examine the socialization of girls and the treatment women receive in the congregation or parish. The curriculum should include biblical stories of how women and girls participated in Israel's history and in the history of the early church, stories that bring out the importance of neglected female characters. Feminist biblical interpretations have brought many of these to light—Hagar, the first woman recorded in the Bible to receive both an epiphany and a birth announcement (Gen 16:11; 21:17–18), the courageous leadership roles of the Hebrew midwives Shiphrah and Puah in the salvation history of the Israelites (Ex 1:15–21), Deborah the judge (Judg 4, 5), Hulda the prophet (2 Kings 22:14–20), the parable of the woman with the lost coin (Lk 15:8–10), Priscilla as a contemporary and highly respected fellow minister with Paul (Acts 18:26; Rom 16:3–4), to mention the most obvious. Such an educational strategy needs to take seriously feminist interpretations of the Bible that help us develop a hermeneutics of suspicion regarding traditional exegesis and interpretation of key passages sometimes used to oppress women. One obvious instance is taking the injunction in Ephesians for wives to be subject to their husbands (Eph 5:22–24) out of context without prefacing it with the injunction in verse 21 to "be subject to one another out of reverence for Christ" and without following it up with the exhortation for husbands to love their wives as Christ loves the church (Eph 5:25–33). Another instance is citing 1 Timothy 2:11–12, "Let a woman learn in silence. . . . I permit no woman to teach or have authority over a man" to keep women from preaching or exercising leadership, while ignoring such historical facts as a long tradition of women prophets in first-century Corinth.[37]

Another educational strategy is encouraging the use of a variety of images for God and using inclusive language in prayers and hymns. The fact that there is no gender difference in the third-person singular in the Chinese, Korean, and Japanese languages should not be used as an excuse not to pay attention to inclusive images and inclusive ways of addressing God.[38]

---

37. For a fascinating study on this topic, see Antoinette Wire's volume, *The Corinthian Women Prophets* (Louisville, Ky.: Westminster/John Knox, 1991), the premise of which is that Paul's Corinthian "opponents" were spirit-filled women prophets in that pioneering Christian community.

38. For discussion of these points in more detail, see Greer Anne Wenh-In Ng, "Inclusive Language in Asian North American Churches: Non-Issue or Null Curriculum?" in *Journal of Asian and Asian American Theology* 1:2 (1996): 21–37.

It is also important to provide alternative role models by making it possible for women to take on nontraditional leadership roles such as being elected as elders and serving on the church board or parish council (roles that are well established in some Pacific-Asian North American churches, but not in others), by occasionally inviting ordained women clergy to preach, and by encouraging women in the congregation to enter seminary with a view toward ordination.[39] The thinking and writing of women of color who are theologians can also encourage Pacific-Asian North American women in naming their own voices and working out their own theological reflection.[40]

Theological/Biblical Reflection and Spiritual Practice

While most missionary-educated Pacific Asian-American Christians tend to follow what they perceive as orthodox belief and personal spirituality, they have initiated, in the last quarter of the twentieth century, a movement that appropriates some of the distinctly Asian modes of spirituality and does theology in a way that takes seriously the context of Pacific-Asian experience in North America. Asian and Asian-American theologians such as Kosuke Koyama (*Water Buffalo Theology*), C. S. Song (*Theology from the Womb of Asia*), Kwok Pui Lan (*Discovering the Bible in the Non-Biblical World*), Chung Hyun Kyung (*Struggle to the Sun Again*), Roy Sano (*Pacific Asian American Theologies*), and Paul Nagano (*Asian American Theology: Multicultural Communities*) are paving the way for doing theology from this perspective. The publication *Journal of Asian and Asian American Theology* (founded in 1994) provides both a distinctly North American perspective and the kind of contextualization that has been missing from the excellent resources coming out of Asia.[41] Religious educators working with Pacific-Asian North American Christians can introduce both themselves and their

---

39. For an extended discussion on this topic, see "Toward Wholesome Nurture: Challenges in the Religious Education of Asian North American Female Christians," by Greer Anne Wenh-In Ng, *Religious Education* 91 (spring 1996): 238–54.

40. A suggested resource is *Sisters Struggling in the Spirit: A Women of Color Theological Anthology*, ed. N. B. Lewis, L. Hernandez, H. Lockyear, R. M. Wimbush (Louisville, Ky.: Presbyterian Church [U.S.A.], 1994).

41. This journal may be subscribed to by contacting Sung Do Kang, managing editor, *Journal of Asian and Asian American Theology*, Center for Pacific Asian-American Ministries, School of Theology at Claremont, 1325 North College Ave., Claremont, CA 91711-3199. Theologies written from a Pacific-Asian perspective: Kosuke Koyama, *Waterbuffalo Theology* (London: SCM), 1974: C. S. Song, *Theology from the Womb of Asia* (Maryknoll, N.Y.: Orbis), 1986; Chung Hymn Kyung, *Struggle to Be the Sun Again: Introducing Asian Women's Theology* (Maryknoll, N.Y.: Orbis), 1991; Kwok Pui Lan, *Discovering the Bible in the Non-Biblical World* (Maryknoll, N.Y.: Orbis), 1995; Roy Sano, comp., *The Theologies of Asian American and Pacific Peoples: A Reader* (Berkeley, Calif.: Asian Center for Theology and Strategies, Pacific School of Religion), 1976; Paul M. Nagano, *Asian American Theology and Multicultural Communities:*

learners to these theological discoveries for more relevant ways of thinking about God and God's ways with humanity and the world.

Interpreting Scripture from an Asian-North American perspective is an integral part of the attempt to construct what are called "local theologies."[42] It is encouraging to note that an early attempt in this direction came from religious educators, rather than biblical scholars, in the form of the curriculum resource *Sojourners in Biblical and Asian American History*, which was followed by two sets of curriculum of five volumes each covering ages kindergarten through adult. *Choosing Sides*, a study of the life and ministry of four protagonists from the book of Judges using the latest biblical scholarship, relates the situation of the early Israelite confederation of oppressed tribes to the situation of Asians in North America. *One in Christ*, a study on the letter to the Galatians, compares the unquestioned demand for Asian Christians to become Westernized to the demand for early Gentile converts to be circumcised. An "indigenous" feature of both sets is the inclusion of stories, poetry, and artwork by Asian-American Christians of all ages, thus giving voice to and validating their experience, empowering these Christians to make theological sense out of their pain and struggle.[43] On the other hand, resources such as *Tabi: Journey through Time, Stories of the Japanese in America*, and *Tayo Na: Let Us Go*, begin from the experience of specific groups of Asian-Pacific Americans to reach back to Scripture to illuminate their struggle, much as Latin American base Christian communities resort to the Bible to comment on the "text" of their lives.[44]

A dimension of Asian-North American theological reflection and biblical interpretation that religious educators need to consider carefully is making room for the experience and perspectives of girls and women. Christian

Redirecting the Ministries of the Church into the Life of the Community (San Pablo, Calif.: n.p., 1992).

42. Robert Schreiter's book *Constructing Local Theologies* (Maryknoll, N.Y.: Orbis, 1985) is the classic volume on contextualizing theologies equally applicable to former mission fields such as Africa, Asia, and South America, and the local contexts of North America.

43. A product of the Asian-American Christian Education Curriculum Project, unfortunately no longer available, this set of five books from kindergarten/grade 2 to college/adult was published jointly by the Office of Ethnic and Urban Church Affairs and the Office of Education, Golden Gate Mission Area of the Synod of the Pacific, United Presbyterian Church (U.S.A.).

44. Yoshiko Uchida, *Tabi: Journey through Time: Stories of the Japanese in America* (Nashville: Graded Press, 1980), offered both as a student book and as a teacher's book, contains four units of three sessions each. Fe R. Nebres, *Tayo Na: Let Us Go* (New York: United Church Press, 1988), was developed by the multicultural curriculum resources of the Hawaii Conference, United Church of Christ, to promote multicultural awareness in church schools. It contains in three units of four sessions each of the experiences and faith stories of Filipino/a-American Christians.

women in Asia have made an excellent beginning in this work (for instance, through the magazine *In God's Image* and books such as *Reading the Bible as Asian Women, We Dare to Dream: Doing Theology as Asian Women, Struggle to Be the Sun Again, Women of Courage: Asian Women Reading the Bible*, and others).[45] Biblical interpretive work in the North American context needs to be further encouraged. However, it is possible that much more is being done than has either been recorded or published. This would be especially true of Bible studies conducted at denomination caucus meetings, church gatherings, and denominational and ecumenical conferences.[46] A strategy worth trying is to start exchanging Bible study designs of this category either electronically or through newsletters such as that produced by PAACCE. Such a strategy could also make use of the resources already produced by ethnic minority theologians and biblical scholars in North America.[47]

Concomitant with the contextualizing trend, members of the Pacific-Asian Christian communities in North America began to discover (or, more accurately, to give themselves permission to acknowledge) how their Asian religious collective consciousness continues to color their mode of spiritual practice. Faced with the more manifestly multifaith nature of North American society in the twenty-first century, Asian Christians

---

45. *In God's Image* is published four times a year by Asian Women's Resource Centre for Culture and Theology, Sun Ai Lee Park and Chung Hyun Kyung, eds. Address: Cheonji, 181-7 Inheon-Dong 2-Ga, Dhun-Gu, Seoul, Korea. Telephone: 82-2-263-3168. *Reading the Bible as Asian Women: Twelve Bible Studies on Mobilizing Women in Struggle for Food, Justice, and Freedom* (Singapore: Christian Conference of Asia [Women's Concerns Unit], 1986); Virginia Fabella and SunAi Lee Park, eds., *We Dare to Dream: Doing Theology as Asian Women* (Hong Kong: Asian Women' Resource Centre for Culture and Theology; Manila: Women's Commission in Asia, Ecumenical Association of Third World Theologians [EATWOT] 1989); Chung Hymn Kyung, *Struggle to Be the Sun Again: Introducing Asian Women's Theology* (Maryknoll, N.Y.: Orbis, 1991). Lee Oo Chung, Choi Man Ja, Sun Ai Lee-Park, Kim Elli, Mirza Rodriquez, Debra Goodsir, eds., *Women of Courage: Asian Women Reading the Bible* (Seoul, Korea: Asian Women's Resource Centre for Culture and Theology, 1992).

46. A small sampling of Bible studies from an Asian or minority perspective conducted in the early 1990s includes the following: a study on Hagar by Kay Cho and Greer Anne Wenh-In Ng that was presented at the United Church of Canada's Ethnic Ministries Convention in Montreal in June 1992; on Orpah by Leonida Baybay at the United Church of Canada's National Consultation of Women in Halifax, Nova Scotia, October 1993; on Deborah and Jael, Vashti and Esther, by Greer Anne Wenh-In Ng at the Chinese Presbyterian Church in Oakland, Calif., spring 1994. The design for the Vashti and Esther study is included as a resource in *People on the Way*, ed. David Ng.

47. Two of these are *Out of Every Tribe and Nation: Christian Theology at the Ethnic Roundtable*, ed. Justo Gonzalez (Nashville: Abingdon, 1992), and *Coming Together: The Bible's Message in an Age of Diversity*, by Curtiss Paul DeYoung (Valley Forge, Pa.: Judson, 1995).

may find themselves in situations where their acquaintance with Eastern religions is assumed by others. In order to help both themselves and others develop a more holistic approach to the practice of spirituality, they first need to explore the Eastern dimensions of their own spirituality, which their cultures have already embedded in them. Such a phenomenon has been called variously "interreligious dialogue within the self," "dual religious belonging," and "multiple religious participation." Korean theologian Chun Hyun Kyung writes that her Christian mother created a peace between her faith and certain Confucian practices. She participated comfortably in ancestral memorial observances and the celebration of Buddha's birthday. Kwok Pui Lan, a theologian from Hong Kong, advocates using Asian life experiences and art forms like myths, lullabies, proverbs, and poetry as resources for doing theology.[48] Eastern cultural influence is a dimension in the religious and spiritual nurture of Pacific-Asian North American Christians that finally needs to be acknowledged and attended to.

Racism Issues: Justice, Discipleship, and Citizenship

Pacific-Asian Christians in North America have always had to face racism in one form or another, as Fumitaka Masuoka's study on emerging themes in Asian-American churches has proved.[49] From the nineteenth to the mid-twentieth century, racist legislation persisted, as in the Exclusion Act against the Chinese between 1923 and 1946, the Orders in Council decreeing the internment of Japanese Canadians during World War II in Canada, and the prohibition against property ownership and the relocation of residents and citizens of Japanese origin in the United States. After the civil rights movement in the United States won certain basic rights for racial ethnic minority groups, racism against Asians has been expressed more subtly in the form of the "glass ceiling," reluctance to sell or rent houses to individuals and families of Asian origin, and similar acts of discrimination.

Although mainline denominations have from time to time developed programs on antiracism education, they have not focused on the special brand of racism endured by Asians. Action was not taken until anti-Asian racism manifested itself in more violent forms, for example, the murder of Vincent

---

48. See discussion in Greer Anne Wenh-In Ng's "Toward Wholesome Nurture," *Religious Education* 91 (spring 1996): 244–45, and "The Asian North American Community at Worship," chap. 7 in *People on the Way*, ed. David Ng, pp. 147–75.

49. Fumitaka Masuoka, *Out of Silence: Emerging Themes in Asian American Churches* (Cleveland, Ohio: United Church Press, 1995). Masuoka traces the racially discriminatory treatment experienced by Asian-American Christians and churches, but ends on a challenging note. See especially chapter 3, "A Stone That Cries Out: An Alternative Understanding of Community Amidst a Racist Society," pp. 85–120.

Chin by Detroit auto workers who had been laid off because of Japanese car imports. Chin, a Chinese American, was thought by the autoworkers to be Japanese. In 1989 a group of concerned Asian American/Canadian denominational staff persons formed the Ecumenical Working Group of Asian Pacific Americans (EWGAPA), joining forces with secular agencies to engage more intentionally in educational and advocacy work with an antiracism focus, including the production of some excellent program resources.[50]

Confronting racist attitudes and behavior in work, school, and denominational spaces is something Asian Christians, taught as they are not to stir up trouble by resisting or protesting, must learn to do better. That racism has not been a part of the explicit curriculum of Asian congregations in North America may be due both to a cultural characteristic of trying to live in harmony with others and to a presumed concern for good citizenship. The last thing recent immigrants want to be accused of is being ungrateful to the host country. Consequently, it has instead become part of their "null curriculum." By omitting discussion of racist incidents, this curriculum teaches that they are not relevant to religious education and should be tolerated. Religious educators and church leaders whose consciousness has been raised must make up for this neglect, both by involving their congregations in any denominational or ecumenical effort in antiracism education and by offering themselves as a resource to deal with overt or covert racist incidents happening in their communities. Religious educators, learners, and other church members need to be empowered to acknowledge this harsh reality of their North American life. They must come to see that resistance and advocacy around this issue are consonant with the practice of faithful discipleship and good citizenship. Church groups offer a safe place for youth and adults to explore issues of racism through activities like discussion, role-play, and simulation games.[51] Such efforts can be reinforced by doing theology from an Asian-North American perspective that emphasizes a God who liberates the oppressed to provide a sound theological and Scriptural base for a church ministry of advocacy and resistance.

---

50. These are *"It's Just Not Fair!" Racially Motivated Violence against Asians in the U. S.,* by Wallace Ryan Kuriowa [study guide by Victoria Lee Moy] (New York: Ecumenical Working Group of Asian Pacific Americans, 1989) and *Beyond the Crucible: Responses to Anti-Asian Hatred*, by Brenda Paik Sunoo (New York: Ecumenical Working Group of Asian Pacific Americans and Canadians, 1994). The Evangelical Lutheran Church of America has produced *No Hate Allowed: A Resource for Congregations for Action against Racial Hate Crimes* (Chicago: Commission in Multicultural Ministries, Evangelical Lutheran Church of America, 1995).

51. Examples of these activities are included in Donald Ng, ed., *Asian Pacific American Youth Ministry* (Valley Forge, Pa.: Judson, 1988), pp. 113–21.

DOING RELIGIOUS EDUCATION IN
PACIFIC-ASIAN NORTH AMERICAN CHURCHES

Given the above histories, contexts, and issues that face Pacific-Asian American/Canadian churches, what factors do religious educators need to consider as they go about their teaching-learning enterprise in these faith communities? This section considers some of the nitty-gritty elements of doing religious education in these congregations to offer some signposts or guidelines. It looks briefly at possible *subject matter* to be covered that is specific for these churches, along with the range of *instructional practice* likely to be most effective, the religious education *approaches* deemed appropriate, the *contexts and settings* in which such practice takes place, and the *leadership development and resources* needed to engage effectively in Pacific-Asian North American religious education.

Subject Matter

As with all Christian faith communities, a central responsibility of the Pacific-Asian North American church is the formation and nurturing of members in the Christian tradition and Christian discipleship. Christians of Euro-Anglo descent have a cultural identity that is formed and affirmed without extra effort, since it coincides with that of North American society in general. But Asian Christian communities need to give specific attention to the formation, affirmation, and development of their members' ethnocultural identity, especially that of their younger members. In addition to telling the biblical story, they must immerse members in liturgies and symbols of the Christian faith, grounding them in the doctrines, beliefs, and lifestyles of the Christian church. Religious education in these churches also needs to tell ancestral stories/legends and the community's immigration and settlement history and celebrate the ancestral culture's festivals with their distinctive symbols. In this way, the church can support and supplement the efforts of families at socializing younger members into the customs, values, and ethos of their particular heritage culture (what Tillich calls "inducting education"[52]), thus nurturing both the Asian and the Christian dimensions of their members' being.

The church can become a place for first-generation immigrants to address their questions about how far to acculturate or assimilate. The church can provide space, community, and programming for second and later generations to learn about and recover the culture of their ancestors. A contemporary example is the Sansei Legacy Project initiated by Buena Vista United

---

52. Paul Tillich, *Theology and Culture* (New York: Oxford University Press, 1959), p. 147.

Methodist Church in Alameda, California, which undertook to address the sansei's identity concerns through open dialog across generational lines concerning the internment camp experience. The project aims to provide a forum whereby the wounds of past experiences can be understood and interpreted for the sake of the future of Japanese Americans as a people.[53] Both these efforts will entail at least some study of the immigration history of the Asian communities in North America, making use of a resource such as Ronald Takaki's *A Different Mirror*,[54] if not also some knowledge of their ancestral nation in Asia.

To tend to the "education" dimension as distinct from the "formation" dimension of religious education, planned programs may be offered to raise consciousness around the issues discussed earlier in this chapter— issues of generational and gender dynamics in family and church, issues of racism, issues of theological reflection, biblical interpretation, and spiritual practice—taking "Asianness" and Asian perspectives into account. Assisting parishes, congregations, groups, and individuals to identify emerging issues, to analyze them, and to plan ministry action in faithful response becomes an important task of religious educators, pastors and church leaders. At times some of these responses may take the shape of educating toward new directions in pastoral care and counseling (in, for example, interracial and interfaith marriages).[55] At other times, it may mean educating in prophetic resistance or political advocacy. Surfacing areas of hitherto "null curriculum"—confronting racism in society, attacking sexism and reverse ageism in the church, and other justice issues—is not easy. Yet not to touch such sensitive issues means continuing to ignore significant hurdles in Christian maturity and Christian discipleship.

Instructional Practice

High on the list for instructional practice is cultural and contextual appropriateness for the learning groups in Asian-American churches. Religious educators need to become aware of distinctive Asian educational philosophies, styles of learning and teaching, and other factors leading to educational strategies and teaching methodologies different from the

---

53. Masuoka, *Out of Silence*, p. 69. See pp. 69–73 for how third-generation Japanese-Americans found that their parents' and the niseis' silence about those experiences prevented the sansei from addressing the "Japanese part" of themselves.

54. Ronald T. Takaki, *A Different Mirror: A History of Multicultural America* (Boston: Little, Brown, 1993).

55. A useful reference work on this topic is *Racially Mixed People in America*, Maria P. P. Root, ed. (London: Sage, 1992). Two curriculum resources are *Tales of Interracial Marriage*, ed. Greer Anne Wenh-In Ng (Toronto: United Church of Canada, 1993) and *Stories of Interfaith Families*, ed. Freya Godard (Toronto: United Church of Canada, 1994).

dominant culture's. This is especially true for first-generation or immigrant-generation members. One example is the lifelong hierarchical relationship between teacher and student, and the respect for external authority that exist in both Confucian cultures (Chinese, Korean, Japanese, Vietnamese of Chinese ethnicity) and indigenous Pacific cultures. The teacher is seen as master or mentor with "ascribed" (who she or he is) as well as "achieved" authority (what he or she knows), someone who should know more about the subject and be in a position to guide the student. This attitude leads to extreme deference and respect, which is demonstrated in, for example, never addressing the teacher by first name and accepting and expecting a didactic mode of teaching over against the inquiry mode set in place by John Dewey.[56] Such practice preferences greatly facilitate the transmission of a body of knowledge, values, and behaviors in cases where Christian tradition and values are "learned." But these may not be the preferences of 1.5 or second and subsequent, more acculturated, generations, who are more used to experiential learning, small-group discussion, and sharing their perspectives and opinions, even when they contradict the ones held by their teachers and leaders. This contrast shows up most starkly in group Bible study, where first- or immigrant-generation members expect the leader or teacher to do all the exegetical and interpretative work ahead of time and then deliver the results, while second- and subsequent-generation members expect active participation, opportunity to ask questions, and involvement in searching for clues and answers. Adult religious education practice, therefore, should not be transferred wholesale, but must be appropriately employed or introduced, depending on the generational makeup of the group. Caution must be employed in the use of bodily senses among adults of mixed generations, especially in dramatization and physical touching, since perceptions of what is appropriate behavior will differ. Special challenges also arise in approaches that image the Christian life as a journey and expect teachers and learners to share faith questions and clues together without respect to age or status. This will become clear when the "faith community" approach to religious education is discussed below.

An expectation inherited from centuries of religious teachings in Asia is that any teacher of religion will be a person of high moral integrity and deep spirituality. This may place an unfamiliar demand on church professionals who have been influenced by the "technical expert" model.[57] In all cultures any significant perceived moral shortcoming or any inability to integrate espoused beliefs or convictions with practice tends to lessen the teacher's effectiveness. But, this phenomenon seems to be more pronounced

---

56. See Robert J. Radcliffe's "Confucius and John Dewey," *Religious Education* 84 (spring 1989): 215–31.

57. For a fuller discussion of this point, see Victoria Urubshrurow's "Tibetan Buddhist Pointers on Religious Education," *Religious Education* 89 (spring 1989): 201–14.

in Pacific-Asian cultures, and it continues to be so among these cultures in North America.

Difference of expectations between more traditional and more assimilated or Westernized members, even in the same church, also applies to the adoption of specific learning activities. Where storytelling might work well with some, formal classes in a more transmissive style may be expected by others, and indeed may work more effectively.[58] One aspect of teacher/leader training in these congregations may be to learn about these differences and to be clear about which target group needs which teaching style and approach, remembering that with very young children parental expectation and practice would have socialized these children into a similar style and attitude.

Approaches and Structures

To what extent are five contemporary approaches to Christian Education relevant or helpful to these churches? In what relation do structures and approaches stand to one another, and is there any approach unique to such faith communities? The five approaches, slightly modified from Seymour and Miller's volume, *Contemporary Approaches to Christian Education*, include religious instruction, faith community, spiritual development, liberation, and interpretation.[59]

The traditional "religious schooling" approach to religious instruction may be effective in churches with a significant proportion of recent immigrants because of the high esteem in which immigrants hold formal education and schooling. Parents in these churches will not only expect this approach for themselves—for instance, Bible study classes, new membership classes, or classes to prepare parents and sponsors for infant and child baptism—but also for their offspring in their first few years. The Sunday school or parish religion class remains very much the expected and approved paradigm, as does the use of catechisms. In this connection, the question might arise as to the appropriateness of a contemporary, adult-education-centered approach such as that employed by the Catholic religious education program Religious Christian Initiation of Adults (RCIA). Religious educators need to consider what modifications might be needed for such a program to be successful with recent immigrants from Pacific-Asian regions, both from a pedagogical and from a culture-specific point of view.

---

58. See David Ng's "Sojourners Bearing Gifts," pp. 16–23, for an excellent discussion of this topic, as well as suggestions for developing Pacific Asian-American Christian education.

59. These approaches are described and analyzed in *Contemporary Approaches to Christian Education*, ed. Jack Seymour and Donald Miller (Nashville: Abingdon, 1980). See especially pp. 11–34.

In contrast to the "schooling" approach to religious instruction, the "faith community," or "enculturation," approach utilizes all expressions of congregational life—celebrations of their corporate past and identity, liturgy, rituals, and rites of passage—as occasions for education and faith nurture.[60] Such an approach should work well for Pacific Asian-American churches, since the desire for and actual practice of enculturating younger members into a specific ethnocultural community would give parents and church leaders an affinity for, an understanding of, and practice in the skills of socialization or enculturation into Christian tradition as well. After all, "high context" cultures such as those from Asia and the Pacific already place stronger emphasis on communal life and loyalty.[61] Such an approach breaks down, however, when intergenerational learning, as well as worship and social life, are expected to take place. The prevailing attitudes toward hierarchy, authority, reverse ageism, and the teacher-learner relationship all conspire to make parents, grandparents, and teachers resistant to the idea that they have anything to learn from those younger, those less qualified, or those occupying positions lower than theirs. Even where openness to such an approach exists, the same weaknesses facing mainstream churches using this approach apply: the problem of how to ensure the faithfulness of that parish or congregation and the problem of how such an approach would be undercut if younger or middle-age members did not show up at gatherings of the community.

The "spiritual development" or "faith development" approach, which utilizes structural developmental models mainly from psychology, needs to be assessed from a cross-cultural perspective for it to be culturally appropriate.[62] Structural developmental models devised mostly in European-American cultures, such as Erikson's eight psychosocial ages, Fowler's faith development stages, and Gillespie's faith situations, need to be accompanied or modified by the inclusion of the racial-cultural identity development considerations that are very much a part of the psyche of Pacific-Asian North American Christians. In the spiritual development

---

60. Proponents of this approach include John H. Westerhoff, *Will Our Children Have Faith?* (New York: Seabury, 1974); C. Ellis Nelson, *Where Faith Begins* (Richmond, Va.: John Knox, 1974); Charles R. Foster, *Educating Congregations: The Future of Christian Education* (Nashville: Abingdon, 1994); Maria Harris, *Fashion Me a People: Curriculum in the Church* (Mahwah, N.J.: Paulist, 1989).

61. "Contexting" as a way of analyzing social values in cultures was introduced by anthropologist Edward Hall in *The Silent Language* (New York: Doubleday, 1959) and was further developed by Dorothy Chave Herberg in *Frameworks for Cultural and Racial Diversity: Teaching and Learning for Practitioners* (Toronto: Canadian Scholar's Press, 1993), pp. 29–68.

62. For a succinct summary of the findings of Randall Furishima's substantial study on this question, see his article "Faith Development in a Cross Cultural Perspective," *Religious Education* 80 (summer 1982): 447–67.

approach, the teacher or leader is a spiritual guide. The relation between mentor/guides and learners is complicated by the stages of their respective racial-cultural identity development. If that is taken seriously, however, such mentoring or guiding may yield significant dividends, with clearer understanding as to where each is "coming from" and therefore fewer unrealistic expectations placed on either the mentor/guide or the learner. This complex of dynamics helps explain why it may be more practical (as well as more peace producing) for second-generation, English-speaking members to worship and even function as a separate congregation rather than remain an integral part of their immigrant parents' congregation.

The "liberation" approach should be highly effective for Pacific-Asian North American faith communities and groups aware of their marginalized status, either in their denomination or in society at large. It can be effective as well in dealing with racism and other justice issues as a way of working for ecclesial and social transformation. It can provide internally marginalized segments such as women and youth the means to deal with sexism and reverse ageism within congregations or parishes and to work for social and cultural transformation in their particular faith and ethnic communities. It would not be a feasible approach for churches that do not want to disturb the status quo.[63]

The "interpretation" approach, like Groome's "shared praxis,"[64] requires naming the learners' present social minority realities and their marginalized histories, plus engaging the biblical story from a Pacific-Asian North American perspective so as to yield faith insights that emerge out of that dialectic. Where there is lack of awareness of minority realities and resistance to or lack of practice in engaging the story, the potential of this approach for Pacific-Asian North Americans will be greatly impaired. This shared praxis approach is most effective when it undergirds not just the educational endeavors of a congregation but also its pastoral care, liturgical, and other ministry practice.[65]

It appears, therefore, that each approach is potentially useful if a specifically Asian-Pacific dimension is intentionally employed, and if religious educators are cognizant of what factors render an approach incomplete or problematic. To achieve this, a redeveloped, integrative approach with

---

63. For further insights, see *Religious Education Encounters Liberation Theology*, by Daniel S. Schipani (Birmingham, Ala.: Religious Education Press, 1988), especially pp. 9–64; 228–35.

64. Thomas H. Groome, *Christian Religious Education* (San Francisco: Harper & Row, 1980), pp. 184–206.

65. In *Sharing Faith: A Shared Praxis Approach to Christian Religious Education* (San Francisco: HarperSanFrancisco, 1991). Thomas Groome provides both food for thought and practical hints on how to do this.

diverse facets for specific generations and developmental phases could be worked out by using an ethnocultural lens as an overall framework.

Contexts and Settings

Contexts for religious education in Pacific-Asian North American churches will depend to a large extent on the particular approach or combination of approaches used. As a rule, a classroom setting is expected when religious education is following curriculum resources for age-specific groups. But there are numerous family-oriented occasions that even grown children and married children and their families are expected to attend—extended family celebrations over milestones such as births ("full moon" dinners) and deaths, weddings, sixtieth and other significant birthdays for senior members, and the like. Religious as well as cultural socialization can happen when members participate in their ethnocultural festivals within or outside their churches. Intentional learning can take place when these festivals are reflected upon in community in terms of their place and relationship to Christian festivals, liturgy, or faith practice.

The religious educational role of the pastor, priest, or minister takes on a particular character in Pacific-Asian North American churches. The teaching aspect of the pastor's ministry is highlighted in Chinese and Korean because the term for *pastor* is made up of the written characters for *shepherd* and *teacher*. As a result, the teaching role of clergy is ingrained, and Asian pastors are expected to be heavily involved in their congregation's educational ministry, more than their Caucasian counterparts. Consequently, Pacific-Asian North American congregations employ coordinators or ministers of religious education only rarely, although many do have assistant ministers for English-speaking youth ministry.[66]

Although many Pacific-Asian American and Canadian congregations are Roman Catholic or belong to identifiable Protestant denominations,

---

66. Discussing the role of the pastor, Sun Bai Kim comments that he finds the Korean immigrant churches too clergy centered. He encourages Korean-American churches to change the "minister-dependent" pattern to an "every-member-participant" pattern in which teaching is the responsibility of both ministers and laity. See "The Ministry of the Laity," in *Korean American Ministry*, ed. Lee and Moore, pp. 75–84. Also on the pastor's role in religious education, see Charles R. Foster, "The Pastor: Agent of Vision in the Education of a Community of Faith," in *The Pastor as Religious Educator*, ed. Robert L. Browning (Birmingham, Ala.: Religious Education Press, 1989), pp. 22–32. Other excellent resources include *A Teachable Spirit: Recovering the Teaching Office in the Church*, by Richard O. Osmer (Louisville, Ky.: Westminster/John Knox, 1991) and "Pastors as Teachers," by William H. Willimon, in *Rethinking Christian Education: Explorations in Theory and Practice*, ed. David S. Schuller (St. Louis, Mo.: Chalice, 1993), pp. 47–56.

there are also many independent congregations, both large and small. Denominational hierarchies and staff need to understand that denominational identity is only one of the many ways (and often not a highly significant way) in which Christians whose ethnicity is the primary constituent of their identity experience a sense of belonging. Nevertheless, "one of a kind" Asian churches in a particular diocese or presbytery may find that as a matter of sanity (if not survival) they need to connect and act together with similar ethnic faith communities in spite of different denominational labels, which, after all, are often residues of colonial and overseas missionary expansion and a repetition of those historical spheres of power in North America. We have seen how this acting together has already happened in the establishment of movements and organizations such as PACTS and PAACCE. Christian churches in China have led the way into a postdenominational church, not, as K. H. Ting observes, because they feel superior to others, but because the churches exist in a particular historic situation.[67] A situation demanding self-government, self-support, and self-propagation developed when foreign missionaries were expelled and foreign denominational aid was lost under the People's Republic. This situation was exacerbated during the ten catastrophic years of the Cultural Revolution (1966–76). Perhaps, out of the realities of their current situation, Asian-Pacific congregations in North America will also signal more cross-denominational functioning for religious education in the future.

Resources and Leadership Development

Pacific-Asian churches face some unique issues, which occasionally call for specific resources, including church school curricula and other materials such as Bible study designs, gender-awareness workshops, and contextualized liturgies and music.[68] Translations of denominational or ecumenical resources produced for mainstream consumption without contextualizing are often not helpful except in cases of basic information for new members or professional ministry personnel. The following questions need to be asked of mainstream resources, even those with inclusive stories and graphics:

---

67. K. H. Ting, "Fourteen Points from Christians in the People's Republic of China to Christians Abroad," in *A New Beginning: An International Dialogue with the Chinese Church*, ed. Theresa Chu and Christopher Lind (Toronto: Canada-China Program of the Canadian Council of Churches, 1981), p. 113. See especially point 6, "The Unity of the Chinese Church," pp. 112–13.

68. For a listing of some educational resources, see "Church School Curricular and Other Congregational Resources" in the appendix, "Resources for Pacific Asian-American Religious Education."

- Do we use the resource as is? If so, do we need to make it bilingual? This is often the case with official documents, liturgies, and hymns of a denomination.
- Do we adapt or modify existing religious resources to make them culturally and pedagogically more appropriate?
- Do we create religious education supplements to provide the necessary contextualization and to address those issues missing from mainstream materials? Such adapting, supplementing, and producing require financial commitments as well as special training for writers and editors. How committed is our denomination to providing some of these? If the commitment is low, what are our alternative sources of funding?
- Do religious educators employ an alternative strategy such as making use of day-to-day general (read *secular*) resources that deal with relevant issues and can be used for both theological reflection and lifestyle choices? How can we best make use of existing general resources in this category with Asian and Asian North American content or focus, such as newspaper items pertaining to Asians in North America or plays and novels dealing with their concerns and questions, to relate life situations to faith issues?

To try any of the above strategies requires strong support for leadership development. When recruiting leaders and teachers, it is important to be aware of cultural factors such as age seniority and kinship expectations, leadership styles, and styles of conflict management between recruiter and recruitee, especially if one of them does not belong to a Pacific-Asian ethnic group or another racial-ethnic minority group. These factors can become part of awareness raising during in-service training events. Decisions also need to be made about whether or not to provide interpretation services for Asian-language-speaking leaders, especially if the event is a denominationally sponsored one offered in English only. To what extent minority participants are involved in the denomination's committee work and in the planning of training events is well worth monitoring. Much empowering and educating of adult church leaders can happen while they serve national, regional, or local committees and task forces. Participating in cross-denominational ethnic caucuses can be one educationally effective and cost-effective way of providing such lay leadership training. Because females still labor under secondary status among the laity in Pacific-Asian North American churches, special efforts are required to develop the leadership potential of girls and women.[69]

---

69. For the issues surrounding Asian women's leadership, see chapter 5, "Asian North American Women in the Workplace and the Church," by Young Lee Hertig, in *People on the Way*, ed. David Ng, pp. 105–27. For a more detailed discussion concerning the nurturing of women and girls for leadership, see "Culture, Theology, and Leadership," by

LOOKING AHEAD: RELIGIOUS EDUCATION AND PACIFIC-ASIAN NORTH AMERICAN CHURCHES IN THE TWENTY-FIRST CENTURY

As the twenty-first century unfolds, what are the prospects for religious education in Pacific-Asian North American congregations? This section begins by looking at several realities of these churches in general.

Sojourners No Longer: A Response to "Won't the Asian Church Disappear?"

One of the questions most frequently asked of Pacific-Asian American or Canadian Christians by mainstream church leaders is, Do you see the Asian church continuing in the future, or do you see it merging into mainstream congregations as more and more younger English-speaking members replace heritage-language-speaking first-generation members? Behind the question is an assumption that ethnic congregations are "bridge" communities, communities in transition, making this state of affairs temporary and somehow not normal. This in turn assumes that language and culture make up the chief incentive to forming distinct parishes or congregations. The question also assumes that English-speaking Asian-American/Canadian Christians who are more or less acculturated to Euro-Anglo cultures will naturally feel at home in mainstream congregations. And it assumes that mainstream congregations will welcome Pacific-Asian North American Christians into their midst without much trouble, nay, even eagerly. If these assumptions were correct, a major task of religious education in Pacific-Asian North American churches might be to "acclimatize" the members of these churches into a Euro-Anglo Christian ethos so that the transition into membership in mainstream congregations could be as smooth as possible. But to what extent are these assumptions correct?

Historically speaking, the establishment of distinct ethnocultural and distinct linguistic faith communities has accompanied significant increases in immigration. The assumption that these are only temporary and transitory churches, however, has been disproved by the continuing existence of Asian-American and Canadian congregations over decades, a few even over a century or more.[70] This has happened even in cases where congregational

---

Julia Matsui-Estrella and Greer Anne Wenh-In Ng, in *Woman of Power* no. 24 (1995): 68–70.

70. Some of these were founded as mission stations in the nineteenth century. For example, the Vancouver Chinese United Church celebrated its centennial in 1985, ahead of the centennial celebration of the founding of the city of Vancouver. In 1994 Chinese United merged with "mainstream" Chown Memorial to form what is now an integrated bilingual church, Chinese and Chown Memorial United Church.

strength has shifted to later generations and only a handful of Asian-language speakers remain, as in the case of the Centennial Japanese United Church in Toronto. Why? Why has such a phenomenon not been paralleled by continuing minority European-speaking Protestant congregations such as Scandinavian, Hungarian, or German ones, all of which started with similar motivations and patterns?

I believe the clue can be found in the issues around identity and racism explored earlier in this chapter. In his book, *The Dragon Pilgrims,* Karl Fung cited the mistaken prediction of his predecessor at the Chinese Community Church in San Diego in 1955, that within twenty-five years "Chinese Christians will be accepted into the life of the White Anglo-Saxon Protestant (WASP) churches, and that ethnic church[es] would cease to exist."[71] What actually happened, of course, was that within thirty years it was the ethnic churches that were in the forefront of new church development, in contrast to the dwindling membership of many mainstream congregations. He goes on to point out how, conversely, the efforts of the Japanese United Church of Christ in that city to assimilate by changing their church names into WASP-sounding church names did not attract Americans of other races to their sanctuaries.[72] As long as racism—or rather, white supremacy—remains part and parcel of North American society, there will always be ethnic churches where Asian and other minority Christians can feel safe as they worship, can be spiritually nurtured, and can work out their discipleship together. For religious education, this means being alert to the needs of the changing membership, and offering more and more programs in English instead of the ancestral language, without shortchanging the cultural relevance of the subject matter. It is also important to be proactive in nurturing the leadership capacities of these second- and subsequent-generation Christians so that they can assume the necessary positions of leadership when their elders are no longer there or when they form their own communities of worship.

As long as North American-born Pacific Asian-American and Canadian Christians have to wrestle with questions of ethnocultural identity because of their bicultural or biracial heritage, they will need a space where such wrestling can take place with understanding and assistance. One possible scenario is that "pan-Asian" congregations such as the Evergreen Baptist Church in Los Angeles may become less and less of a novelty.[73] In such

---

71. Karl Fung, *The Dragon Pilgrims: A Historical Study of a Chinese-American Church* (San Diego, Calif.: Providence, 1989), p. 140.

72. Ibid., p. 141.

73. One vibrant example is Evergreen Asian American Church in Los Angeles, pastored by Ken Fong, a second-generation Chinese-American clergyman. He speaks of his experience and discusses pan-Asian American ministry in *Insights for Growing Asian-American Ministries: How to Reach the Increasing Numbers of Americanized Asian Americans for Christ* (Rosemead, Calif.: EverGrowing, 1990). A more pluralistic

churches, commonality rests on an experience of being second-, third-, or subsequent-generation English-speaking and therefore finding it difficult to participate fully and equitably in their own Korean, Chinese, or Japanese American/Canadian churches. As interethnic and interracial marriages take place, the membership of such English-speaking Asian North American congregations and parishes may become more and more racially and ethnically mixed. Religious education will need to plan specific ministries to address the needs of this latter group, as well as facilitate theological and biblical reflection about what it means to be biracial/cultural or multiracial/cultural in one's own family as well as place of worship. The struggles and efforts at such living and "faithing" will become gifts this group can offer to the total Christian community in North America in its increasing diversity.

Why is it considered unnatural or undesirable for Christians who have grown up together and have faced hardship together to want to remain together? Would we have expected anything different from any of the mainstream churches? Pacific-Asian North American churches in the future will be filled with settlers, not sojourners. As settlers, they should be encouraged, as were the European settlers of our continent, to form their own religious communities and thrive in them.

Bearing Gifts Still

Pacific-Asian North American sisters and brothers who are "no longer sojourners," however, still come bearing gifts for the total Christian faith community and for North American society. Some of these gifts, rooted in Confucian and Taoist traditions, will have continuing impact: a capacity for hard work, family cohesiveness, valuing the communal, respecting elders and their wisdom, living as part of nature rather than over against nature. The very ability of Pacific Asians to survive as minorities within a dominant culture is a skill sorely needed by mainline churches and their members who find themselves in danger of becoming a "sideline" in society.

Another significant gift that is emerging with more globally connected Pacific Asians is their ability to help the total church live into its global reality in a nonpaternalistic mode. By their natural family and friendship ties with individuals and institutions in Asia on a more personal and human level, these Christians can facilitate exchanges that are more equal—more like partnerships rather than the customary Euro-dominant benefactor-recipient exchanges. As a challenge to traditional Western missiological concept and practice, an exchange of religious educational resources and ways of

---

approach is taken by David Ng in "Varieties of Congregations for Varieties of People," chapter 13 in *People on the Way*, ed. David Ng, pp. 281–300.

educating religiously might lead to fresh ways of relating and cooperation between the faith communities of North America and Asia.

But how will these gifts be received? On the North American continent, churches of Pacific-Asian ancestry could grow spiritually by taking their missioning role more seriously, moving from a survival and maintenance mode to a more participating and sharing mode. Through worship and proclamation, religious education and pastoral care that incorporate special strengths from their cultural and religious heritages, these churches have much to contribute to the health and strength of the total church. They have had experience transferring cultural values and practices not wholesale, but by contextualizing them to North American culture. This experience can provide some useful modeling for the necessity and the possibility of contextualizing mainstream faith and cultural values as well. Such a move, of course, will only be possible if the majority part of the church learns to graciously accept these gifts—learns how to be *missioned to*, for a change. This means that in the total ecology of religious education on the North American continent, there should be give-and-take between mainstream churches and ethnic-specific churches. For example, local and regional religious education committees can disseminate literature about their activities in each of the languages of their denomination's churches, and make sure representatives from ethnic churches are invited to sit on regional religious education committees. These and other important ways to achieve missioning together can form a challenging focus in multicultural religious education.

SOME CLUES FOR PACIFIC-ASIAN NORTH AMERICAN CHURCHES: GLEANINGS FROM FUTURING EXERCISES IN RELIGIOUS EDUCATION

If Pacific-Asian churches are here to stay in North America, and if they have true gifts to bring for the total church, what direction might their religious education assume in order to live out this calling? I propose to seek a few clues by drawing on the results of two of the varied futuring or visioning consultations, conferences, and research projects pertaining to the field of religious education taking place near the end of the twentieth century. One is the ecumenical consultation on curriculum held in Nashville, Tennessee, in spring 1995 by former partners of JED (Joint Educational Development, publisher of the four-stream *Christian Education: Shared Approaches* resources). The other is the six-denomination U.S. research project carried out over almost four years in the late 1980s by Search Institute.

Three "Futuribles" Relevant to Religious
Education in the Twenty-first Century

From 1987 to 1990 six major denominations in the United States took part in a wide-ranging study conducted by the Search Institute. The study, which involved over 11,000 adults and youth and 561 congregations, aimed to investigate in depth the teaching function of the church, guided by four concepts: maturity of faith, growth in faith, congregational loyalty, and denominational loyalty.[74] Based on the findings of this study, Richard Osmer, in the concluding chapter of *Rethinking Christian Education* (in which leading thinkers in religious education reflect on the implications of the Search study), proposes three "futuribles" for mainline Protestant churches.[75] Osmer's suggestions apply equally well to Catholic and Eastern Orthodox churches. They include (1) shifting from the churches' existing "pastoral ecclesiology" to a "teaching ecclesiology," (2) intentionally viewing themselves as "cognitive minorities" in the culture, and (3) recommitting themselves to social criticism. In passing, Osmer points out how a "futurible" differs from simply "futuring" by being "a future we actively create" rather than "a future we passively accept."[76]

To what extent do these possible scenarios apply to Pacific-Asian North American churches' educational ministry?

Shifting from a pastoral to a teaching ecclesiology, the first of Osmer's futuribles, is not a concept that is foreign to these churches. Asian pastors have never accepted the role of manager/therapist as fully as their European-American counterparts because their people's expectations have firmly anchored them to the role of pastor/teacher. In fact, the two Chinese characters making up the term *minister* are *mu-shi*, "pastor master/teacher," or, in

---

74. Schuller, *Rethinking Christian Education*, p. 4. Denominations involved were the Christian Church (Disciples of Christ), the Evangelical Lutheran Church in America, the Presbyterian Church (U.S.A.), the United Church of Christ, the United Methodist Church, and the Southern Baptist Convention. For an overview of the findings of the study, see Peter L. Benson and Carolyn H. Eklin, *Effective Christian Education: A National Study of Protestant Congregations—A Summary Report on Faith, Loyalty, and Congregational Life*. The study is available from Search Institute, Thresher Square West, 700 South Third St., Suite 210, Minneapolis, MN 55415. Telephone 800-888-7828. Additional resources produced from the study and available from Search Institute are *Exploring Christian Education Effectiveness*, by E. Roehlkepartain; *Exploring Faith Maturity: A Self-Study Guide for Adults*, and *Exploring Faith Maturity: A Self-Study Guide for Teenagers*, by E. Roehlkepartain and D. Williams; and *The Power of Christian Education Video Series*, produced by J. Gambone. Also see *The Teaching Church: Moving Christian Education to Center Stage*, by E. Roehlkepartain (Nashville: Abingdon, 1993).

75. Richard Osmer, "Three Futuribles for the Mainline Church," in *Rethinking Christian Education*, ed. David Schuller, pp. 125–39.

76. Stephen Toulmin as quoted by Richard Osmer in *Rethinking Christian Education*, ed. David Schuller, p. 126.

written and more refined phraseology, *jiao-mu,* "teaching-shepherding."
The both/and orientation of Asian *yin-yang* culture has always insisted that
clergy teach as well as pastor.

What we need to rethink here is *how* pastors teach and how those already
engaged in religious educational ministry can be recognized and nurtured.
An "invitation from the future" might be for teacher/pastors to affirm the
teaching ministry of other leaders and teachers in the congregation to teach
in an egalitarian manner. Shifting from a "meeting the people's needs"
mentality to one of "school house of faith" for the church[77] might still
be uphill work for consumer-style Christians, who pick pastoral services
and denominations much as they select items in a supermarket or a cafe-
teria. Pacific-Asian North American Christians share in this contemporary
phenomenon, often seeking the relatively congenial and comfortable environment of ethnic and linguistic-specific churches because of personal
and social needs occasioned by the culture shock and resettling process of
recent immigration or refugee experience. To shift to a mentality of learning
to deepen and widen personal faith beyond private and family "coping"
requirements to one encompassing life-affirming values, advocating social
change, and acting and serving (three of the eight "core dimensions" of
mature faith as defined in the Search study),[78] will indeed take much teaching
and learning on the part of both lay and professional church leaders.

The church as a consciously "cognitive minority," Osmer's second
futurible, has already been a historical reality for Pacific-Asian North
American churches, which for all of their existence have had to "actively
resist assimilation by the surrounding culture in order to maintain their
cultural identity."[79] Mainstream Protestant and Catholic churches, therefore,
have much to learn from these churches, and culture resistance could well
become a topic for the religious educators of both kinds of churches to
develop together. On the other hand, in so far as Pacific-Asian churches
have tried to become acceptable not only to the dominant social culture
that surrounds them but also to the ecclesial or denominational one,
they have had to compromise their uniqueness. Such adjustments can
range from putting their family name last rather than first (as have Asian
feminist theologians Chung Hyun Kyung and Kwok Pui Lan) to adopting
Western-style funeral rituals. Sorting through the complexities of being

---

77. Osmer, in Schuller, *Rethinking Christian Education,* p. 130.

78. The eight "core dimensions of faith" posited by the Search study for mature
Christians can be summarized as follows: (1) trusts in God and believes in Jesus;
(2) experiences well-being, security, and peace; (3) integrates faith and life; (4) seeks
spiritual growth; (5) seeks to be part of a community of believers; (6) holds life-affirming
values; (7) advocates social change for greater justice; (8) serves humanity through acts
of love and justice. See also E. Roehlkepartain, *The Teaching Church,* pp. 36–37.

79. Osmer, in Schuller, *Rethinking Christian Education,* p. 132.

a recognizable minority as circumstances and forces change presents a continuing task for both mainstream and racial ethnic minority churches in the twenty-first century. It will tax the ingenuity, patience, and courage of the religious educators of the future.

A recommitment to social criticism is Osmer's third futurible. Two of his three specific strategies in this category, involving churches in outreach projects and the institution of awe-inspiring rites of initiation and transition, hold potential for Pacific-Asian North American churches. In particular, the latter strategy can be extended to include actual physical transitions such as immigrant and refugee families' resettlement in an unfamiliar land. Osmer's caution that it not give rise to sectarian imperialism or intellectual isolation need not concern Pacific-Asian North American churches to the same extent, since continuing racial discrimination will make it almost impossible for these churches to fall into those dangers.

"All Things New"

The Nashville consultation "All Things New," held in April 1995, was attended by representatives from over sixty denominations covering a range of theological perspectives. Pacific-Asian religious educators were visible not only among the participants but also in the leadership. From the list of nineteen projects coming out of the final strategizing, this section singles out for comment those that are most pertinent to Pacific-Asian North American churches in terms of ethos/approach, subject matter/topics, methodology/technology, and settings.[80]

Ethos/Approach: Crossing Boundaries: Judging from the type of projects proposed, there seems to be a general readiness among the consultants to cross traditional boundaries, whether they be boundaries of congregation, denomination, or culture. Many of the proposals call for doing things together, including ecumenical youth conference on spirituality (proposal 7),

---

80. The following list of nineteen projects emerged from the Nashville consultation's module 9 "Planning for the Future" interest groups: (1) Afrocentric Curriculum, (2) African American Publishers' Association, (3) Beyond Denominations, (4) Bilingual Curriculum Development, (5) Cross-Congregational Conversation/Interaction, (6) Cross-Cultural Spiritual Formation, (7) Ecumenical Retreats for Spiritual Formation of Early Adolescents, (8) Electronic Curriculum, (9) Faith Mentor Program for Children and Youth, (10) Home Study Curriculum, (11) Involving Lay Leaders in Curriculum Development, (12) Intercultural/Anti-racism/Multicultural Education, (13) Learning and Being in Intergenerational Groups, (14) Program Curriculum of Ordered Learning for Adults, (15) Setting the Congregation Free to be Educator, (16) Teachers Fulfill the Role of Facilitator in Nurturing Faith, (17) Training on CD-Rom, (18) What Works, (19) Working Groups on Research. For information on any of the above, write to your denominational Christian education office or to Sidney D. Fowler, United Church of Christ, 700 Prospect Avenue, Cleveland, OH 44115.

children's cross-cultural storytelling and spiritual formation (proposal 6), and cross-congregational sharing/interaction (proposal 5). This general tendency would certainly be welcomed by Pacific-Asian North American churches. They have (as indicated earlier in this chapter) out of necessity already been planning and strengthening religious education across congregational, denominational, and national lines.

There was also a high level of awareness among the consultants for a much more cross-cultural approach, a dimension present in at least six out of the nineteen projects (numbers 3, 4, 5, 6, 7, 12). The added dimension of crossing ethnocultural lines within Asian cultures themselves was also evident. At some point, crossing minority culture lines among Latino/a, black, native, and Asian groups in both the United States and Canada, groups that pursue similar religious educational goals, would indeed be a demanding challenge. At the same time, such a challenge could lead to mutual learning and solidarity.[81]

As religious educators think ahead to doing things cross-congregationally, cross-denominationally and cross-culturally, however, they must exercise caution on two fronts. First, in the majority-minority interchanges involved in such crossing of boundaries, planners must learn to be aware of an inherent power imbalance so that it can be addressed in conception, planning, and implementation.[82] Second, they must ensure that Pacific-Asian North American groups make their own decisions about how far they wish to participate. As with other minority cultures in North America, Pacific-Asian religious education tends to make its best contribution to multicultural religious education by being culture-specific rather than multicultural. Put another way, whereas multicultural efforts are perceived primarily as efforts at inclusivity from the perspective of the majority segment, from the perspective of the minority, they are most authentic as efforts to acknowledge and celebrate a particular ethno-cultural group's specific voice and experience. As implied in an exchange between a Native Canadian elder and a European-American on a Globalization of Theological Education Summer Institute in 1990, "You need globalization; we need indigenization."[83] An example from the Nashville consultation is the goal to implement a plan for preparing curricular resources for Pacific and

---

81. To pursue this topic further, see the author's chapter, "Asian North American Relationships with Other Minority Cultures," in *People on the Way*, ed. David Ng, pp. 229–37.

82. Eric Law points out this imbalance throughout his book *The Wolf Shall Dwell with the Lamb: A Spirituality of Leadership for a Multicultural Community* (St. Louis, Mo.: Chalice, 1993).

83. See the report on "Efforts Toward the Globalization of Theological Education in the Association of Theological Schools of the United States and Canada," by Greer Anne Wenh-In Ng, in *Ministerial Formation* 70 (July 1995): 22–26.

Asian American/Canadian congregations.[84] Combined with the proposal to develop bilingual curricula for Hispanic, Korean, and other Asian immigrant congregations (fourth on the list of projects), this should affirm efforts already under way and encourage similar activity in the future. At the same time, it points to a tension between ethnocultural-specific churches, with their need of culture-specific educational programming, and multicultural congregations or parishes with their equally valid interest in programming that combines a variety of cultural needs.

Subject Matter/Topics: Several topics emerge among the nineteen proposed projects as high learning priorities. Spiritual formation (especially of children and young people), the biblical story (interpreted from contemporary perspectives), linking faith questions with life experiences, the importance of diversity, and learning to live in intergenerational groups are some examples. Most of these can be endorsed by Pacific-Asian North American churches, especially the last two, since concerns of diversity and cross-generational living continue to remain hot issues in Pacific-Asian communities, no matter how long their members have been in North America.

Methodology/Technology: Pacific-Asian Americans and Canadians may have a sense of "coming home" with several proposed innovations in the way we educate or teach. Developing a faith mentoring process whereby adults mentor children and youth would not be unfamiliar in cultures that make much of a master-disciple model of learning. Emphasizing story making (constructing one's own life and faith stories), story telling (telling a story [which was made or received] to one's community and to younger generations), and story sharing (sharing stories between groups or communities) for purposes of spiritual formation and nurture would make a lot of sense to cultures that depend heavily on oral transmission of traditions, for example Pacific Islander and Laotian/Cambodian/Hmong cultures. Story telling and story sharing between original-language-speaking parents or grandparents and younger English-speaking generations, or between one language group and another, will need the specialized ministry of bilingual speakers and educators. How to make storytelling a viable tool for mutual learning will require hard work on the part of religious educators, especially in view of the general Asian tendency for the older and more senior members to speak and the younger to listen only. In fact, how to introduce a nonauthoritarian style of leadership or mentoring is a strong challenge in cultures where authority resides so much in teachers and parents. That is why another proposal, the one to prepare volunteer teachers and other religious educators primarily as facilitators in nurturing faith (number 16), may not work as well in these communities, since the teacher is expected to be the expert and the authority.

---

84. From the Curriculum Project Summary as one of the projects identified out the consultation with possibilities for ecumenical partnership in curriculum development.

The strong interest in moving religious education into the realm of CD-ROMs and electronic curricular resources will be taken in stride by the Asian communities in North America, since many are already aware of the viability of such a direction by their experience in business before coming to North America. At the same time, such a trend might set up negative tension for highly literate East Asian cultures that prize "book learning" above oral, visual, and performing practices.

Settings/Contexts: Pacific-Asian North American congregations have always utilized spaces outside the sanctuary for purposes of socialization and formation—in their homes, their family and clan gatherings, at banquets, funerals, and other life cycle communal events.[85] The effectiveness of using camps, retreats, and the outdoors as contexts for religious education purposes, however, will again depend on how receptive a particular Asian culture is to rural, natural, primitive (in the sense of "less civilized") settings. Older generations and more urbanized segments of highly literate cultures (Chinese, Korean, Japanese), will tend to value formal "schooling" contexts over against less structured, more informal settings. Segments still in touch with their indigenous popular religiosity, which include practices of, among Koreans for instance, "going to the prayer mountain," may make greater use of outdoor settings, provided that as Christians they have overcome the fear of remaining in the grip of earlier shamanistic religiosity.

What seems to be missing from the Nashville project list is any explicit reference to educating around multifaith issues. Nevertheless, learning to live with respect for adherents of the world's great faiths now making their home in North America should be high on the agenda of all churches.[86] Traditionally, attention to multifaith realities and issues has not been a priority for Pacific-Asian Christians in North America, owing to the still prevalent fear of being "contaminated" by non-Christian faiths. Their practice has generally been one of cooperation on community and relief/charity projects, but noninvolvement in religious matters. Religious educators need to ask if the time has come in their religious communities for more explicit reflection and study of these relationships as well as other religious practices and beliefs. If the answer is yes, what conditions must prevail within these Christian communities in order for this kind of exploration to begin? What persons within these Christian communities are conscientized enough to begin to give leadership?

---

85. For example, see Ellen Tanouye, "Festivals: Celebrating Community, Story, and Identity," in *People on the Way*, ed. David Ng, pp. 177–88.

86. An excellent introduction to the necessity of doing multifaith Christian education is Martin Marty's chapter, "Christian Education in a Pluralistic Culture," in *Rethinking Christian Education*, ed. David Schuller, pp. 17–30. Also helpful is *Religious Pluralism and Religious Education*, ed. Norma H. Thompson (Birmingham, Ala.: Religious Education Press, 1988).

To complicate matters, the issue goes beyond mere dialogue or encounter with others: for Pacific-Asian Christians in North America, an interreligious dialogue might be occurring within themselves as well. This is because elements of Asia's great faiths (Buddhism, Hinduism, Confucianism, Taoism) or its indigenous religions (shamanism, Shintoism) and spiritual practice have been ingrained into the collective consciousness of these Christians and are part of their cultural heritage. For example, the connection with one's ancestors and the departed can provide a vital approach to the Christian concept of "the communion of saints." For the most part, Pacific-Asian Christians have denied any such connection ("I am a Christian pure and simple and all these pagan religions do not concern me") or have resorted to a state of compartmentalization ("Christianity is my faith; those others— whether Confucian, Taoist, Shintoist practice, or popular religious elements in cultural festivals—are simply cultural phenomena").[87] In the increasingly multifaith reality of North America, however, along with the trend to retain or reclaim cultural roots, such denial or compartmentalization will no longer be tenable. It is a religious education task to help Christians acknowledge the possibility of such dual or multiple religious belonging and struggle with their very real fears of self-imposed or externally imposed charges of syncretism or "heresy." With critical assessment of this delicate situation, and the care of the learner that it entails, these Christians will have a chance to live life "in all its fullness" rather than continuing to live compartmentalized or truncated spiritual lives. Then, along with their mainstream sisters and brothers, they can add their unique perspective and improved understanding to meeting the crucial task of living faithfully as integrated Christians in the pluralistic world of the twenty-first century.

RESOURCES FOR PACIFIC-ASIAN
NORTH AMERICAN RELIGIOUS EDUCATION

Church School and Congregational
Curricular Resources

Asian American Christian Education Curriculum Project (Presbytery of San Francisco, Presbyterian Church, U.S.A.). *Choosing Sides: The Book of Judges from an Asian American Perspective.* 5 vols. Kindergarten-Grade Two through College-Adult, 1985.

---

87. This point is illustrated and discussed more fully in two articles by the author, "The Dragon and the Lamb: Chinese Festivals in the Life of Chinese Canadian/American Christians," by Greer Anne Wenh-In Ng, *Religious Education* 84 (summer 1989): 368–83, and "Toward Wholesome Nurture: Challenges in the Religious Education of Asian North American Female Christians," *Religious Education* 91 (spring 1996): 238–54.

————. *One in Christ: The Letter to the Galatians from an Asian American Perspective.* 5 vols. Kindergarten-Grade Two through College-Adult, 1985.

Godard, Freya, ed. *Stories of Interfaith Families: A Resource for Families and Congregations.* (Toronto: Division of Mission in Canada and Division of World Outreach, United Church of Canada, 1994).

Kawano, Roland, ed. *Creating a Nation: Seeking Our Identities in a Developing Canada.* Toronto: United Church of Canada, 1995.

Nebres, Fe R. *Tayo Na: Let Us Go.* A course of study developed to promote multicultural awareness in church schools by the Multicultural Curriculum Resources Project of the Hawaii Conference, United Church of Christ. New York: United Church Press, 1988.

Ng, Greer Anne Wenh-In, ed. *Tales of Interracial Marriage.* Toronto: Division of Mission in Canada, United Church of Canada, 1993. With study guide.

————. *Generations Trying to Live Together.* Toronto: Division of Mission in Canada, United Church of Canada. 1995. With study guide.

Nishioka, Rodger, and Mary Lee Talbot. *My Identity: A Gift From God.* New York: Program Agency, Presbyterian Church (U.S.A.), n.d. Senior high age. Three linguistic versions in one volume—English, Spanish and Korean.

Tanouye, Ellen. *Learning Parenting Skills Together in an Asian-American Context.* Vols. 1-2. Japanese Presbyterian Conference, 1991–92.

Uchida, Yoshiko. *Tabi—Journey through Time: Stories of the Japanese in America.* Nashville: Graded Press, 1980. Grades 5–8. Separate student and teacher's books.

Handbooks and Manuals

Ng, Donald, ed. *Asian Pacific American Youth Ministry: Planning Helps and Programs.* Valley Forge, Pa.: Judson, 1989. For youth ministry coordinators and leaders.

Chud, Gyda and Fahlman. *Early Childhood Education for a Multicultural Society.* Vancouver, Canada: Pacific Education Press, 1985.

Ng, David. *A Colorful Community: Ministry with Racial/Ethnic Minority Youth.* Network Papers: A Periodical of Theory and Practice, no. 41. New Rochelle, N.Y.: Don Bosco Multimedia/The Center for Youth Ministry Development, 1991.

Sunoo, Brenda Paik. *Beyond the Crucible: Responses to Anti-Asian Hatred.* New York: Ecumenical Working Group of Asian Pacific Americans [and Canadians], 1994.

[Toronto] Metropolitan Separate School Board. *Race and Ethnic Relations and Multicultural Policy: Guidelines and Procedures.* Toronto: Metropolitan Separate School Board, 1986.

Liturgical and Music Resources

Loh, I-to, ed. *Sound the Bamboo*. Shatin, Hong Kong: Christian Conference of Asia, Asian Institute for Liturgy and Music, 1989.

Japanese Presbyterian Worship Handbook Committee. *Worship Handbook for Japanese American Lay Leaders and Ministers*. Sacramento, Calif.: Sierra Mission Area Asian Ministers' Language and Cultural Seminar, 1981.

Pacific Asian American Canadian Christian Education Ministries (PAACCE). *Asian American/Canadian Worship Resources*. In progress. Write the Christian Education or Asian/Multicultural Ministry office of these denominations: American Baptist Churches, Valley Forge, PA 19482 (Rev. Donald Ng); Episcopal Church, USA, 815 2nd Avenue, New York, NY 10017 (Rev. Dr. Winston Ching); Evangelical Lutheran Church in America, 8765 West Higgins Road, Chicago, IL 60631; Presbyterian Church in Canada, 40 Wynford Drive, Don Mills, ON, Canada M3C 1J7 (Rev. Paul Ryu); Presbyterian Church (U.S.A.) 100 Witherspoon Road, Louisville, KY 40202-1396; Reformed Church in America, P.O. Box 1868, Maraysville, CA 95901 (Ella Campbell); United Church of Christ, 700 Prospect Ave., Cleveland, OH 44415-1100 (Rev. Vilma Machin): United Church of Canada, 3250 Bloor Street West, Etobicoke, ON, Canada, M8X 2Y4 (Rev. Richard Choe); United Methodist Church, Nashville, TN 37202. Or send inquiries to PAACCE, c/o Dorothy Savage, Ministries of Christian Education, National Council of Churches, 475 Riverside Drive, New York, NY 10027.

Takenaka, Masao, and Ron O'Grady. *The Bible through Asian Eyes*. Auckland, New Zealand: Pace Publishing/Asian Christian Art Association, 1991.

————. *The Place Where God Dwells: An Introduction to Asian Church Architecture*. Auckland, New Zealand: Pace Publishing/Asian Christian Art Association, 1995.

United Methodist Church. *Hymns from the Four Winds*. Nashville: Abingdon, 1984.

7

HISPANIC RELIGIOUS EDUCATION

Esperanza Ginoris

Every culture serves to fulfill the needs of its particular group and provide the necessary support for its survival. As members of a culture, people learn and behave and form their cultural patterns according to their own personal experiences influenced by the significant people in their lives, such as parents, teachers, and church ministers. Members of Hispanic cultural groups are no different. Hispanic culture, although existing in different countries and in various forms, has developed its distinct characteristics as a consequence of the extended family concept, by which everyone is seen as a brother or a sister. The extended family includes in-laws, neighbors, and friends. The extended family concept also influences how laws, rules, and regulations are considered. It affects cultural ideas about communication between persons, about time, about religious devotions, and about religiosity itself.

In *Strangers and Aliens No Longer* Joseph Fitzpatrick asks the question, What happens when people are viewed through the lens of culture? The answer is, first, many of people's greatest needs come into focus and, second, appreciation of culture leads to appreciation of a people's greatest gifts and strengths. The authors conclude that if we want unity among cultures, we must develop a sense that each culture has plenty to learn from every other.[1] Anyone looking at Hispanic peoples through the lens of culture quickly sees

---

1. Joseph Fitzpatrick, *Strangers and Aliens No Longer, Part One: The Hispanic Presence in the Church of the United States* (Washington, D.C.: NCCB/USCC Office of Research, 1992). This is a useful resource for anyone interested in the multicultural experience in the United States. It profiles cultural groups and gives insights into the church's vision of culture and the process of inculturation.

that hospitality is an important part of their daily lives. In Hispanic culture everyone has a place—in-laws, neighbors, and friends. This very tribal concept, in which everyone is seen as a sister or a brother, was probably learned from the indigenous Americans who form part of the Hispanic heritage. For Hispanics, the extended family relation is a special gift from which emerges the spirit of *fiesta* that gathers everyone to celebrate, no matter what the occasion is. Hispanics who live in the United States readily add to their familiar celebrations those that are not part of their own culture, such as Thanksgiving and Halloween.

Extended family, hospitality, celebrations—these are important characteristics of Hispanic cultures everywhere. In spite of these shared characteristics, however, Hispanics are not a single race. They are of different colors and countries—the white Hispanic of European descent, the mestizo of Indian and Spanish heritage, the mulattos of African and Spanish origin. All have links of language, culture, and Christian faith that unite them. For this cultural conjoining of ethnically disparate peoples many employ the term *mestizaje*, a rich complexity forged by culture into an integrated whole.[2]

Hispanics are found in all socioeconomic strata. Many came to the United States as political refugees. Some represent a thriving middle class. Others came looking for a solution to the lives of poverty and hunger they knew in their own countries. Some have family in United States who can receive them in their homes, where there is always room for one more. Others arrive penniless, without papers, families, or friends to support their move. They look for solidarity in the struggle to survive, so they turn to Mother Church for help in securing basic human needs for shelter, food, and clothing. There they expect to find a friendly response, not administrative rules and regulations. Sometimes the dominant culture of the United States and its strong institutional church make them feel unwelcome. That church may not be the same as the one they knew in their homeland, but they turn to it nevertheless.

The church Hispanic immigrants find is an American church. Both the Hispanic newcomer and the Anglo Christian may feel challenged or frustrated by the behavior patterns of the other. Time-conscious, highly scheduled Anglos may not understand the Hispanic concern for the event itself—We're running over! versus What's your hurry? Most of this frustration is rooted in ignorance or fear of the unknown. Either party may discriminate against the other as a way to relieve the frustration. People usually judge other cultures according to their own cultural expectations. They forget that their own cultural patterns as well as the cultural patterns of others are unconscious. Human beings do not ask to be born in a certain culture, they are just born into it! They seldom question why they behave

---

2. Loida Martell-Otero, "En Las Maños del Señor: Ministry in the Hispanic Context," *The Apple Seed: A Christian Forum for Reconciliation*, Winter 1994, p. 20.

as they do. But cultural patterns are valuable and need to be respected and preserved. As the documents of the Second Vatican Council (1962–65) stated, "The unity of mankind is being fostered and expressed in the measure that the particular characteristics of each culture are preserved."[3]

To respond effectively to Hispanics, and also to people of other cultures, religious educators must learn how to approach them without stereotyping and labeling them. They need to be familiar with some of the general characteristics of their culture. It is helpful, for instance, to know that Hispanics generally respond best to person- and family-centered activities such as blessings, celebrations, and similar means of making newcomers feel welcome in the group. Treating their cultural traditions with respect and thus encouraging their ethnic pride, offering programs in their own language, taking care personally of their pastoral and personal needs, trying to understand their anxieties, fears, and hopes—all are important ways to draw them in. Many are going through crises and sufferings, and many are struggling for survival in the promised land, looking for political asylum or for better economic opportunities.[4]

As Joseph Fitzpatrick has noted, the prominent cultural trait *personalismo* means that "Hispanics . . . relate to persons rather than to organized patterns of behavior efficiently carried out."[5] With a strong faith in relatives and friends, an orientation toward personal relationships, and an emphasis on cooperation (due in part to accustomed interdependence of family members), Hispanics are more likely to become involved in religious education activities if they have a personal relationship within the group. Since they respond to interpersonal warmth, they prefer a personal invitation or a phone call to a written note. Being sensitive to the differences that their culture presents, even in these small ways, encourages people to participate and says that different does not mean inferior.

Cultural Patterns and Religious Education

Any religious educator assigned to a community that has a large Hispanic population must realize that he or she is called to be a bridge person. Bridge persons need to know both sides of the bridge. They need to be aware of their own culture's perceptions of God, values, and concepts of life and the world while understanding and appreciating the differences in the other.

---

3. *Gaudium et Spes*, Documents of Vatican II no. 53, 54, 1965.

4. R. A. Gutiérrez, "Historical and Social Science Research on Mexican Americans," in *Handbook of Research on Multicultural Education*, ed. James A. Banks (New York: Macmillan, 1995), pp. 209–10, and S. Nieto, "A History of the Education of Puerto Rican Students in U.S. Mainland Schools: "Losers," "Outsiders," or "Leaders?" in *Research on Multicultural Education*, ed. James Banks, pp. 406–7.

5. Joseph Fitzpatrick, *One Church, Many Cultures: The Challenge of Diversity* (Kansas City, Mo.: Sheed & Ward, 1987), p. 133.

The list below summarizes contrasting elements of Hispanic and other Western cultures and helps identify some characteristics peculiar to the Hispanic culture.

Figure 7.1: Contrasting Characteristics of Culture

Hispanic Culture	*Other Western Cultures*
Relational	Independent
Intuitive	Rational
Cyclical	Linear
Traditional	Futuristic
Subjective	Objective
General	Particular
Symbolic	Literal
Cooperative	Individualistic

A well-known study by Ramirez and Castañeda found that of four ethnic groups—Mexican Americans, European Americans, Native Americans, and African Americans—Mexican Americans showed the strongest tendencies toward a field sensitive cognitive style, represented by the left side of Figure 7.1.[6] All of these particular characteristics help to shape and form the different cultures, and all demonstrate the richness and diversity of God's creation. Some characteristic patterns of Hispanic culture are described more fully below.

Authority Patterns: Hispanics traditionally believe strongly in parental authority. Although masculine dominance is still central to the family and the wife is expected to respect, obey, and serve her husband, traditional patriarchal structures are gradually evolving into a more typical Anglo pattern. Moral and emotional support also come from religious ties, as, for example, *compadrazco*—the coparenting relationship that exist between godparents and parents, extending kinship beyond the family. *Compadres* may be baptismal godparents, confirmation sponsors, or wedding sponsors.[7] Church ties are strong. Many Spanish-speaking immigrants, particularly

---

6. The original study, *Cultural Democracy, Bicognitive Development and Education*, by Manuel Ramírez III and Alfredo Casteñeda (New York: Academic, 1974), is discussed in *What Color Is Your God: Multicultural Education in the Church*, by James and Lillian Breckinridge (Wheaton, Ill.: Bridgepoint, 1995), p. 116. Also see Christine I. Bennett, *Comprehensive Multicultural Education: Theory and Practice* (Boston: Allyn & Bacon, 1986), pp. 98–108.

7. Marta Alvarado, "Ministering to Major Cultural Groups—Hispanics," in *Christian Education Foundations for the Future*, ed. R. E. Clark, L. Johnson, and A. K. Sloat (Chicago: Moody Press, 1991), p. 377.

among the elderly, show an almost blind submission toward clergy. They may pass this concept on to the family clan more or less effectively, depending on how close-knit the family unit is.

Economic Patterns: Economic patterns often have an orientation toward the present, rather than the future, with the major concern being to provide adequately *now* for the family. Most income goes toward basic necessities, but rather expensive items can be considered necessities—encyclopedias, electronic toys, a television set, and so on. Generally speaking, Hispanics spend their money as they earn it. They may ignore the mainstream concern for having a savings account in the bank.

Health Concerns: Traditionally, Hispanics have been extremely concerned about becoming ill, as sickness has been considered a matter of destiny. Therefore they have been less likely to direct efforts to promote or preserve good health. Most express happiness at enjoying good health and wish each other *salud* ("good health"). When asked, What is the worst thing that could happen? their response is often, Lose my health. This fear has been explained in connection with the extended family dimension, the illness of one of the members affecting everybody in the family. Among Hispanic immigrant communities, religious education should include identifying and providing pastoral ministry to those in need of health care.[8]

Social Life and Social Barriers: Hispanic newcomers, especially, may restrict themselves to their own ethnic group and have little social contact with Anglos. This is due primarily to the language barrier, but even for the English-speaking there are other, more subtle barriers. The verbal communication used in mainstream U.S. culture is direct and concise. In the Hispanic culture, the language is indirect, subjective, and digressive. Sometimes Hispanics perceive these differences in the dominant culture as expressions of rudeness or lack of feeling. It is very difficult for Hispanics to express themselves without giving details (which may be perceived by Anglos as digressions) or displaying emotions and feelings. One writer advises leaders in Hispanic churches to teach with their hearts as well as their heads. Communication should not just be logical; it must be logical and *warm,* with personal illustrations and pointed examples.[9]

Another barrier may be the different concept of time. The Hispanic culture is oriented toward polychronic time—time can be extended; mainstream U.S. culture is monochronic time-oriented—things must happen now. As a group, Hispanics are extremely generous with their time. They do not consider long conversations a waste of time because for them the person

---

8. Maria Luisa Gastón, "Leadership Development in the Hispanic Community," in *Faith and Culture: A Multicultural Catechetical Resource* (Washington, D.C.: Dept. of Education, United States Catholic Conference, 1987), p. 38.

9. Alex D. Montoya, *Hispanic Ministry in North America* (Grand Rapids, Mich.: Zondervan, 1987), p. 116.

is more important than any project. In the neighborhood you see people talking for long periods of time in a supermarket aisle, on the sidewalks, even from car to car in the middle of the street. They cannot understand the criticism that their behavior provokes among task-oriented Anglos!

Hispanic culture as a whole is intuitive, affective, personal, sensorial, present-time oriented, traditional, philosophical, and emotional—all with a strong sense of community. Hispanics enjoy practicing hospitality; even the poor characteristically share what they have. They prefer forms of recreation that the entire family participates in, for example, visiting in homes and dancing *quinceañeras* (sweet fifteen), a celebration with both religious and social connotations among Mexican Americans.

Describing the impact of Hispanic social patterns on the life of the urban church, Loida Martell-Otero says that it is no coincidence that the Spanish word for town, *pueblo*, is also the word for people. "In the church, when a person has a transforming experience with Christ, it is not uncommon to see whole families come to the altar simultaneously, or soon afterward. This eventually includes the extended family (friends, neighbors, *compadres* as well as blood relatives)."[10] Another consequence of this sense of community is that the achievements of one person in the community (or the failures) bring honor (or dishonor) to the whole community. Religious education is well placed to respond to this strong sense of community, since in its lifelong learning focus it provides opportunities for instruction, worship, and service for family members at every age.

Acculturation vs. Integration

Hispanics often seem to resist acculturation, remaining faithful to their language, culture, heritage, and traditions. Although culture, being dynamic rather than static, is subject to development and change, and the process of integration occurs for Hispanic immigrants as a normal process, complete assimilation is seen as unacceptable, just as extreme ethnicity or nationalism is also unacceptable.[11]

Hispanic people are an integral part of the United States. The United States is the fifth-largest Spanish-speaking country in the world, exceeded only by Mexico, Spain, Argentina, and Colombia. A quarter of a century before the Pilgrims landed at Plymouth Rock, Spanish-speaking people were in North America. It is not surprising, then, that Hispanic people

---

10. Martell-Otero, "En las Maños del Señor," p. 17.

11. Acculturation is understood as the process by which newcomers to a culture and their offspring gradually acquire the language, values, beliefs, and behaviors of the dominant group. For an interesting discussion of how different levels of acculturation seem to affect the achievement of second and third generations, see "Quantitative Educational Research with Ethnic Minorities," by Amado Padilla and Kathryn Lindholm, in *Research on Multicultural Education*, ed. James Banks, pp. 107–8.

want to keep their language, faith, and cultural traditions as part of their self-being. This is a blessing to both cultures. The Cuban bishop in exile, Eduardo Boza Masvidal, has said, "Great enrichment is possible whenever two cultures come together in a spirit of mutual respect, each contributing some of its values. This constitutes a healthy integration, and both benefit. However, the opposite occurs when one culture absorbs the other because the assimilated culture has lost its identity and its values."[12]

Hispanics tolerate cultural integration better than acculturation or assimilation. The integration process allows people to maintain the values and seek the goals of their own culture while learning and adapting some values and practices of the mainstream culture. In acculturation, individuals so identify with the dominant culture that they lose their cultural distinctives. The Hispanic family is a very strong influence in the anti-acculturation process because respect for the traditions, symbols, rites, history, and practices that take place within the privacy of the family perpetuates the roots of their culture. Among the different groups that share a Hispanic heritage, some are more vulnerable than others to finding acculturation and assimilation as means of survival against the cultural stripping action of American society, which does not value immigrant groups as people with cultures, languages, traditions and histories worthy of being preserved.[13]

It is very difficult for a minority group to obtain success and power as a group. However, one example of an Hispanic group that has achieved this is the Cuban population of Miami. The first Cuban political immigration occurred in the early 1960s, and was mainly composed of professional people and their children. They remained in South Florida and have obtained political, social, economic, and ecclesiastic leading positions without being assimilated by the mainstream system. They have even established the same schools that they had in their native Cuba to preserve their language, religion, traditions, and history. Children from other parts of South America, Central America, and the Caribbean are among the ten thousand children who attend these schools. The Hispanic experience in South Florida is unique.

Ideally, the many cultures in the United States should coexist and enrich each other. None should have to fight to preserve their identity. For many Christians, the idea of a homogeneous America seems against God's plan for humanity. The kind of unity that most Christians pursue is impeded by uniform expectations of people that do not allow differences to be a source

---

12. Eduardo Boza Masvidal, "Unity in Pluralism," in *The Proceedings of II Encuentro Hispano de Pastoral*, (Washington, D.C.: U.S. Catholic Conference, 1977), p. 16. This publication is out of print, but is available from Sepi Book Service, Miami, Fla. 33155.

13. For a discussion of immigrant acculturation in America, see "Immigrants and Education," by Michael R. Olneck, in *Research in Multicultural Education*, ed. James Banks, pp. 310–13.

of richness. Religious education should nurture appreciation and respect for religious traditions unique to different cultural communities.[14]

Language Preservation

The preservation of their language is a primary value among Hispanics in North America. While the majority of Hispanic Americans are native-born U.S. citizens, they are also bilingual. In her book *Puerto Ricans: Born in the USA*, Clara Rodriguez reports that 91 percent of Puerto Ricans living on the eastern seaboard say they speak Spanish at home, and 70 percent say they speak English "very well." On the West Coast, 64 percent of Mexican Americans speak Spanish in the home, and 42 percent say they speak English very well. This implies a need for a religious education ministry that takes their bilingualism seriously, celebrating it and including both languages in teaching and worship.[15]

There is much to support the concept of a right to bilingual communication. One of the most frequently named rights of the U.S. Constitution is the right of free speech. It is also true that the language of each people expresses its core, the soul and spirit of that people, which emerges from their way of being, feeling, and appreciating the world in accordance with their specific historical environment. People have the right, therefore, to remain faithful to their particular language, since it is one of the most important elements of their received culture. Particularly in religious education, hearing and speaking the central teachings of the faith in their own language is a paramount need of Hispanic Christians.

The book Acts tells the story of Pentecost. The passage describes the mystery of many tongues expounding a simple faith in words understandable to all. "Each of us hears them speaking in his own tongue about the marvels God has accomplished."[16] Virgilio Elizondo has said in regard to the inculturation of Hispanic faith, "If you will listen to our prayer form, take part in processions, devotions, and liturgical fiestas, listen to our ordinary first names and see the decoration in our bodies, you will quickly discover that faith for us is not an abstract formula or merely a Sunday affair, but the reality of our lives."[17]

---

14. In 1990 the National Council of Catholic Bishops, Washington, D.C., published a pastoral letter, *Heritage and Hope: Evangelization in the United States*, in observance of the five hundredth anniversary of the coming of the gospel to the Americas. The Church recognizes that in the process of bringing Christianity to this hemisphere, the European colonization was responsible for the destruction of Indian civilization, cultural oppression, and usurpation of land. The Church does not deny its share of responsibility for those abuses and has pledged to protect and preserve the freedom and cultural heritage of the people.

15. Reported in Martell-Otero, "En Las Maños del Señor," p. 16.

16. Acts 2:1–11 NAB

17. Virgilio Elizondo, in a speech to the National Council of Catholic Bishops, Washington, D.C., 1990. The term *inculturation* as used here refers to the process by

Religious educators seeking sensitivity to authentic cultures and a real sense of what is required by the process of inculturation may take Psalm 98:2 (NAB) as reference: "The LORD has made his salvation known: in the sight of the nations he has revealed his justice." Christ prays in the upper room to the Father: "I do not pray for them alone. I pray also for those who will believe in me through their word."[18] Everyone is included in Christ's prayer. A critical analysis of personal Hispanic cultural and social reality is needed to move Hispanic people to a life conversion, to transform cultural values that are against the gospel and reinforce those in the Hispanic culture and heritage that incarnate the message of the gospel.

Hispanic Faith Expression

In 1968 the United States Catholic Conference (USCC) opened a division for Hispanic affairs within its Department for Social Action in recognition of the uniqueness of Hispanic faith expression in the American church. The year 1972 saw the first Encuentro Nacional (National Meeting) of Hispanic Catholics take place—a significant focus for Hispanic ministry that would continue through subsequent decades—as well as the creation of the Mexican-American Cultural Center (MACC) in San Antonio, Texas, with a specific purpose to train religious educators for Hispanic ministry.[19]

Church leaders concerned with the religious education of Hispanics have noted the centrality of religious expression to Hispanic identity. In general, Hispanics are a religious people: 83 percent say they consider religion important.[20] Hispanic spirituality puts a strong emphasis on the humanity of Jesus, especially his suffering, his passion, and his death. It is a notably devotional spirituality; holy places and practices are very important. Joseph Fitzpatrick wrote in 1987 that the dynamic and communal style of Hispanic faith and worship was impacting the American church, predicting that the Hispanic population would give a particular character to the Catholic Church in the United States during the twenty-first century, just as Catholic immigrants from Europe did during the twentieth century.[21] While Protestant Hispanic churches represent a more recent and much smaller segment of the Hispanic population (from 80 to 90 percent of Hispanic Americans are Roman Catholic),[22] the experiential and devotional nature of their faith is

---

which a specific religious faith is expressed in a particular culture. See Fitzpatrick, *One Church*, pp. 50–51.

18. John 17:20 NAB

19. Marina Herrera, "Hispanic Americans," in *Harper's Encyclopedia of Religious Education*, ed. Iris V. Cully and Kendig Brubaker Cully. (San Francisco: Harper & Row, 1990), pp. 292–93.

20. National Conference of Catholic Bishops, *The National Plan for Hispanic Ministry* (Washington, D.C.: NCCB/USCC 1987), p. 13.

21. Fitzpatrick, *One Church*, p. 125.

22. Herrera, "Hispanic Americans," p. 292.

similar. Caleb Rosato believes that churches and their educational forms in America must avoid an impersonal "sanitized and antiseptic environment" and become one with the Hispanic people they are trying to serve.[23]

In order to minister to people, religious educators have to know their needs, life history, level of education, family values, and life experiences. Sometimes this is difficult, particularly when a different culture is involved. Groups can develop some negative attitude patterns—passivity, submissiveness, fear of earning a living, familism, and sense of being discriminated against. These patterns are not helpful in dealings with the dominant culture. Attitudes toward immigrants should reflect that of Saint Paul, who, while being a Jew, became Greek to the Greeks and a Roman to the Romans. Religious educators, too, should see and accept immigrants' human and Christian values, over and above their own set of national standards and differences of language and culture. Teachers and other church leaders have to go far beyond any form of paternalism (often expressed as concern for "this poor Hispanic immigrant minority"), which implies that no matter what their numbers are, they will always be a minority, always be the problem child, so we must help them conform to established so-called living standards so they can learn and become like the rest of society. Such an attitude suggests that religious educators value people for the way they eat, speak, socialize, express their faith, and even for the way they dress.

On the more positive side, there are elements very strongly rooted in the Hispanic community that are based on the central core of the Christian message that tells us to love God and love our neighbors. These elements provide good soil for evangelization. They include the presence of God in daily life; a hospitable and welcoming attitude that inspires a spirit of celebration; a desire to share, generosity, and a sense of humor; trust in the providence of God; communal bonds; respect for elders and authorities; the prized virtues of faith, hope, and charity, which relegate everything else to a secondary role; gratitude to God for the gifts of life and health. Popular piety, symbols, stories, poems, songs, rites, devotions, proverbs, and art all speak of God to Hispanic people, the Emmanuel and his option for the poor and his total obedience to the Father, an awareness of sin and the need to expiate it, respect and remembrance for the dead, and for Christ as a king who comes to rule and serve.

While religious educators have identified these values as present in the everyday life and in popular religion among Hispanics, they must nevertheless seek ways to incorporate Hispanics more fully into the life of the Church. They must, by maintaining an educational methodology that allows dialogue and contact with family as a whole, seek a conversion that

---

23. Caleb Rosato, "The Church, the City, and the Compassionate Christ," in *VOCES: Voices from the Hispanic Church*, ed. Justo L. González. (Nashville: Abingdon, 1992), p. 76.

is both intellectual and affective, one that can inspire a response of faith from both mind and heart.

Teaching/Learning Style

One general principle of the religious education process says that educators must know the people they teach; this means they have to discover the learners' positive and negative values, inclinations, and desires. Teachers do not impose ideas or knowledge, but affirm learners' positive values and guide them away from obstacles that can interfere with emotional and spiritual growth. Religious educators should develop a methodology for Hispanic learners that reflects the reality in which they find themselves. They need a pedagogy that (1) leads them to a deeper experience of faith through their sense of community, (2) connects them with the central teaching of salvation history, and (3) takes advantage of the teachable moments built into their lives and cultural values. Such a wholistic approach touches specific needs in people's lives. An academic approach may be rejected as "too much like school."

Some Highlights for Teachers Working with Hispanics

The following list below highlights Hispanic teaching and learning styles. Many items are relevant to the evangelization purposes of religious education.

1. Hispanic learners are people oriented and work well in cooperative groups. This is due in part to the accustomed interdependence of family members.
2. Some Hispanic learners may receive information passively.
3. Hispanic learners show a preference for instruction related to global concepts rather than analytical instruction.
4. Hispanic learners prefer essay-type, memory/action tests over tests based on analysis and discussion.
5. Curriculum objectives for Hispanic learners should be culturally and experientially oriented.
6. Hispanic learners respond well to social rewards. They respond better to praise and reinforcement from others than to internal self-motivation. They are very sensitive to criticism.
7. Hispanic learners often seek feedback from their teachers. Plan to offer opportunity for personal contact.
8. The preferred teaching style is basically lecture and memorization.
9. Hispanic learners frustrated in class may choose to withdraw rather than experience failure, or they may rebel and behave belligerently.

10. They expect the teacher to tell them what to do. They may not adapt
    easily to the role of active participant in discussions. This can conflict
    with the competitive Anglo style of learning.

To sum up, Hispanics learn more by global methods than analytical ones.
They work well in cooperation and often seek contact with others. Their
family system makes them people-oriented. Many may be passive learners
in the classroom. Since their preferred teaching style is by lectures, talks,
and stories, their evangelization must emphasize the spoken word over the
written. The use of audiovisuals is beneficial. Storytelling, celebrations,
plays, or skits are good ways to proclaim the gospel, since Hispanics prefer
this style of communication.[24]
   In less formal settings there may be much personal sharing. Hispanics
do not consider it bad taste to show emotions and they may express their
feelings very frankly. This creates a warm climate for interaction in a
group. However, Anglo teachers may react negatively to the pace and
style of the interactions. It is quite acceptable for several persons to be
involved in different conversations at the same time, something mainstream
Americans consider rude and unacceptable. This behavior is a manifestation
of a cultural pattern due in part to the accustomed interrelation among the
members of the extended Hispanic family. These familiar patterns mitigate
against taking turns to establish a conversation. Thinking and feeling levels
must be taken into consideration when working with Hispanic learners.
Their only means of validating the experience of moving from a culture in
which they were born and reared to the dominant culture, are those means
that sustained previous newcomers and helped them adapt a set of behavior
patterns at cognitive, affective, and cultural levels.
   The dominant American culture values capacity for action, work, and
objectivity. The Hispanic culture values capacity for endurance, feelings,
and creativity. As a result of their orientation toward personal relationships,
Hispanics are more intuitive-affective than pragmatic. Hispanic learners, for
example, may be less motivated by competitive activities. Hispanic children
are often motivated by personal support or affirmation. Family life and social
values are strengths of the Hispanic culture that can serve learning very well,
for example, children's sense of responsibility for siblings and respect for
older persons can make teaching across age-groups especially effective.
Families, including fathers, should be encouraged to participate in their
children's religious education.[25] If religious educators want their message

---

   24. For further discussion of the learning styles of Hispanics and recommended
teaching practices, see "Learning Styles and Culturally Diverse Students: A Literature
Review," by J. J. Irvine and D. E. York, in *Research in Multicultural Education*, ed.
James Banks, pp. 490–91.
   25. Alvarado, "Ministering to Major Cultural Groups," p. 383.

to get through, they must consider these characteristics when planning teaching events, conferences, didactic materials, Bible study circles, and other means of religious education.

A Case Study: Hispanic Farm Workers

Churches must not ignore migrant workers, or farm workers, as they like to be called. These are people on the move, itinerant laborers. They are poor among the poor, thousands of people moving from one state to another following the harvest. They come mostly from Mexico, but also from Guatemala, El Salvador, Ecuador, and other countries. They live below the poverty level in trailer camps. Their situation challenges all of us who live in a country that proclaims equality and justice for all.

The second Encuentro Nacional Hispano de Pastoral in 1977 proposed the elaboration of material specifically for farm workers. Religious educators, as all Christian ministers, must assume responsibility to empower the migrants and reaffirm their dignity as human beings, so that they realize through the teaching of the Word of God Jesus' option for the poor and oppressed. These people live in a cycle of poverty that never ends. Their children rarely go to school. They work in the fields with their parents or stay at home taking care of their brothers and sisters. Many of them can neither read nor write. Their pilgrimage across the nation is a prophetic voice, calling us to make a commitment to justice—to be the voice of these brothers and sisters marginalized and waiting to be evangelized.

Some people see the migrants as a burden, which others ignore their presence. Nonetheless, they are a reality across the United States—a sad reality in the world's most powerful nation. Many Christians look for a faraway mission land like Africa, Latin America, or even China. That is good, but they have to know that in their own backyard are people living sometimes without running water or a bed to sleep in, without adequate food, without opportunity for an education or for health care, living in old trucks, *la troca*, or in trailers, *la traila*, shared with others.

These migrants are very anxious to listen to the word of God, to know more about what it means to be a child of God and to learn how to make Christian decisions. Religious educators have the responsibility as good Christians to reach out to these marginalized, oppressed, and neglected people who are still waiting for a messiah to come and give meaning to their lives. As we read in Isaiah 61 (NAB): "To proclaim liberty to the captives and release to the prisoners." Religious educators must be advocates for the migrant workers, walking with them, empowering them, integrating social action with pastoral action. They must instruct and develop leaders able to identify themselves with the rural environment and mentality, leaders who will be instruments in God's hands not only for the growth and spiritual development of these farmers but for their physical and social life as well.

As a consultant for the archdiocese of Miami, Florida, the author has trained migrant religious educators for seven years and can say that this work has lead her to encounter the true, suffering Christ and to understand better God's option for the poor. Also evident is the meaning of one of the conditions that lead us to the kingdom of God. Mark 10:13–16 says that we have to accept the reign of God like little children. In a genuine way, migrants depend on God's will and providence. This dependency causes Christ's disciples to be like children. More than ever, religious education methodology has to recognize the migrants' reality in order to identify their economic, political, moral, and religious needs. Their particular Hispanic background can vary from camp to camp. A camp composed mainly of Mexicans differs from those camps of Salvatorian, Guatemalan, and Equatorian Hispanics. Symbols, stories, proverbs, songs, rites, and devotions play an important part in their evangelization and conversion, but vary from one ethnic background to another, although there are key elements common to all Spanish people. Religious educators need to be aware of the historical and cultural differences among these Hispanic groups.

There are few religious education materials prepared specifically for Hispanic farmworkers, but there is a booklet published for Hispanics and others called *Journeying Together toward the Lord*.[26] The bilingual edition, *En Marcha Hacia el Señor*, is an important resource for religious education with migrants and has been widely used with farmworkers across the nation for the formation of religious educators among migrant communities. The educational methodology and religious themes in this booklet are excellent and unique. It was prepared for the most part by migrant leaders who emerged from the rural community itself.

In spite of their many sorrows, the stories of Hispanic Americans hold much beauty. Hispanics are a *pueblo* who know how to celebrate, sing, and share. In spite of their poverty, there is much that enriches their lives. Reflecting on her years of growing up in the city, one Hispanic minister recalls her mother saying that her people knew how to "make a new blouse out of papa's old shirt." The ministry with Hispanic Americans, says Martell-Otero, particularly ministry in an urban context, is a constant source of challenge and joy. "The minister must work in an environment of violence, poverty, social indifference (at best), and malignant racism (at worst). He or she must learn to make 'new blouses out of papa's old shirt,' struggling to make do with precious little resources or networking." Yet the result is also reflected in an old saying among her people that Hispanics, for all their trials, are *un pedazo de musica andante* (a walking piece of music).[27]

---

26. This resource was edited in 1982 by the Department of Education of the Catholic Conference in Washington, D.C. It was revised in 1992 through the efforts of the National Committee for Catechesis.

27. Martell-Otero, "En Las Maños del Señor," p. 19.

Encounters with Faith and Religious Instruction

Most parish ministers, including religious educators, would probably agree that in their religious expression Hispanics are more tied to ritual protocol than some other cultures are. They seem to experience a profound sense of "being church" in small groups and in the context of their own language, sharing their life experience of faith within their own culture. These essential elements are introduced among Catholics through the small, church-based communities that promote a communitarian evangelism and a missionary model of church life. In the *Comunidades de Base* (Basic Ecclesial Communities) occurring in neighborhood or family gatherings, participants "read and reflect on the scriptures, pray together, and seek to . . . be of service to their neighbors."[28] Through these means of religious education, participants are able to establish close personal relationships, knowing each other, sharing their struggles, happiness, and family events, and celebrating their faith together as a community.

Apostolic movements represented by charismatic and lay involvement are very popular among Catholic Hispanics who try to find their identity and commitment to the Christian vocation within a Church that often seems to them more institutional than missionary or servant to the poor. Churches must promote fuller participation of Hispanics so they can celebrate their faith at a personal and communitarian level. They need to double efforts to increase the number of people ministering to Hispanics in order to facilitate communication between grassroots communities, the unchurched, and the "Church." Resources for religious education need to be developed "by Hispanics for Hispanics." St. Mary's Press began an effort in 1988 to identify religious educators who were working successfully with Hispanic youth and could help write and produce such materials.[29]

In the year 2000 there will be more than 31 million Hispanics living in the United States. Many Christian churches, Protestant as well as Catholic, recognize a need to open their doors to the Hispanic population, making them feel welcome, discovering their needs and interests, encouraging them to be part of their community. With such goals in mind, the United Methodist Church approved more than $2 million to prepare ministers and leaders to minister to Hispanics. Methodist theologian Justo Gonzalez, noting that his denomination had created a committee to develop a national plan for Hispanic ministries, urged churches to place the needs of Hispanics before the needs of a particular denomination. "We must build bridges to other Hispanics . . . in other denominations, and we must seek to develop, throughout the Church at large, a theology and a practice that is more consonant with the needs and the experiences of Hispanic people. I see signs

---

28. Fitzpatrick, *One Church*, pp. 138–40.
29. Herrera, "Hispanic Americans," p. 293.

of this approach, . . . and for that we must rejoice." Gonzalez maintains that the gospel should be taught in a way that makes theology accessible to young and old in Hispanic communities, educated and uneducated, the great and the "least of these."[30]

Other Protestant groups are producing curriculum resources for Hispanic religious education. The Southern Baptists have Spanish-language curricula graded for preschooler through adult Sunday school classes. The Evangelical Lutheran Church also produces Spanish-language educational resources. Gospel Publishing House's English curriculum, *Radiant Life* (*Vida Radiante*), used largely by Pentecostal churches, has been translated into Spanish and adapted for Hispanic culture. Independent evangelical publishers Gospel Light and Scripture Press provide a Spanish edition of their curricular materials for distribution from Mexico. Some churches find it useful to employ some curricular materials in both Spanish and English, so teachers or learners can work bilingually. Marta Alvarado advises church teachers to adapt for their own learners the limited resources that are available, using them creatively and with an interactive teaching style.[31]

Implementing National Goals for Hispanic Religious Education

Throughout American history many Hispanics have suffered from discrimination and prejudice, resulting in the loss of self-esteem. Ministers of religious education must affirm and support the dignity of all sons and daughters of God and make learners aware both of the value of human beings as created in the image of God and the responsibility for each human being for active participation in the mission of Jesus. To this end, the Catholic Hispanic community that lives in the United States started the process of national assemblies called Encuentro in June 1972. The Third Encuentro took place in 1985, but as an event the Third Encuentro process lasted three years. It involved consultations throughout the United States as well as meetings at both regional and local levels. This culminated in a national meeting in August 1985 held in Washington, D.C. It was a major social, cultural, ecclesial, and faith event. From the Third Encuentro came a pastoral plan for Hispanics and a pastoral letter, "The Hispanic Presence: Challenge and Commitment," from the Catholic bishops. The bishops showed that the Catholic Church is sensitive to the needs of the Hispanics and also recognizes the gifts that Hispanics bring to the so-called American Church and the pastoral actions this requires. The Third Encuentro generated a pastoral plan at the national level—a goal that the Church wanted to achieve and that the Hispanic community viewed as

---

30. Gonzalez, *VOCES*, pp. 170–71.
31. Alvarado, "Ministering to Major Cultural Groups," p. 283.

the real meaning of this key event. There were participants from different ethnic backgrounds, lay leaders as well as religious men and women from different regions of the country, Mexicans, Mexican Americans, Puerto Ricans, Cubans, South and Central Americans. The Encuentro planners also invited the socially and economically marginalized, for example, migrant farm workers, unemployed, undocumented, immigrant men and women, and a very important element—Hispanic youth. The participants represented the whole Hispanic community, and everyone had a voice in this historic process. Joseph Fitzpatrick concludes, "There is much evidence that Hispanics are taking their religious life in their own hands and are showing impressive signs of strength." Outcomes include an emphasis on ministry and teaching in Spanish with the continuity of *personalismo,* and a family style of religious practice and public celebrations, particularly the familiar processions. Any attempt to transform Hispanic religious practices too hurriedly to dominant-culture model was discouraged.[32]

What the pastoral plan requires is action toward an "integral education," one that acknowledges the urgency to include all the aspects of human life: personal, familial, and social. Each aspect must be founded in religious education that has a clearly evangelical dimension of spiritual formation and proposes to meet the needs of human beings in their totality—body and mind.

Religious educators among Hispanics must apply three basic principles of education to implement such goals effectively:

1. Know each person—establish a personal, cordial and ongoing dialogue. This requires time, respect, and a true Christian love that inspires trust. Understand each person's situation, the transformation, and the obstacles that may have been experienced with a change in environment. Be able to communicate in their own "language." Each cultural group, community, and family his its own "cultural language" by which it expresses values, deep feelings, and needs. It is not limited to what is spoken, but includes customs, rites, and traditions. Religious educators must discover this familiar "language" in order to communicate in depth.

2. Know how to present the importance of the theme of the instruction. Motivate a continuing education, by which learners will continue to be taught the fundamental elements of the faith.

3. Discover God's presence and action in the world. Live the values of the gospel in all aspects of life.

One suggested means of instruction is to lead participants through four steps. (1) See: The religious educator discusses his or her own experience in relation to the theme, be it positive or negative. (2) Judge: Discuss how God reveals himself in these situations, what God tells us and asks of us.

---

32. Fitzpatrick, *One Church*, pp. 154–56.

In positive experiences we see and feel God's merciful love, in negative ones we hear Christ's call to unite ourselves in his Paschal ministry, to fight against evil and to work with his Church to build a better world. (3) Act: Find ways of answering God's call personally, in the community, and through social Christian action. (4) Celebrate: Through prayer and liturgy, celebrate what has been learned.[33]

An important effort to help the development and growth of the Hispanic ministry among Catholics was the 1992 Congress, Roots and Winds, that provided the opportunity to recognize the achievements of dedicated religious educators and other ministers working with Hispanic communities. The congress focused on reaching out to professional, bilingual, cultural Hispanics. There was recognition of the apostolic movements that have made and continue to make important contributions to Hispanic ministry. This congress offered conferences and workshops highlighting present-day Hispanic ministries. It offered a process for developing greater commitment to the National Plan for Hispanic Ministries, and a dialogue with Hispanic-Latino leaders in society, politics, and business. Another congress, Roots and Wings, has also been prepared.[34]

The goals of the Third Encuentro, with all its resulting plans, must not be seen as merely serving a minority group in search of power but rather as part of the body of Christ living here and now. It must not be seen as just one more event in the history of the Hispanic people living in the United States, but as a process that marked a truly important step in the journey of faith for Hispanic people. Through these goals, religious education can help lead Hispanic Christians toward the unity and solutions that will benefit the Church as a whole in the United States. Although participants considered Third Encuentro a success, growth, development, and implementation of the pastoral plan for Hispanics has been slow, unknown to many, unsupported by others, and inadequately funded to accomplish such a goal. A great deal of work and dedication are needed, not only to develop but also to gain support for this pastoral plan. Parishes differ in their effectiveness. A recent study of the religious education goals and needs of four thousand Catholic parishes showed that most Hispanic parishes were located in the inner city (40 percent) and in rural areas (48 percent), but not in more affluent suburbs. Among the bishops and diocesan religious education leaders surveyed, 73 percent noted a "serious or very serious" lack of family-focused programs, and 69 percent agreed that a lack of recognition

---

33. Excerpted from·the catechetical supplement to the Pastoral Plan for Hispanic Ministry, approved by the National Conference of Catholic Bishops in 1987. The author has used this process and has found it effective in training religious educators in many areas of the United States.

34. *St. Mary's Press Newsletter*, Christian Brothers Publications, 702 Terrace Heights, Winona, MN 55987-1320.

of minority cultural conflicts was a "serious or very serious" problem for the parishes.[35] Implementation of the pastoral plan, in particular its religious education component, would greatly assist many of these parishes.

A Task For The Future

No matter where it is undertaken, and by whatever denominations, accomplishing the task of Hispanic religious education ministry demands well-trained leaders with a high degree of sensitivity, knowledge of the language, commitment, ample materials, and spiritual resources to satisfy people's needs. Speaking especially to Protestant religious educators, Loida Martell-Otero says that religious educators of today and tomorrow must be bilingual and multicultural, knowing the idiosyncrasies and idioms of the varied groups they face every day. "As a new generation of Hispanic Americans arises, better educated, more professional, the [religious educator] must respond to the questions posed by a generation no longer satisfied with the formulas of the past." She sees the challenge facing the religious educator as ensuring that educated persons do not assume the cultural biases of the dominant society so completely that they abandon the faith of the *pueblo*. To minister to the *pueblo* is to witness to the power of the crucified Christ who brings life and renewal. In this context the religious education minister continues to see stories of healing, of transformation and of empowerment— evidence of miracles every day.[36]

In looking to the future of Christian faith in the United States, Joseph Fitzpatrick has also stressed the significance of the next Hispanic generation. Writing in 1987, he maintained that it would be the second and subsequent generations that would achieve "a new cultural expression of the faith," a dynamic blend of both Hispanic and American influences. He welcomed such a possibility: "If this takes place, the Church of the next century could radiate a new life that would have a significant impact on the Church and the nation."[37]

SUGGESTED READINGS

Blubaugh, J. A., and Dorothy L. Pennington. *Crossing Difference, Interracial Communication*. Columbus, Ohio: Charles E. Merrill Publishing, 1976. This book is particularly important for students because it includes

---

35. *Supplementary Final Report of a National Study of Catholic Religious Education/Catechesis* (Washington, D.C.: Office of Educational Testing Service, 1994), pp. 1, 9.
36. Martell-Otero, "En Las Maños del Señor," p. 19.
37. Fitzpatrick, *One Church*, p. 161.

exercises to help them explore and deal with individual and group response and how to facilitate the understanding of interpersonal communication between people of different races.

Cotera, Martha, and Larry Hufford. *Bridging Two Cultures*. Austin, Tex.: National Education Laboratory Publishers, 1980. This work is written with the characteristics of a bicultural community in mind.

Elizondo, Virgilio. *Christianity and Culture*. San Antonio, Tex.: Mexican American Cultural Center, 1983. This work covers the anthropological and psychological characteristics of Mexican Americans, their faith, spirituality, and popular religious practices. Excellent resource for anyone wishing to understand the bicultural community.

———. *Galilean Journey: The Mexican American Promise*. Maryknoll, N.Y.: Orbis Books, 1985. The founder of the Mexican American Cultural Center writes eloquently of the Mexican-American heritage and of the struggles and gifts of Latino/Hispanic peoples in the United States.

Fitzpatrick, Joseph. *One Church, Many Cultures, The Challenge of Diversity*. Kansas City, Mo.: Sheed and Ward, 1987. Chapters 5–6 are extremely helpful for a better understanding of the relationship of culture to the faith of Hispanic Christians.

———. "The Hispanic Poor in the American Catholic Middle-Class Church." *Thought: A Review of Culture and Ideas* 63:249 (1988): 189–200. This article points out the difference between the middle-class Church in the United States and the Hispanic poor and how the Church attempts to evangelize them. Important to understanding Hispanic spirituality and religious formation.

———. *Strangers and Aliens no Longer, Part 1: The Hispanic Presence in the Church of the United States*. Washington, D.C.: NCCB/USCC Office of Research, 1992. This is the first of three books. It is intended to serve as a useful resource on the Hispanic presence in the American church for seminarians, researchers, and all who are interested in or involved with the multicultural experience in the United States. It contains profiles of cultural groups produced by the latest census data and insights into the Church's vision of culture and the processes of inculturation. It considers questions that remain to be answered by researchers if we are to better serve a given culture.

Gonzalez, Justo L. ed. *VOCES: Voices from the Hispanic Church*. Nashville: Abingdon, 1992. Twenty-three contributors—Catholic and Protestant, male and female—address concerns that cut across denominational and confessional lines.

Hall, Edward T. *The Silent Language*. Garden City, N.Y.: Anchor, 1963. The author discusses the richness of communication and how to better understand a culture group. He examines nonverbal communication and how it is affected by culture.

Heritage and Hope: Evangelization in the United States. Washington, D.C.: NCCB/USCC Hispanic Affairs, 1990. The pastoral letter written by

U.S. Catholic bishops for the five hundredth anniversary of the coming of the gospel to the Americas.

Isasi-Diaz, Ada, and Yolanda Tarango. *Hispanic Women: Prophetic Voice in the Church*. San Francisco: Harper & Row, 1988. This work makes a good contribution to a spirituality for Hispanic women, especially those living in the United States. It is based on many interviews that show experiences of Hispanic women.

"Journeying Together Toward the Lord" \En Marcha Hacia El Señor. Bilingual edition, Publication No. 565–8 United States Catholic Conference, Washington, D.C. Revised edition, 1993. Valuable resource for leaders in migrant communities, who will later direct the catechesis in migrant camps.

Maldonado, L. *Introduccion a la Religiosidad Popular*. Edicion Sal Terrae Santander, Spain, 1985. The author explains popular religiosity and the role it plays in the faith expression of the people. It describes that even after the reforms of Vatican II the Church did not know how to use the best of popular religiosity for evangelization purposes.

Martell-Otero, Loida. "En Las Manos del Senor: Ministry in the Hispanic Context." *The Apple Seed: A Christian Forum for Reconciliation,* Winter 1994. The journal of the ethnic American ministry program of Seminary of the East, New York City, invites Christians from all racial and ethnic backgrounds engaged in ministry to teach and learn from each other.

Padilla, Amado M. *Acculturation: Theories, Models and Some New Findings*. Washington, D.C.: American Association for the Advancement of Science, 1980. This book covers acculturation among Cubans, Mexican Americans, and Puerto Ricans. It focuses on environmental adaptation, sex roles, and biculturalism.

Portes, Alejandro, and Robert L. Back. *Latin Journey: Cuban and Mexican Immigrants in the U.S.A.* Berkeley: University of California Press, 1985. This work is particularly important because there are few books that include both Cuban and Mexican immigration factors. It also helps in understanding other ethnic groups.

Prophetic Voices. Washington, D.C.: Office for Hispanic Affairs NCCB, 1986. Explains the process of the III Encuentro Nacional de Pastoral Hispana. It describes the work of Hispanics across the nation and their leadership.

Saint Mary's Press Newsletter. Christian Brothers Publications, 702 Terrace Heights, Winona, MN 55987–1320.

The Puerto Rican Americans. Englewood Cliffs, N.J.: Prentice-Hall, 1987. This book describes the Puerto Rican community in New York City and explains how religion helps understand Puerto Rican spirituality.

8

NATIVE AMERICANS AND RELIGIOUS EDUCATION

Jace Weaver

There are birds of many colors—red, blue, green, yellow—yet it is all one bird. There are horses of many colors—brown, black, yellow, white—yet it is all one horse. So cattle, so all living things—animals, flowers, trees. So men: in this land where once were only Indians are now men of every color—white, black, yellow, red—yet all one people.

—Hiamovi, Cheyenne[1]

He put in your heart certain wishes and plans, in my heart he put other and different desires. Each man is good in his sight. It is not necessary for eagles to be crows.

—Sitting Bull, Hunkpapa Lakota[2]

The title for this chapter is apt—Native Americans *and* religious education. When the indigenous peoples of the Americas have impinged at all upon the consciousness of religious educators, it has been as the subjects of missionization rather than as living beings whose culture and worldview have something important to contribute to our understanding of the Creator

---

1. Hiamovi, a Cheyenne chief, quoted in *The Gift Is Rich*, by E. Russell Carter, rev. ed. (New York: Friendship, 1968), pp. 80–81.
2. W. W. Penn, *The Absence of Angels* (Sag Harbor, N.Y.: Permanent, 1994), p. 6.

and the created order. Religious education given to Native Americans has reflected a monocultural imposition on a multicultural reality.[3] What then does multicultural religious education mean to America's Native population?[4]

Multicultural education has been defined in four distinct and very different ways. It has been used to mean education of the culturally different, education about cultural differences, education for cultural pluralism, and bicultural education.[5] Native Americans have experienced almost exclusively education of the first type. European-Americans have typically assumed that Native Americans come from "deficit" home environments and dysfunctional cultures. The role of education thus has been to "increase compatibility" between the home and the dominant culture.[6] The goal of such education has been the destruction of Native cultures and assimilation into the dominant society. For non-Natives, multicultural education has largely been of the second type, namely, education about cultural differences.

This dichotomy creates a number of problems for religious education in general and multicultural religious education in particular. For Natives, the question is how to teach persons from widely diverse cultures and traditions while respecting those traditions and without imposing European-American cultural values—that is to say, without pushing toward assimilation. For non-Natives, the issue remains how to educate concerning Native cultures

---

3. It needs to be pointed out that both *Native American* and *American Indian* are, in fact, social constructs. There is tremendous diversity in traditions and thought worlds among various Native nations, and, despite growing pan-tribal discourse, an Indian's primary identification remains the tribe. No single ethnicity can take fully into account the more than five hundred tribes, eight major language groups, and at least three distinct racial (Amerindian, Athabascan, and Aleut and Innu) strains usually lumped together under the collective term *Native American* or *Indian*. In general, tribes of the same language group share similar, though still very distinct, cultures. Athabascans are as different from Cherokee (of the Iroquoian language family) as, for example, Chinese are from Arabs. See *Struggle for the Land: Indigenous Resistance to Genocide, Ecocide, and Expropriation in Contemporary North America*, by Ward Churchill (Monroe, Me.: Common Courage, 1993), p. 19; "Roots," by Robsen Bonnichsen and Alan L. Schneider, *The Sciences* (May/June 1995): 30.

4. Although I am aware of more restrictive definitions of religious education, in formulating this essay, I have thought of the term in its broadest application. Behind my usage is an assumption that there is "a commonality in religious education which cuts across faiths" and various levels and aspects of the educational process. Norma H. Thompson, "The Role of Theology in Religious Education: An Introduction," in *Religious Education and Theology*, ed. Norma H. Thompson (Birmingham: Religious Education Press, 1982), p. 15.

5. Frederic R. Gunsky, "Multicultural Education: Implications for American Indian People," in *Multicultural Education and the American Indian*, ed. Jack Forbes (Los Angeles: American Indian Studies Center, University of California, 1979), p. 70.

6. Ibid.

without continuing the pattern of their exploitation. The problems are hardly new.

HISTORICAL PATTERNS OF RELIGIOUS EDUCATION AMONG NATIVE AMERICANS

Jorge Noriega states that the "formal education of the indigenous population of the Americas began at virtually the same moment as the European drive to colonize the hemisphere."[7] That education was religious education. Catechistic rituals such as *las posadas*,[8] created by Augustinian Father Diego de Soria in 1587, were introduced to teach Natives Christian concepts and practices while, at the same time, deliberately subverting indigenous concepts of deity that the religious educators regarded as pagan and diabolical.

At almost the very inception of the colonial enterprise in the Americas, missionaries developed the so-called reductionist model of evangelism and religious education. Under this paradigm, Indian converts and catechists left their villages and moved into compounds, or *reducciones,* supervised by missionaries. According to Catholic apologist Aloysius Roche, these *reducciones* were designed "to protect the natives from their rascally exploiters." He declares, "A royal ordinance had provided that no converted Indian could be enslaved, and so the Jesuits determined to found reservations or enclosures, and then to get the Indians to move into them, lead their own life and receive instruction. This was the origin of the *Reductions,* so called because the natives were recalled (*reducir*) from the jungle, into which their oppressors had driven them, to live in proper communities under Christian laws." Roche notes that because of the ever-present danger from slave hunters, Indians flocked to the *reducciones.*[9] In fact, potential Native converts were "physically and politically separated from their communities and families" so that instruction could be carried out unimpeded by "pagan" influences.[10] The primary purpose was to speed conversion and prevent relapse by removing the Natives from their traditional culture and surrounding them with exclusively Christian examples. According to George

---

7. Jorge Noriega, "American Indian Education in the United States: Indoctrination for Subordination to Colonialism," in *The State of Native America: Genocide, Colonization, and Resistance,* ed. M. Annette Jaimes (Boston: South End, 1992), p. 371.

8. *Las Posadas* is a service of shelter for the Holy Family, traditionally celebrated by Hispanic peoples over a number of nights during the Advent season.

9. Aloysius Roche, *In the Track of the Gospel* (London: Burns Oates, 1953), pp. 94–95. Emphasis original.

10. George Tinker, *Missionary Conquest: The Gospel and Native American Cultural Genocide* (Minneapolis: Fortress, 1993), p. 18.

Tinker (Osage/Cherokee), the system was first advanced by Bartolome de Las Casas, the Spanish Dominican priest often hailed as a reformer and a protector of the Indians.[11] Among its earliest written justifications is a letter written in 1628 by Jonas Michaelius, a minister sent to establish the first Dutch Reformed Church at New Amsterdam. The letter is worth quoting at length. Writing to a colleague in the Netherlands, Michaelius said:

> As to the natives of this country, I find them entirely savage and wild, strangers to all decency, yea, uncivil and stupid as garden stakes, proficient in all wickedness and ungodliness, devilish men who serve nobody but the devil, that is the spirit they call Menetto,[12] under which title they comprehend everything that is subtle and crafty and beyond human skill and power. They have so much witchcraft, divination, sorcery, and wicked arts that they can hardly be held in by any bands or locks. They are as thievish and treacherous as they are tall, and in cruelty, they are altogether inhuman, more than barbarous, far exceeding the Africans. . . .
>
> How these people best be led to the true knowledge of God and of the Mediator Christ is hard to say. I cannot myself wonder enough who it is that has imposed so much upon Your Reverence and many others in the fatherland concerning the docility of this people and their good nature, the proper *principia religionis* and *vestigia legis naturae* which are said to be among them, in whom I have as yet been able to discover hardly a single good point, except that they do not speak so jeeringly and so scoffingly of their Creator as the Africans dare to do. . . . Now, by what means are we to prepare this people for salvation? . . .
>
> Shall we then leave the parents as they are and begin with the children, who are still young. Let it be so. But they ought in youth to be separated from their parents, yea, from their whole nation. For, without this, they would forthwith be as much accustomed as their elders to the heathenish tricks and deviltries which of itself are kneaded into their hearts by nature by a just judgment of God, so that having once, by habit, obtained deep root, they would, with great difficulty, be brought away from it. But this separation is hard to effect, for the parents have a strong affection for their children and are very loath to part with them, and when this happens, as has already been proved, the parents are never fully contented but take them away stealthily, or induce them to run away.
>
> Nevertheless, we must proceed in this direction, although it would be attended with some expense, to obtain the children by means of presents and promises, with the gratitude and consent of the parents, in order to place them under the instruction of some experienced and godly schoolmaster, where they might be instructed, not only to speak, read, and write our language but especially in the fundamentals of our Christian religion, and where, besides, they will see nothing but good examples of virtuous living. But they must sometimes speak their native

---

11. Ibid., pp. 18–19.
12. I.e., Manitou.

tongue among themselves in order not to forget it, as being evidently a principal means of spreading the knowledge of religion through the whole nation.[13]

This reductionist paradigm became, with slight variation, the model for missions and education among Natives, for both Catholics and Protestants, until well into the twentieth century. The goal was to create a system under which the indigenes could eventually become self-colonizing.[14]

Christianity and United States Government Indian Policy

The new American nation took up the task from its European forebears immediately. In 1776 the Continental Congress began to recruit and send Christian ministers and teachers to the Indians.[15] In 1819, when Congress established a so-called Civilization Fund for the education of the native nations, the contours of U.S. educational policy among Native Americans were taking shape.[16] By 1820 boarding schools began to be set up, following the philosophical end that "Indians would be made over into Christian farmers and would fit the mold of American society as represented by the Jeffersonian agrarian matrix."[17] The best and brightest Indian youths would be removed from their culture and assimilated into European-American culture, including Christianity, and then returned to serve "as a virus, a medium through which to hurry along a calculated process of sociocultural decay 'from within,' thus speeding the day in which Native America might be predicted to become fully integrated into the Euroamerican state structure."[18]

The best-known of these boarding schools, the Carlisle Indian School in Pennsylvania, was founded in 1879, headed by Richard H. Pratt, an army officer who had once served as commandant of Fort Marion, the infamous Indian prison camp in Florida. At Carlisle, students spent half their day in

---

13. Letter from Jonas Michaelius to Adrian Smoutius, 11 August 1628, reprinted in Mortimer J. Adler, et al., eds., *1493–1754: Discovering a New World* vol. 1 of Annals of America (Chicago: Encyclopedia Britannica, 1976), pp. 92–94.

14. Tinker, *Missionary Conquest*, pp. 18–20.

15. Floyd O'Neil, "Multiple Sources and Resources for the Development of Social Studies Curriculum for the American Indian," in *Multicultural Education*, ed. Jack Forbes, p. 113.

16. Terry Tafoya and Roy De Boer, "Comments on the Involvement of Christian Churches in Native American Affairs," in *Christians and Native American Concerns in the Late 20th Century*, ed. Marilyn Bode et al. (Seattle: Church Council of Greater Seattle, 1981), p. 17. See also Henry Warner Bowden, *American Indians and Christian Missions* (Chicago: University of Chicago Press, 1981), pp. 134–67, passim.

17. O'Neil, "Multiple Sources," p. 113.

18. Noriega, "American Indian Education," p. 379.

classroom and religious instruction. The remainder was dedicated to manual labor. Military-style discipline was strictly enforced.[19]

It was not unusual for Native children to be removed from their homes at age six or seven. They did not see their families again until they were seventeen or eighteen. Noriega points out that at that age, consistent with the aforementioned "virus" concept, they were often *sent* back, thoroughly alienated from their culture and with little idea of the role they were supposed to fulfill within it.[20] Mary Crow Dog relates finding a poster among her grandfather's effects, listing the rules of the boarding school he attended. The rules run as follows:

- Let Jesus save you.
- Come out of your blanket, cut your hair, and dress like a white man.
- Have a Christian family with one wife for life only.
- Live in a house like your white brother. Work hard and wash often.
- Learn the value of a hard-earned dollar. Do not waste your money on give-aways.
- Be punctual.
- Believe that property and wealth are signs of divine approval.
- Keep away from saloons and strong spirits.
- Speak the language of your white brother. Send your children to school to do likewise.
- Go to church often and regularly.
- Do not go to Indian dances or to the medicine men.[21]

According to Noriega, "Altogether, the whole procedure conform[ed] to one of the essential criteria—the forced transfer of children from a targeted racial, ethnic, national, or religious group to be reared and absorbed by a physically dominating group—specified as a Crime Against Humanity under the United Nations 1948 Convention on Punishment and Prevention of the Crime of Genocide."[22]

The most direct component in the alliance forged between Christianity (and religious education) and official U.S. government policy occurred, however, in 1869, ten years before the founding of Carlisle Indian School, when President Grant inaugurated his "peace policy," whereby military personnel were replaced by men from a variety of Christian denominations

---

19. Robert A. Trennert Jr., "Bureau of Indian Affairs Schools," in *America in the Twentieth Century*, ed. Mary Davis (New York: Garland Publishing, 1994), p. 84.

20. Noriega, "American Indian Education," p. 379.

21. Mary Crow Dog with Richard Erdoes, *Lakota Woman* (New York: Weidenfeld, 1990), p. 31.

22. Noriega, "American Indian Education," p. 381.

who were given exclusive control over seventy-three Indian agencies. The denominations were prohibited from interfering in affairs on each other's reservations and, in fact, missionaries from one denomination could enter a reservation administered by another only with permission. Churches also exercised control over disbursement of funds and procurement. Attendance at church worship services was compulsory, while traditional Native spiritual practice was outlawed. For example, in 1923 U.S. Indian Commissioner Charles Burke instructed his agents that traditional dances be limited to one each month and that no person under fifty years of age be permitted to take part.[23]

To become Christian meant to stop being Indian. It meant to surrender one's culture. This "cultural genocide"[24] caused Christians to view the Native population as a dying race. D. P. Kidder, a professor at Drew Theological Seminary in the nineteenth century, wrote, "Without enumerating or discussing causes, the fact must be recognized that throughout the whole continent the aboriginal races are dying out to an extent that leaves little present prospect of any considerable remnants being perpetuated in the form of permanent Christian communities. Still missions are maintained in the Indian territories and reservations, and the government of the United States is effectively cooperating with them to accomplish all that may be done for the Christian civilization of the Indians and Indian tribes that remain."[25] The unenumerated causes were assimilation on the one hand and wholesale extermination on the other. The cooperation of the U.S. government is Grant's peace policy. Though the kind of ecclesiastical serfdom described above officially ended in the 1930s, with the institution of the Indian New Deal under Franklin Roosevelt and his Indian Commissioner John Collier, its effects continue to the present.[26]

Because of their supposed involvement in the ghost dance movement—the apocalyptic, religious renewal movement that gained wide acceptance among Natives and led ultimately to the Wounded Knee Massacre—Mormons were barred from Native missions in the 1890s. They resumed evangelization efforts in 1942, greatly expanding them in the 1950s. Today they

23. Leonard A. Carlson, "Government Policy: 1900–1933," in *Native America*, ed. Mary Davis, pp. 215, 217; Jace Weaver, "Missions and Missionaries," in *Native America*, ed. Mary Davis, p. 347.

24. Tinker, *Missionary Conquest*, p. viii.

25. D. P. Kidder, "Missions," in *Cyclopedia of Biblical, Theological, and Ecclesiastical Literature*, ed. John McClintock and James Strong, (New York: Harper, 1867–87), p. 375.

26. John Collier, *Indians of the Americas* (New York: Norton, 1947), pp. 261–87; Jace Weaver, "Native Reformation in Indian Country: Forging a Relevant Spiritual Identity among Indian Christians," *Christianity and Crisis*, 15 February 1993, pp. 40–41.

rank second among Christian denominations in Native adherents.[27] A principal component of the Mormon religious education for Natives has been the Indian Placement Program, a variation of the boarding school system that in twenty-five years placed more than sixty thousand Native youths with Mormon foster families. Operating as a modern-day *reduccion*, the program secures the children (beginning at eight years of age) an education and trains them in Mormon belief, practice, and lifestyle. Parents are discouraged from visiting, especially during the first year. Though officially phased out beginning in the 1970s, when it came under criticism for removing of children from their parents and tribal cultures, the program continues to the present. It is downplayed because of Native opposition. According to Joann Sebastian Morris (Sault Ste. Marie Chippewa), "several studies have raised questions about the extent to which the placement program and its suppression of tribal identity produce psychological stress, anxiety, and alienation among Indian students."[28] George Patrick Lee, the only Native ever to rise through the hierarchy of the Church of Jesus Christ of Latter-Day Saints, was excommunicated for criticizing the program.[29]

Contemporary Missionary Activity Among Native Americans

George Tinker has written that an illusion with which contemporary American denominations live "too comfortably . . . is the historical interpretation of the churches' missionary outreach to the native peoples of this continent."[30] And while most Americans now probably acknowledge at least a part of the churches' unsavory past in regard to Native peoples, many are surprised to find out that missionaries are still at work in Indian country. William Baldridge, a Cherokee who taught at Central Baptist Theological Seminary in Kansas City, stated that he continues to be impressed by the number of people active in the life of various denominations who are shocked to hear about the realities of current mission programs to Native Americans and who express the assumption that "we stopped doing missions like that a hundred years ago."[31] Baldridge joined with Kim Mammedaty,

---

27. Approximately 25 percent of the Native population in the United States is Christian. There are roughly 265,000 Native Roman Catholics, 75,000 Native Mormons, 35,000 Native Episcopalians, and 17,500 Native United Methodists. If one accepts the 1990 U.S. Census figure of 1.8 million Native Americans, these four denominations account for almost 22 percent of that number.

28. Joann Sebastian Morris, "Churches and Education," in *Native America*, ed. Mary Davis, p. 115.

29. Ibid.; see also Weaver, "Missions," p. 348.

30. Tinker, *Missionary Conquest*, p. 2.

31. William Baldridge, "New Visions for the Americas: Religious Engagement and Social Transformation," in *Reclaiming Our Histories*, ed. David Batstone (Minneapolis: Workers Press, 1993), pp. 23–32.

a Kiowa and an ordained member of the clergy, in calling for an end to continued "spiritual oppression." Challenging the church to recognize its "complicity in evil," the pair called for the American Baptist Church to bring its missionaries home.[32]

The issue of evangelization of Native Americans remains a sensitive one among Natives because of the history of mission activity and because of the minority position of Christianity among them. It has caused much internal division and jealousy. Many Natives, both Christian and traditional, oppose any evangelization of Natives whatsoever, preferring to see something akin to the agreement between mainline denominations and Jews against such attempts at conversion. Others, following the lead of Roman Catholics and conservative, evangelical Protestant denominations, still take the position that it is incumbent upon all Christians to spread the gospel. The matter is further complicated by interdenominational rivalries and by the fact that many fundamentalist Indian Christians have internalized the assimilationist, culture-denying Christianity first brought to them by missionaries decades ago.[33] In fact, in terms of religious education, many Natives are still taught such a faith, despite the fact that their denominations may have long ago abandoned such teachings for non-Natives "for a more contemporary articulation of the gospel."[34] According to George Tinker, "One must at least suspect that the process of Christianization has involved some internalization of the larger illusion of Indian inferiority and the idealization of white culture and religion. Some have called it internalized racism, and as such it surely results in a praxis of self-hatred."[35]

In many locales missionary activities have not changed since the inauguration of Grant's peace policy. Vine Deloria Jr. (Standing Rock Sioux) pointed out the truth of this in his book *Custer Died for Your Sins*. In 1967 he asked a Presbyterian missionary in charge of that denomination's work among the Shinnecocks of Long Island, New York, "how long [they] intended to conduct mission activities among a tribe that had lived as Christians for over three hundred and fifty years." The minister replied impassively, "Until the job is done."[36] As recently as 1985, Carl Starkloff, a Jesuit priest who has worked among Natives and who continues to write extensively about them, stated, "The task of the Church remains missionary, in that as yet there does not exist a self-supporting, self-governing and self-propagating body that is a native Indian Protestant church save in a few

---

32. Jace Weaver, "Native Reformation," p. 40.

33. I have called the faith of such fundamentalist, culture-denying Native Christians "apple piety." "Apple," the Indian equivalent of "Oreo" among African Americans, is a derogatory term meaning red on the outside and white on the inside.

34. Tinker, *Missionary Conquest*, p. 3; Weaver, "Native Reformation," pp. 39–41.

35. Tinker, *Missionary Conquest*, p. 3.

36. Vine Deloria Jr., *Custer Died for Your Sins* (New York: Macmillan, 1969), p. 112.

local cases—and even fewer in Roman Catholicism."[37] James Treat (Creek) points out that Starkloff "does not seem to consider the possibility that it may well be the Church's missionary stance which is the only thing *preventing* the widespread establishment and maturation of indigenous Christian bodies."[38]

Even among those religious educators who are seemingly most sympathetic to Native cultures, traditional religions are devalued. For instance, E. Russell Carter, who served for seventeen years as religious work director at the Haskell Institute (later Haskell Indian Nations University) in Lawrence, Kansas, speaks of traditional religions as "marvelous bridges over which Indian people find a passage into a new and meaningful faith" through Christianity.[39] He contends that the great mistake of most missionaries was one of missed opportunity. He cites with approval the statement to the National Fellowship of Indian Workers by Robert L. Bennett (Oneida), the first Indian to become commissioner of the Bureau of Indian Affairs: "The churches were presented with an unusual opportunity to capitalize on an existing spiritual life, *just as the Government was presented an unusual opportunity to capitalize on an existing temporal life.* Perhaps neither body, the religious nor the secular, fully recognized the opportunity it had, and chose, therefore, to offer their *contributions* as substitutes for, rather than supplements to, the Indian way of life."[40]

CONTEMPORARY PROBLEMS OF NATIVE CHRISTIAN RELIGIOUS EDUCATION

For many Natives today, to become Christian *still* means to stop being Indian. Sister Gloria Davis, a Choctaw-Navajo nun, puts it succinctly when she states, "The missionaries . . . said we had no religion, that we were pagans, even though we believed we were in harmony with the Creator and that he took care of us. But even now we are told by the church not to be too Indian."[41] Donald Pelotte, an Abenaki and Roman Catholic bishop of Gallup, New Mexico, echoes Sister Gloria, saying, "It's terrible that some denominations won't let Indians be Indians."[42] This continued subjugation

---

37. Carl F. Starkloff, "Religious Renewal in Native North America: The Contemporary Call to Mission," *Missiology* 13, no. 1 (January 1985): 83.

38. James A. Treat, "Native Americans, Theology, and Liberation: Christianity and Traditionalism in the Struggle for Survival" (Master's thesis, Pacific School of Religion, 1989), p. 77. Emphasis original.

39. Carter, *Gift Is Rich*, p. 57.

40. Ibid., pp. 104–6. Emphasis mine.

41. Catherine Walsh, "Native American Catholics at a Crossroads," *America*, 31 October 1992, p. 329.

42. Donald Pelotte, interview with author, 4 January 1993.

by the institutional church contributes to what another Native nun, Marie-Therese Archambault, termed "the terrible irony" of being both Indian and Christian.[43] Multicultural religious educators who are seeking to interpret Native cultures to their learners need to be aware of the way Natives experience their lives as Americans, as members of a particular Native culture, and (in some cases) as Christians. Similarly, religious educators who are working in a multicultural context that includes Native Americans need to be aware of the identity crisis that challenges many, particularly the young, who try to live as Native Christians. According to James Treat, "Native Americans face challenging and confusing circumstances as they attempt to reconcile traditional cultural and spiritual understanding with the dominant white society. Having accepted the religion of their oppressors, they face questions raised by the dilemma of living in two worlds, questions that contribute to a crisis of identity. And while many Americans view domestic oppression as a thing of the past, the five-hundred-year-old assault on Native American sovereignty . . . mistreatment and coercive conversion of Native Americans by Christian missionaries also impacts theological reflection."[44]

Those in the European-American dominant culture, in fact, always have been amazed by the survival of Native cultures and identity. Whites have always assumed that Natives would accept an option not open to African Americans, Asian Americans, or other minority groups—simply to be white. As Terry Tafoya (Taos Pueblo) and Roy De Boer (Lummi) succinctly point out, "Over and over again, a central theme of Federal relationships with American Indians is an attempt to 'remake' Indians into a darker hue of White people."[45] This policy has in turn shaped the way that the broader culture views Natives. To this way of thinking, those few remaining Natives who clung to their identity were recalcitrant throwbacks who would eventually fade from the scene. During the 1950s and 60s, Time-Life publisher Henry Luce expressed the epitome of this belief when he banned coverage of Natives and Native issues from his publications, believing modern-day Indians to be "phonies."[46]

When modern-day Indians are not viewed as degraded cultural recalcitrants, they are expected to conform to a stereotype born of romanticized, white-produced representations of the nineteenth century. When confronted by a Native who does not fit this image, other North Americans judge her or

---

43. Weaver, "Native Reformation," p. 40.
44. Treat, *Native Americans, Theology, and Liberation*, pp. 1–2.
45. Tafoya and De Boer, "*Comments on Involvement*," p. 17.
46. Alvin Josephy, "New England Indians: Then and Now," in *The Pequots in Southern New England: The Rise and Fall of an American Indian Nation*, ed. Laurence M. Hauptman and James D. Wherry (Norman, Okla.: University of Oklahoma Press, 1990), pp. 7–8.

him to be "inauthentic." Regularly, Natives are expected to "look Indian."[47] Cherokee author Thomas King, appearing for a radio show, was once told to "sound Indian."[48] A whole host of non-Native "wannabes" (i.e., "I wanna be Indian") pass themselves off as "part Indian"—or even simply as Indian. The New Age movement, the so-called men's movement (popularized by Robert Bly and others), and the dominant European-American culture at large have appropriated Native imagery. Many actual Natives pander to white desires by creating colonialist fantasies for the eager consumption of non-Natives. As George Tinker writes, "The truth is . . . that Indian people have internalized this illusion [of the colonizer] just as deeply as white Americans have, and as a result we discover from time to time just how fully we participate in our own oppression. Implicitly, in both thought and action, we too often concede that the illusion of white superiority is an unquestionable factual reality."[49]

In all too many cases, we have become the self-colonizers envisioned by religious educators, missionaries, and government policy makers. And as Tunisian postcolonialist Albert Memmi wrote, "In order for the colonizer to be a complete master, it is not enough for him to be so in actual fact, but he must also believe in [his] legitimacy. In order for that legitimacy to be complete, it is not enough for the colonized to be a slave, he must also accept the role."[50]

Yet despite attempts at suppression of Native culture and identity, and contrary to white expectations, Natives and their traditions survive. The gods of Native North America have never left themselves without witness.[51] It has even been suggested that it was the very act of suppression itself, the forcing of traditional religions and practices underground, that permitted their survival.[52]

NATIVE RELIGIOUS EDUCATION
AND WORLDVIEW

To speak of religious education and Native Americans is to engage in a kind of incommensurate discourse. The Western, European-American

---

47. Jace Weaver, "Gaming in the Fields of the Lord: Indian Gambling and New England," *Zion's Herald*, 9 October 1992, p. 6.

48. Thomas King, interview with author, 27 January 1993.

49. Tinker, *Missionary Conquest*, p. 2.

50. Albert Memmi, *The Colonizer and the Colonized*, sp. ed. (Boston: Beacon, 1967), p. 89.

51. Though Native religions were officially suppressed until 1934, they continued underground. See Collier, *Indians of the Americas*, p. 261.

52. O'Neil, "Multiple Sources," p. 153.

worldview common to most religious educators is quite different from the Native worldview.[53] This incommensurability and the near impossibility of translating from one thought world to the other complicate the task of the religious educator.

The thrust of the Western Enlightenment rationalist tradition has been to confine religion in its own peculiar sphere, separate from science and everyday existence.[54] Natives recognize no such separation. For them, religion is life as it is lived in its entirety. Traditional religions are not sets of principles, creeds, or theology. They are integrated into daily activity. Thus as Charles Eastman (Sioux), one of the foremost Native writers of the early twentieth century, observed, "Every act of [an Indian's] life is, in a very real sense, a religious act."[55] It is therefore "impossible to speak of *any* aspect of Indian life without discussing religion."[56] The implications of such a difference in worldview are clear, and they infinitely complicate the task of the religious educator. If the educator's objective is to enable learners to *live* their religion, the Native conceptualization has much to offer. Such a "lived" religion is not possible if "religion" is separated from day-to-day life.[57]

Ward Churchill (Creek/Cherokee Métis) depicted the difference in Native and European-American views graphically. Diagram 1 below shows the European conceptualization. Diagram 2 reflects the Native.[58]

Western thought is essentially linear. Vine Deloria writes, "An old Indian saying captures the radical difference between Indian and Western peoples quite adequately. The white man, the Indians maintain, has ideas; Indians have visions. Ideas have a single dimension and require a chain of connected ideas to make sense. . . . The vision, on the other hand, presents a whole picture of experience and has a central meaning that stands on its own feet as an independent revelation."[59]

---

53. Despite the tremendous diversity among the indigenous peoples of the Americas (fn. 3), there are certain commonalties in worldviews and epistemology that make it possible to discuss them together in broad terms.

54. See Paul Boyer, "Living Spirituality," *Tribal College: Journal of American Indian Higher Education*, fall 1994, pp. 4–5. For a more fulsome discussion of Native worldviews, see Dennis H. McPherson and J. Douglas Rabb, *Indian from the Inside: A Study in Ethno-Metaphysics* (Thunder Bay, Ont.: Centre for Northern Studies, Lakehead University, 1993).

55. Charles Eastman, *The Soul of the Indian* (Boston: Houghton Mifflin, 1911), p. 47.

56. Carter, *Gift Is Rich*, p. 55.

57. For a discussion of similar ideas in a non-Native context, see James Michael Lee, *The Shape of Religious Instruction* (Mishawaka, Ind.: Religious Education Press, 1971), pp. 6–9; 81–86; see also, generally, Thomas H. Groome, *Christian Religious Education* (New York: Harper & Row, 1980).

58. The diagrams come from Ward Churchill, "White Studies: The Intellectual Imperialism of Contemporary U.S. Education," *Integrated Education* 18 (1984): 54.

59. Vine Deloria Jr., "A Native American Perspective on Liberation," *Mission Trends* 4, (July, 1977): 262.

Figure 8.1 European and Native American Worldviews

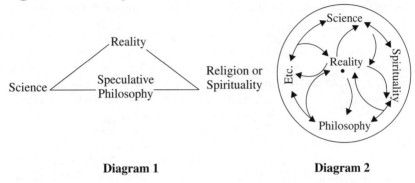

Diagram 1   Diagram 2

This view of religion as "a whole picture of experience" or as the totality of existence is described eloquently by Jack Forbes (Powhatan/Lenape/Saponi): " 'Religion' is, in reality, 'living.' It is not what we profess, or what we say, or what we proclaim; our 'religion' is what we do, what we desire, what we seek, what we dream about, what we fantasize, what we think—all these things—twenty-four hours a day. One's religion, then, is one's life, not merely the ideal life but the life actually lived. . . . 'Religion' is not prayer, it is not a church, it is not 'theistic,' it is not 'atheistic,' it has little to do with what white people call 'religion.' It is our every act. If we tromp on a bug, that is our religion; if we experiment with animals, that is our religion; if we cheat at cards, that is our religion; if we dream of being famous, that is our religion; if we gossip maliciously, that is our religion; if we are rude and aggressive, that is our religion. All that we do, and are, is our religion."[60] Because of this attitude toward spirituality, most Native languages do not even have words for "religion."[61] Highlighting this difference in regard to Western traditions, Forbes has speculated somewhat ironically that perhaps there is no need for a word for religion until a people no longer have religion.[62] In Cherokee, the word sometimes translated as "religion," *eloh'*, also means land, history, and culture.[63] Perhaps there is no need for religions of theology until these things have been lost as well.[64]

---

60. Jack D. Forbes, *Columbus and Other Cannibals* (Brooklyn, N.Y.: Autonomedia, 1992), pp. 26–27.

61. For example, Joe S. Sando, *Pueblo Nations: Eight Centuries of Pueblo Indian History* (Santa Fe, N.M.: Clear Light, 1992), p. 30.

62. Forbes, *Columbus*, p. 26.

63. Jimmie Durham, quoted in *Stolen Continents: The Americas through Indian Eyes since 1492*, by Ronald Wright (Boston: Houghton Mifflin, 1992), p. 311.

64. Again, in a non-Native context, for a not unrelated discussion of the meaning of religion, see James Michael Lee, *The Content of Religious Instruction* (Birmingham, Ala.: Religious Education Press, 1985), pp. 2–3, 650.

A second difference between European-American and Native religion and modes of thinking is related to the linear nature of Western thought. Because of the linear character of its thought, Western humanity tends to perceive itself chronologically. George Tinker has observed that the Western intellectual tradition "functions out of a base that is quintessentially temporal. That is, time is the ordinate category, while space is subordinate."[65] By contrast, Native peoples are spatially oriented. Native religions are usually rooted in the land—and not just any land, but the traditional lands of a given tribe. This can be seen in the tribes' creation myths. These stories, as Deloria points out, are not so much, as in the Jewish-Christian traditions, stories of "what happened then" as they are accounts of "what happened here" (i.e., on the lands of the nation).[66] There is no *creatio ex nihilo*, and there is scant interest shown in the origins of the cosmos as a whole. This is clearly demonstrated by the origin myth of the Cherokee. While superficially an account of the creation of the *whole* world, it is in reality a depiction of the formation of old Cherokee country in the American Southeast.

Mircea Eliade has pointed out this fundamental difference between what he calls "modern" and "archaic" or "primitive" humanity. According to him, "archaic" humanity (i.e., indigenous, traditional peoples) sees itself as related and connected to the entire cosmos; by contrast, "modern" humanity views itself as linked to history.[67] Given the devastation wrought upon the environment since this shift to a "modern" perception of reality, it may be that the true nature of the fall of humanity is to be condemned to live only in history.

This leads to the third major difference between Western and Native religions. Unlike Christianity, traditional Native religions are not primarily religions of theology or belief, but, to use Tom Driver's phrase, religions of "ritual observance."[68] For instance, the Lummi of the Northwest coast speak of ritual as the "umbilical cord" that binds humanity to the cosmos. And in the case of most Native religions, these rituals often cannot be practiced *anywhere*, as can Christianity, but must be performed at specific sites or on specific lands.[69]

---

65. George Tinker, "Theological Education and Cross-Cultural Inclusiveness," (unpublished paper, Denver, Colo., 1989) p. 9.

66. Vine Deloria Jr., *God Is Red: A Native View of Religion* 2d ed. (Golden, Colo.: Fulcrum, 1992), p. 78.

67. See, generally, Mircea Eliade, *The Myth of the Eternal Return*, rev. ed. (Princeton: Princeton University Press, 1965).

68. Tom F. Driver, *The Magic of Ritual* (San Francisco: HarperCollins, 1991), p. 38.

69. In so writing, I am not unaware that many Roman Catholics, both Native and non-Native, would aver that Catholicism is a religion of "ritual observance." The Mass, they would argue, cannot be performed anywhere, but should be performed over the bones of a saint—following Christian tradition since the catacombs. The dichotomy

These three fundamental differences between Western and Native thought worlds have produced devastating effects for traditional Native religions, both in the ways that such religions are viewed by the church and with regard to their protection in the American courts. Christian missionaries and the church have, like Eliade, viewed Native religion as primitive and "pagan"—something to be eradicated and replaced by more "enlightened" rationalistic concepts. Similarly, the Western concept of "religion," as embodied in the U.S. Constitution and enforced by the courts, cannot encompass religions which so permeate life that they cannot be separated into their own distinct spheres, nor that are site specific, nor that are primarily religions of practice and not mere belief. Recent legal decisions, couched in terms of "freedom of religion" and the First Amendment, have eroded severely the protection afforded traditional Native religions, including decisions that affected sacramental use of peyote and limited access to traditional sacred sites. It has been left to the legislative process as to whether or not these Native faiths will be protected.[70]

MULTICULTURAL RELIGIOUS EDUCATION PRACTICES AND NATIVE AMERICANS

Any discussion of multicultural religious education must be divided into two parts, reflecting, broadly speaking, the different definitions discussed at the outset of this chapter. The first part involves education of non-Natives about Indian culture and religion. The second involves the religious education of Natives themselves.

In most churches today, religious education concerning Natives and their culture and spiritual traditions is limited usually to annual "basement" gatherings in which an Indian is invited to come and speak to the members of the congregation or parish. These talks are typically scheduled to coincide with Columbus Day or Thanksgiving. All too often the invitation is to speak only to the *children* of the congregation or parish. Such an invitation to address only the young may reflect a deep subconscious racism which assumes that Native culture, history, and tradition are appropriate subject

---

holds, however, in that there is a long and strong tradition of Catholic theology from the earliest origins of the church to the present day.

70. Jace Weaver, "In the Absence of the Holy: Native Land and Religious Freedom Claims and American Jurisprudence" (paper delivered at the fourth International Native American Studies Conference, Lake Superior State University, Sault Ste. Marie, Michigan, 9 October 1993). See also Jace Weaver, *Then to the Rock Let Me Fly: Luther Bohanon and Judicial Activism* (Norman: University of Oklahoma Press, 1993), pp. 44–50.

matter only for children and youth. In some bookstores and libraries, for instance, books about Indians are classified as children's literature; in others they are placed in the folklore section.[71] Not surprisingly, both youthful and adult audiences are disappointed when a Native arrives to speak to them who does not conform to the stereotyped nineteenth-century image. Both expect to see the fantasy Indians of James Barrie's *Peter Pan*. Often Natives are asked to bring drums with them or to perform rituals for the eager non-Native audiences, who are angered by refusal. Yet, would the same groups, inviting in an African American during African-American history month or for Martin Luther King's birthday, request that their guest perform an African ritual for them?

Misunderstandings about Native Americans and their cultures need to be addressed in the religious education process, and their cultures need to be treated sensitively as living, vibrant, evolving cultures—not as static relics of a nostalgic past.[72] All too often they are still treated like the latter. Natives are uniformly expected to live on reservations. They are expected to know everything about the traditions of every tribal group, reflecting the homogenized view of Indians held by most people in the dominant culture. I was once asked, "How long have you known you were Indian?" When I answered, "All my life," the response was, "You're so privileged!" Many wannabes have come lately to a "recovery" of their Native ancestry since Indians have become chic. Non-Natives eager for validation proclaim that they have participated in a sweat lodge (an important purification ceremony in many Native cultures) or other ceremony, often adding that although the ritual was "authentic," there were no Natives present.

Multicultural Religious Education Curricula for Non-Native Learners

Very few denominations have developed religious education curricula to educate non-Native churches about Native Americans, even among denominations with significant Christian Native memberships.[73] Two exemplary curriculums, however, should be noted.

The first is *Christians and Native American Concerns in the Late 20th Century: A Study for Congregations*. Produced in 1981 by the Church Council of Greater Seattle and written by Marilyn Bode with significant Native participation, the study was a response to a 1978 call by the National

---

71. In the Columbia University bookstore in New York, for example, this author recently found books by Gerald Vizenor, one of the preeminent current Native novelists, who writes novels in a postmodern idiom, in the folklore section.

72. For a discussion of the always evolving nature of cultures, see "The Man with the Spear," *Nature Conservancy*, January/February 1995, p. 30. No author is listed.

73. See fn. 27.

Congress of American Indians for churches to educate their constituents on Native issues "for the purpose of developing understanding and respect, and, ultimately, advocacy."[74] It consists of six sessions: (1) "Why Do I Care about Justice in Native American Issues?" dealing with dominant culture stereotypes and attitudes; (2) "How Did We Come to be in Possession of This Land?" the conquest and the realities of modern Native life; (3) "Can We Have Nations Within a Nation?" tribal sovereignty; (4) "Can a Group of Citizens Have What Seems to Be Unique Rights?" the special status of Native nations under the U.S. Constitution and pursuant to treaty; (5) "How Do Treaty Rights Affect Natural and Human Resources?" control by Natives of natural resources on their lands and self-determination; (6) "What Part Can We Play in the Resolution of Conflicts to Assure the Survival of Native Americans?" action responses to improve relations between Natives and non-Natives.[75]

In 1992, largely through the efforts of the Native American International Caucus, the General Conference of the United Methodist Church acknowledged its failure to treat Natives as full partners in the church. It passed the Confession to Native Americans, which confessed its sins against the indigenous peoples of the Americas. It suggested that local congregations develop and use their own similar confessions "as a way of fostering a deep sense of community with Native Americans."[76] It also established a four-year comprehensive initiative to focus on Native American ministry and participation in the church. The plan contains religious education components, including a program of leadership training events for Native laity. The workshops provide instruction on (1) Native cultural and spiritual values, (2) identification of community resources, (3) local congregation development, outreach, and administration, and (4) United Methodist resources, polity, history, and doctrine.[77] One concrete outgrowth of this Methodist emphasis on Native American concerns is a three-session unit entitled Native Americans and U.S. Society. The unit focuses on ongoing racism against America's Native population. It is part of a wider twelve-session multicultural study on racism in American society for church religious education groups. The educational goals of the three sessions deal with dispelling dominant culture stereotypes and misconceptions; providing some knowledge of the historical background of Native peoples, the role

---

74. Marilyn Bode, *Christians and Native American Concerns in the Late Twentieth Century: A Study for Congregations* [leader's guide and study papers] (Seattle: Church Council of Greater Seattle, 1981), p. 2.

75. Ibid. (participant's book), pp. 2–12.

76. "Confession to Native Americans," in *The Book of Resolutions of the United Methodist Church 1992* (Nashville: United Methodist Publishing House, 1992), pp. 210–11.

77. "Native American Comprehensive Plan on Its Way to the Year 2000," *Echo of the Four Winds*, February 1995, p. 4.

Christianity has played in disruption of Native cultures, and the realities of contemporary Native life; and encouraging understanding of Native demands for sovereignty and self-determination and the part the church needs to play in supporting such demands.[78]

As noted earlier, people in church congregations and parishes are generally ignorant of the history of relations between the dominant culture and Natives within the church. Two resources written by Native persons provide profitable study material for church groups. The first is *Missionary Conquest: The Gospel and Native American Cultural Genocide* by George Tinker; the second is *First White Frost,* by Homer Noley (Choctaw).[79] Both books deal with the confusion by the church of European-American cultural values and the gospel churches purport to proclaim. A third volume, older and in some respects dated but nonetheless still relevant, could provide the basis for a church study course of relations between whites and Native Americans. *Nations within a Nation: The American Indian and the Government of the United States*, by A. T. Anderson (Iroquois), deals with a wide range of Native issues that have religious education implications for Christians wanting to live faithfully with their neighbors.[80] Both Roman Catholics and United Methodists provide video presentations (with accompanying leadership guides to facilitate group study) on Native American concerns for non-Native congregations. *Circle of the Spirit: A Saga of Native Americans in the Catholic Church*, produced by the United States Catholic Conference, deals with the experiences of two tribes of the northwestern United States, the Coeur d'Alene of Idaho and the Lummi of Washington. Including comments by Bishop Charles Chaput, one of the two Native American Catholic bishops, the film attempts to help viewers appreciate both the religious and the cultural differences inherent in trying to be both Indian and Catholic.[81] *Living the Dream* and *Faith That Endures*, both from the United Methodist Church, depict Native ministries in Oklahoma and North Carolina and are designed as interpretive videos to encourage support of that denomination's Native American Awareness Sunday.[82]

78. Jace Weaver, "Native Americans in U.S. Society," in *Challenge: Racism*, ed. Donn Downall (Nashville: United Methodist Publishing House, 1994).

79. Homer Noley, *First White Frost: Native Americans and United Methodism* (Nashville: Abingdon, 1991).

80. A. T. Anderson, *Nations within a Nation: The American Indian and the Government of the United States* (Chappaqua, N.Y.: Union Carbide Corporation, 1976). The author served as special assistant to the U.S. government's American Indian Policy Review Commission in the mid-1970s.

81. "Circle of the Spirit: A Saga of Native Americans in the Catholic Church" (Washington, D.C.: United States Catholic Conference, 1990).

82. "Living the Dream" and "Faith That Endures: A Videotape Celebrating the Past, Present, and Future of the Oklahoma Indian Missionary Conference" (Nashville: Discipleship Resources, 1994–95).

The above resources are all suitable for study by adults. The task of finding resources for children is more difficult. Ready-made religious education curricula espousing a Native point of view are not readily available. Two secular multicultural resources, however, could be adapted for religious education purposes. First, a special issue of *Rethinking Education,* entitled *Rethinking Columbus,* was published in 1991.[83] Although its focus is primarily on the quincentenary (the five hundredth anniversary of Columbus's "discovery" of the "New World"), its articles remain useful in developing a multicultural religious education curriculum including Native Americans. In addition, *Through Indian Eyes: Native Experience in Books for Children,* edited by Beverly Sapin and Doris Seale, provides a useful resource.[84] Designed for childhood educators "interested in responsible multicultural education," the volume contains essays, poetry, and fiction by Natives. It also contains reviews of more than one hundred children's books with Native themes and extensive bibliographies. Especially helpful is the section entitled "How to Tell the Difference," a guide to aid in assessment of whether potential books and curricula present accurate depictions of Native persons and groups.[85]

In using any of the above-mentioned resources, however, it would be wise to hear the admonition of Roger Buffalohead (Ponca): "It is not hard to find a bibliography that says, 'Here are Indian contents, here are all the books written, here are all the articles.' It is one thing to identify the content. It is another thing to put that content and then teach it from a point that supports Indian perspective."[86] What this means for religious educators from the dominant culture interested in multicultural religious education inclusive of a Native voice is a commitment to first educate themselves and then to so teach the materials that learners can stand in solidarity with Natives in their struggles for dignity and sovereignty. To do less is, at best, to engage in paternalism; at worst, it is to perpetuate the racism and ignorance that too often characterized the dominant culture's relations with Natives from the earliest encounters to the present.

Seminaries and Native American Experience

This discussion about multicultural education of non-Natives has focused on religious education of laity in the local church. The situation is, however, even more dire in seminaries and schools of theology where future religious

---

83. September 1991.

84. Beverly Sapin and Doris Seale, *Through Indian Eyes: The Native Experience in Books for Children*, 3d ed. (Philadelphia: New Society, 1992).

85. Ibid., pp. 240–64.

86. Roger Buffalohead, quoted in "Developing Indian Content in Social Work Education: A Community-Based Curriculum Model," by Timothy Shaughnessy and Eddie F. Brown, *Multicultural Education*, ed. Jack Forbes, p. 157.

educators are being taught. Curricula at such institutions are almost totally devoid of courses with Native content. When Natives are taken into account, it is most often as subjects of missionization. All too frequently, faculty members with no previous knowledge of, nor interest in, Native peoples are asked to teach *something* about Indians as a nod toward "inclusiveness."[87] Without guidance as to resources these reluctant pedagogues wind up employing works written by "plastic medicine men" like Wallace Black Elk or Dhyani Ywahoo[88] or by reported frauds like Jamake Highwater or Harley "SwiftDeer" Reagan.[89] As a result, sincere, unsuspecting non-Native seminarians believe that they are getting legitimate information about Indians when they are not. They are left confused and bewildered about what is genuine and what is not. Vine Deloria stated the problem succinctly: "The realities of Indian belief and existence have become so misunderstood and distorted at this point that when a real Indian stands up and speaks the truth at any given moment, he or she is not likely to be believed, but will probably be publicly contradicted or 'corrected' by the citation of some non-Indian and totally inaccurate 'expert.' "[90]

The problem is exacerbated by the paucity of Native scholars at schools of religion. In 1996 only two theological schools (Iliff School of Theology and the School of Theology at Claremont) had full-time Native faculty members working in Native studies.[91] Steve Charleston, a Choctaw theologian, left academia to become Episcopal bishop of Alaska. To my knowledge, only

---

87. This becomes patently clear at the American Academy of Religion, where scholars in this unenviable position crowd around Natives and non-Native experts, stating this fact and inquiring as to resources.

88. The term, despite its apparent gender exclusivity, "refers to individuals of both genders trading in the commercialization of indigenous spirituality." Ward Churchill, "Spiritual Hucksterism" in *Fantasies of the Master Race: Literature, Cinema and the Colonization of American Indians*, ed. M. Annette Jaimes (Monroe, Me.: Common Courage Press, 1992), p. 220. The persons cited are merely two examples of a growing phenomenon. See, for example, Wallace Black Elk and William S. Lyons, *Black Elk: The Sacred Ways of a Lakota* (San Francisco: HarperCollins, 1990); Dhyani Ywahoo, *Voices of Our Ancestors: Cherokee Teachings from the Wisdom Fire* (Boston: Shambhala, 1987). The former must not be confused with Nicholas Black Elk, the noted Lakota visionary of the late nineteenth and early twentieth centuries, immortalized by John Neihardt in *Black Elk Speaks*.

89. See, for example, Jamake Highwater, *The Primal Mind: Vision and Reality in Indian America* (New York: Harper & Row, 1981); Bill Wahlberg, *Star Warrior: The Story of SwiftDeer* (Santa Fe, N.M.: Bear, 1993). Although the latter of these works lists Wahlberg, a psychotherapist, as its sole author, it is told almost exclusively in the first person from Reagan's point of view. For a discussion of Highwater's Native identity, see "Letters: Highwater Marks," *Publishers Weekly*, September 14, 1992, p. 8.

90. Vine Deloria Jr., quoted in "A Little Matter of Genocide," by Ward Churchill in *Fantasies of the Master Race*, ed. M. Annette Jaimes, pp. 190–91.

91. Jace Weaver, "Native Reformation," p. 39.

one other such institution, Union Theological Seminary in New York, has course offerings examining Native cultures and spirituality from an indigenous perspective. Cook College and Theological School (formerly Cook Christian Training School) in Tempe, Arizona, offers an A.A. degree in pastoral studies for Natives. Over its eighty-two year history it has prepared students from more than ninety tribes for college and seminary work. Its faculty is approximately 50 percent Native, and its president, Joseph Iron Eye Dudley, is a Yankton Sioux. In wider academic circles, over 85 percent of those who teach Native studies in universities and colleges are white.[92]

Several years ago, Native seminarians at Duke Divinity School attempted to get a course in Native cultures instituted. The administration's rationale in turning down the request was that there were not enough Native seminarians at the school to justify the addition. The response, sadly, is not unique, but has been replicated at institutions all across the country. It willfully perpetuates the ignorance referred to earlier as characteristic of the dominant culture. Such an academic offering would benefit not only, nor even primarily, Native students but also non-Native students, many of whom will influence Native American ministries through work in their various denominations' national boards and commissions and almost all of whom will be involved in religious education in one venue or another. Recognizing this fact, the same general conference of the United Methodist Church that enacted the Confession to Native Americans passed ecclesiastic legislation entitled "Education Responsibilities Concerning Native American Cultural Traditions." The resolution acknowledged that non-Natives were being appointed to serve Native United Methodist churches who had "little or no awareness of the history, culture, and language of Native Americans in that particular community." Realizing the potential for insult and injury through insensitivity and ignorance, the general conference commissioned the National United Methodist Native American Center, a body run by and for Natives themselves, to develop a curriculum to be made available to all United Methodist seminaries.[93]

Multicultural Religious Education Curricula for Native Americans

For Natives, the problems entailed in fostering multicultural religious education are related to those described above but are far from identical.

---

92. See Achiel Peelman, *Christ Is a Native American* (Maryknoll: Orbis, 1995), p. 44; David Young and Jean-Guy Goulet, eds., *Being Changed by Cross-Cultural Encounters: The Anthropology of Extraordinary Experience* (Peterborough, Ontario: Broadview, 1994).

93. "Education Responsibilities concerning Native American Cultural Traditions," in *The Book of Resolutions of the United Methodist Church, 1992* (Nashville: United Methodist Publishing House, 1992), pp. 247–48.

Education of all types in the United States has acted as the "great massifier," seeking to bring the diverse and disparate elements of American society into a monocultural, European-American system. The book *Cultural Literacy* by E. D. Hirsch is a particular manifestation of this impulse. Hirsch includes a list compiled by himself, Joseph Kent, and James Trefil (all professors at the University of Virginia). The list, styled "What Literate Americans Know," includes five thousand dates, names, places, and concepts that its authors believe any knowledgeable citizen should know. This onymasticon was alarming in its Eurocentric and male bias. As a corrective, Rick Simonson and Scott Walker edited a volume entitled *Multi-Cultural Literacy: Opening the American Mind.* Composed primarily of essays by people of color on the topic of multiculturalism, it also included a preliminary list to supplement the one by Hirsch and his colleagues. Omissions cited by Simonson and Walker included James Baldwin, Zora Neale Hurston, and Simon Bolivar. From a Native standpoint, additional entries included Native reservations, Wounded Knee, Black Elk, and Quetzalcoatl.[94]

This important, albeit tentative, corrective highlights a reality for Native peoples. As for other racial/ethnic groups in America, all education, including religious education, has always been bicultural. In schools and in churches they have been socialized in the ways of the dominant culture. Education in their own culture has been left to traditional training in their communities. Even this traditional education has been deliberately suppressed by the dominant society.[95] With Native communities fractured by more than five hundred years of colonialism and genocide, traditional Native paths of cultural continuity can no longer be relied on exclusively. The pressing need is to break the concept of education as a "great massifier" and introduce Native content, both substantive and structural, into Indian education.[96] The church should be the first institution to reject the "massifier" concept in favor of a truly multicultural religious education for Native Americans.

A COMMUNITIST RELIGIOUS EDUCATION

Religious education of Natives must become what I term *communitist* in its approach. This neologism is a combination of the words *community* and *activism*. A new term is needed because no other adjective from the

94. Rick Simonson and Scott Walker, *Multi-Cultural Literacy: Opening the American Mind*, The Graywolf Annual, no. 5 (St. Paul, Minn.: Graywolf, 1988), p. 191.

95. See, for example, David A. Rausch and Blair Schlepp, *Native American Voices* (Grand Rapids, Mich.: Baker, 1994), pp. 99–105; 134–35; 142–46.

96. On subject matter being the substantive content and methodology being the structural content of religious education, see Lee, *Content*, p. 8.

root *communitas* (e.g., communitarian, communist, communal) conveys the precise sense required. Community is the highest value in Native society, and fidelity to it is a primary responsibility.[97] Communitism is related to "indigenism," a movement that takes the rights of indigenes as the foremost priority. Whereas, however, indigenism "draws upon the traditions . . . evolved over many thousands of years by native peoples the world over" and sees its commitment as being to indigenous peoples everywhere,[98] communitism focuses specifically on Native America. Communitism requires a pro-active commitment to Native American communities, to their survival, integrity, sovereignty, and healing after the dislocations of more than five centuries of ongoing colonialism.[99] To be communitist means to be committed to the traditional values of Native American culture. Religious education must be communitist in that it must involve an active commitment to the needs of Native communities.

Vine Deloria has written that the European-American educational approach, of which Christian religious education has been a large part, has produced a "strange generation of Indians." To remedy the omissions and errors of this approach, Deloria says,

> we need to devise a realistic program that understands the cultural gulf between Indians and the rest of American society. We need to develop an educational program which enables Indians to understand fully their own cultural roots and to have increasing reliance on the usefulness and rationality of tribal customs. Related to these patterns must be a general humanistic-liberal arts-social science complex whereby Indians can learn the most important general ideas which underlay specific institutions in American life. These theories would constitute for Indians a set of tools which would enable them to relate to the specific application of information as it is propagated in western civilization. The very things which non-Indians take for granted, the 'common sense' understandings of behavior, are for most Indians a puzzling and unrelated set of actions and Indians need to find an intellectual context in which they can learn about them. At those points where Indian and non-Indian concerns are tangent regarding substantial differences in emphasis or points of view, we can easily demonstrate the ways that each confronts problems and offer solutions. With two clear alternatives marked out, it will be relatively simple for Indians to make a choice and justify their decisions.[100]

---

97. See, for example, Vine Deloria Jr., "Sacred Lands and Religious Freedom," *American Indian Religions*, winter 1994, pp. 75–76.

98. Ward Churchill, *Struggle for the Land*, p. 403.

99. See "The Spectrum of Other Languages: An Interview with Joy Harjo," *Tamaqua*, spring 1992, p. 21, for a discussion of healing Native communities.

100. Vine Deloria Jr., "Education and Imperialism," *Integrated Education* 18 (1984): 61. This entire volume of *Integrated Education* is devoted to Native education. It includes

The approach suggested by Deloria is communitist, and although he writes in a secular context, I believe his ideas have utility in the area of religious education as well. Because Native traditions recognize no split of the secular and the sacred, any education in Native culture will be, by definition, religious education. From a Native standpoint, Jack Forbes writes that education "is not primarily the acquisition of specific skills or factual knowledge. Rather it is learning how to be a human being. That is, how to live a life of the *utmost spiritual quality.* A person who has developed his [or her] character to its highest degree, and who is on that path, will also be able to master specific skills. But if they don't have that *spiritual core,* they will use those skills to hurt other people. . . . So knowledge without the spiritual core is a very dangerous thing."[101] He goes on to state, "The main thing I want to emphasize is that there can be no education that is multicultural involving the Native American tradition unless it gets into this area of the meaning of life, unless it gets into the area of values. If it just pays attention to painting or basketry or material culture, it is nowhere close to that which constitutes the real meaning of the Native struggle in this American land."[102] In so speaking, Forbes is using the language of communitism. He is also affirming that for Natives all education in their culture is religious education. Anyone engaged in religious education of Natives must incorporate this communitist element. He or she must respect Native cultures and let their teachings, beliefs, values, and approaches dictate both the content and the structure of religious education. For non-Natives, not deeply immersed in— or even familiar with—such cultures, this is all but impossible.

Problems with a Communitist Element in Native Religious Education

Both Deloria and Forbes acknowledge that introducing this communitist element into Native religious education is no easy task.[103] In their attempts to do so, Native Christians encounter multiple problems.[104] The first problem relates directly to the nature of contemporary Native existence in America. Largely as a result of federal government relocation programs

---

essays by notable Natives including Deloria, Annette Jaimes, and Bea Medicine, and it provides a useful resource to anyone interested in multicultural education.

101. Jack Forbes, "Traditional Native Philosophy and Multicultural Education," in *Multicultural Education,* ed. Jack Forbes, p. 11. Emphasis mine.

102. Ibid.

103. Deloria, "Education and Imperialism," pp. 61–63; Forbes, "Traditional Native Philosophy," pp. 11–12.

104. The problems of teaching Natives in the classroom are well limned by Greg Sarris (Coastal Miwok/Pomo), a professor at UCLA, in two essays in his volume *Keeping Slug Woman Alive* (Berkeley: University of California Press, 1993).

in the 1950s,[105] over two-thirds of the country's 1.8 million Indians live in diaspora in cities, according to the 1990 U.S. Census. They are distanced from tribal lands and often from their tribes themselves. Poet and novelist Gerald Vizenor (Anishinabe) refers to these city-dwelling Natives as living in a world of pan-tribal urban emptiness where "people are severed like dandelions on suburban lawns, separated from living places on the earth."[106] Though these Natives may to the untrained eye seem indistinguishable from the population at large, often being mistaken for Italians, Jews, Hispanics, or Asians, they still earn less, die younger, and go to jail in disproportionate numbers compared to the dominant culture.[107]

The second problem emerges as these Natives seek community. They find it at Native community houses, at powwows, and at churches. Evidence, anecdotal but significant, shows that Natives in cities usually attend the local Indian church without regard for denominational affiliation. Thus a Native living in Denver may have been raised Lutheran and may attend Lutheran-affiliated Living Waters Indian Church. But if she moves to St. Paul, she will seek out the Native congregation or parish, which happens to be Episcopalian, rather than go to a predominantly white Lutheran church. The problem that is created is less one of denominational doctrine or polity and more one of culture. The diversity of tribal backgrounds found in such local churches, despite certain common elements, creates as much of a problem for religious education as does the culturally diverse non-Native population.

The third problem concerns the paucity of Native churches in urban areas. Despite the fact that New York City ranks third among urban areas in Native population, according to the 1990 U.S. Census, there is no identifiable Native church in the area. For several years I myself served as associate pastor of a 250-person congregation, composed of approximately 50 percent African-American and Caribbean blacks, 20 percent South Asians (i.e., Indian and Pakistani), 20 percent Hispanic, and 10 percent Anglo. The preaching and religious education functions were complicated by this rich and rewarding diversity. Imagine a religious educator with a numerically similar membership consisting of an amalgam of persons representing thirteen different tribal traditions. Such an example is not hypothetical. It is the reality of Native ministry in urban America. To be sensitive to and inclusive of all learners is the religious educator's challenge.

---

105. For a full discussion of this program, which was designed to terminate reservations and with them federal responsibility for Natives, see Donald L. Fixico, *Termination and Relocation: Federal Indian Policy, 1945–1960* (Albuquerque: University of New Mexico Press, 1986).

106. Gerald Vizenor, *Landfill Meditation*, quoted in "Trickster among the Wordies," by Jace Weaver, *Christianity and Crisis*, 17 August 1992, p. 286.

107. See Lynda Shorten, *Without Reserve: Stories from Urban Natives* (Edmonton: NeWest Press, 1991).

Any of the above problems is complicated infinitely if the religious educator is non-Native, lacking even the base of commonalties Natives share. Such a person must teach while respecting various cultural taboos (all foreign to him or her), beliefs, and attitudes. Such respect is a baseline minimum for the communitist objectives of Native religious education. The problems posed for non-Native teachers by such Native diversity, along with some helpful suggestions, are well presented by James Mark Mahan and Mary Kathryn Criger in their article "Culturally Oriented Instruction for Native American Students."[108] Non-Native religious educators can adapt many of these suggestions to religious instruction contexts.

Curricular resources produced by Protestant denominations are geared toward non-Native audiences. Although some Protestant denominations produce religious educational materials for their racial/ethnic groups other than Native Americans, Native learners both in cities and on reservations suffer from a lack of culturally oriented curriculum. Even when the subject matter is Indian, as in the case of materials cited earlier, the projected readership is non-Native.

Courses of study for Roman Catholics and other resources for Christian religious education of Native Americans are provided by the Tekakwitha Conference National Center, Great Falls, Montana. These include a Native catechism entitled *Finding a Way Home*; a series of ten workbooks under the collective title, *Native First Communion*; a study for Native kindergarten students entitled *Stories That Jesus Told: Dakota Way of Life*; a volume of comparative theology, *The Pipe and Christ*; and an edited volume of stories by and about Catholic Natives, *The Story and Faith Journey of Seventeen Native Catechists*.[109] Sister Kateri Mitchell (Mohawk) describes the purpose of such resources as "to provide a process that will aid our people to help one another live in harmony with God, our Creator, with self, with one another, and with all creation in light of the 'good news.' "[110] This is in

---

108. James Mark Mahan and Mary Kathryn Criger, "Culturally Oriented Instruction for Native American Students," in *Understanding and Counseling Ethnic Minorities*, ed. George Henderson (Springfield, Ill.: Charles C. Thomas, 1979); reprinted from *Integrated Education* 15 (1977): 9–13.

109. Patrick J. Twohy, *Finding a Way Home* (Spokane: University Press, 1983); Gilbert F. Hemauer, *Native First Communion Series*, rev. ed. (Great Falls, Mont.: Tekakwitha Conference National Center, 1987); Charles Palm, *Stories That Jesus Told: Dakota Way of Life* (Sioux Falls, S.Dak.: American Indian Research Center of Blue Cloud Abbey, 1985); William Stolzman, *The Pipe and Christ: A Christian-Sioux Dialogue*, 4th ed. (Chamberlain, S.Dak.: Tipi, 1992); Gilbert F. Hemauer, *The Story and Faith of Seventeen Native Catechists* (Great Falls, Mont.: Tekakwitha Conference National Center, 1982).

110. Kateri Mitchell, "Program Development and Native American Catechesis," in *Faith and Culture: A Multicultural Cathechetical Resource* (Washington, D.C.: Dept. of Education, U.S. Catholic Conference, 1986), pp. 86, 100–102.

keeping with the broad mandate of the Catholic Church that "at all times catechesis must respect the personal dignity of minority group members, avoiding condescension and patronizing attitudes. The ultimate goal is that minority groups be able to provide for their own catechetical needs, while remaining closely united in faith and charity with the rest of the Church."[111] Unfortunately, these resources are problematic on a number of grounds. First, although some were prepared with Native input, all were written by non-Natives. Despite the best of intentions, the "subtle nuances of language, the memories of tribal life, and the strong sense of the past and its integration with the present are lost even to the most gifted [non-Native] writer."[112] Second, though these resources are distributed and used in pan-Indian contexts, they most often deal only with a single tribal tradition, usually the Sioux. This tends to homogenize discourse with Natives and fails to respect the diversity of cultures and worldviews. Finally, these resources too often reflect a successionist theological viewpoint. They portray Christianity as the displacement or fulfillment of Native religions, or, alternatively, demonstrate the "hidden Christianity" within Native religious traditions. In *The Pipe and Christ*, for example, William Stolz compares Lakota Sioux religion to Judaism and discusses it as a "second-stage revelation" as compared to Christianity's "third-stage revelation in Salvation History."[113] Such discussions demean traditional Native religions and cultures and rightly anger many Native persons.[114]

Thus Native churches are left with two broad alternatives: (1) to use existing study plans, teaching them from a Native perspective and injecting Native content into them, or (2) to develop their own curriculum. The first alternative is unsatisfactory because underlying Western assumptions and values are difficult, if not impossible, to weed out. The second is too time-consuming and difficult for most churches. Some Native churches, however, are coming up with alternative solutions to the curriculum problem. Their experiences may be helpful to churches of other denominations seeking creative solutions. At the Native American United Methodist Church in Norwalk, California, a suburb of Los Angeles, Marvin Abrams (Seneca) and his congregation have struggled to add a Native perspective to a denominationally produced set of curricula in which their voice is silent. Together they have embarked on an intentional program to foster traditional Native American values among urban Natives, largely starting from scratch because of

---

111. No. 194. *Sharing the Light of Faith: National Catechetical Directory for Catholics of the United States* (Washington, D.C.: Dept. of Education, U.S. Catholic Conference, 1979), pp. 116–18. Quoted in Hemauer, *Story and Faith*, p. vii.

112. Wilma Mankiller, in *The Witch of Goingsnake and Other Stories*, by Robert J. Conley (Norman: University of Oklahoma Press, 1988), p. x.

113. Stolzman, *The Pipe and Christ*, pp. 211–12.

114. Ibid., p. 212.

the unavailability of Native-oriented resources and the unsuitability of other religious education resources that are available. At the Garfield Church in Phoenix, Arizona, founded by Harry Long (Muskogee),[115] Pastor Evelene "Tweedy" Sombrero (Navajo) is involved in a similar project.[116] In efforts that could be called communitist, both churches feature outreach programs that honor traditional values. The Phoenix church, for instance, has incorporated sweat lodges into its total church life. Both churches are intentional in their worship styles and religious education programming so that they appeal to Native persons whose religion is primarily traditional.[117] Sombrero has noticed that whenever an older person talks, the children of the congregation become very quiet and attentive out of both respect and eagerness to learn about the old ways. Further, many urban Natives in various stages of recovery use Native Christian churches as a means to be in community with other Natives before reintegrating into their traditional cultures. Similar models are followed at the Bay Area Native American Ministries in Northern California and at the Living Waters congregation in Denver, two interdenominational ministries established by George Tinker. They too incorporate sweat lodges and other traditional ceremonies into their church life. They regularly have medicine men and other traditional Native practitioners come, as a part of both worship and religious education.

A lack of liturgical and worship resources also presents a problem for the religious educator in Native churches, since religious education takes place in a variety of contexts other than the classroom, including the worship service. The majority of "Native" hymns and prayers have been written by white missionaries.[118] These employ Native imagery to put a red patina on Christianity in an effort to speed evangelism. Although a service such as *las posadas* evolved originally for the religious education of Indians, it is of little value to contemporary Natives who do not have a Hispanic heritage. Similarly, to incorporate Indian traditions in worship resources for all churches is not appropriate. When a Native Christian developed a version of the green corn ceremony (one of the most sacred ceremonies of

---

115. Long is somewhat of a legend among Native Christians. Still serving a church in Oklahoma in his seventies, he has served Native ministries in Oklahoma, California, and Arizona. Although he never attended seminary, he is referred to by many Natives as their "bishop." See Toby Smith, "Street Scene: Harry Long in Phoenix," *New World Outlook* (November/December, 1985), p. 26.

116. Donald K. Small, "Native American Awareness Sunday," *Interpreter*, February/March 1993, pp. 9–10.

117. Noley, *First White Frost*, p. 230.

118. See, for example, the 1989 *United Methodist Hymnal* (Nashville: United Methodist Publishing House, 1989) or The Presbyterian Hymnal, the hymnal of the Presbyterian Church (U.S.A.) (Louisville: Westminster/John Knox, 1990). Although a few of the resources contained therein are from actual Native sources, the majority fit the pattern described in the text.

many eastern tribes) for *The United Methodist Book of Worship*, published in 1992, its inclusion was successfully challenged by Natives because of the potential for abuse by non-Natives.[119] In 1993 that denomination produced a hymnal supplement expressly for Native congregations, containing truly Native resources.[120] As in the case of the religious education curricula discussed above, individual Native congregations have also developed their own resources. These have been spread through networks of pastors and laity throughout North America.

Communitist Religious Education and the Seminary Experience of Natives

The problems encountered by Natives in seminaries have already been alluded to. Deloria writes that young Indians in universities are being trained to view themselves and their cultures in the terms prescribed by white experts *rather than* in the traditional terms of the tribal elders. Deloria sees the process as automatically setting the members of Indian communities at odds with one another, "while outsiders run around picking up the pieces for themselves. In this way, the experts are perfecting a system of self-validation in which all semblance of honesty and accuracy are lost. This is not only a travesty of scholarship, but it is absolutely devastating to Indian societies."[121] This "ideological/conceptual subordination of Indian people"[122] occurs no less in theological schools than in the secular academy. The crying need is for the introduction of communitist values into the experience of seminarians who will be responsible for the religious education of fellow Natives.

In an essay on revisioning religious higher education entitled "Theological Education and Cross-Cultural Inclusiveness," George Tinker relates an incident that occurred at Harvard Divinity School. For several years, a colloquium of doctoral candidates and faculty met to discuss particular authors and issues. The seminar operated on what was described as a "hermeneutic of generosity" whereby "texts were to be read with a sole focus on the 'ideas' presented . . . without reference to the cultural, political, social or economic context of the author." This hermeneutical presupposition came under criticism when students of color and women took part. Tinker writes:

---

119. Many Natives object to any use of this sacred traditional ceremony in a Christian context. Further, certain elements are suitable only for performance by Natives with other Native participants. To include such a ceremony, even in an adapted form, presents the potential for abuse.

120. Marilyan M. Hofstra, ed., *Voices: Native American Hymns and Worship Resources* (Nashville: United Methodist Publishing House, 1993).

121. Deloria is quoted in "A Little Matter of Genocide," by Ward Churchill, in *Fantasies of the Master Race*, ed. M. Annette Jaimes, pp. 190–91.

122. Pam Colorado, quoted in "A Little Matter of Genocide," p. 191.

To some of us whose reference communities are communities of color . . . it seems preposterous that contemporary theologians would still make that sort of argument. We had thought that there was a common assumption today that every theologian, like every philosopher, every historian and every newspaper reporter, writes or speaks out of a sociocultural context—whether it is acknowledged or not. Surely we no longer believe that texts 'speak for themselves' or that texts are 'trying to say' anything at all. It is human beings who speak through the medium of text, and every textual utterance, theological or otherwise, will defy understanding in any sense of fullness until a significant attempt is made to understand the sociocultural context of the utterer—the speaker/writer of the text. . . . We had thought that this minimum had become our common intellectual heritage, a foundation for theological and philosophical discourse across cultural boundaries.[123]

Tinker contends that difficulties such as those encountered by students of color and women in the Harvard colloquium will continue to occur until a critical mass of faculty and students is reached.[124] Yet he also makes it clear that increasing the percentages of racial/ethnic students and faculty is not enough. "Without an openness to the transformation of the structures of theological education multicultural theological education will become yet one more tool of cultural imposition on and oppression of racial/ethnic people."[125] Such a disastrous outcome for multicultural religious education is equally possible, and unacceptable. The issue thus becomes how to integrate alternative models of discourse into multicultural education at both the theological and religious educational levels.

For Natives this means shaping a discourse that takes seriously the differences in worldviews and epistemologies discussed earlier. This will require modification of curriculum. According to Tinker, "The argument is this: to ensure the nurture of all students in a culturally diverse student body, curricular revision should move toward allowing students of color to replace some existing required courses with others more suitable to the development of ministerial proficiency in their communities."[126] Specifically with regard to Native students, courses in, for instance, the history of Christian missions in North America or perspectives in Native American worldview should be offered, perhaps substituting for other requirements in church history or systematic theology. Both of these proposed listings are part of the curriculum required by the now defunct Native American Theological

---

123. Tinker, "Theological Education," pp. 7–8.
124. Today Native Americans make up less than one-tenth of one percent of the total number of students in seminaries. The number of faculty members has already been discussed.
125. Tinker, "Theological Education," p. 5.
126. Ibid., p. 10.

Association, which sought to covenant with institutions of higher learning to ensure "that every American Indian student [was] exposed to certain curricular components specifically designed to meet the needs of that student and the Native American community" of which that student is a part.[127] Thanks to Tinker, these changes *are* being implemented at the Iliff School of Theology where he teaches. Such an approach is communitist in that it respects Native experiences, needs, and cultural diversity. It makes a commitment to Native communities by committing itself to their survival. In addition, Tinker points out that "it becomes imperative for 'Perspectives in Native American Worldviews' that the instructor live and more and have her being in the Native American community,"[128] though it is recommended that the person teaching the histories of missions course be Native.

There are other aspects of current theological training that must be re-envisioned in accordance with communitist goals. One of these is the area of clinical pastoral education. While the goals of CPE may be admirable, the program itself remains "an ethnocentric discipline."[129] Like other pedagogical practices involving a therapy model, clinical pastoral education needs to be reexamined carefully to expose its Eurocentric bias. It presupposes a certain set of cultural values. When those values are present, the program works reasonably well. Problems arise, however, when those values are not present. In the case of Native persons, the values in place are often directly contrary to those assumed by the process. Again, George Tinker offers an example from a Native perspective:

> The group dynamics process used by every CPE program I am aware of makes an implicit cultural assumption which works well for the dominant culture. An assumption is that a group of like-minded people who are complete strangers can very quickly and easily form most intimate relationships based on openness and trust. Indeed, White Americans are renowned world-wide for their overt friendliness and the ease with which they move into relationships. Native American people on the whole form relationships much more slowly, and crosscultural intimacies come at an even slower pace. The imposition, then, of Anglo-American instant intimacy, however well intentioned, would be an act of violence against most American Indian people, even in many cases where individuals would seem on the surface to respond well to that kind of treatment. It is an imposition of a cultural value which may be inappropriate.[130]

A further difficulty arises from the fact that clinical pastoral education is based on a more or less confrontational pedagogical model. By contrast,

---

127. Ibid., pp. 16–18.
128. Ibid., p. 20.
129. George Tinker, conversation with the author, 25 October 1993.
130. Ibid.

confrontation does not function as a pedagogy in Native cultures, where cooperation is given priority. The use of these models, both in counseling and in religious education, needs to be studied, and alternative forms developed for Native participants. Such forms need to be sensitive to the culture from which Native learners come and in which religious educators will exercise their ministry.

MULTICULTURAL RELIGIOUS EDUCATION: MANY PATHS, MANY ROADS

The discussion in this chapter is intended to be both a critique and a challenge to religious educators. Jack Forbes defined *multicultural* in a Native idiom by saying that it means "many paths, many roads." He writes, "The way people do things, the way people behave, the way people think, the ideas they have in their minds, all cause them to follow certain paths or roads. So we'll just call [multicultural education] 'many roads to education.' "[131] In education, whatever else those many roads mean, they mean more than merely respecting other paths. Thomas Roughface (Ponca), a former chair of the Native American International Caucus, says, "We need to come down and say, 'Look, how can we reach across the fences? How can we build gates?' We need to deal with each other honestly. We need to have more dialogue. We've got to get beyond 'respect.' I can 'respect' you until the end of your days but I may never really appreciate who you are."[132] "Many roads to religious education" means teaching in such a way that other paths are respected and that their continued use is supported and encouraged for those communities who have traveled them traditionally. "Many paths, many roads" means a proactive commitment to those communities by supporting their struggles for dignity and sovereignty. It means communitist education that validates Native culture and strengthens Native languages and worldviews.[133] It means seeing traditional Native religions as more than mere predecessors to Christianity in the economy of "salvation history."

In 1969 Vine Deloria stated that the "impotency and irrelevancy of the Christian message" for Native Americans was leading to a widespread revival of traditional spirituality.[134] Although he believed at the time that "an Indian version of Christianity could do much for our society," he was convinced that white-dominated American churches, with much invested

---

131. Forbes, "Traditional Native American Philosophy," p. 4.

132. Tom Roughface, "How Can We Reach Across Fences" (offprint, n.p., n.d.).

133. Joseph C. Dupris, "The National Impact of Multicultural Education: A Renaissance of Native American Culture through Tribal Self-Determination and Indian Control of Education," in *Multicultural Education*, ed. Jack Forbes, p. 49.

134. Deloria, *Custer*, p. 112.

in conventional assimilationist missions, would never permit it to happen. He asked, "Can the white man's religion make one final effort to be real, or must it too vanish like its predecessors from the old world?"[135] Besides the U.S. government, the institution that has had the most impact on Native Americans has been the church. For five hundred years, the church has gone out to American Natives as a message bearer. Now it is time for the church to listen.

Ironically, two years before Deloria penned the above-quoted words, Cecil Corbett (Nez Perce), an ordained Presbyterian minister, told the National Fellowship of Indian Workers, "*A new day is here!* The church has a second chance. A second chance in that before, the ministry was *to* and *for* Indians. This conference has clearly stated that the ministry in this new day is to be *with* and *by* the Indians themselves."[136] Unfortunately, Corbett was woefully premature in his assessment. It is therefore understandable that many Natives would greet similar comments made more than a quarter of a century later with a high degree of skepticism. Yet within Christian bodies, Natives are beginning to assert themselves. New voices such as George Tinker, Steve Charleston, Bill Baldridge, and Homer Noley are making themselves heard as both theologians and religious educators. Tinker, in words that seem to echo Corbett, declares:

> Now a new day is emerging. Following on the renaissance of traditional tribal spirituality, many Indian clergy, lay people, and whole congregations are insisting on natural indigenous categories of our tribes for structuring our faith. Hence the old ways of tribal spirituality are beginning to be as much at home in Indian churches as they are in traditional ceremonies. The values that define Indian existence, Indian community, traditional spirituality and culture are being articulated in Indian preaching and theology in our churches. Traditional forms of prayer, considered by missionaries to be pure paganism, are making their way into the heart of our Christian liturgies: the drum, the eagle feather, four directions symbolism, and rites of smudging.[137]

I have also added my own modest voice to this growing theological and educational discourse.[138] The day, however, as Tinker states, is *emerging*, not

135. Ibid., p. 124.

136. Cecil Corbett, quoted in Carter, *Gift Is Rich*, p. 107. Emphasis original.

137. George Tinker, "Native Americans and the Land: 'The End of Living, and the Beginning of Survival,'" in *Lift Every Voice: Constructing Christian Theologies from the Underside* ed. Susan Brooks Thistlethwaite and Mary Potter Engels (San Francisco: Harper, 1990), pp. 142–43. The drum, eagle feather, four directions, and smudging are important symbols and rituals in many traditional Native religions.

138. See Jace Weaver, "A Biblical Paradigm for Native Liberation," *Christianity and Crisis*, 15 February 1993, p. 40; idem, "Interpreting a Vision of a Red Bear," *Native Journal*, August 1992, p. 4.

yet *emergent*. It is still in the process of being formed. As Steve Charleston writes,

> The Native People's Christian theology is being overlooked, because it is born in silence. That silence is so strong, so pervasive, so smothering that even the shout of a human voice cannot escape it. Not alone. But within each day that passes, more and more voices are beginning to take up the cry. In little backwater reservation chapels. In urban slums. In Arizona and Alaska and Minnesota and California and Manitoba. In sweat lodges and camp meetings. In Christian homes and Traditional homes. In Cheyenne homes and Mohawk homes. In tribes all across Native America. . . . Native People are shouting into the silence of Western colonialism. They are shouting their names. They are saying that they are still the Tribe of the Human Beings. The Memory is coming back and with it the voice of a whole nation. Against that kind of power, no silence will long endure.[139]

If Natives ever do regain control of their own destinies and produce a genuine Native Christianity, it will be, as William Wantland (Seminole) envisions it, "strange, if not alien, to people of European background. It will be something far different from English or Scottish Christianity."[140] Whether it results in a "coming out," as Deloria suggests, or it takes some form within existing Christian traditions, it will not be merely a red patina on a white happening. This means incorporating traditional spiritual practice, belief, and ways of teaching. It means acknowledging the power and truth in the old ways and stories. Such a Christianity must not only be rooted in Native culture, it must be in the hands of Natives to define as well. It must be a faith that, in its preaching, worship, instruction, and action, promotes Native liberation, both spiritual and sociopolitical. It must be, simply, a Christianity of our own.

---

139. Steve Charleston, "The Old Testament of Native America," in *Lift Every Voice*, ed. Thistlethwaite and Potter, pp. 60–61.

140. William Wantland, Episcopal bishop of Eau Claire, Wisconsin, in an interview with the author, 21 December 1992. This is true, just as African and Asian expressions of Christianity are often very different from the Eurocentric Christianity of much of the world.

PART III

EDUCATIONAL PRACTICE IN MULTICULTURAL RELIGIOUS EDUCATION

9

EFFECTIVE TEACHING AND MULTICULTURAL RELIGIOUS EDUCATION

Deborah L. Bainer
and
Jeffrey W. Peck

In Sunday morning worship services they were peppered throughout the congregation, trying to sing the hymns of the faith with great gusto. They were Kampuchean teenagers, recently resettled to the American Midwest, and members of Deborah Bainer's Sunday school class. Each week she could not help wondering: Do these church routines make sense to them? Do they understand what they are singing? Are they here to improve their English? Or because they think it is the American thing to do? Am I getting through to them at all?

Readers of this chapter may have similar concerns relating to their work in religious education, especially if they work with children or adults whose cultural or socioeconomic roots are different from those of the majority culture. Because members of diverse cultural groups bring different experiences, competing expectations, variant explanations, and individual values and attitudes into the religious education setting, meeting their learning and spiritual needs can be challenging.

The purpose of this chapter is to examine what is known about effective teaching and learning in multicultural settings and to apply that knowledge to religious education settings. Specifically, the chapter will explore the following questions: What is known about the unique learning styles of minority learners? What does a religious educator need to know to be an effective teacher of minority learners? What is known about the kinds of teaching that will best meet the religious education needs of minority learners?

COGNITIVE STYLES AND TEACHING STYLES

Most people are aware that they like to study some topics more than others and that they learn well in certain ways. Some people enjoy studying art and music, while others enjoy discussing religious philosophy. Still others prefer studying and investigating the natural sciences or mathematics. Further, people prefer to obtain and process information in distinctive ways. Some prefer to work alone, while others enjoy group experiences. Some people learn well when information is presented visually; others learn better by hearing the information or through physical manipulation. Even children as young as four or five years of age display observable preferences.[1]

People's learning styles are as distinctive as fingerprints. Psychologists and educators have tried for years to understand, describe, and measure individual learning preferences and styles. *Learning styles* can be thought of as descriptions of individual "learning personalities." A learning style is the consistent pattern of behavior and performance by which an individual approaches educational experiences. It is deeply embedded in the personality and reflects how a person views the world. Learning style is influenced by the individual's neural organization and personality as well as by cultural experiences at home, school, and in the community.[2]

The aspect of individual learning style that has been the most extensively measured and described by psychologists is *cognitive style*. The term itself comes from psychological research into how people perceive and organize information from the world around them. Cognitive styles are distinctive personality types evidenced in part by the way people approach and adapt to the world as they see it.[3] Some aspects of cognitive style have been linked to cultural differences.

Field Sensitivity/Field Independence
Researchers locate learners along a continuum from "field dependent" to

---

1. Marlin Languis, T. Sanders, and S. Tipps, *Brain and Learning: Directions in Early Childhood Education* (Washington, D.C.: National Association for the Education of Young Children, 1980), p. 30.

2. James W. Keefe and Barbara R. Ferrell, "Developing a Defensible Learning Style Paradigm," *Educational Leadership* 46, no. 2 (1990): 59.

3. Keefe and Ferrell, "Defensible Learning Style Paradigm," p. 58.

"field independent."[4] Banks replaces the label field dependent with a more positive term—field sensitive.[5] Field-sensitive learners rely heavily on cues from the environment, while field-independent learners are less bound by situations in which they find themselves.

Generally, field-sensitive learners manifest a strong interest in other people and in interpersonal relationships. They need and desire to be physically close to people, and are very attentive to social cues from others.[6] They are most comfortable learning material that has social content and relevance. For example, they enjoy studying how Jesus interacted with others and the parables he used to relate eternal principles to their everyday lives. They also appreciate the letters of Peter, John, and Paul because of the relevance these books hold for their lives. These learners seem particularly well suited for working in cooperative situations, although they may tend to focus more on getting to know the other group members than on the learning task at hand! Teachers must be careful to structure cooperative learning experiences to ensure that these learners achieve the stated learning goals.

Field-sensitive learners tend to draw upon those around them for guidance, for information in unfamiliar or ambiguous situations, and for help in solving problems. They tend to be responsive to praise and other kinds of reinforcement, but to be adversely affected by criticism. Because field-sensitive learners are so responsive to the advice and opinions of significant others, religious educators can exert a profound impact on their lives.[7]

In contrast, field-independent learners tend to be more analytical than field-sensitive learners. Generally, they are good at working with unstructured information and reorganizing it. Field-independent learners may be able to make sense out of even difficult biblical passages. They are generally less gregarious or people-oriented than field-sensitive learners, and they tend to prefer working on their own or with reference materials. Because many field-independent learners enjoy learning for its own sake, religious educators may need to help them go a step further and focus on the relevance and everyday applications of Scripture passages. They also may need to be taught how to "read" or consider the context in understanding social information in the Bible, as well as how to work collaboratively with others in Bible study.

Cognitive styles tend to change somewhat over time because of developmental changes. For example, a field-sensitive child can be expected to

---

4. See Herman A. Witkin, Carl Moore, Donald Goodenough, and P. Cox, "Field-dependent and Independent Cognitive Styles and Their Educational Implications," *Review of Educational Research* 47 (1977): 1–64.

5. See James Banks, *Multiethnic Education* (Boston: Allyn & Bacon, 1988).

6. Barbara J. Shade, "Afro-American Cognitive Style: A Variable in School Success?" *Review of Educational Research* 52, no. 2 (1982): 229.

7. Shade, "Afro-American Cognitive Style," pp. 219–44.

become more field independent until the middle teen years. Late in adulthood, most people become more field sensitive. An individual's orientation remains fairly stable throughout life, however, with respect to others along the field sensitive/independent continuum.[8]

More important to this discussion, research suggests that field sensitivity is related to cultural heritage. For example, Mexican-American children and African-American children tend to be more field sensitive than European-American children, who tend toward the field-independent end of the continuum.[9] This information takes on additional significance when it is recognized that traditional education approaches, in society as well as in the church, reflect a field-independent style, thus putting field-sensitive learners at a disadvantage. Specifically, the instructional procedures and substantive content of traditional religious education programs hold little appeal for learners who require educational events saturated with social emphasis and immediate practicality.

Analytical/Relational Modes

Another way of discussing cognitive styles is by describing analytical and relational modes of conceptual organization.[10] Learners with an analytical style tend to focus on detail and generally exhibit sequential and structured thinking. They have a good memory for abstract ideas and information that is not immediately relevant, and they learn impersonal or inanimate information with relative ease. Further, individuals described as having an analytical style are task oriented in learning situations, tend to persist even at unstimulating tasks, and are less affected by the opinions of others. In educational situations, analytical learners are often model students who learn in spite of the teacher. The problem in religious education contexts is that although analytical learners may readily acquire biblical information, they may isolate it and not allow it to affect their values and daily lives. Religious educators all too frequently reinforce this focus by stressing only information in their teaching. However, it is important to push analytical learners beyond the facts to examine how principles impact their lives and relationships, which was, after all, Jesus' emphasis and concern (Mt 23:23; Jn 15:12).[11]

---

8. Anita E. Woolfolk, *Educational Psychology* (Boston: Allyn & Bacon, 1990), p. 148.

9. Manuel Ramirez III and Douglass R. Price-Williams, "Cognitive Styles of Children of Three Ethnic Groups in the United States," *Journal of Cross-Cultural Psychology* 5, no. 2 (1974): 216, 217.

10. James A. Anderson, "Cognitive Styles and Multicultural Populations," *Journal of Teacher Education* 39, no. 1 (1988): 7.

11. Anderson, *Journal of Teacher Education*, pp. 5–9.

In contrast, learners with a relational style perceive information as part of a total picture and generally exhibit original and intuitive thinking. They are most successful at learning when the material has human or social content and is experientially or culturally relevant. Relational learners have a good memory for information and ideas that they *hear* (as opposed to *read*), especially if the material is relevant to them. This is because they prefer social encounters to learning situations, and they withdraw from tasks that they consider purely cognitive or irrelevant. Learners with this cognitive style challenge religious educators to make the learning experience practical or of immediate concern to the individual's life, or they will tend to ignore it. Relational learners tend to be influenced by statements of confidence or doubt in their ability expressed by authority figures, as they are also by the opinions of their peers. Because of this, relational learners often have hearts that are sensitive and open to God at a very early age. This openness to the voice of authority can also be a problem, however. Relational learners seem to be able to entertain conflicting ideas or theories presented by authority figures without confusion because the information is compartmentalized rather than integrated in their minds. Paul encountered this situation with the Greeks who wanted to include all deities in their worship (Acts 17:16–34).

The analytical/relational modes of cognitive style have also been linked to cultural groups. Individuality and independent thinking and work, which characterize the European-American worldview, reflect an analytical style. In contrast, Shade's research found that African-Americans frequently evidence a relational style.[12] Similarly, others have found that Asian Americans, Native Americans, and Mexican Americans tend to value group identity, conformity, and collective behavior.[13] These qualities reflect a relational style. The Vietnamese culture, for example, emphasizes maintaining harmony among people. Candor and directness are considered rude, so there is a reluctance to contradict someone directly, even in learning situations or class discussions.[14] Furthermore, it is unthinkable to question recognized authorities, whether that authority is the written Word of God or the religious educator. One Taiwanese doctoral student, for example, did not question the contradictions between the biblical account and Chinese folklore regarding the origin of life. She professed to sincerely believe both accounts.[15]

---

12. Shade, *Review of Educational Research*, p. 229.

13. Christine Bennett, "Teaching Students As They Would Be Taught: The Importance of Cultural Perspective," *Educational Leadership* 36, no. 4 (1979): 265; Voung G. Thuy, "The Indochinese in America: Who Are They and How Are They Doing?" in *The Education of Asian-American and Pacific-American Children and Youth* (Washington, D.C.: National Institute of Education, 1981), pp. 130–54.

14. Barbara Garner, "Southeast Asian Culture and Classroom Culture," *College Teaching* 37, no. 4 (1989): 128.

15. Deborah L. Bainer, *Student Interviews* (Columbus: Ohio State University, 1991).

Satellizers/Nonsatellizers

A third way of describing cognitive style is to place it along a continuum from "satellizers" to "nonsatellizers." Satellizers have an intrinsic sense of self-worth that is independent of what they accomplish. Conversely, nonsatellizers lack intrinsic feelings of self-worth and feel a need to prove themselves through accomplishments.[16] This aspect of cognitive style is also evident among cultural groups. In one study, European-American children showed a greater need for achievement than did Mexican-American children, who desired affiliation and succor or comforting.[17] This descriptor of cognitive styles suggests that religious educators need to interact with and encourage learners in varied ways.

Affective/Cognitive Domains

As has been seen, learners with different cognitive styles bring different needs and attitudes to learning situations. Religious educators should be aware of these differences and should design learning experiences to meet the needs of all their students. This includes integrating the affective domain of learning, which involves feelings, motivation, and reaction to others,[18] with the cognitive domain, as well as providing opportunities for practical application.[19] Cognitive activities such as lecture, questioning, group discussion, and reflection should be balanced by activities that access the affective domain—music, artwork, role-play, storytelling.[20] There is strong empirical support for benefits to all learners (1) when learning is made relevant to daily life; (2) when learners can actively participate in learning situations, especially in cooperative situations; and (3) when instruction addresses application to daily living, including actual opportunities to provide service

---

16. See David P. Ausubel, *Educational Psychology: A Cognitive View* (New York: Holt, Rinehart & Winston, 1968).

17. Ramirez and Price-Williams, "Cognitive Styles," pp. 212–18.

18. Kenneth E. Hyde, *Religion in Childhood and Adolescence: A Comprehensive Review of the Research* (Birmingham, Ala.: Religious Education Press, 1990), p. 397. See also pp. 46–47; 362–63 for the realm of the emotions in religious understanding.

19. Thomas Lickona, *Educating for Character: How Our Schools Can Teach Respect and Responsibility* (New York: Bantam Books, 1991), pp. 50–62; Kevin Ryan and Thomas Lickona, "Character Development: The Challenge and the Model," in *Character Development: In Schools and Beyond*, ed. Kevin Ryan and Thomas Lickona, 2d ed. (Washington, D.C.: The Council for Research in Values and Philosophy, 1992), pp. 14–21.

20. Particularly for young children, but frequently for others as well, affect is the dominant psychological process. See J. M. Lee, "How to Teach: Foundations, Processes, Procedures," in *Handbook of Preschool Religious Education*, ed. Donald Ratcliff (Birmingham, Ala.: Religious Education Press, 1988), pp. 189–91.

to others.[21] Active participation may include, for example, children learning about prayer by planning and conducting a prayer service for their peers, youth learning about diversity by visiting and sharing with a youth group in another ethnic church, or adults forming a task force to study and help resolve a community problem. For learners with a more relational cognitive style, such experiences are particularly indicated.

Other Influential Factors

Although the notion of cognitive styles is appealing, it is often overstated. Support from empirical research for the direct impact of cognitive styles on learning is weak. Further, differences among learners in multicultural learning situations are not due solely to cognitive style. The notion is helpful in drawing attention to the varied approaches to learning exhibited among different groups and by individuals within those groups, but the issue of cognitive style differences remains mired in debate and uncertainty.[22] Therefore, it may be more useful to shift the discussion of effective multicultural religious education to other influencing factors, such as motivation, and from learning styles to teaching styles.

MINORITY GROUP DIFFERENCES

While differences in cognitive styles may help us understand why learners respond differently to learning and religious education, much is left unexplained. For example, why do individuals from some minority groups adjust well, cooperate, and excel in majority culture school, church, and community activities, while members of other minority groups remain disengaged from the majority culture? This suggests that differences in learning and motivation are due to more than having a culture, language, and cognitive style that is different from the majority culture. Based on considerable empirical research, Ogbu contends that differences within the minority communities themselves, termed "community forces," have a major impact on what and how individuals learn in educational settings and social institutions.[23] In other words, identifiable forces within minority

---

21. For a further discussion of ways to make learning values a part of one's life, see William Damon, *The Moral Child* (New York: Free Press, 1988), pp. 115–30.

22. Gloria Ladson-Billings, "Culturally Relevant Teaching: The Key to Making Multicultural Education Work," in *Research and Multicultural Education: From the Margins to the Mainstream*, ed. Carl A. Grant (Washington, D.C.: Falmer, 1992), pp. 106–21.

23. John U. Ogbu, "Adaptation to Minority Status and Impact on School Success," *Theory Into Practice* 31, no. 4 (1992): 289.

communities greatly impact group members' motivation. A prerequisite to effective teaching of minority learners, then, is to understand these community forces, which can work for or against the success of learners in religious education as well as in other educational contexts.

Ogbu says that differential educational success across groups and sub-groups of minorities can be explained in part by their cultural and language frames of reference. These frames of reference are either ambivalent and oppositional or nonoppositional. Voluntary minorities, such as Chinese and South Korean immigrants, came to this country seeking economic well-being, better educational opportunities, or political freedom. Voluntary minorities are characterized by nonoppositional frames of reference. This nonoppositional frame leads voluntary immigrants to interpret difficulties and problems that they experience in society, schools, and churches merely as hurdles between them and their goals for a new life. They believe that they can overcome these obstacles through education and hard work. Further, voluntary minority groups tend to trust or acquiesce in their relationship to majority culture leaders. As a result of this frame of reference, voluntary minority communities strongly endorse education and persistent efforts to succeed in European-American society. Thus, the problems that voluntary immigrants initially experience due to culture and language differences are overcome as the minority group succeeds or even outperforms majority group members. In learning situations, they shine as highly motivated or even model participants.[24]

Ogbu points out that involuntary immigrants, in contrast, are often characterized by ambivalent and oppositional frames of reference. Involuntary populations, including African Americans, Mexican Americans, Native Americans, and Native Hawaiians, originally became part of the United States against their will through colonization, slavery, or forced labor. These oppositional frames may hinder learning and coping in the mainstream culture. Among involuntary minorities, learning tends to be equated with adopting the culture and language of European Americans and displacing their own social identity, sense of community, and self-worth. Involuntary minorities tend to distrust European-American authorities in social institutions. They realize that even if they do successfully learn to "act white" or succeed in white social institutions, they will not be fully accepted by the majority culture. Nor are the rewards and opportunities provided to European Americans available to them as members of minority groups. Involuntary minorities typically lack strong motivation to "play the game" in school, at church, and in other social institutions. Their experience discourages involuntary minorities from adopting the standard attitudes and behaviors that enhance learning and success in the majority culture and makes them

---

24. John U. Ogbu, "Understanding Cultural Diversity and Learning," *Educational Researcher* 21, no. 8 (1992): 5–14, 24; idem, *Theory into Practice*, pp. 287–95.

appear ambivalent. They are more likely than voluntary minority group members to need or demand culturally compatible curriculum resources and appropriate teaching styles, communication styles, and interactional styles than the ones traditionally offered in schools and churches.[25] Individuals within involuntary minority cultures who want to succeed in the majority culture often do so by adopting coping strategies to shield themselves from peer pressure and distractions in the ambivalent minority community that hinder their success. These adoptive strategies include emulating whites, accommodation without assimilation (i.e., following white norms at school but black norms in the home community), having a mentor, attending private schools, and, interestingly, becoming involved in church activities.

Differences among minority groups regarding their approach to majority culture social institutions, including the church, exist because of complex community forces. These community forces are evident through different relations between their culture and the American mainstream culture. It is important to note that although they may appear similar on the surface, the cultural problems related to learning and religious education that arise from voluntary and involuntary minorities appear for very different reasons. Further, the expectations and motivations that different minority group members bring to churches will vary, and they must be taken into consideration by religious educators. Is a minority youth internalizing a Christian lifestyle or merely adopting certain behaviors to gain acceptance from those in the youth group? Why do some minority learners appear to be indifferent, while others are ambivalent? Are they rejecting God and biblical principles, or are they actually rejecting a dominant-culture approach to religious education?

CULTURALLY RESPONSIBLE PEDAGOGY

It is apparent, then, that community factors may influence a minority member's motivation to cooperate and learn. But this does not help us understand how to teach or how to bring about learning in multicultural religious education settings. Sadly, according to Sleeter and Grant, discussions of multicultural education have virtually overlooked the instructional process and pedagogical procedures.[26] While it is doubtful that there is even one magic bullet, let alone an arsenal of them, that provides a sure method of teaching minority learners effectively, there are guidelines that can assist with these endeavors.

---

25. Ogbu, "Understanding Cultural Diversity," pp. 8–13; idem, *Theory into Practice*, pp. 290, 291.

26. Christine Sleeter and Carl A. Grant, "An Analysis of Multicultural Education in the United States," *Harvard Educational Review* 57, no. 4 (1987): 434.

Culturally responsible pedagogy is the term used to describe efforts by teachers to accommodate the variety of learners in multicultural educational contexts. Culturally responsible pedagogy involves preparing a relevant curriculum and conducting it in such a way that minority learners are more comfortable in the learning environments. In addition, the religious educator utilizes strategies that research and experience have shown to be effective in bringing about learning for minority group members.

Culturally responsible pedagogy addresses three aspects of teaching. First, it addresses content knowledge. Although religious educators must have an adequate understanding of biblical/theological content, Christian discipleship, and church history, this basic knowledge is not enough to enable them to present that information in a culturally responsible way. They must also be knowledgeable about the culture and background of the minority learners in the group, and how their history or present situation relates to what is being taught. For example, a study of the life of Solomon should include exploration of African and other cultures associated with his reign. A study of the gospels should note that Simon of Cyrene, who helped carry Jesus' cross, is believed by many to be black.[27] But where was the city of Cyrene? And what was Simon doing in Jerusalem? Did he end up following Christ's teachings? The point is not to distort biblical history to make minority group members feel good, but to point out how Western history has distorted contributions made by people of color. Unfortunately, this information is difficult to find in traditional biblical commentaries and religious education resources. (See chap. 4 for theological and biblical insights.)

Second, culturally responsible pedagogy addresses teacher attitudes. Religious educators must possess attitudes that promote rather than inhibit minority learners' success and spiritual development. Baptiste and Baptiste present eleven attitudes, "cultural competencies," which are characteristic of effective minority educators.[28] In short, minority members should not be viewed as victims of inescapable situations who are less capable of difficult learning or are crude and less sophisticated than other students. Rather, educators must believe in their learners, insist that they are able to overcome barriers, and provide them with challenging ideas and tasks. Educators must respect the tremendous task that minority learners engage in when they juggle two cultures, and through their expectations and modeling help them work toward equilibrium.[29] Ethnic minority parents and church

---

27. Cain Hope Felder, *Troubling Biblical Waters: Race, Class, and Family* (Maryknoll, N.Y.: Orbis, 1989).

28. H. Prentice Baptiste and Mira Lanier Baptiste, *Developing the Multicultural Process in Classroom Instruction: Competencies for Teachers* (Washington, D.C.: University Press of America, 1979).

29. Deborah L. Bainer, "Essential Skills for Effective Minority Teacher Education," *Teacher Education Quarterly* 20, no. 3 (1993): 19–29.

members, by their active participation in community life and by working with their children's schools and organizations, can model the self-respect and sense of purpose youth need to emulate.

Third, religious educators practicing culturally responsible pedagogy utilize instructional skills that are effective with minority group members. Even if attitudes take time to change, making changes in the teaching process can have an immediate impact on learning in a diverse religious education setting. The following discussion focuses on instructional skills and strategies that seem to be most effective in multicultural learning contexts.

Skills for Effective Teaching in Multicultural Contexts

Many ethnic minority learners are taught in their churches by members of their own cultural group, but many others are not. Teacher logs indicate that instructing learners from a culture different from one's own, even with increased sensitivity, is not easy.[30] Yet religious educators do not have to share the same race or ethnicity of their learners to identify and capitalize on the cultural and cognitive assets of minority populations.[31]

The bad news is that, according to Brown, being a good teacher is not enough. A diversity of learning styles means that what traditionally might have been considered good teaching in a majority culture situation may not necessarily be effective teaching in a multicultural setting.[32]

The good news is that the teacher does not have to make major changes to achieve effectiveness with minority learners. Making minor changes in one's teaching style can result in vast increases in minority members' motivation, attitudes, and learning. More important, the strategies that will improve minority learning will also enhance the learning and motivation of others in the group. All learners benefit when teachers utilize procedures that are associated with increased learning for minority group members.

Guskey and Easton found that instructors who were effective with culturally diverse learners shared many teaching characteristics and instructional practices, but few personal characteristics.[33] The following section examines four areas that are related to teaching effectiveness: the lesson, the curriculum, the learning environment, and the teacher's personality.

---

30. Nancy Davis Burstein and Beverly Cabello, "Preparing Teachers to Work With Culturally Diverse Students: A Teacher Education Model," *Journal of Teacher Education* 40, no. 5 (1989): 14.

31. Anderson, *Journal of Teacher Education*, p. 7.

32. T. J. Brown, *Teaching Minorities More Effectively: A Model for Educators* (Washington, D.C.: University Press of America, 1986).

33. Thomas R. Guskey and John Q. Easton, "The Characteristics of Very Effective Teachers in Urban Community Colleges," *Community/Junior College Quarterly* 7, no. 3 (1983): 265–74.

The Lesson

The lessons taught by teachers who are effective in multicultural contexts share certain characteristics. Guskey and Easton found that a variety of procedures can be effective in teaching minority learners, if they are carried out appropriately.[34]

Many religious educators utilize didactic instructional methods, such as lectures or teacher-centered discussions, for most of their lessons. Because many minority members prefer a relational approach to learning, religious educators should attempt to balance the use of a direct instruction approach when working with multicultural groups or groups with predominately minority members. That having been said, religious educators can take certain steps to significantly improve their level of success when they decide to use a direct instruction approach. The lesson must be clearly and systematically organized and yet be open enough to allow for learner-generated discussion. At the beginning of the learning experience, whether it be a CCD class, a youth Bible study, or an adult seminar, it is best to give an overview of the plans for the session. The objective should be clearly communicated in terms of what the learners should be able to do by the end of the session. For example, telling the learners that by the end of the session they should be able to: name the twelve disciples, explain in today's terms what Jesus meant in telling the parable of the lost coin, or suggest incidents in Solomon's childhood and youth that may have influenced him to request wisdom over wealth or fame. Informing learners of the direction and objective of the session helps them to listen for and focus on the main points.

It is important to avoid using jargon while teaching. This is especially difficult for religious educators who grew up in the church and so naturally "speak the language" of the church. Even if the minority learners speak English fluently, many of them will have difficulty with the formal language used in the church and in some books. They may not understand what they hear and what they read, especially traditional versions of the Bible and religious education curriculum materials. It is essential to avoid formal language and to summarize what has been said after the discussion. Further, passages should be summarized after they are read. Any religious jargon or unfamiliar biblical terms should be printed on the chalkboard or a poster, pronounced, defined, and discussed. Unfamiliar terms and concepts must be contextualized so that they are more accessible to the learners. For example, when explaining that Christ was a "sacrifice" for our sins, it would be helpful to explain the Old Testament practice of bringing a spotless lamb to the temple for a sin offering.

It is important to provide visual and verbal cues throughout the session to help learners structure and remember the information. Verbal cues include

---

34. Guskey and Easton, "Very Effective Teachers," p. 272.

identifying the main points as first, second, third, and so on. The teacher can strengthen this with a visual cue by holding up the appropriate number of fingers. Sequencing terms like *next, last,* and *finally* and rhetorical questions such as What does this mean? or Why is this important? are also effective. A printed, general outline will help many learners make sense out of the lesson, focus on the important points, and see how they are related. Also use plenty of examples and nonexamples when teaching new concepts or information. For example, when teaching about Paul, point out that he was a leader in the early church but not one of the twelve disciples. This helps to clarify who the disciples and apostles were and how they received those distinctions.

It is important to "read" the learners and use specific questions to check for their understanding of concepts or directions throughout the teaching event. It is surprising and disheartening to realize how little minority individuals (and others!) actually learn in teaching sessions. For example, when academically successful minority students at one Christian university were asked if they understood their courses, they estimated that their comprehension was limited to 25 percent of the content presented.[35] Simply asking, Are there are any questions? at the end of the Bible study or youth group session is ineffective in determining if participants have heard and understood the teaching. Instead, pose questions throughout the session and phrase them in a way that elicits thoughtful answers. "In what places did Paul and Barnabas have an effective ministry?" "Why did they agree to part ways?"

It is also important to provide learners with frequent, specific feedback on their progress throughout the session and to point out how much they have learned. It is not enough to congratulate them at the end of the session on a good Bible-times craft project or for insights shared during group discussion. Providing feedback and encouragement throughout the learning experience increases motivation to keep listening and participating.

At the end of the lesson, teachers need to review to see that the objective of the session has been accomplished. Psychologists tell us that providing this closure is vital to learning.[36] Closure can be accomplished by summarizing the main points of the lesson in a few sentences. Asking learners to summarize or react to the topics of discussion is even better. You can also remind them of how today's information was built on previous learning and points toward next week's lesson. Asking learners to suggest practical applications ensures that learning is relevant to the individual. This approach also moves the focus of learning beyond the memorization of facts to include changed lives.

---

35. Deborah L. Bainer, *Student Interviews* (La Mirada, Calif.: Biola University Press, 1988).

36. Myron H. Dembo, *Applying Educational Psychology* (White Plains, N.Y.: Longman Publishing Group, 1994), pp. 268, 269.

Because of the differences in preferred modes of processing information cited above, some minority learners may have difficulty with a linear, step-by-step approach to learning. Others will experience difficulty with the lesson because of their limited English proficiency. In such a case, it may be beneficial to try a more holistic approach using sheltered instruction.[37] Sheltered instruction includes overviewing the lesson briefly at the beginning of the session, preferably in the minority students' primary language, then teaching the lesson, and finally summarizing it at the end in the learners' primary language as well as in English. With older children and adults, it is often effective to have a learner present the overview and summary in his or her own words, even with learners whose primary language is English.

Using Diverse Methods for Building Concepts: In addition to verbal instruction, a variety of teaching methods have been shown to be effective in multicultural contexts. Generally, lessons that actively involve participants in learning and that apply information to their immediate world are most effective. Religious educators must keep in mind that, while the focus in religious education often involves teaching abstract concepts or ideas, a major goal of religious instruction must include learner response and life application, which are also a matter of attitude, beliefs, and behavior. However, when building concepts is the goal of instruction, thematic lessons tend to work better than sequential lessons that progress through a book or series of lessons, as some traditional religious education materials suggest. When introducing a concept or discussing an idea or principle, it is important to engage individuals in a direct experience that will connect the idea to life application. For example, a visit to a homeless shelter could precede a study of the prophet's concern for doing justice and loving mercy.

If a direct experience is not possible, a vicarious experience, such as a demonstration, a news event, or a specific personal story related to the concept, may also be used to introduce biblical-theological concepts. Storytelling and readings that involve learner participation work especially well in teaching concepts, as is evidenced by Jesus' extensive use of parables to teach eternal truth. Incorporating poetry, music, and movement in the teaching of concepts enhances the learning experience.[38]

For learners of all ages with limited English proficiency, the religious educator should use many large pictures, nonverbal books, line art drawings, charts, and graphs to illustrate and show the relationship among concepts.

---

37. L. Davidman and P. Davidman, *Supervising with a Multicultural Perspective: Adding a New Dimension to Clinical Supervision in a Preservice Program* (San Luis Obispo, Calif.: California Polytechnic State University Press, 1989).

38. Several authors have written on this topic, including Dorothy Jean Furnish, *Living the Bible with Children* (Nashville: Abingdon, 1979); Jerome Berryman, *Godly Play* (San Francisco: HarperSanFrancisco, 1991); and Gretchen Pritchard, *Offering the Gospel to Children* (Cambridge, Mass.: Crowley, 1992).

When telling a story, giving directions, or explaining rules, it is important to illustrate the key points or steps with simple drawings on the chalkboard or poster paper. For example, if the directions are to cut, color, and then paste a picture, the teacher might, while giving oral directions, print the word *cut* followed by a sketch of scissors, then print the word *color* followed by a picture of a crayon, and finally print *paste* followed by a glue bottle. Similarly, while giving adults directions to break into groups of four and come up with three verses from Proverbs that talk about rearing children, the religious educator might draw a group of four stick figures followed by the numeral three and a child stick figure. Finally, in addition to telling learners what is desired, the teacher needs to show them. The religious educator can model the series of directions by completing one of the pictures or by giving one example of an acceptable verse from Proverbs. This enables learners to understand the directions through one of a variety of modes and encourages their success in the learning experience.

Working in Cooperative Groups: As previously discussed, many minority group members prefer to work cooperatively in small group situations because, in part, of their cognitive style. Often teachers assume that having participants work in small groups is the ultimate learning approach. They assume that in small groups more individuals are actively engaged in learning and that there are tremendous social benefits to having learners work that way. Unfortunately, research shows that just the opposite is often true: frequently, fewer students are generally engaged in the learning task. Many students drift away from the learning task and some withdraw. Further, students who tend to be dominant or passive are even more so in small groups, thus inhibiting true teamwork.[39] This suggests that, especially in diverse classrooms, small group learning situations must be planned rigorously. Small groups are most successful when (1) the group task is carefully outlined and structured, (2) learners are thoughtfully assigned to various groups, and (3) the teacher continuously monitors each group's progress and redirects floundering groups by briefly joining in their discussion.[40]

Several simple types of cooperative learning can be used profitably in religious instruction. Assigning learning partners is a nonthreatening approach to implementing cooperative learning situations. Partners can

---

39. Mary McCaslin and Thomas L. Good, "Compliant Cognition: The Misalliance of Management and Instructional Goals in Current School Reform," *Educational Researcher* 21, no. 3 (1992): 4–17.

40. Dembo, *Applying Educational Psychology*, pp. 409–15, provides a discussion of effective practices for instructing culturally diverse students, including the use of cooperative groups.

discuss answers to questions and then present their opinions to the larger group. A more involved approach called "jigsawing,"[41] in which each member of a small group "teaches" the rest of his or her group, has also been demonstrated as effective with diverse learners.[42] When properly structured, cooperative learning situations have been observed to provide many benefits to relational-style learners, including building a sense of community and emphasizing the importance of all the members of the class or group.[43]

Adjusting the Pace of the Lesson: Finally, many minority members tend to prefer a relaxed teaching and learning pace. Pacing deals with whether the work is at the appropriate level of difficulty for the learners in the group and how rapidly the teacher covers the material. By carefully planning the lesson, materials, and structure in advance, religious educators can ensure that even difficult concepts will be offered on the students' level and that each point will be illustrated with clear, practical examples and nonexamples. In addition, this careful planning has benefits for the religious educator, since it enables him or her to exhibit a more confident, relaxed pace during the session and thus to increase the chances that participants will learn.

Interestingly, Waxman's research found that different groups of minority students respond positively to different aspects of instruction. Specifically, African-American students who perceived that the teacher set a learning tone in the classroom that kept them engaged in the learning process showed increases in learning. Structuring comments throughout the lesson, such as providing an overview at the beginning and end of instructional sequences and frequently checking to ensure that the learners understood what the teacher was talking about, were also cited by African-American students as helpful to their learning. In contrast, Hispanic students reported that

---

41. In "jigsawing," a topic of study is divided into sections that are later fit into a whole. The teacher introduces a topic and then divides the learners into small "home groups." Members each receive a number and one aspect of the topic to study, along with appropriate materials and directions. They disperse and regroup into "expert groups" with members of other home groups who have been assigned the same number and topic aspect to study, explore, and discuss, helping each other "become experts" on the topic. After the allotted time they return to their home groups, where they are responsible to teach their group what they learned in the expert group. High learner involvement and repeated opportunities to explain what was learned are the strengths of the jigsaw model. See Robert Slavin et al., eds., *Learning to Cooperate, Cooperating to Learn* (New York: Plenum, 1985), p. 10–11.

42. Thomas Lickona, *Educating for Character: How Our Schools Can Teach Respect and Responsibility* (New York: Bantam Books, 1991), pp. 185–207. Lickona devotes a chapter of this book to the use of cooperative learning in the teaching of values.

43. See Lickona, *Educating For Character*, pp. 186–89, for a discussion of the benefits of using cooperative learning in the teaching of values, especially with diverse groups of learners.

the pacing of the lesson was most closely related to their learning. Those who felt that the instruction was most appropriately paced for them did significantly better in learning situations.[44] Religious educators should note that it was *the learners' perceptions* of the lesson that influenced their success in learning. Learners' perceptions of a lesson and instruction can be assessed only when the teacher asks for this feedback in a systematic way.

The Curriculum

The curriculum that is effective in a culturally diverse educational setting is noticeably different from the curriculum that is usually found in traditional religious education materials. An effective curriculum is one that has been modified by the religious educator to make it relevant to the learners' immediate lives and experiences, as well as to their overall lives and goals.

Relevance and Meaning: For all learners, interest and attentiveness are linked to their perceptions of the relevance and purposefulness of the topic under examination.[45] These perceptions of relevance, however, vary across minority groups in a culturally diverse situation. Brown points out that while white, middle-class learners are generally content to believe that what they are learning may someday be of use to them, African-American and Hispanic learners need to see the immediate relevance of what is being taught.[46] Deferred relevance is often insufficient to motivate them to pay attention or to engage in the learning experience. Brown encourages multicultural educators to take as much time as necessary for learners to grasp how the topic or experience relates to the real, immediate world in which they live. Further, the needs of minority learners should be recognized and revisited with frequent applications in order to validate the curriculum.

The curriculum must have meaning for all the learners in a diverse group. This suggests that religious educators may need to present multiple purposes for the curriculum and for each learning activity. To successfully engage and motivate all the individuals and cultural groups within a multicultural setting, the curriculum must be viewed by the learners as meeting their specific needs, both immediate and deferred.

Cultural Affirmation: The curriculum and each lesson taught should stress cultural affirmation and utilize teaching procedures that draw on learners' cultural strengths. The curriculum should be set up to ensure

---

44. Hersholt C. Waxman, "Urban Black and Hispanic Elementary School Students' Perceptions of Classroom Instruction," *Journal of Research and Development in Education* 22, no. 2 (1989): 60.

45. Robert F. Biehler and Jack Snowman, *Psychology Applied to Teaching* (Boston: Houghton Mifflin, 1992).

46. Brown, *Teaching Minorities More Effectively.*

that learners use their personal experiences and cultural backgrounds to understand and interpret the concepts under discussion.[47] A simple way to do this is to ask learners to give personal examples or to relate incidents from their lives that illustrate topics under consideration. Finally, the curriculum and illustrations used should reflect what is known about minority members' learning. For example, school-aged European-American learners tend to do better than learners from most other ethnic groups on analytic tasks. Compared to school-aged Mexican-American learners, European-Americans learn material that is inanimate or impersonal more easily. In contrast, Mexican-American learners tend to learn material most easily that is humorous, has social content, or is characterized by fantasy.[48] For this reason, creative and interpretive dramatics, role-play of biblical scenarios, and simulations relating biblical passages to current issues are good methods to use. For example, a group might perform a modern version of the good Samaritan set in an urban area with the diverse religious characters of a modern city. Not only are these effective ways to encourage learning with some minority group members, but they also provide a relaxed atmosphere and occasionally stimulate a few laughs.

It is not easy for religious educators to make the changes in religious education curricula that are necessary to enhance minority learning. To make these modifications, it is necessary to abandon Eurocentric ways of thinking, feeling, and interpreting religious truths. This means that religious educators must believe that minority learners, as individuals and as cultural groups, have special strengths that need to be explored and used in the learning situation.[49] Although it is often difficult, dominant-culture teachers must recognize that religious principles and practices may apply to minority learners in ways that the teacher can scarcely imagine. Religious educators must keep in mind that formal classroom lectures alone do not present the best learning experience to many minority members.[50] The learning situation or class should be reciprocal and oriented toward interaction, not transmission.[51] To be effective, religious educators must take on the role of facilitator and colearner, abandoning the traditional role as giver of knowledge and final authority on religious truths. The greatest challenge is to draw out even the most reluctant learners and to lead them to examine and apply spiritual realities to their lives and goals.

---

47. Luis C. Moll, "Some Key Issues in Teaching Latino Students," *Language Arts* 65, no. 5 (1988): 465–72.

48. Anderson, *Journal of Teacher Education*, p. 5.

49. Ladson-Billings, "Culturally Relevant Teaching," pp. 106–21.

50. Christine Sleeter and Carl Grant, *Making Choices for Multicultural Education*, 2d ed. (New York: Merrill/Macmillan, 1993), p. 66.

51. Jim Cummins, "Empowering Minority Students: A Framework for Intervention," *Harvard Educational Review* 56, no. 1 (1986): 18–36.

In addition, effective curriculum modifications require a disciplined effort on the part of the religious educator to investigate and actually experience minority cultures. In any geographic or economic area, opportunities abound to accomplish this. One obvious way to become informed about other cultural groups, especially regarding the problems and issues they face in your particular area, is by reading the local newspaper or, even better, a newspaper targeting a specific minority group. There are many quality books and films that provide an understanding of minority group cultures and concerns. Amy Tan's novels provide excellent insights into the struggles experienced by Chinese Americans as they attempt to balance two cultures. Lawrence Yep's books, although they are written for children, provide similar cultural insights into Chinese culture. Mystery novels by Tony Hillerman are laced with perspectives and beliefs of various Native American groups. Films such as *Malcolm X*, *Mississippi Burning*, and perhaps *Dances with Wolves*, alert religious educators to cultural perspectives held by other minority groups. Public and university libraries have an abundance of informative and appropriate resources. It can also be helpful to invite a group of minority students from your church or youth group into your home for dinner or an entertaining evening. By talking with them and listening to them, you can gain many cultural and personal insights.

Religious educators can become more effective by increasing their familiarity with the communities in which their learners reside. Walk through the ethnic communities, shop and eat dinner in local establishments, attend a worship service in an ethnic church, tutor new immigrants in English and learn their language at the same time. These experiences often produce feelings of discomfort or stress, which are themselves informative. The multicultural religious educator benefits by knowing how it feels to be the only minority group member in the youth group or CCD class.

Involving Members in Curriculum Decisions: It is even more important, however, to involve minority learners and their parents, leaders in the minority community, and minority members of the congregation or parish in decision making regarding the curriculum.[52] By eliciting help from minority group members, it is possible to develop a curriculum that is relevant to learners and embraces and honors their cultural background and personal experiences.

Given the limited knowledge that most religious educators have of the experiences and cultural background of other ethnic group members, how can these curricular modifications be made wisely? It is good to begin by surveying the cultural characteristics represented in the group.

---

52. D. First and W. Crichlow, "Effective Teachers' Knowledge and Practice in Working with 'At-Risk' Students in an Urban School District: A Collaborative Investigation by Teachers and Researchers," (paper presented at the Tenth Annual Ethnography in Education Research Forum, University of Pennsylvania, Philadelphia, February 1989).

Saville-Troike developed a set of questions that can help educators identify what they need to know (see below).[53] Applicable to a wide variety of groups, the questions focus attention on sociocultural elements relevant to education and religious education—differences related to ethnicity, religion, language, and other cultural characteristics that should be considered when modifying the curriculum.

Table 9.1 Survey of Cultural Group Characteristics
(adapted from Saville-Troike, 1978)

General
1. What major stereotypes do you and others have about each cultural group? To what extent are these stereotypes accepted by members of the group being explored?
2. To what extent and in what areas has the traditional culture of each minority group changed as a result of contact with the dominant American culture? In what areas has it been maintained?
3. To what extent do individuals possess knowledge of or exhibit characteristics of traditional groups?

Family
1. Who is in a "family"? Who among these (or others) live in one house?
2. What is the hierarchy of authority in the family?
3. What are the rights and responsibilities of each family member? Do children have an obligation to work to help the family?
4. What are the functions and obligations of the family to the larger social unit?
5. What is the degree of solidarity or cohesiveness in the family?

The Life Cycle
1. What criteria define the stages, periods, or transitions in life?
2. What are the attitudes, expectations, and behaviors toward individuals at different stages in the life cycle?
3. What behaviors are appropriate or unacceptable for children of various ages? How might these conflict with behaviors taught or encouraged in a class or learning situation?
4. How is the age of children computed? How is the child's birth commemorated and when?

Roles
1. What roles within the group are available to whom, and how are they acquired? Is education relevant to this acquisition?
2. What is the knowledge of and perception by the child, the parents, and the community toward these roles, their availability, and possible or appropriate means to access them?

---

53. Muriel Saville-Troike, *A Guide to Culture in the Classroom* (Washington, D.C.: National Clearinghouse for Bilingual Education, 1978).

3. Are class differences involved in expectations about child role attainment? Are these realistic?

Interpersonal Relationships
1. How do people greet each other? What forms of address are used between people in various roles?
2. Do girls work and interact with boys? Is it proper?
3. How is deference shown?
4. How are insults expressed?
5. Who may disagree with whom? Under what circumstances?

Communication
1. What languages, and varieties of each language, are used in the community? By whom? When? Where? For what purposes?
2. What are the characteristics of "speaking well"? How do these relate to age, sex, context, or other social factors? What are the criteria for correctness?
3. What roles, attitudes, or personality traits are associated with particular ways of speaking?
4. What gestures or postures have special significance or may be considered objectionable? What meaning is attached to making direct eye contact? To eye avoidance?
5. Who may talk to whom? When? Where? About what?

Decorum and Discipline
1. What counts as discipline in terms of the culture and what doesn't?
2. What behaviors are considered socially acceptable for students of different age and sex?
3. Who (or what) is considered responsible if a child misbehaves?
4. Who has authority over whom? To what extent can one person's will be imposed on another? By what means?
5. How is the behavior of children traditionally controlled, to what extent, and in what domains?

Religion
1. What is considered sacred and what secular?
2. What religious roles and authority are recognized in the community? What role do children play in religious practices?
3. What taboos are there? What should not be discussed? What questions should not be asked? What student behaviors should not be required?

Health and Hygiene
1. Who or what is believed to cause illness or death?
2. Who or what is responsible for curing?
3. How are specific illnesses treated? To what extent do individuals utilize or accept modern medical practices by doctors and other health professionals?
4. If a student is involved in an accident, would any common first-aid practices be unacceptable?

Food
1. What is eaten? In what order? How often?

2. What foods are favorites? What are taboo? What are typical?
3. What rules are observed during meals regarding age and sex roles within the family, the order of serving, seating, utensils used, and appropriate verbal formulas (e.g., how, and if, one may request, refuse, or thank)?
4. What social obligations are there with regard to food giving, preparation, reciprocity, and honoring people?

Dress and Personal Appearance
1. What clothing is typical? What is worn for special occasions? What seasonal differences are considered appropriate?
2. How does dress differ for age, sex, and social class?
3. What restrictions are imposed for modesty?
4. What is the concept of beauty or attractiveness? What characteristics are most valued?
5. What constitutes a compliment? What form should it take?
6. Does the color of dress have symbolic significance?

History and Traditions
1. What individuals and events in history are a source of pride for the group?
2. To what extent is knowledge of the group's history preserved? In what forms and in what ways is it passed on?
3. How and to what extent does the group's knowledge of history coincide with or depart from scientific theories of creation, evolution, and historical development?
4. To what extent does the group in the United States identify with the history and traditions of its country of origin? What changes have taken place in the country of origin since the group or individuals emigrated?
5. For what reasons and under what circumstances did the group or individuals come to the United States (or did the United States come to them)?

Holidays and Celebrations
1. What holidays and celebrations are observed by the group and individuals? What is their purpose (e.g., political, seasonal, religious)?
2. What cultural values are they intended to inculcate?
3. Do parents and students of immigrant children know and understand church holidays and behavior appropriate for them (including appropriate nonattendance)?

Education
1. What is the purpose of education?
2. What methods for teaching and learning are used at home (e.g., modeling and imitation, didactic stories and proverbs, direct verbal instruction)? Do methods vary with the setting or according to what is being taught or learned?
3. Is it appropriate for students to ask questions or volunteer information?
4. What constitutes a positive response from a teacher to a student?
5. Do parents, teachers, and students hold different expectations with respect to different groups, for example for boys versus girls?

Work and Play
1. What range of behaviors are considered work? Play?
2. What kinds of work are prestigious and why? Why is work valued?

3. Are there stereotypes about what a particular group will do?
4. What is the purpose of play?

Time and Space
1. What beliefs or values are associated with concepts of time? How important is punctuality? How important is speed of performance when taking a test or completing projects or assignments?
2. How do individuals organize themselves spatially in groups (e.g., in rows, circles, around tables, on the floor)?
3. What is the knowledge and significance of cardinal directions (north, south, east, west)? At what age are these concepts acquired?
4. What significance is associated with different directions or places (e.g., heaven is up, people are buried facing west)?

Natural Phenomena
1. What beliefs and practices are associated with the sun, moon, comets, and stars?
2. Who or what is responsible for rain, lightning, thunder, earthquakes, droughts, floods, and hurricanes?
3. Are particular behavioral prescriptions or taboos associated with natural phenomena? What sanctions are there against individuals violating restrictions or prescriptions?
4. To what extent are traditional group beliefs still held by individuals within the community?

Pets and Other Animals
1. Which animals are valued, and for what reasons?
2. Are particular behavioral prescriptions or taboos associated with particular animals?
3. Do any animals have religious significance? Historical importance?

Art and Music
1. What forms of art and music are most highly valued?
2. What media and instruments are traditionally used?
3. Are there any behavioral prescriptions or taboos related to art and music (e.g., depiction of the human form; desecration of living things)?
4. How and to what extent may approval or disapproval be expressed?

Expectations and Aspirations
1. How is success defined?
2. What beliefs are held regarding luck and fate?
3. What significance does adherence to the traditional culture of the group have for the individual's potential achievement?
4. What significance does the acquisition of the majority culture and the English language have?
5. Do parents expect and desire assimilation of children to the dominant culture as a result of education and the acquisition of English?
6. Are the attitudes of community members and individuals the same as or different from those who speak for the community?

The Learning Environment

Even a curriculum that is carefully adapted to reflect the cultural background and personal experiences of minority learners will be ineffective unless the learning environment is inviting. That is, the psychological environment in multicultural learning contexts should communicate that the teacher or group leader has confidence in the minority learners' abilities, holds high expectations for their success, behavior, and learning, and respects them as individuals and members of a complex cultural group. The physical environment of the meeting room should also demonstrate a commitment to including members of minority groups, since an accepting physical environment can enhance the psychological environment as well.

The Physical Environment: An inviting meeting room provides a variety of instructional and social arrangements and situations to maximize learning, interaction, and success. It provides a variety of experiences, including both structured and unstructured activities, so that learners can find something at which they can frequently succeed. Especially for those with limited English proficiency, it is essential to make the room a highly literate environment in which many language experiences can take place. There are several ways in which a rich, literate environment can be created. Visual illustrations of current biblical or other religious education subject matter should be hung at the learners' eye level. The walls can be decorated with pictures and simple captions of a personal nature. One group member can be featured each month, a corner of the room being dedicated to a display of that person's interests, accomplishments, favorite things, and family background. A message center near the door where weekly messages are posted for each person and where members can post messages for each other encourages a rich, interactive environment. A collection of newspaper articles that recount the learners' accomplishments can be displayed in a visible place. Group members can even post their favorite cartoons and jokes. After all, an inviting learning environment testifies of the personalities and interests of those who spend time there. Too often our meeting rooms look like motel rooms, devoid of personality and character. In contrast, inviting rooms reflect the humor, experiences, and cultural background of both the leader and the learners.

The Psychological Environment: An important aspect of establishing an inviting learning environment is ensuring that the participants feel safe. Maslow's hierarchy (see chap. 3) suggests that all humans need to have sufficient food and shelter and need to feel safe, appreciated, and accepted by significant others. Only when these basic needs are met are persons free to address needs for intellectual challenge, aesthetic appreciation, and self-fulfillment. This suggests that the religious education environment must be perceived as safe, predictable, and nonthreatening if group members are to feel emotionally safe and free to explore, ask questions, and learn. Jackson found that students drop out of school, not because they cannot handle the academic work, but because they were unable to "read," or understand how to follow procedures and how to have their needs met in order to succeed.[54] This suggests that children, youth, and adults may walk away from religious education efforts simply because they cannot figure out how to gain the attention, esteem, and the related emotional support they need to satisfy their basic human needs.

How can you make a learning environment safe and nonthreatening? First, establish routines and structure in the classroom or other meeting place. Develop specific routines that you clearly communicate to group members and consistently implement. There are a variety of routines that meet members' basic needs—routines for greeting one another on arrival, deciding where to sit, using the rest room, and knowing how and when to gain the leader's attention. Routines are also needed to get the session started, provide supplies, give directions, call on learners, and clean up after activities. Teachers should develop routines for greeting learners who arrive early and guide their behavior, and routines for dismissing the group in a friendly but orderly way when the session is over. Are refreshments provided for adults and children? If so, there should be a routine for smoothly integrating them into the session's activities. While some educators may fear that routines can stifle learner creativity, such is not the case. Instead, a structured environment has the opposite effect: it frees learners from expending considerable emotional energy trying to figure out what behaviors are expected, and it enables them to focus on learning and instruction.[55]

Teacher-Learner Interaction: A third factor that is essential to establishing a learning environment that minority members find inviting deals with teacher-learner interactions. Unfortunately, many educators are unaware that in the process of interacting with minority group members, they frequently offend them. Jenkins and Bainer synthesize a list of teacher behaviors that are offensive to minority college students:

1. Avoiding eye contact with minority group members while making eye contact with majority students.
2. Calling directly on majority students but not minority students.
3. Waiting longer for majority students to respond.
4. Interrupting minority students more often than majority students when they do respond.

---

54. Philip W. Jackson, *Life in Classrooms* (New York: Holt, Rinehart & Winston, 1986).

55. Donald R. Cruickshank, Deborah L. Bainer, and Kim K. Metcalf, *The Act of Teaching* (New York: McGraw-Hill, 1994), pp. 369–80.

5. Using probing or additional explanation to coach majority students toward a fuller or correct answer, but not probing minority students.
6. Responding more extensively to comments made by majority students and assuming a more attentive posture when they respond.
7. Using a tone that expresses interest or delight with majority students. Conversely, using a patronizing or impatient tone when minority students respond.
8. Habitually standing closer to majority students than to minority students.
9. Making well-intentioned comments which imply that minority students are not as competent as majority group members.
10. Reacting to comments or questions offered in a minority language style as if they are less insightful or less valuable than comments from majority students.[56]

According to minority students, these teacher behaviors have an adverse effect on their interaction and learning. The minority students surveyed state that these behaviors discourage them from participating in class and from seeking help or counsel outside of formal group meetings. The teacher behaviors also tend to undermine the minority member's confidence. Further, they often cause learners to avoid the class or to leave the institution, in this case the church, altogether.[57] Religious educators need to be alert to their own unconscious habits of interaction in order to encourage, rather than unintentionally alienate, minority members. It can be helpful to have a colleague come in to observe and point out behaviors that need to be changed.

Group discussions and participation are the most common type of teacher-learner interaction in religious education. Therefore, it is important to recognize that participation is often linked to cultural characteristics. Some cultures consider it inappropriate or disrespectful to compare or analyze another person's ideas or actions, even in a learning situation. One American company, for example, attempted to market baby diapers in Japan using television commercials that compared the absorbency rate of their diaper with that of a competitor. The Japanese found the commercials confrontational and offensive, so diaper sales were low. When the advertising was changed to present only their product, the company's diaper sales soared.

---

56. Carol A. Jenkins and Deborah Bainer, "Educating for Equity: Issues and Strategies for Effective Multicultural Instruction," in *Ethnic Minorities and Evangelical Christian Colleges*, ed. D. J. Lee (New York: University Press of America, 1991), pp. 259–89.

57. Roberta M. Hall, "The Classroom Climate: A Chilly One for Women?" *Project on the Status and Education of Women* (Washington, D.C.: Association of American Colleges, 1982).

To most religious educators, learner participation is important because it shows whether or not they are grasping and applying the material being presented. It is important, then, to encourage a high level of participation and discussion. Group participation can be increased if the religious educator, by monitoring his or her teaching behaviors, encourages everyone to participate. For example, it is important to react to learner-initiated comments or responses in a way that builds confidence and reinforces participation. This means that when reacting to learner comments, leaders should praise the effort ("Thanks for sharing that." or "Good point!"), as well as providing feedback on the quality of the answer ("Important contribution!" or "Interesting point, I've never thought about it in that way."). Participation can also be encouraged by redirecting questions, that is, asking a question, inviting someone to respond, and then asking another learner to respond to the same question or to react to the first learner's answer.

Sometimes it is easier for minority learners and others who hesitate to respond to open up in "safer" small group situations rather than in front of the entire group. Participation can be encouraged by using a "neighbor nudge." The teacher asks learners to share their answers with the person sitting next to them, rather than the entire group. Finally, reluctant participants can be encouraged by having them respond in writing on an index card, then collecting and reading or commenting on the anonymous written responses. If you are working with group members who have limited English proficiency, try giving each of them a card containing one or two questions that the teacher will ask them during the next session. This gives them an opportunity to find and rehearse a response to the questions for the next meeting, as well as to become more confident in both the quality of the response and their English presentation. Because it eliminates much of the risk of responding, this method is effective in creating a safer environment and drawing out many minority and nonresponding learners.

Finally, it is essential to recognize that many minority group members respond and learn better in situations that are learner-centered rather than task-oriented or teacher-centered. We have already discussed this preference as one aspect of learning style. For example, African-American children showed improved conduct, higher attendance, and greater belief and trust in a teacher who was student centered rather than task centered.[58] Because many minority group members value group cohesiveness over individual competition, it may be important for teachers to avoid calling attention, either positive or negative, to individuals in a culturally diverse classroom. It is better to comment on small group or whole group efforts and successes.[59]

To summarize, then, what do teachers do to effectively establish an inviting learning environment? They show kindness, optimism, understanding,

58. Ladson-Billings, "Culturally Relevant Teaching," pp. 106–21.
59. Bennett, "Teaching Students," pp. 265, 266.

adaptability, and general warmth in a learner-centered environment. This provides a learning environment that is both psychologically and physically appealing. Further, they are driven by a deep commitment to their learners and to the minority community, and they interact in ways that communicate that concern and respect.[60]

Teachers' Personal Qualities

Other than the attitudes just mentioned, which aid in establishing an inviting learning environment, Guskey and Easton found no other shared traits for teachers who were effective in culturally diverse classrooms.[61] Scollon's research, however, suggests that in cross-cultural situations learners want an involved and interested teacher. His research shows that the quality of teacher-learner relationships is linked to growth and learning.[62]

In short, Scollon found that teachers who are effective in cross-cultural situations demonstrate their humanness. They regularly share personal information with learners and display objects that conveyed their personality and interests. Religious educators can do this by displaying family pictures, talking about their favorite books and Bible characters, and sharing their own spiritual struggles with the group members. This encourages learners to open up and lend their personalities to the group as well. Further, it is easy to display a positive, personal regard for learners at all times by showing interest in them as people, not just as learners in the religious education context. How can this be done? In simple ways such as learning the proper pronunciation of learners' names and using those names in and outside of the learning context, greeting group members as they come through the door, commenting on new articles of clothing or recent achievements, and inquiring about family members and school events. Above all, be yourself. Learners easily pick up on a teacher's sincerity, sense of humor, and personality, traits that endear the teacher to the learner and, in turn, to the message that the teacher relates.[63]

CONCLUSION

What does all of this mean to religious educators? First, they must recognize that there are tremendous differences among the learners in religious education groups, based in part on differences in learning style. Everyone

---

60. Ladson-Billings, "Culturally Relevant Teaching," pp. 106–21.

61. Guskey and Easton, "Very Effective Teachers," pp. 265–74.

62. Ronald Scollon, *Teachers' Questions about Alaska Native Education* (Fairbanks: University of Alaska Center for Cross Cultural Studies, 1981).

63. Cruickshank, Bainer, and Metcalf, *Act of Teaching*, pp. 316, 317.

in the group will not learn in the same way that the leader does. This means that to be effective in a multicultural learning situation, it is essential to utilize a variety of methods and approaches.

Second, it means that motivation will differ among the participants in the group. Some will be eager, almost overbearing. Others will be hesitant, reluctant, or even ambivalent. These differences in motivation exist for very complex reasons. They should not be interpreted as personal responses to the religious educator. Instead, leaders should try to understand the community forces that impact the learners and help them work through those issues.

Finally, it suggests that a conscious effort must be made to teach appropriately in multicultural learning situations. It is important to note that adjusting the instructional approach, the curriculum, and the learning environment in the aforementioned ways does not mean that personal standards or the holiness of the Scriptures and Christian lifestyle are compromised. Adjusting the instructional approach merely makes learning more accessible to learners whose cultural backgrounds and learning styles differ from the leader's, or from the background and style of the majority culture. The adjustments in teaching approach and in curriculum help minority group members acquire comparable information and experience religious truths, but through a different path.

The importance of adjusting teaching style and approach to accommodate cultural differences is perhaps most poignantly summarized by the apostle Paul. An effective crosscultural religious educator, for the sake of the gospel he became all things to all people that he might by all means save some (1 Cor 9:19–23).

10

CURRICULUM AND MULTICULTURAL
RELIGIOUS EDUCATION

Laura B. Lewis
Ronald H. Cram
James Michael Lee

Is there a special curriculum for multicultural religious education?

We are a monocultural congregation. Can we "do" multicultural religious education?

We would like to be involved in some kind of multicultural religious education—can that emphasis be added to the curriculum we already have in place?

The questions above and others like them are raised with more and more frequency by lay and ordained religious education leaders in the church in the context of ethnic and cultural diversity. In this chapter we will consider current curricular thought with respect to appropriate goals and approaches to multicultural religious education, and then we will explore some of the possibilities and challenges that cultural diversity offers those who attempt to fashion multicultural curriculum resources.

Diane Hoffman believes that educators must approach multicultural education by candidly admitting that they really do not know how to do multicultural education, despite many claims to the contrary. It is essential for educators to shed all ideology if genuine multicultural education is to take place. Teachers and curriculum builders should approach various cultures as young children do, with open hearts and minds, as explorers who are able simultaneously to transform and to be transformed by their encounters with other cultures.[1]

A CONCEPTUAL FRAMEWORK FOR UNDERSTANDING CURRICULUM

What is meant by the term *curriculum*? Curriculum is defined in divergent ways. Some understand curriculum to be as broad as life itself, while others see it simply as printed instructional materials.[2] What is often forgotten is that whatever the definition, there are a wide range of possible approaches to teaching, learning, and content present in all curricula. Many people who teach on an occasional or even weekly basis in a church-related educational program rarely take the time to evaluate the pedagogical assumptions that are embedded in the instructional resources they use. The risk is that religious educators may inadvertently be teaching in a way that is incongruent with their own assumptions and values. Every curriculum resource has some pedagogical "ax to grind." Three of the more common pedagogical assumptions found in curricula are described in this section. As readers consider these different assumptions, they should ask themselves, "Do any of these assumptions ring true for me? If so, why? If not, why not?" Those who find their anger flaring at any particular approach deserve hearty congratulations! What few teachers realize is that all religious educators have deep feelings about teaching, learners, and subject matter. To feel strongly (and know why one feels strongly) is a mark of a good teacher.

Guiding Themes for Curriculum

There are many different ways of understanding the aim of curriculum.[3] Three representative "guiding themes" for curriculum, based on different assumptions, can be identified as (1) a classical approach, (2) a democratic-dialogical approach, and (3) a life-experiences approach. A classical approach to curriculum assumes that there are unchanging and eternal truths

---

1. Diane M. Hoffman, "Culture and Self in Multicultural Education: Reflections on Discourse, Text, and Practice," *American Educational Research Journal*, 33 (fall 1996): 565.

2. For a summary of these divergent positions, see James Michael Lee, *The Content of Religious Instruction* (Birmingham, Ala.: Religious Education Press, 1985), p. 10. See also Iris V. Cully, *Planning and Selecting Curriculum for Christian Education* (Valley Forge, Pa.: Judson, 1983), p. 107.

3. An annotated list of resources that may be of value to readers wishing to explore various ways of understanding curriculum as discussed in this section is included in the appendix at the end of this chapter.

that have been passed on through generations. These truths are contained in books or other documents that are referred to commonly as classics. The classical book or document is at the core of the instructional process recommended in these resources. The learners' experiences or feelings are typically devalued. The purpose of teaching in such a curriculum approach is to conform the learner's heart and mind to the eternal truths of the classic, and the teacher's role is to be an expert in the classical document or text (in religious education, the Scriptures) that is to be taught.[4]

Another guiding theme for curriculum arises from the ideal that has shaped public and much religious instruction in the twentieth century throughout the world—the political and philosophical theme of democracy. Where democracy has become the guiding frame of interpretation for the curriculum, teacher and learner have been understood to be equals. In the language of educators in the 1920s, the teacher is a guide who walks beside the student in mutual learning. This language of the teacher as guide reemerged with great strength in Christian religious education circles in the 1980s and continues to be a crucial metaphor for many teachers in the church. The basic aim of such an educational approach is social reconstruction based on democratic ideals. Terms like *liberation, dialogic imperative,* and *gender equity* are quite common in such an approach. Experience-centered production of knowledge is favored over the transmission of eternal truths from one generation to another. In democratic, or "dialogical," teaching models, students and teachers may revise or reject what has previously been understood to be a classic, based on their experience or their commitment to social action and democratic principles.[5]

A third guiding theme for religious-education curriculum assumes that there are persistent life situations that must be addressed by the learner and teacher in order for both to become productive citizens of the world. The persistent life situation curriculum was first developed in a comprehensive, systematic form by Florence Stratemeyer in her influential book, *Developing a Curriculum for Modern Living.*[6] This approach to the curriculum was especially popular among Catholic and Protestant groups during the 1950s and early 1960s. Near the end of the twentieth century it seemed to be regaining popularity among many religious groups. This approach to teaching and learning presumes that the content of the curriculum needs to focus on such

---

4. See Elliot W. Eisner, *The Educational Imagination: On the Design and Evaluation of School Programs* (New York: Macmillan, 1985), pp. 66–69. Harold Burgess discusses some of the leading religious education theorists of this position in chapter 5, "The Evangelical/Kerygmatic Model of Religious Education," in *Models of Religious Education: Theory and Practice in Historical and Contemporary Perspective* (Wheaton, Ill.: BridgePoint, 1996).

5. Eisner, *The Educational Imagination,* pp. 74–79. Also see Burgess, "The Classical Liberal Model of Religious Education," in *Models of Religious Education,* pp. 75–107.

6. See the second edition of this book (New York: Teachers College, Columbia University, 1957).

everyday situations as family life, life in the workplace, life in leisure, inter-personal relationships, health, and aesthetic appreciation, for example. Spe-cial attention is given in these curricula to the social sciences and behavioral sciences in order to provide insight for the teacher on how to help learners function effectively in all aspects of public and private life. This curriculum approach encourages learners to engage the classical texts (the Scriptures) in a dialogue that focuses on present life experiences, while the role of theological reflection may be minimal.[7] These three approaches characterize how very different the aims of teaching and learning may be, depending on the assumptions one makes about teacher, learner, and subject matter.

Curriculum and Culture

Theodore Brameld developed an influential view of curriculum. Of im-portance for multicultural religious education is that Brameld perceived curriculum in cultural terms with a concern for how the curriculum (and the teachers) approach pedagogy in relation to the culture.

For Brameld, there are three major kinds of curriculum: (1) progres-sivism, that is, education as cultural transition; (2) essentialism and perennialism, both education for cultural conservation; and (3) reconstruc-tionism, which is education as cultural renaissance.[8] Until 1970 Catholic and Protestant religion curricula for persons of all ages were, by and large, perennialist in orientation. While most Catholic and all evangelical Protes-tant religious curricula have remained perrenialist, a few Catholic religion curricula and some mainline Protestant curricula became reconstructionist after 1970, largely influenced by educational philosopher Paulo Freire and the political theologians. It is interesting to note that three of the major late-twentieth-century religious-education writers are largely in the recon-structionist camp—James Michael Lee, who comes out of a holistic social-science approach, Gabriel Moran, who comes from a linguistic perspective, and Thomas Groome, who comes out of the liberationist approach.

Defining Curriculum

Most curriculum specialists define curriculum as the set of learning expe-riences that an institution or a teacher is responsible for. This definition shows that a curriculum is not tied only to formal settings (such as a school or a Sunday school), but includes informal settings such as a home, a restaurant, or a ballpark where a religious educator may talk with a

---

7. Eisner, *The Educational Imagination*, pp. 69–74. Also see Burgess, "The Mid-Century Mainline Model of Religious Education," in *Models of Religious Education*, pp. 109–44.

8. Theodore Brameld, *Patterns of Educational Philosophy* (Yonkers-on-Hudson, N.Y.: World, 1950).

learner. This definition highlights the central educational role of the local church: everything the local church is responsible for is the curriculum of that church.

To gain perspective on the values at work in a curriculum, three questions may be asked: How is the teacher understood? What is the role of the learner? What is considered to be the subject matter of teaching and who decides what subject matter content is worth knowing?

Curriculum As The Interplay of Texts

Regardless of one's assumptions about teacher, learner, and subject matter, it is possible to conclude that all curriculum is a basic form of communication among persons about social reality. Curriculum as defined in this chapter may be best understood as the interplay of texts. In this definition texts may be literary or nonliterary; they include, but are not limited to, written or spoken texts. In this sense, the term *texts* is not the equivalent of written documents, but means the whole existential-cultural ecology out of which we live our everyday lives.[9] Used in this way, *texts* may be described as a universe of interdependent vehicles of communication—including beliefs, ritual practices, art forms, ceremonies, stories, and rituals of daily life.[10] All of these provide different kinds of texts by which people's behavior is guided.

When we attentively "read" those texts that surround us, we have a good sense about what counts as socially accepted understandings of meaning and of social reality.[11] For example, in a local congregation the texts of ritual and belief are deliberate ways a particular worldview is rehearsed and lived.[12] Charles Foster describes the curriculum for teaching and learning in faith communities as emerging from "the interplay of historic texts (biblical and theological) that illumine the events and relationships that structure our corporate experience and the questions and issues that a congregation faces

---

9. The word *texts* was originally used in this way by certain philosophical linguists. It was borrowed from them by some Scripture scholars and subsequently passed into liberal mainstream Christian theology. We use this term here as an effort in multiculturalism, deliberately interfacing religious education with philosophical and theological hermeneutic.

10. Ann Swidler, "Culture in Action: Symbols and Strategies," *American Sociological Review* 51 (April 1986): 273. Swidler sees culture as a "tool kit" of symbols, stories, rituals, and worldviews that people use in various combinations to respond to many kinds of problems (pp. 273–86).

11. Peter L. Berger and Thomas Luckmann, *The Social Construction of Reality: A Treatise in the Sociology of Knowledge* (Garden City, N.Y.: Doubleday, 1966), pp. 19–24.

12. For a theologian using the term *texts* in this way, see Mark Kline Taylor, *Remembering Esperanza: A Cultural-Political Theology for North American Praxis* (Maryknoll, N.Y.: Orbis, 1990), pp. 3–4.

as it seeks to engage faithfully in worship and service."[13] Different cultural groups—which are distinct social systems with presumed worldviews—have different texts that tend to shape group members' attitudes and behaviors. In a Korean-American church, adult Christians entering the church building for any reason go first to the sanctuary for a few moments of silent worship, and then proceed to the kitchen, classroom, or office for work or a meeting. This contrasts with the more task-oriented behavior many American churchgoers take for granted. Different cultural groups, therefore, embody different understandings of what counts as normal or real. In a complex and interdependent whole, these many texts communicate stories or narratives about the ways in which such important social concerns as gender, race, ethnicity, socioeconomic class, religion, linguistic choice, and national origin are to be understood and acted on. Cultural narratives blur the distinction between "what *ought* to be" and "what *is*." But the most important thing to remember here is that when the many different texts of a given community are viewed as a whole, a single story with power and depth is being told.

For example, one cultural group may understand the role of women in the church to be limited to submissive service. Ordination of women would be unimaginable in such settings. Another cultural group may understand the role of women in the church to be that of equal, nonhierarchical participation and leadership. Ordination of women would be taken for granted in such a setting. The reality-generating function of culture is hard at work in both contexts, with members of each group believing the truthfulness of their approach to meaning and life. The plot, which is the meaning-making core of any narrative, is a human construction, as is the plot of any cultural "text."[14]

Within Christian religious education, we have come to recognize that the texts of action and the texts of oral and written communication cannot be understood separately. Action and reflections, behavior and attitudes, are interdependent—different sides of the same coin. This understanding of the relation of action and reflection, behavior and attitudes, however, rarely shapes our common understanding of curriculum for the church. We know that curriculum includes both written and spoken texts. But curriculum also includes the "texts" of cultural action—including decisions, motivations, and those formal and informal social processes that seek to legitimate a particular worldview.[15]

---

13. Charles R. Foster, *Educating Congregations* (Nashville: Abingdon, 1994), p. 140.

14. See Hayden White, "The Value of Narrative in the Representation of Reality," in *On Narrative*, ed. W. J. T. Mitchell (Chicago: University of Chicago Press, 1981), pp. 1–24.

15. Calvin O. Schrag, *Communicative Praxis and the Space of Subjectivity* (Bloomington: Indiana University Press, 1986), p. 24. The basic understanding of "text" in this chapter is adapted from this book.

Understanding curriculum as the interplay of texts that intentionally communicate through attitudes, values, and behaviors, leads to understanding it as being fundamentally contextual and fundamentally political.[16] Curriculum is a basic form of communication that intentionally carries within it a vision of the world as it ought to be. The contextual and political dynamics of curriculum viewed as a network of communication systems give urgency to the importance of reflective teacher practice in Christian religious education.[17]

The primary task of Christian religious education is to help persons see things as they are, as well as how they ought to be, and to respond in a way that harmonizes with the good news of God's love for the world through Jesus Christ. No individual's human experience is normative for all other human beings. Our values and assumptions are almost always embedded in our "personal experiences." Christian religious education helps the church recognize that *all* human experience is a social product and process and that there are times when personal experiences are both faithful to the gospel *and* unfaithful to it. For example, self-delusion is a common behavior at the community and personal levels. How is it possible that some local Christian congregations are functionally racist, while other local Christian groups seek to work for justice and peace among all persons, including Jews, Muslims, and Buddhists? The perception and interpretation of experience, including the possibility of self-delusion, take place within the imagined world of cultural texts, where patterns of cultural experience alien to a religion may nevertheless influence it.[18] To *see* is to do so only by means of culturally produced (and simultaneously culture-shaping) experiences, or texts. Therefore, cultural and textual analysis—including analysis of the dynamics of power and discrimination—is a crucial first step for those interested in curriculum evaluation.

It is worth remembering when considering texts (or anything else in this chapter) that a cardinal goal in developing a successful multicultural religious education curriculum is that the curriculum be teachable. An effective multicultural religion curriculum is one that contains within it the

---

16. Maria Harris sees teaching as political in the sense that it strives to build the church as the kind of body whose form and polity aims to serve one another and the wider society. *Fashion Me a People: Curriculum in the Church* (Louisville, Ky.: Westminster/John Knox, 1989), p. 112.

17. The idea of reflective practice comes from Chris Argyris and Donald A. Schön, *Theory in Practice: Increasing Professional Effectiveness* (San Francisco: Jossey-Bass, 1975). See especially pp. 3–34.

18. This view is congruent with what George Lindbeck refers to as a cultural-linguistic approach. Lindbeck uses the example of warlike cultures that brought changes to the practice of both Christianity and Buddhism at certain periods and places. See *The Nature of Doctrine: Religion and Theology in a Postliberal Age* (Philadelphia: Westminster, 1984), pp. 32–34.

necessary dynamics to help the religious educator better enact it in practice. Furthermore, a good multicultural curriculum is constructed not only to help learners but to help both the learner and the religious educator grow in multiculturality.[19]

A BIBLICAL EXAMPLE OF A
MULTICULTURAL RELIGION CURRICULUM

One biblical example of a multicultural religious-education curriculum is the narrative passage of the cross-cultural encounter between Peter and Cornelius in Acts 10:1–11:18. This story, which is recounted three times in this passage, forms the climax of the first half of the Acts of the Apostles.[20] It introduces an important theological rationale that forms one important basis for the multicultural stance of the early Christian church.[21] Close examination of this narrative yields important insights on crucial dimensions of contemporary curriculum development for multicultural religious education.

In the wake of Stephen's murder (Acts 7), the church in Jerusalem experienced persecution, and all Christians but the apostles left Jerusalem for the countryside of Judea and Samaria (Acts 8:1). Yet the church continued to grow as these believers proclaimed and lived the gospel. Philip conducted a successful mission in Samaria, and the Ethiopian eunuch was converted (Acts 8:26–40). Paul was converted and chosen for a ministry that would include Gentiles (Acts 9:1–19). The apostles in Jerusalem, however, had not yet ventured forth to preach to the Gentiles living in Judea, Galilee, and Samaria, although some, such as Peter, proclaimed God's good news to Jews in the villages and towns in these areas. Peter's encounter with Cornelius, a Gentile centurion living in Caesarea, indicates that the apostles' reluctance to pursue the Gentile mission in their own backyard, so to speak, stemmed from a cultural and religious prejudice against Gentiles whom they regarded as unclean.[22]

The story of Peter's encounter with Cornelius presents a kind of multicultural curriculum text-in-action that merits close attention. This passage

---

19. Deborah Loewenberg Ball and David Cohen, "Reform by the Book: What Is— or Might Be—the Role of Curriculum Materials in Teacher Learning and Instructional Reform?" *Educational Researcher* 25 (December 1996): 8.

20. Beverly Gaventa, *From Darkness to Light: Aspects of Conversion in the New Testament* (Philadelphia: Fortress, 1986), p. 122.

21. Charles H. Talbert, *Acts* (Atlanta: John Knox, 1984), p. 44.

22. Robert C. Tannehill, *The Narrative Unity of Luke-Acts: A Literary Interpretation*, vol. 2: *The Acts of the Apostles* (Minneapolis: Fortress, 1990), p. 135. See also Johannes Munck, *The Acts of the Apostles* (Garden City, N.Y.: Doubleday, 1979), p. lxvi, and William Willimon, *Acts*, Interpretation (Atlanta: John Knox, 1988), pp. 95–100.

portrays an extended learning event in multicultural religious education. As the narrative literally moves back and forth between Peter, the Jewish Christian, and Cornelius, the devout Gentile, it models a multicultural religious-education exchange that gives the young church and its leaders a clearer understanding of God's vision for their shared life together as Jew and Gentile in Christ. Robert Tannehill observes that "the visions in question here have the specific purpose of opening a relationship between persons of different cultures. Each is a vision which leads its recipient to be open to a stranger's experience of God. God works from two sides at the same time to achieve this goal."[23]

We believe this narrative also highlights six significant characteristics of a multicultural curriculum for religious education today. These six characteristics are incomplete personal visions, openness to the cultural other, face-to-face encounter, multiple perspectives, conflict and public debate, and reciprocal hospitality.

Incomplete Personal Visions

Both Cornelius and Peter, two men separated by geographical, cultural, and religious distance, receive a vision from God, to whom they each pray. At prayer in his home in Caesarea, Cornelius is told to seek out Simon Peter, who is staying in Joppa with another Simon, a tanner, in a house by the sea. The next day, also while praying, Peter is told in a vision to kill and eat from among animals classified as clean and unclean according to Mosaic dietary laws. Peter steadfastly refuses this command, however, even when the vision and its explanation—"What God has made clean, you must not call profane" (10:15)—are repeated three times.

The content of the vision each man receives in this narrative is different, and in itself, incomplete.[24] *Each vision depends on the other to make complete sense.* Cornelius and Peter must respond to each other and share what they have heard to learn what God has to say to them both. Each one is dependent on the response and perspective of the other to understand fully what God intends. The curriculum for the religious education developed here employs both cross-cultural experience and interdependent learning to assist Peter and Cornelius in ascertaining God's will.

Openness to the Cultural Other

The next act of this drama takes each man on a journey beyond himself and his incomplete understanding of God's intention. Although in the cultural

---

23. Tannehill, *The Narrative Unity of Luke-Acts*, p. 131.

24. Ibid., p. 128. See also Luke T. Johnson, *The Acts of the Apostles*, Sacra Pagina Series (Collegeville, Minn.: Liturgical, 1992), pp. 185, 187.

traditions of Cornelius such a meeting between Jew and Gentile is unusual, and from Peter's perspective it is against religious law, both men ultimately are open to God's command and are willing to risk personal contact that dares to cross cultural boundaries.

Cornelius acts first on the limited information given him in the vision and immediately sends two slaves and one of his soldiers to Joppa to find Peter and invite him to his home. Cornelius also tells these men the details of his vision, translating his private experience into public discourse.[25] They arrive the following day while Peter, who has just received his own vision, is puzzling over its meaning. These messengers provide additional information as they tell Peter about Cornelius's vision and ask Peter to come to Caesarea to tell Cornelius whatever he has to say. Although the meaning of Cornelius's invitation and its relationship to Peter's vision is still not clear, Peter accepts the Spirit's guidance that he should go, and accedes to the men's request. Peter also takes the cultural risk of inviting the Gentile slaves and the Roman soldier to spend the night in his borrowed lodging. Thus, the first move toward open hospitality by Cornelius is reciprocated by Peter as both men move haltingly toward a face-to-face encounter.

The next day the community that surrounds each man expands as others are included in the cross-cultural meeting. Peter travels to Cornelius and takes along believers from Joppa who are willing to join him in going to a Gentile's house. Meanwhile in Caesarea, Cornelius gathers members of his household and some close friends to await Peter's arrival. The importance of the gathered community of Jews and Gentiles is underscored here as an integral aspect of the multicultural curriculum being fashioned.

Face-to-Face Encounter

In Acts 10:25 the moment of face-to-face encounter occurs. The dialogue previously carried on through their messengers now takes place between Peter and Cornelius. Significantly, the first exchange is nonverbal, but powerful. Against the cultural and religious law Peter has carefully observed all his life as a Jew living under Roman rule, he enters the centurion's house.[26] Cornelius—a Gentile, a Roman officer, and a member of the ruling cultural group in occupied territory—lies prostrate at Peter's feet.[27] Both

---

25. Johnson, *Acts of the Apostles*, p. 183, n. 8.

26. Part of the temple purity system required "careful avoidance of contact with all that was judged impure or unholy (sinners, lepers, blind, lame, menstruants, corpses, toll collectors, Samaritans, Gentiles)" as noted by John H. Elliot, "Temple versus Household in Luke-Acts: A Contrast in Social Institutions," in *The Social World of Luke-Acts: Models for Interpretation*, ed. Jerome H. Neyrey (Peabody, Mass.: Hendrickson, 1991), p. 221.

27. Paul W. Walaskay in *'And So We Came to Rome'* (London: Cambridge University Press, 1983) observes that this was "an act of obeisance reserved for divine beings and

actions at their meeting go against the norms of the culture that each man represents.

Peter quickly brings Cornelius to his feet, however. As they stand eye to eye, he says more than even he has been able to recognize fully until this meeting: "Stand up; I am only a mortal" (10:26). In coming to the awareness that Cornelius, the Gentile, was not unclean or profane in God's sight, but fully human, Peter also has to examine himself more closely. He is no better than Cornelius is in God's sight. Indeed they are, as Peter says, two men whom God chooses to value equally as human beings. Thus, the two men meet as equals and enter the house together. They demonstrate their common humanity first through nonverbal action and then through spoken words, which become part of an interplay of texts as this multicultural religious education curriculum unfolds.

Out of the separate, incomplete visions by which God summoned each man to the other, and as a result of their face-to-face encounter, Peter and Cornelius undertake the joint task of shaping a new, shared perspective on their relationship with each other and with God, as well as shaping new attitudes and new behavior. Peter sums up what he has learned in a public statement to the gathered community of Jewish Christians and Gentile believers: "God has shown me that I should not call anyone profane or unclean" (10:28).

Part of the theological foundation for multicultural religious education is laid here in Peter's declaration, but the interplay of texts continues. There are other lessons to be learned in this interdependent cross-cultural encounter. The meaning of Peter's rooftop vision is now clear. He understands that he can associate freely with all people. All are acceptable to God as they are. The meaning of Cornelius' vision remains a mystery, however, until Peter asks his host why he has been summoned. Peter still depends on whatever insight Cornelius has in order to complete his own understanding of the vision. Only as they share their different perspectives do these two men come to understand what God wishes the multicultural community gathered in Cornelius's home to learn.

Multiple Perspectives

In response to Peter's question, Cornelius shares the story of his vision. His telling of it resembles the account that his servants gave Peter when they arrived in Joppa, but then Cornelius adds his own perspective on the

---

human authorities of the highest order. A Roman centurion of the Italian cohort lying prone before a Galilean peasant would certainly make exciting reading for the Christian community. One might ask, however, what a Roman magistrate might have thought of such a scene" (p. 84 n. 110).

purpose of their meeting: "So now all of us are here in the presence of God to listen to all that the Lord has commanded you to say" (10:33).

Earlier Peter had said more than he knew when he raised up the centurion lying at his feet. So now Cornelius says more in his reply than he knows by asking Peter to tell him "all that the Lord has commanded." From Peter's perspective, such an invitation is a request to speak the good news of the one he has come to know as *his* Lord, even Jesus the Christ. Therefore, Cornelius's request becomes the catalyst for the startling insight that emerges as these men share what they have experienced in the hope of learning more about the one who has brought them together. Even more profound than Peter's first insight that to God no human being is profane or common, nor should be treated that way, is the revelation about God that Peter comes to "truly understand" (10:34) when Cornelius asks him to speak what the Lord had commanded.

In Peter's vision the Lord did not command him to speak, but it is no mystery to Peter what the one whom Cornelius names Lord would want him to say. By assessing the situation from Cornelius's point of view, Peter now comes to the threefold theological understanding that he elaborates aloud to the assembled company (10:34–36). It is this: (1) God does not discriminate or show partiality among people or nations; (2) everyone who fears God and does what is right (an apt description of the Gentile Cornelius) is acceptable to God; and (3) the one Peter had previously claimed as *his* Lord is actually the Lord of *all*. This cross-cultural encounter and dialogue with Cornelius makes clear to Peter that the gospel story entrusted to him is not an exclusive message to be hoarded or protected from those outside his own culture. It is, rather, an inclusive message to be shared with all—even Gentiles in Cornelius' household.[28] As Peter tells the story of God's saving work through Jesus Christ from his own particular perspective as a son of Israel,[29] the Holy Spirit falls on the Gentile hearers to the astonishment of the circumcised Jewish believers present (10:44). Peter then responds by authorizing the baptism of Cornelius and the other Gentiles who have heard and responded to God's good news in the power of the Spirit.

It is important for understanding the dynamics of a multicultural curriculum that in this narrative both persons' individual perspectives, which grow out of their particular cultural experiences, make vital contributions

---

28. Mark A. Plunkett, "Ethnocentricity and Salvation History in the Cornelius Episode," in *Society of Biblical Literature 1985 Seminar Papers*, ed. Kent H. Richards (Atlanta: Scholars Press, 1985), pp. 478–79.

29. Robert Tannehill notes (in *The Narrative Unity of Luke-Acts*), the significance of Peter's rehearsal of the gospel story from his perspective as a Jew. Peter retains the story's Jewish setting and does not transform Jesus into a Gentile or a Gentile environment. "It is Jesus the Jew through whom God is working for all, and the witness of his first followers who accompanied him 'in the land of the Jews and Jerusalem' has permanent value" (p. 142).

to the new, shared perspective that emerges. Without Cornelius' vision and his request to hear the words that the Lord had commanded Peter to speak, Peter might have remained unaware that the proclamation of his own experience of the gospel was God's intention for these Gentiles. Since his vision had not included a command to speak, Peter might have missed the significance of what he came to "truly understand" about God's impartiality and about the inclusive nature of Jesus as Lord. Similarly, without Peter's new understanding of Jesus the Messiah as Lord of all and his subsequent sharing of the gospel as he experienced it, the Gentiles gathered in Cornelius's house might not have encountered God's saving activity in Jesus Christ as meant for them as well as for Israel. The diversity of experiences, attitudes, and perspectives that are shared and pondered during the multicultural exchange in Cornelius' house makes clear that seeking out multiple perspectives is a vital dimension of the multicultural curriculum in progress in this passage.

Like Peter and Cornelius and the other Gentiles in this biblical narrative, all the learners whom religious educators teach come from multiple worlds: the world of family, of neighborhood, of culture, of ethnic background. An important task of the multicultural religious education curriculum is to assist learners to navigate successfully the border crossings of their multiple worlds, so that their faith lives may become broader and less provincial.[30]

Conflict and Public Discussion of Differences

A curriculum that promotes significant multicultural learning also may generate a certain amount of conflict and discussion as participants engage in dialogue on substantive issues of difference. Jaime Wurzel notes that one role of multicultural education is to ameliorate conflict, to accept its inevitability and to recognize it as a positive element in the learning process.[31] Donald Bossart also emphasizes the positive element of conflict by locating it within a context of interdependence. Bossart holds that "there must be a mutual, vital concern that affects the well-being of both parties to bring the forces into conflict. This same interdependence offers the hope for positive growth in every interdependent system." If these common values are kept in view, Bossart says, "then growth for all can result from the

30. Patricia Phelan, Anne Locke Davidson, and Hanh Cao Yu, "Students' Multiple Worlds: Navigating the Borders of Family, Peer, and School Cultures," in *Renegotiating Cultural Diversity in American Schools*, ed. Patricia Phelan and Ann Locke Davidson (New York: Teachers College Press, 1993), pp. 52–88.

31. Jaime S. Wurzel, "Multiculturalism and Multicultural Education," in *Toward Multiculturalism: A Reader in Multicultural Education*, ed. Jaime S. Wurzel (Yarmouth, Me.: Intercultural, 1988), p. 2. See also C. Ellis Nelson, "Some Educational Aspects of Conflict," in *Tensions Between Citizenship and Discipleship*, ed. Nelle G. Slater (New York: Pilgrim, 1989), pp. 195–218.

conflict, as all are drawn together by their common shared values."[32] The curriculum example of Acts 10–11 follows this pattern. Conflict arises when the news that the Gentiles in Caesarea had received the word of God reaches the other apostles and church leaders in Jerusalem (11:1). This controversy leads to a strengthening of the new multicultural Christian community as it identifies its common bond in Jesus Christ (11:18).

In this biblical narrative there is no avoidance of conflict or public discussion. Peter and those believers from Joppa who had witnessed the events in Cornelius's home do not hesitate to share their experiences as a source of religious education for those who question their conclusions. Peter acts as a religious education mediator by offering an experiential account of his change of mind and heart during the multicultural encounter. Without pressuring those who question the Gentile baptisms and table fellowship, he rehearses for them the sequence of events as he experienced them, to promote empathy and increased understanding of what has transpired. Tannehill compares the Jerusalem audience to Peter, with his "previous assumptions about how a Jew should behave. A sequence of events led Peter to change his mind. Now his audience is being led through the same sequence of events so that they can appreciate and share Peter's new insight."[33] It required a dynamic interplay of verbal, cultural, behavioral, and attitudinal texts to bring about these changes.

As a mediator, Peter brings together the recent events and the past promises of God through the saving action of Jesus Christ in order to offer the community a new way to interpret the conflict.[34] Peter's account takes the community's beliefs and experiences seriously and demonstrates what he now sees as continuity between God's action in the past and God's action for change in the present. Finally, Peter presses the community to consider and discuss how they would have responded in similar circumstances: "If then God gave them the gift he gave us when we believed in the Lord Jesus Christ, who was I that I could hinder God?" (Acts 11:17).

For this multicultural learning event to be the transforming religious-education experience that God intended, it could not be limited to a private understanding between Peter and Cornelius. Nor could it be an isolated common agreement between a small group of Jewish Christians in Joppa and a small group of baptized Gentiles in Caesarea. The new communion that was forged through multicultural encounter and dialogue in Cornelius' house is tempered by the experience of conflict and public discussion at the center of the church's life in Jerusalem. Johnson observes of Acts 10–15 that the entire passage describes "the stages of a church decision

32. Donald E. Bossart, *Creative Conflict in Religious Education and Church Administration* (Birmingham, Ala.: Religious Education Press, 1980), p. 11.

33. Tannehill, *Narrative Unity of Luke-Acts*, p. 144.

34. Talbot, *Acts*, p. 47.

concerning the admission and status of Gentiles. With literary artistry and genuine theological sensitivity, Luke shows through the narrative itself how the diverse experiences of God's action by individuals are slowly raised to the level of a communal narrative, which in turn must be tested by the entire community in a difficult and delicate process of disagreement, debate, and discernment of the Scripture."[35] Only by dealing directly with this new diversity of cultural traditions and beliefs that had emerged through the design of the multicultural encounter could the Jerusalem church verify and confirm the new thing happening in its midst—a new thing that appeared to shake to their core existing cultural and religious beliefs and practices.

The community's honoring of multiple perspectives even in conflict had resulted in concurrence with Peter's conclusions and a greatly enlarged vision of what kind of community it was to be in Jesus Christ (11:18). Certainly disagreement over inclusion of Gentiles and their practices did not end with this experience, as the ongoing Jerusalem Council debate in Acts 15 clearly demonstrates. However, much had been learned by the whole church from the "multicultural-curriculum event" of Acts 10–11, which it could not have learned if it had suppressed the emerging conflict and had avoided dealing with it publicly.

Reciprocal Hospitality

The theme of hospitality—particularly with respect to shared lodging and table fellowship—runs throughout this narrative, but it is especially emphasized at the close of the scene in Cornelius's home. Following their baptism, the new Christians invite Peter and the Jewish believers to stay with them for several days (10:48). Spiritually and culturally Peter has come quite a distance, from praying on his roof in Joppa while waiting for a kosher meal to breaking bread in a centurion's house with newly baptized Gentile believers. Similarly, the new bond that the centurion Cornelius now shares with Peter, first as his brother in Christ and second as his table host, constitutes an amazing transformation in roles. Yet the way in which each group has practiced hospitality toward the other throughout this multicultural experience can hardly be considered coincidental. Instead, it is another essential quality of the multicultural curriculum in this narrative. Gaventa underscores this significant dimension of the text when she writes, "By means of the hospitality issue Luke demonstrates that the conversion of the first Gentile required the conversion of the church as well. Indeed, in Luke's account, Peter and company undergo a change that is more wrenching by far than the change experienced by Cornelius."[36]

---

35. Johnson, *Acts of the Apostles*, p. 16.
36. Gaventa, *From Darkness to Light*, p. 109.

It is not altogether surprising, then, to discover in the final scene of the biblical narrative that the scandal of cross-cultural hospitality and table fellowship becomes the source of challenge and conflict that first tests and then establishes the basic lesson in multicultural religious education that the curriculum modeled in this narrative teaches. The six important dimensions of a multicultural curriculum found in this biblical passage can help shape approaches to curriculum designs that are multicultural.

HISTORICAL TRENDS IN MULTICULTURAL RELIGIOUS EDUCATION CURRICULUM

Whenever religious instructional resources (one important kind of "text" in the church's religion curriculum) are developed, the theory, design, and subsequent materials have within them overt and covert understandings of the relation of culture and Christian religious education. Whether overt or covert, these understandings have very practical theological as well as religious educational consequences.

In the most general of terms, religious educational resource development in the nineteenth century in the United States will be remembered for three kinds of instructional materials: (1) catechisms, (2) linguistic translation resources, and (3) ecumenical and denominational resources.[37] All three types of instructional resources, generally speaking, embodied a monocultural standard in regard to Christian religious educational concerns.

Catechisms, in both Protestant and Roman Catholic contexts, presumed that the primary responsibility of instructional materials was to teach a particular mode of understanding the interpretation of tradition, the Bible, and human experience. Catechisms became important educational tools during the Reformation and the Counter-Reformation, and their long history is a testimony to their durability.[38]

Catechisms do many things very well. They provide a particular religious worldview in a concise and direct way. They are interested in correct belief, and therefore presume that there is such a thing as a uniform basis for belief in a religious community. Catechisms assume that memory and religious identity go hand in glove, and that a common religious language is both possible and necessary in the church. Catechisms do not seek, however, to take contextual pluralism seriously. A catechism is presumed to be as valid in Rome, Georgia, as in Rome, Italy. This decontextualization assumption presumes not only the possibility of the unerring expression of universal

---

37. See Frank G. Lankard, *A History of the American Sunday School Curriculum* (New York: Abingdon, 1927), pp. 99–236.

38. See Marianne Sawicki, *The Gospel in History, Portrait of a Teaching Church: The Origins of Christian Education* (New York: Paulist, 1988), pp. 246–47; 250–51; 279–80.

truth but also the ability for indigenous groups to conform to the pattern of belief and action expressed by the catechism.

The catechism, then, downplayed the importance of personal experience or context in the life of faith. A catechism approach to religious education tends to presume that religious belief and community arise from doctrinal texts given to a cultural group. Conformity to a catechism as an act of faithfulness and an expression of orthodoxy often presumes a particular approach to the understanding of Scripture. It could be argued that the catechisms of many denominations were best understood as lenses through which the Bible and human experience could be read. In many ways, this approach to religious education curriculum is extremely congruent with contemporary trends in sociolinguistics.[39]

At first, catechism teaching may appear to be rather heavy-handed. Certainly such an approach may be used in ways that ignore cultural specificity and require conformity to European (or other) culture. Yet this has not always been the case. Marianne Sawicki cites examples of some Catholic missionaries who endeavored to express the gospel in terms of specific cultures as early as the sixteenth century.[40] Many missionary educational efforts in the United States during the nineteenth century attempted to balance verbal content and experiential content. These missionary efforts could be described as "linguistic translation." Curriculum resources were developed by missionaries for Native Americans in several areas of the country. Catholic missionaries, for example, worked arduously throughout North America both to translate the Bible into Native American languages and to develop various curriculum resources.[41] Presbyterian missionary activity among the Cherokee Indians resulted in such literary productions as a translation of the Gospel of Matthew, a little hymnbook, and a tract that included selected Bible verses. But missionary activity included other kinds of texts as well. In what might be called "texts of decision and action," missionaries sometimes became advocates for the cultural integrity of Native American groups within which literacy programs and accompanying instructional resources were being developed. These actions provided a way

---

39. George Lindbeck writes in *The Nature of Doctrine* that "a religion can be viewed as a kind of cultural and/or linguistic framework or medium that shapes the entirety of life and thought. . . . It is similar to an idiom that makes possible the description of realities, the formulation of beliefs, and the experience of inner attitudes, feelings, and sentiments. Like a culture or a language, it is a communal phenomenon that shapes the subjectivities of individuals rather than being primarily a manifestation of those subjectivities" (p. 33).

40. Sawicki, *Gospel in History*, p. 247.

41. Jay P. Dolan, *The American Catholic Experience* (Garden City, N.Y.: Doubleday, 1985), pp. 43–68.

for the learners to understand what faithfulness to the gospel looked like in the missionaries' policies and behavior.[42]

An example of such actions in a representative mainline Protestant denomination concerns the imprisonment of two Presbyterian missionaries by the state of Georgia in 1831. As the state of Georgia attempted to force the Cherokees off their land, the missionaries stood in solidarity with the Native American peoples and forcefully advocated humane treatment—and allowing the Cherokee people to stay on their own land. The state of Georgia understood this stance by the missionaries as interference in political affairs, and it imprisoned the two missionaries for four years.[43]

If we understand curriculum texts only as the literary materials and translations that were produced for the Cherokee people, then we must conclude that the curriculum was, if not imperialistic, at least monocultural. On the other hand, if we understand the curriculum to include those "texts of decision and action" that the missionaries composed with their lives, then the missionary curriculum was approaching what many in the field of missiology are referring to as "intercultural." Gerloff and Mazibuko, specialists in multicultural education in the church, write that the term *intercultural* includes the social, political, and economic dimensions of the life of a people. "It does not mean to learn the language of others in order to 'sell one's product' more efficiently but rather to be able to respond to the needs of others on a level of mutual respect and equality."[44]

Clearly, these missionaries to the Cherokee people were not unsullied models of a multicultural/intercultural curriculum development process. On the other hand, when curriculum is understood broadly as an interplay of many intersecting texts—verbal, behavioral, and affective—the curriculum that the Presbyterian missionaries developed was not purely monocultural either. Along with the literary verbal texts they translated, they also offered themselves as "living texts" for the Cherokee people to study. Aspects of openness to the cultural other, face-to-face encounter, and recognition of multiple perspectives were present to various degrees.

No curricular attempt is ever going to embody fully the biblical ideal. Multicultural religious educators do not attend to negative examples of curriculum in order to blame, but rather to reflect more faithfully on the meaning of the gospel for today. The actions or policies of all communities of faith sometimes conflict with and at other times are congruent with their own written texts of belief. Multiculturalism does not call us to an inhuman perfectionism, but to an ongoing humble mindfulness and hospitality.

---

42. This information on Presbyterian missionary activity is recorded in *The Missionary Herald* (Boston: Crocker & Brewster, 1831), pp. 247–50; and *The Missionary Herald* (Boston: Crocker & Brewster, 1832), pp. 43–45.

43. Ibid.

44. R. Gerloff and B. Mazibuko, "Forum for Ecumenical Intercultural Learning," *Mission Studies* 7, no. 1 (1990), p. 35.

With a more narrow understanding of curriculum as instructional resources that are in print, much of the curriculum for the African-American
churches during the nineteenth century could be disregarded. As early as
1823, Sunday schools for African-American children had been established
by Anglo-American congregations.[45] It could be concluded that, when
viewed as objects of benevolent Anglo-American Sunday school teachers,
African Americans had no religion curriculum of their own. We should
not presume, however, that where the Christian religious faith within the
African-American community was based on oral tradition, curriculum was
not present. Curriculum, when understood as the interplay of many kinds of
texts, does not presume that literacy is the only criterion of communication.
Most of the curriculum of the African-American religious community of the
nineteenth century is today unknown, but many recent studies of African-
American churches in the United States give testimony to its presence.
Clearly, the African-American Christian communities generated curriculum
as the interplay of texts within the community's oral culture.[46] As the world
enters what many have called an image-based, post-Gutenberg form of
communication, assumptions about the relationship of print resources to
curriculum will need to be questioned again and again.

Denominational and interdenominational curriculum resources during
the nineteenth century were saturated with two major concerns: moral
education and "Americanization." In this they were in concert with public
school resources of the day, which also gave prominence to these two
concerns. Probably no other print materials in the United States have lasted
longer than the McGuffey readers. Since 1836, more than twenty-two million copies of the McGuffey reader (in its various permutations) have been
sold. While elementary school readers may not come to mind immediately
as instructional resources of the Protestant churches in the United States,
the McGuffey readers were perhaps the most important curriculum resource
of American popular culture of the nineteenth century.[47]

The 1837 edition of the McGuffey reader was filled to the brim with
Scotch-Irish Presbyterian views of sin, death, salvation and God. By the

---

45. See Ronald H. Cram, "The Origins and Development of the Philadelphia Sunday
and Adult School Union," *Christian Education Journal* 10, no. 3 (spring 1990): 51–52.

46. A splendid example in this regard is C. Eric Lincoln and Lawrence H. Mamiya,
The Black Church in the African American Experience (Durham, N.C.: Duke University
Press, 1990). Much of the oral culture of early African-American churches, in touch with
the harsh realities of oppression, was simply not recorded in literary form. This does
not negate the fact, however, that slave narratives, music, movement in worship, and
resistance of oppression were curricular "texts."

47. For one account of the scope and influence of the McGuffey readers, see Lawrence
A. Cremin, *American Education: The National Experience, 1783–1876* (New York:
Harper & Row, 1980), pp. 69–73. For a fuller account, see John H. Westerhoff III,
McGuffey and His Readers (Nashville: Abingdon, 1978). This helpful volume grew out
of Westerhoff's doctoral dissertation.

1879 edition, most of the overt Scotch-Irish Presbyterianism had vanished in favor of those moral attributes needed by any "good" American. Both understood the United States as a melting pot—a place where a new citizen was being forged out of many diverse peoples. Monocultural and imperialistic in tone and content, the McGuffey readers were congruent with the social Anglo-Protestant hegemonic ideology of the era. Said another way, what was taught in Anglo-Protestant churches was congruent with the values expressed in these volumes. It is possible to suggest that nothing produced by denominational publishing houses in the era of the McGuffey readers was incongruent with their inherent values.[48]

The post-Civil War focus on national unity, combined with an understanding of the "oneness of God," led to national Protestant curriculum resource materials produced by centralized publishing houses by the late 1800s. In 1872 the interdenominational Protestant Committee on Uniform Lessons endorsed the Uniform Lesson Series—a series still used in many congregations today.[49] By 1900, some five million Protestant Sunday school students were using the uniform lessons. Monocultural in tone and content, the lessons stressed good moral character, biblical knowledge, and disciplined study habits. Clearly modeling a transmissive approach to education, the implicit message of the curriculum resources was still very much in the melting pot tradition.

Textbooks in religious education in the American Catholic Church took on a pattern and coloration that differed from their Protestant counterparts.[50] For Catholic children and youth in the eighteenth, nineteenth, and first half of the twentieth century, the primary and in many cases the sole textbook in the United States was the catechism, a pithy book presenting the major

---

48. See Ronald H. Cram, "Eclectic Readers, by William H. McGuffey," *American Presbyterians: Journal of Presbyterian History* 66, no. 4 (winter 1988): 241–44.

49. See Cully, *Planning and Selecting Curriculum*, pp. 13–14.

50. Much of the material in this paragraph is drawn from the meaty historical article by Berard L. Marthaler, "The Development of Curriculum from Catechism to Textbook," *Living Light* 33, no. 2 (winter 1996): 6–19. Readers should note, however, that the words *Douay Catechism* as listed by Marthaler in his article (p. 7) are really an abbreviation of the Douay/Rheims Catechism, a name taken from the anglicization of the French town of Douai where Catholic refugees from the bitter religious persecutions in England had fled and had established a Catholic college for English persons. This college temporarily moved from Douai to Reims (1578–93). The first major translation of the Bible into English under official Catholic auspices was begun in England and completed at Douai and Reims. Hence this translation is often called the Douay/Rheims Version. (*Rheims* is an anglicization of the French *Reims*, the English having a regrettable tendency to anglicize the names of towns in other lands.) The two major weaknesses of this version lie in its use of the Latin Vulgate rather than the original languages as its source and in its reliance on previous English Protestant translations. For a concise history of the Douay Version, see Jack L. Lewis, "Douay Version" in the *Anchor Bible Dictionary*, vol. 2, ed. David Noel Freedman et al. (New York: Doubleday, 1992), pp. 227–28.

points of Catholic cognitive doctrine in very concise question-and-answer form. The major advantage of the catechism in the minds of Church officials was that it was easy to understand and easy to memorize (memorization was a major ingredient of Catholic religious education in former times).

Berard Marthaler's careful historical research has led him to conclude that the first catechism used in the United States was edited by Robert Molyneaux in 1788. Other catechisms soon followed, including the Carroll Catechism and the David Catechism, to mention just two of the more prominent ones. But far and away the most influential catechism ever published in the United States was the Baltimore Catechism (1885), which was encouraged and even decreed by the Third Plenary Council of Baltimore. Even to this day, the Baltimore Catechism, typically in revised form, is used as a basic textbook in conservative Catholic schools and parish religious education programs.

Though the catechism was the principal textbook in Catholic religious education for a great many years, biblical history textbooks were also used as auxiliary resources. The first of these was written by Joseph Reeve in 1784, and the most famous by Richard Gilmour in 1869. This book recounted biblical history in simple language and was tastefully illustrated with lovely engravings. The last seventy pages of this three-hundred-plus-page book gives the history of the Catholic Church from the subapostolic period to what was then the present.[51]

Graded textbooks for religious education purposes first made their appearance in the early part of the twentieth century with the series edited by Peter Yorke. They came into wide use only with the advent of the *Highway to Heaven* series published by the Bruce Publishing Company between 1931 and 1934. Other series soon followed, including the *Jesu-Maria* series. These two series relied heavily on the Baltimore Catechism for inspiration and substantive content. After the conclusion of World War II, Catholic publishing companies grew more innovative. The *On Our Way* series published by Sadlier Publishing Company used the new kerygmatic theology as its inspiration.[52]

With the issuance of official religious education documents emanating from Rome and from the American hierarchy beginning in 1971, major Catholic religion textbook publishers such as Benziger, Silver Burdett,

---

51. The third-named author of this chapter recalls studying from both the Baltimore Catechism and the Gilmour Bible History while in Catholic elementary school. He especially treasures the memories of the Gilmour Bible History for affective as well as cognitive reasons. He read from this book to his three children when they were young. The Gilmour volume occupies a special place in his *auctorium*, the small room in which he writes his books and articles.

52. Possibly the best treatment of the influence of kerygmatic theology on Catholic religious education is Mary C. Boys, *Biblical Interpretation and Religious Education* (Birmingham, Ala.: Religious Education Press, 1980).

Tabor, as well as the commercially hard-hitting Sadlier, made sure that their graded series conformed to the new official church decrees.

In terms of multicultural religious education, it should be understood that while the various catechisms did not highlight multiculturality, nonetheless there was an underlying multicultural cast to them. The children and youth who studied from these catechisms came from immigrant families or from the sons and daughters of immigrant families. Until well into the middle of the twentieth century, "real Americans" were typically regarded as Anglo-Saxon Protestants. Catholic Americans in colonial days, and most especially in the era of the great Irish Catholic immigration in the late 1830s and 1840s, as well as the huge waves of Italian and German Catholic immigrants in the last third of the nineteenth century, were deeply aware that they were culturally different. They were profoundly cognizant that they were not considered "real Americans" by Anglo-Saxon residents. After all, the immigrants were neither English nor Protestant. The catechisms were culturally neutral in that they appealed to Catholics from a whole host of cultures ranging from Irish to Italian. Catholic children and youth were well aware, without being told by the catechisms, that what they learned from the catechisms applied vigorously to their own particular culture. It would supply them with the basic cognitive doctrines that would preserve their faith in the American culture, which either persecuted them (through groups such as the Know-Nothing movement of the mid-nineteenth century) or resented them.

Since the late 1970s two separate strands have infiltrated Catholic graded series in religious education. The first of these strands was the official Church's renewed emphasis on social justice. As a result of this emphasis most curriculum series included important material on multiculturality and stressed the need for every Catholic to accord social justice to persons of all cultures. The second strand was the 1994 publication by the Vatican of the official *Catechism of the Catholic Church*.[53] The melding of social justice emphasis and the teachings of the official Catholic catechism gave the new multicultural content of the religious education textbook series a certain ring of orthodoxy.

While some religious educators, like Herbert Betts in his 1924 book *The Curriculum of Religious Education*, recognized the challenge of ethnic communities in urban settings for curriculum resource development,[54] the

---

53. Of acute multicultural interest is that the Scripture quotations in the American translation of this catechism, at least in the Loyola University Press publication, are taken from the Revised Standard Version and the New Revised Standard Version, both Protestant translations of the Bible, rather than the official but less linguistically elegant Catholic New American Bible.

54. George Herbert Betts, *The Curriculum of Religious Education* (New York: Abingdon, 1924).

very mode of publishing materials worked against such concern. Instructional resources became market driven, centrally produced, noncontextual tools that shaped teacher and student interactions in uniform ways. Profit margins became a major (often unspoken but assumed) factor in curriculum materials. Most mainline Protestant curriculum materials are produced by the denominational publishing house. The United Methodist Church, for example, funds the pension fund for retired clergy from profits made by the United Methodist publishing house. A solid, dependable source of income comes from sale of religious education resources to local Methodist churches. The Catholic Church in America does not have a denominational publisher. Curriculum resources and teaching materials are all produced by private corporations. In such a situation profit may become not only a major incentive but the *raison d' être* of the publishing company.

Even before midcentury, then, the emphasis on moneymaking and on producing "safe," nonprophetic religion curriculum materials resulted in the decontextualization of resource materials and placed a heavy responsibility at the local level to "adapt" the resources—something as difficult for the average consumer to accomplish then as now. Interestingly, while cognitive developmental issues became increasingly important to publishers, concern for ethnicity continued to be ignored under the influence of national consumer patterns. In functional terms, these centrally produced instructional resources served the same basic function as the catechism. They became lenses through which the Bible could be interpreted by everybody in the same way. The developmental psychology of the day presumed Western studies of children's learning and did not take into account the possibility of culturally specific learning patterns. It is fair to say that this presumption continues to be the case in the majority of instructional resource production by the church today.[55]

Viewed as a whole, the twentieth century can be described as a time when both Catholic and mainline Protestant denominational and nondenominational publishing houses in the United States struggled with issues related to multiculturalism in economically-driven, erratic, and generally timid ways. It is important to remember that the notion of *pluralism* was not a central issue for the public school system in the United States until after the onset of the civil rights movement in the 1960s. While various missionary-related groups in the United States in midcentury engaged in innovative work among ethnic minority groups, their work was generally considered to be unrelated to the national production of religious educational materials.[56] Even today, it is extremely difficult to find instructional resources that seek

---

55. Reginald L. Jones, *Black Psychology* (Hampton, Va.: Cobb & Henry, 1991).

56. A good example of some fascinating work, basically discounted by national curriculum producers, is recorded in Barbara Anne Roche, "A History of the Special Curriculum Work Done by the Presbyterian Church in the USA Among the Spanish-

to embrace fully a multicultural perspective throughout all printed materials. More often than not, special curricula for specific ethnic groups, such as African-American, Asian-American, or Hispanic are provided for use only within those ethnic communities. Rather than lament the pervasive lack of multicultural awareness among religion-curriculum publishers, however, religious educators should note the major barriers to multiculturalism and seek to move beyond those barriers to explore what curriculum resources might look like if multiculturalism were taken seriously.

Between World War I and World War II, U.S. society affirmed the ideal of the melting pot. Both general educational and religious education models of teaching presumed the existence of the Western code, including the racial and ethnic superiority of the Western European white. The basal readers of post-World War II that were used in general education often included stories about Dick and Jane or their equivalents. They were typically white, middle-class, often suburban, carefree children of homeowners, who had one employed parent—the father. Such a traditional narrative text was common both in public-school and in church-school literature.[57] This image was consistent with a larger attempt by educators in the United States to try to discover how a national educational system could prepare a new generation of students for responsible life within a democracy. Unity could be brought out of postwar societal changes by constructing curricular options that presumed normative and Western images of the individual in society.[58]

Several years earlier, the International Council of Religious Education, in a significant 1946–47 study of the theological and educational foundations of religious education, found itself responding to the changes of the post-World War II era as well. This study explored the rise of rapid communication, the presence of nuclear weapons, technological innovation, and secularization at work in the world. It also presumed that there was, therefore, an "inescapable need for world unity" in which all persons would

---

American and Navajo Cultures in the Southwestern United States Between 1944 and 1947" (M.R.E. thesis, Princeton Theological Seminary, 1960).

57. For an example of the understanding of the traditional nuclear family current in religious-education literature of that period, see Paul H. Vieth, *The Church and Christian Education* (St. Louis, Mo.: Bethany, 1947), pp. 168–92. On Catholic religious education with respect to the melting-pot position, see Harold A. Buetow, *Of Singular Benefit: The Story of Catholic Education in the United States* (New York: Macmillan, 1970), pp. 281–365. Until the late 1970s, Catholics embraced the melting-pot idea because this meant social recognition and economic parity with the Anglo-Saxon Protestant establishment. On the last point, see John Tracy Ellis, *American Catholicism*, 2d ed.

58. See *General Education in a Free Society: Report of the Harvard Committee* (Cambridge, Mass.: Harvard University Press, 1955), especially pp. 3–6; 42–51. This crucial theoretical document helped shape both public and ecclesial education during the latter part of the twentieth century. Its intellectual influence cannot be underestimated.

focus on "the common good."[59] Hence, the study could note with a degree of passion (which seems uncannily current) that "deep cleavages fissure almost all phases of our social life, separating races, classes, religions, political parties, the age levels, labor and management, and the adherents of our competing ideologies. There is no accepted unity of life. Democracy degenerates into the clash of social groups instead of evoking a united devotion to the common good."[60]

This is a crucial statement, for it helps religious educators understand the lack of interest on the part of subsequent Protestant religious education in multicultural options. The authors of this study, which was composed of some of the most talented religious-education specialists of the day, sincerely felt that "a united devotion to the common good" must take precedence over concern with ethnic specificity—*for the good of the future of democracy itself.* The dangers of plurality after World War II weighed heavily on the imaginations of both public and church educators.

How different this approach sounds from the later discussion among many who affirmed pluralism in the 1990s. Compare the 1947 statement of the International Council of Religious Educators with the words of Jacquelyn Zita in 1992. Zita stated that "any universal reading of reality from one perspective can be challenged by the multiplicity of different selves in different locations. For some postmodernists, subjectivities can ambulate into these multiple locations, each generating a particular discursive view of the world, which in turn 'constructs' the subjectivity of that location. The subject becomes a product of discourse or intersecting textualities, as the world becomes a ceaseless play of interlocking and conflicting 'texts,' spoken from different locations and negotiated across different perspectives."[61]

Postmodernism refers to a contemporary philosophical approach that, among other things, questions the validity of human knowledge that is de-contextualized, or disembodied, from the culture in which it is existentially embedded. It is not difficult to recognize that, from this perspective, racial and ethnic specificity could be valued over an ideal such as the common good. In fact, a "common good" from a postmodernist viewpoint would be met with the highest degree of suspicion.[62]

---

59. The Committee on the Study of Christian Education, *The Study of Christian Education*, vol. 2 *Theological and Educational Foundations* (Chicago: International Council of Religious Education, 1947), p. 12. Many of these findings were popularized in Paul Vieth's book *The Church and Christian Education*. The power of the original mimeographed study, however, was not fully reflected in the book.

60. Ibid., p. 13.

61. Jacquelyn N. Zita, "Male Lesbians and the Postmodernist Body," *Hypacia* 7, vol. 4 (fall 1992): p. 109.

62. Leonardo Boff, "Post-Modernity and Misery of the Liberating Reason," in *Centre Ecumenique de Liaison Internationales* 77 (spring 1966): 5.

Many churches find themselves in a state of "in-betweenness" in relation to multiculturalism, caught somewhere between a worldview assuming that pluralism can be destructive and a worldview assuming that pluralism is creative. A response to pluralism that consists of resources in different languages, inclusive pictures in print materials, or heritage curriculum resources do not in themselves deal with the more basic issues at hand. The movement to the pluralistic option requires a major paradigm shift for many Western religious educators, and it has significant theological and social consequences. Religious-education resources for Appalachian persons, Hispanic curriculum resource guidelines, or African-American materials and research do not in themselves constitute a denominational paradigm shift.[63] A paradigm shift means taking seriously the interplay between religion and culture, not merely transmitting one culture's perspective to another culture. Where an illustrative story in a religion curriculum study guide might promote the value of individual initiative, unquestioned in most Western contexts, the same guide might overlook opportunities to reinforce consensual, communal values of the non-Western readers also using this study guide.

Having considered where religious education has been and where it is today with respect to multicultural options, the next task is to examine educational and other social-science research on contemporary approaches to multicultural studies in public education.[64] Public education in the United States continues to debate the place of multiculturalism in schools and over the years has experimented with ways to integrate multicultural concerns into its curriculum.[65] The following section identifies programmatic options arising from educational practice in the public sector that may prove useful in considering future possibilities for multicultural religious education.

PROGRAMMATIC OPTIONS FOR MULTICULTURAL RELIGIOUS EDUCATION

In considering the important issue of programmatic options, two considerations must be kept in mind. First, these options do not work all by themselves.

---

63. For example, see Willard A. Williams, *Education Ministry in the Black Community* (Nashville, Tenn.: Board of Education of the United Methodist Church, 1972); John J. Spangler, "Developing a Handbook for Christian Education in Appalachia," *Religious Education* 75 (September 1980): 592–605; Joint Educational Development Hispanic Christian Education Team, *Hispanic Christian Education Project (Survey Findings)* (Joint Educational Development, 1983); Grace Choon Kim, ed., *Ways to be a Good Teacher: A Manual for Korean-American Teachers Training* (Louisville, Ky.: Education and Congregational Nurture Ministry Unit, Presbyterian Church [U.S.A.], 1992).

64. Allan C. Ornstein and Daniel U. Levine, *Foundations of Education*, 6th ed. (New York: Houghton Mifflin, 1997), pp. 359–69.

65. For example, see Davidman, *Teaching with a Multicultural Perspective*, pp. 1–30.

Programmatic options are simply frameworks or orientations through which and out of which a religious educator works. Successful multicultural religious education, therefore, is not a consequence of the programmatic option in itself, but rather is the consequence of the dynamic, goal-oriented instructional activities of the religious educator working within the general framework of the programmatic option.

Second, it should be emphasized that the word *program* (as in *programmatic option*) is not necessarily to be equated with an educational framework actualized in a formal setting such as a school or a Sunday school. Rather, a multicultural religious education option is just as programmatic when enacted in an informal environment such as a home.

While many Christians tend to delay implementation of multicultural religious education because of the monocultural composition of their parishes and congregations, the multicultural composition of the U.S. population makes it unlikely that a monocultural approach to education for the sake of democracy can be maintained either in schools or in churches. Indeed, an argument currently advanced by some educators is that the effectiveness of the U.S. work force and the well-being of its democratic society ultimately depend on the quality of the multicultural education its citizens receive in the nation's schools. For example, James and Cherry Banks, multicultural-education specialists, argue that multicultural education is "education for life in a free and democratic society," helping learners "transcend their cultural boundaries and acquire the knowledge, attitudes, and skills needed to engage in public discourse with people who differ from themselves." Multicultural education, according to the Banks, is "not only grounded in the nation's democratic traditions, but is also essential for the survival of a democratic, pluralistic nation in the next century."[66]

Based on their extensive review of the literature, Christine Sleeter and Carl Grant identify five different approaches to multicultural education currently used in public schools in the United States: (1) programs for teaching the culturally different, (2) human-relations programs, (3) single-group studies, (4) multicultural education, and (5) multicultural education for social reconstruction.[67] Each option embodies a distinctive conceptualization of multicultural education that shapes its goals, teaching strategies,

66. James A. Banks and Cherry A. McGee Banks, *Multicultural Education: Issues and Perspectives* (Boston: Allyn & Bacon, 1993), p. xiii.

67. Christine E. Sleeter and Carl A. Grant, *Making Choices for Multicultural Education: Five Approaches to Race, Class, and Gender*, 2d ed. (Englewood Cliffs, N.J.: Prentice-Hall, 1994) and "An Analysis of Multicultural Education in the U.S.A.," Harvard Educational Review 57:4 (1987); 421–44. See also Carl A. Grant and Christine E. Sleeter, *Turning on Learning: Five Approaches to Multicultural Teaching* (New York: Merrill/Macmillan, 1989), a volume with model lesson plans for multicultural education with grades 1–12.

and subject matter.[68] While the approach of general education to multi-culturalism is based on a notion of democratic inclusiveness and not the gospel per se, we believe that these options are congruent with the principles identified earlier from the biblical text and that they suggest possibilities for future curricular reform by those religious educators who wish to integrate multicultural education into the life of congregations and parishes. After all, religious education represents one type or specificity of general education. Thus the basic principles and data derived from general education apply to every specific form of general education, including religious education. It is not surprising that most of the teaching advances made in religious education throughout the twentieth century came originally from general education.

Teaching the Culturally Different

The primary goal of programs for teaching the culturally different in public schools is to assist learners whose cultural background, language, learning style, or learning ability differs from the dominant school culture. This approach is most frequently found in special-education or bilingual-education classes where teachers work at building bridges between learners and the body of knowledge that comprises the school curriculum. Teachers recognize and affirm cultural differences by using the knowledge, values, attitudes, and skills that learners already have acquired from their culture to teach the traditional curriculum. Typically, this multicultural option involves adapting teaching procedures to make them more compatible with students' learning styles and cultural background.[69] For example, teachers may offer bilingual instruction or may use more culturally relevant materials and teaching activities to build on the cultural differences that students bring.

This approach represents a step forward in multicultural education because it does not identify cultural differences as deficiencies to be remedied.[70] In terms of multicultural religious education, it points toward

---

68. Additional information on each of Sleeter and Grant's categories may be found in chapter 1 of this book.

69. For a discussion of the relationship between learning styles and culture, see Jacqueline Irvine and Darlene York, "Learning Styles and Culturally Diverse Students: A Literature Review," in *Handbook of Research on Multicultural Education*, ed. James A. Banks and Cherry McGee Banks (New York: Macmillan, 1995) and Rita Dunn and Shirley A. Griggs, *Multiculturalism and Learning Style: Teaching and Counseling Adolescents* (Westport, Conn.: Praeger, 1995). For a more general discussion of different learning style inventories, see also Pat B. Guild and Stephan Garger, *Marching to Different Drummers* (Alexandria, Va.: Association for Supervision and Curriculum Development, 1985); David A. Kolb, *Experiential Learning* (Englewood Cliffs, N.J.: Prentice-Hall, 1984); and Bernice McCarthy, *The 4 MAT System: Teaching to Learning Style with Right/Left Mode Techniques*, 2d ed. (Oak Brook, Ill.: Excell, 1981).

70. For a critique of the cultural deficiency orientation, see S. S. Baratz and J. C. Baratz, "Early Childhood Intervention: The Social Science Base of Institutional Racism," *Harvard Educational Review* 40 (February 1970): 29–50.

the importance of openness to cultural differences as a critical initial step, as it was in the biblical text about Peter and Cornelius examined earlier. However, this option does little to acknowledge the incompleteness of personal visions or the importance of seeking multiple perspectives. Consequently, Sleeter and Grant observe that this approach is often criticized for its essentially assimilist stance. For example, while bilingual classes and other programs do identify and build on cultural differences to motivate and increase the learning of students as individuals, such programs usually remain on the periphery and rarely lead to modification of the traditional school curriculum to embody cultural diversity. Consequently, the cultural differences that students bring to learning in this approach are not often incorporated into the general program of curriculum and instruction as a source of useful knowledge for all. Rather, they are useful data for teachers who want to make teaching and learning more compatible with individual learning styles and cultural preferences.

In multicultural religious education, some parishes or congregations may have special full-scale programs of religious education for those whose cultural background and language differ from the community's dominant culture. There are also other ways that faith communities may use this approach to incorporate learners of different cultures into their educational programs. For example, religious educators can invest time learning about the cultural differences that their learners bring so they can better assist them in learning. They may, for example, employ a relational, affective, or cooperative strategy over a cognitive or individualized one if the learner's cultural differences indicate those preferences. In this approach, however, religious educators are not likely to build into the lessons experiences of cultural difference for the group because their purpose was to plan a specific teaching procedure rather then to augment or revise the religious education curriculum for all students.

Human Relations

A second program option in multicultural education employs a human relations emphasis. The goals of this approach are "to promote positive feelings among students and reducing stereotyping, thus promoting unity and tolerance in a society composed of different people."[71] Human-relations programs deal more directly with the affective dimension of multicultural education by helping learners develop positive attitudes and feelings about themselves and about those who are different from them while also reducing stereotypes by providing accurate cognitive information.[72] As a

---

71. Sleeter and Grant, *Making Choices for Multicultural Education*, p. 85.

72. James A. Banks, "Multicultural Education: Its Effects on Students' Racial and Gender Role Attitudes," in *Handbook of Research on Social Studies Teaching and Learning*, ed. J. P. Shaver (New York: Macmillan, 1991), pp. 459–69.

curricular program, the human-relations option is most effective when it makes up a comprehensive aspect of all learning activities rather than when it is limited to special human relations exercises offered as occasional enrichment. An occasional emphasis on human relations can result in a "tourist curriculum" where students learn interesting facts about different cultures, but do not deal in depth with human relationships. Derman-Sparks notes that "tourist curriculum is both patronizing, emphasizing the 'exotic' differences between cultures, and trivializing, dealing not with the real-life daily problems and experiences of different peoples, but with surface aspects of their celebrations and modes of entertainment. Children 'visit' non-White cultures and then 'go home' to the daily classroom, which reflects only the dominant culture."[73]

The human-relations approach frequently uses experiences drawn from interpersonal and intergroup life within the culture of the community itself before it attempts to generalize to others "out there." It stresses the commonality of people as well as their differences, and it works toward breaking down prejudice by combating ethnic and racial stereotypes. Use of group process, particularly cooperative work in heterogeneous groups where students pursue common goals on an equal-status basis, is a major teaching method of this approach, along with social-skills training that incorporates teaching activities such as modeling, coaching, and role-play.[74] Community-action projects that take students out of the classroom to engage in service projects in the community also provide direct, experiential contact to help students develop empathy with and reduce stereotyping of those from whom they differ.

Sleeter and Grant applaud the human-relations approach for its focus on reducing prejudice, stereotyping, and hostility between different cultural groups. They observe that this is one of the most popular instructional approaches. In Sleeter's research, teachers more frequently equate multicultural education with human-relation studies.[75] An emphasis on face-to-face encounter, openness to the cultural other, and attitudes of mutual hospitality all are prominent in this approach. Sleeter and Grant critique this option, however, for its lack of attention to the more difficult social issues, such as social stratification and institutional racism, which are not always solved by educating people to get along and to value each other's

---

73. L. Derman-Sparks, *Antibias Curriculum: Tools for Empowering Young Children* (Washington, D.C.: National Association for the Education of Young Children, 1989), p. 7.

74. For research studies on the effectiveness of cooperative learning, see S. Sharan, "Cooperative Learning in Small Groups: Recent Methods and Effects on Achievements, Attitudes, and Ethnic Relations," in *Review of Educational Research* 50 (summer 1980): 241–71.

75. See C. Sleeter, *Keepers of the American Dream* (London: Falmer, 1992).

differences. Their review of instructional materials prepared for human-relations studies reveals that such materials often address cultural diversity only when needed "to improve feelings toward self and others," while continuing to accept the status quo "by failing to focus adequately on social problems and inequities."[76]

Sustained efforts to teach about the roots of cultural conflict and to develop students' skills in public dialogue about changes that might be made are less prominent in this approach. Sleeter and Grant conclude that the human-relations approach offers a solid beginning for multicultural education, particularly in early childhood and primary grades where a foundation can be laid for other approaches to multicultural education later. They also observe that the human-relations option can be incorporated into other approaches to achieve a more comprehensive program of multicultural education.

Those who plan multicultural religious education may weave a human-relations emphasis into the curriculum in a number of ways. Instructional materials are available that offer conceptual, relational, and cultural activities to enrich ongoing curriculum themes or to be used as separate units of instruction.[77] An even more effective use of this approach would be the development of religious education programs emphasizing human relationships on a churchwide basis that engage all ages in study, worship, and mission activities to sponsor increased understanding among diverse ethnic and cultural groups.

In religious education based in a local-church setting, *multicultural* means not only races and ethnic groups different from those of the congregation; it may also mean different faith groups. A key ingredient of total multicultural religious education, then, is the interfacing of members of the local church with parishioners belonging to different Christian and non-Christian churches. The human-relations approach to multicultural religious education has been shown to be effective in breaking down the religious prejudices of members of local churches and in helping those persons incorporate the riches of other faith traditions, as appropriate, into their own spiritual lives.[78]

---

76. Sleeter and Grant, *Making Choices for Multicultural Education*, p. 117.

77. Examples of such teaching resources are Kathleen McGinnis, *Celebrating Racial Diversity* (St. Louis, Mo.: Institute for Peace and Justice, 1994); Camy Condon and James McGinnis, *Helping Kids Care: Harmony Building Activities for Home, Church, and School* (St. Louis, Mo.: Institute for Peace and Justice, 1988); and James and Kathleen McGinnis, *Educating for Peace and Justice: National Dimensions* (St. Louis, Mo.: Institute for Peace and Justice, 1985).

78. For a helpful treatment of multicultural religious education for faith pluralism, see *Religious Pluralism and Religious Education*, ed. Norma H. Thompson (Birmingham, Ala.: Religious Education Press, 1988).

Single-Group Studies

A third approach to multicultural education takes the form of single-group studies that focus on one particular ethnic or cultural group. The main goal of the single-group option is to promote "social equality for and recognition of the group being studied."[79] By concentrating on a particular group and seeking information about it at a depth appropriate for the learners, those who choose this option hope to increase awareness and appreciation of the group, as well as a broader understanding of cultural diversity in mainstream culture. This approach often takes the form of elective courses or special units of study as, for example, African-American studies, women's studies, and so forth. Discussions of a group's history and social contributions, biographies of its outstanding people, and attention to its cultural expressions as found in art, drama, music, dance, and ethnic traditions, for example, typically are significant components of the single-group study approach.[80] Members of the study group share their experiences and reflect on major formative events the group has had, including its struggles, achievements, and experiences of oppression and discrimination, as well as how the group has responded. Such shared dialogue among group members also may help identify contemporary issues that still need to be addressed.

Single-group-studies tend to focus more on the content of study than on particular teaching procedures, particularly at the university level where this approach came to prominence with the addition of black studies and women's studies in the late 1960s and early 1970s. Attention is given, however, to teaching procedures that are compatible with the culture and learning styles of the group. Because a single-group study may include both members of the dominant culture and members of the culture being examined, the interaction of the group itself often becomes a significant part of the learning process. Sleeter and Grant suggest that focused single-group studies can contribute to cultural identity formation among group members, as those who are part of the culture being studied may develop a more positive identification with their culture, while group members of the dominant culture, after confronting evidence of discrimination and inequity on the part of their culture, may also move to a "positive identity with their own group" without being "accepting of their group's superior status."[81]

---

79. Sleeter and Grant, *Making Choices for Multicultural Education*, p. 123.

80. For examples of useful information resources for an African-American single-group study, see the following titles in the African American Reference Library Series: Jay Pederson and Jessie Carney Smith, eds., *African American Breakthroughs: 500 Years of Black Firsts* (Detroit: Gale UXL, 1995); Alton Hornsby Jr. and Deborah G. Straub, eds., *African American Chronology*, 2 vols. (Detroit: Gale UXL, 1994).

81. Sleeter and Grant, *Making Choices for Multicultural Education*, p. 135. See also B. D. Tatum, "Teaching about Race, Learning about Racism: The Application of Racial

The single-group-studies approach can also be effective in multicultural religious education. Some churches incorporate a study of different cultures or geographic areas into their educational curriculum on an annual basis. Such a special study may focus on a particular group that is a part of the church's mission emphasis, and it may involve the whole congregation in learning more about the particular group. An adult group studying a new ethnic enclave in the community could first gather background and statistical information and then visit neighborhood shops, restaurants, and institutions to learn firsthand about the culture, family structures, language, strengths, and perhaps needs of the group. Parishes or congregations who wish to explore their own distinctive cultural expressions of the Christian faith may plan single-group ministries and educational programs built around the religious experience of their group.[82]

A variation of the single-group-studies approach is the bicultural education option, which sometimes accompanies bilingual studies in general education. The goal of a bilingual-bicultural program is to engage learners in learning more about the cultures associated with the languages they are learning. Thus in bilingual-bicultural education children can become more fluent in English as their second language and gain competence in the cultural heritage of their first language. In multicultural religious education a bicultural approach may take shape in faith communities as they develop special ministries with persons who are bicultural and wish to address both sides of their identity within the Christian faith. For example, churches may choose a bicultural-studies option to assist teenagers in immigrant families as they struggle to deal effectively with the culture of their parents and the culture of their peers.[83]

An advantage of the single-group-studies approach to multicultural religious education is that it promotes in-depth awareness of a specific culture. In this option we see another way of openness to other cultures in that cultural distinctiveness becomes a legitimate object of study and exploration rather than a bridge to the traditional religious education curriculum. There is a risk, however, of isolating a single group from the rest of the community

---

Identity Development in the Classroom," *Harvard Educational Review*, 62, no. 1 (1992): 1–24.

82. For examples of religious education materials that use a single-group approach, see Nathan Jones, *Sharing the Old, Old Story: Educational Ministry in the Black Community* (Winona, Minn: Saint Mary's Press, 1982) and Donald Ng, ed., *Asian Pacific American Youth Ministry: Planning Helps and Programs* (Valley Forge, Pa.: Judson, 1988).

83. For an example of bicultural and crosscultural approaches to religious educational ministry, see Mary Lou Codman-Wilson, "Transition and Identity: Ministry with Asian-Americans," *The Christian Ministry* 24, no. 4 (1993): 11–16.

and promoting increased tension or conflict with other groups. Another disadvantage of single-group studies is that they often become mere add-ons to the curriculum and are not integrated into the whole. As such, they may be elected only by members of the group being studied, leaving the rest of the faith community relatively uninfluenced by multicultural concerns.

Because the single-group-studies approach gained its impetus from university programs, it has often been conceptualized as being solely school-based and cognitive. However, a single-group-studies approach in multicultural religious education need not be restricted to the school setting or to cognitive reflection. If affective learning and lifestyle learning are indeed more important than cognition in religion, then the more nonschool and the more affective the educational activity the better. For example, a single-group-studies activity in a particular church may alternate its meetings in the homes of persons of different races, ethnic groups, and religions. This kind of personal interfacing will yield rich affective and lifestyle multicultural learning outcomes.

Multicultural Education

The fourth option, multicultural education, differs from the other options Sleeter and Grant describe because it introduces multiple cultural perspectives on all issues studied and engages all learners in critical analysis of these multiple perspectives as its basic teaching strategy.[84] Multicultural education as practiced in this approach includes teaching that is commonly shared content in U.S. culture, as well as the cultural diversity that actually exists. The approach requires that diverse materials be used to present diverse viewpoints. Learners are expected to accept the fact that there is often more than one perspective on an issue. "Rather than believing only one version, they should learn to expect and seek out multiple versions."[85]

Thus, in a social-studies class, a history unit planned from a multicultural-education approach would incorporate multiple perspectives on the historical events being taught. For example, the political concept "manifest destiny" is frequently employed to justify the military acquisition of land and westward expansion of culture from the perspective of the United States as a growing nation. The same historical events that resulted in the acquisition of new western territories for the United States, however, when viewed from the perspective of Mexico might yield a quite different interpretation.

---

84. In constructing their approach framework, Sleeter and Grant note that in actual practice, *multicultural education* frequently serves as an umbrella term to describe many different educational programs that deal with some aspect of the study of different cultures. They label this fourth approach "multicultural education" because it represents the kind of educational practice most multicultural advocates mean when they use the term. See *Making Choices for Multicultural Education*, pp. 167–68.

85. Ibid., p. 186.

United States territorial acquisitions in the Southwest, from Mexico's point of view as the former occupant of the lands, are more likely to be explained as "conquest" than as "manifest destiny." A multicultural interpretation of these historical events engages students in examining and discussing both perspectives.

Similarly, in a poetry unit a teacher using a multicultural approach might invite students to identify similarities and differences in literary form and style within a historical and cultural context by using poetry written by members of different races and cultures. For example, learners might compare two poems that were read at the inauguration of a U.S. president: Robert Frost's "The Gift Outright," read at President Kennedy's inauguration, and Maya Angelou's "On the Pulse of Morning," read at the inauguration of President Clinton.

Faith communities choosing this option to multicultural religious education are challenged to incorporate a variety of cultural perspectives and expressions into their worship, study, fellowship, and service. In a multicultural-education approach to Bible study, for example, attention might be given to the diverse cultural perspectives represented in the biblical texts themselves, as well as to the diverse perspectives present in the different translations and commentaries. Studying Scripture in dialogue groups with Christians from different ethnic and cultural backgrounds is another a way to engage in multicultural Christian religious education. Broadly understood, the multicultural-education option would engage parishes in learning to look carefully at the diversity of theological formulations, religious lifestyles, liturgical practices, and mission efforts that Christianity encompasses as a significant part of the curriculum of religious education.

One advantage of the multicultural-education option is that it is integrated into all aspects of the curriculum rather than being an isolated addition on the periphery. The importance of integrating multicultural education into the whole of the educational enterprise should not be underestimated. In a recent review of the place of multicultural education in American public schools, Dennis Carlson observes that the two major accomplishments of multicultural education have been making the "other" visible in the curriculum and providing "space" within the school program to address explicitly "issues of race, class and gender identity." He notes, however, that multicultural education has not been as successful in "overcoming the marginalization and alienation of minority students or building a diverse democratic community in the schools."[86] Carlson attributes this to the way in which multicultural concerns have occupied an increasingly marginalized place in the "core subject areas" of public education, having been insulated from the core subject areas of math, science, English, and social studies. He

---

86. Gary Carlson, "Constructing the Margins: Of Multicultural Education and Curriculum Settlements," *Curriculum Inquiry*, 25, no. 4 (1995): 408.

points out that multicultural education is often limited to, for example, the recognition of African-American history month, or to special units on the contributions of minorities and women, or to a human-relations workshop on respecting diversity once a year. Carlson sees such structural marginalization as indicative of the value placed on multicultural education, which is often seen as "just one more 'subject' or set of learning objectives among many, for which some limited time and space must be found in a very crowded curriculum."[87]

In addition to structural marginalization from the core-subjects curriculum, multicultural education is often "spatially," or geographically, marginalized. Urban school systems with larger numbers of minority students are more likely to have multicultural activities or special workshops, while predominantly white, suburban schools often have little multicultural emphasis. Carlson contends that the structural and spatial marginalization of multicultural education in American schools has significant implications for public education, since it reinforces a belief that multicultural education is for minority students and is not needed by others, whose white, middle-class culture is already represented in the curriculum. Carlson argues that it is white, middle-class learners who most need multicultural education in order to "begin thinking beyond the notion of a dominant Eurocentric culture that 'allows' various other subcultures to exist at the margins."[88]

According to Cameron McCarthy, the failure of multicultural education to be integrated fully into the public-school educational program may also explain in part the research showing that multicultural education and human relations programs that emphasize attitudinal changes and cultural understanding "have not been very successful in achieving their goal of eliminating majority/minority prejudice."[89]

In terms of the characteristics of a multicultural curriculum that were drawn from the biblical text about Peter and Cornelius, the multicultural-education option comes closest to including all six characteristics while placing particular emphasis on the importance of multiple perspectives, face-to-face encounter, and public discussion of conflict. The strength of this multicultural approach for religious education lies in the integration of these characteristics, although (as discussed above) to be effective, this approach itself needs to be integrated into the core curriculum and into the life of the learning community.

Another strength of the multicultural approach is its position on the importance of recognizing diverse perspectives. Given the diversity that

---

87. Ibid., p. 415.
88. Ibid., p. 416.
89. Cameron McCarthy, *Race and Curriculum: Social Inequality and the Theories and Politics of Difference in Contemporary Research on Schooling* (New York: Falmer, 1990), p. 45.

exists in American society, a multicultural approach strives to cultivate both understanding and appreciation of diverse points of view rather than ignoring or suppressing diversity. Sleeter and Grant comment that in a country as large as the United States, cultural diversity will continue to exist in spite of attempts by the dominant group to assimilate other groups. Forced assimilation, they state, only antagonizes groups. "If some degree of cultural diversity is natural, then it makes sense that schools embrace this diversity rather than pretending that it is not there or that it is harmful to the country."[90] In contrast to the aims of multicultural education, monocultural education, which focuses only on the dominant group's perspective, risks becoming an abridged or partial education because it teaches only one cultural reality, omits diverse views, and does not teach the social skills and attitudes needed to understand and work effectively with people from the diverse cultures. Sonia Nieto argues that a multicultural approach to education offers a truly basic and fundamental education to all students, while a monocultural approach is limited and partial at best.[91] She also points out that students from the dominant cultural group may benefit most from multicultural education. Because multicultural education is "*about* all people," Nieto claims, "it is also *for* all people, regardless of ethnicity, language, religion, gender, race, or class. It can even be convincingly argued that students from the dominant culture need multicultural education more than others, for they are often the most miseducated about diversity in our society. In fact, European American youths often feel that they do not even have a culture, at least not in the same sense that clearly culturally identifiable youths do. At the same time, they feel that their way of living, of doing things, of believing, and of acting are simply the only possibilities. Anything else is ethnic and exotic."[92]

In a church adopting the multicultural-education approach, following some weeks of studying various ethnic or religious groups in their area, youth leaders might arrange for their youth group to meet one week with youth at the local Jewish temple, and another week invite them to meet at the church. Observing and discussing one another's traditions, music, sanctuaries, and scriptures would help them define their own heritage and recognize their common values. Similar exchanges might take place between, perhaps, a black Baptist youth group and members of a predominantly white Catholic Youth Organization. Such exchanges should be an ongoing feature of the religion curriculum, rather than just an isolated unit or a set of adult learning activities.

---

90. Sleeter and Grant, *Making Choices for Multicultural Education*, p. 179.

91. See Sonia Nieto, *Affirming Diversity: The Sociopolitical Context of Multicultural Education*, 2d ed. (White Plains, N.Y.: Longman, 1996), pp. 311–12.

92. Ibid., p. 313.

Critics of the multicultural-education option contend that a focus on multicultural issues throughout the curriculum deters students from mastering the traditional subject matter. However, religious educators should recall that religion, even when conceptualized as a cognitive subject, necessarily includes multiculturalism. Far from being extraneous to religion content, multiculturalism is inextricably a part of the content. Advocates for single-group studies or the "teaching-the-culturally-different" approach raise questions about whether a broad multicultural approach can give adequate attention to the distinctive concerns of particular cultural groups. Another limitation is the tendency of this option to celebrate cultural diversity, while overlooking systemic issues of social inequality and social injustice. Both these issues are dealt with more directly in the final approach.

Multicultural and Social Reconstructionist

The fifth option, education that is both multicultural and social reconstructionist, responds to the critique that multicultural education celebrates diversity but fails in social-action efforts. This approach has much in common with the multicultural education option discussed above. It seeks to construct a curriculum for all learners, which will represent the multiple perspectives and contributions of diverse groups through the entire learning experience. In addition, however, the social-reconstructionist option develops social-action skills to effect change and engages learners in practicing social responsibility in a culturally diverse society. Emphasis is placed on exploring life experiences related to social injustice and social disadvantage in order to develop constructive responses. In this approach, social analysis, which culminates in social-action projects, often emerges from the daily lives of students or from incidents in the classroom. Stacy York describes such an experience from a preschool class where a child's father had difficulty visiting the preschool because he was physically disabled, and the school had no special parking arrangements. The children became aware of the problem, discussed the situation, and worked to create a handicapped parking space in the school's parking lot.[93] Schools, churches, and others who employ this approach to a multicultural curriculum frequently work with local community groups that are involved regularly in social action.

Parishes or congregations that wish to use this approach as part of their multicultural religious education curriculum could incorporate direct experiences of multicultural social action into their curricular plans in a variety of ways. For example, two congregations—one predominantly African-American and the other predominantly European-American—have been working together as partner churches for four years to deepen their

---

93. Stacy York, *Roots and Wings: Affirming Culture in Early Childhood Programs* (St. Paul, Minn.: Red Leaf, 1991), p. 27.

ministries as Christians engaged in multicultural dialogue. Their partnership began shortly after racial violence erupted in Los Angeles in response to the acquittal of police officers charged with the beating of Rodney King in 1992. At a church meeting during this time of racial unrest, a group of church leaders from one of the churches shared their growing concerns about the deep racial divisions that existed in their own city too—much closer to home than they wanted to believe. This honest exchange elicited a candid admission that few of them knew anyone who lived on the other side of the city.

These church leaders decided that there were people whom they and their congregations ought to get to know better as Christians and that seeking out Christians in a partner church across town was a good way to begin. The city's urban-ministry organization helped the church and their pastor find another congregation interested in such a shared dialogue, and the two churches began a new venture in multicultural partnership. Members of these congregations meet together periodically for joint Bible studies and other discussions on topics of mutual concern. Often these gatherings, which alternate between church locations, focus on hopes for the children and youth of each congregation. Over the years both churches have exchanged pastors and choirs during Sunday services of worship, giving each congregation an opportunity to participate in different worship and preaching traditions. The youth groups in both congregations meet together occasionally for sports events and have worked together to plan and conduct worship for the two congregations.

In 1995, in the wake of the controversy widespread in the United States over the verdict in the murder trial of sports figure O. J. Simpson, members of these two congregations, embracing each other across different cultural and racial lines, began to talk frankly about a variety of social issues, including the criminal-justice system. Honoring the different perspectives that exist among them, they became even more committed to finding ways to work together to reduce violence in their city and insure that citizens in all sections of the city are protected and treated fairly under the law. They organized a series of gatherings to meet jointly with the police chief and other law-enforcement officials to express concerns, not only for themselves and their different neighborhoods but also for the public's welfare. A pressing common concern was juvenile crime and the search for alternatives for effective rehabilitation of young people within the criminal-justice system.

The desire of these two churches to know each other as Christians across geographic and racially divisive lines slowly broadened to form a coalition of Christian citizens working together with city officials for the common good. Although the group's initial goal was to develop a deeper multicultural commitment between two Christian churches, they found that their oneness in Christ called them to do more than enjoy each other's friendship and good will. In terms of Sleeter and Grant's framework, these two churches began to incorporate more of the social reconstructionist emphasis in their approach to multicultural religious education.

Similarly, congregations committed to this approach can begin to identify ways in which their present commitments to social justice may move in the social-reconstructionist direction. In response to Jesus' call in Matthew 25:31–46 to feed the hungry, clothe the naked, and welcome the stranger, an adult study group might join hands to build houses for Habitat for Humanity, participate in a CROP walk for hunger, and stock the community food pantry. These are important activities in and of themselves, but they also can be the beginning of even greater commitments to address the systemic causes of homelessness, poverty, unemployment and hunger, as well as to relieve their symptoms.

A strength of this multicultural and social-reconstructionist option is that it is more comprehensive than the other approaches. It includes the positive features of the multicultural-education approach and also involves learners in doing social analysis, exercising decision-making skills, and engaging in cooperative social action. From the perspective of the biblical characteristics of multicultural learning events, this approach is strong in its efforts toward life-changing hospitality and in its ability to acknowledge conflict and engage in public discussion of diversity for the sake of multicultural transformation.

Sleeter and Grant point out in their critique of this approach that not much research literature exists on this option and that there is little specific guidance for teachers.[94] They highlight several aspects of the approach that make it both a promising option and a demanding one—particularly for teachers and planners. Because this approach advocates that multicultural education become involved in social change by teaching learners how to engage in social analysis, exercise decision-making skills, build effective coalitions among social groups, and focus on the dynamics of societal structures as well as individual attitudes and values, this approach demands a great deal in terms of teachers' experience, knowledge, and skills.

Some criticisms of this approach are that its focus on multicultural social change may distract learners from mastering fundamental skills and knowledge, escalate distrust and conflict by emphasizing instances of injustice and prejudice that need to be confronted, dilute an appropriate emphasis on single-group issues by forming coalitions to accomplish changes in society, and undercut other less radical and demanding multicultural options. In public-educational practice, a social-action approach is more frequently employed in peace education, world hunger, and ecology. It is used less often to deal directly with the social injustices related to race, ethnicity,

94. Sleeter and Grant, *Making Choices for Multicultural Education*, p. 235.

and culture.[95] These hazards would no doubt carry over to multicultural religious-education efforts. Nevertheless, the multicultural and reconstructionist approach, in religious as well as in public education, holds promise for making significant change by engaging people in a well-informed, cooperative, and active stance toward multicultural issues that continue to challenge our society. It is, perhaps, the most holistic and integrated of the five options and likely the most demanding.

Analytical frameworks such Sleeter and Grant's serve a number of useful purposes. Such frameworks make clear what are some of the options for multicultural curriculum planning. They articulate the assumptions and goals that support different options so that religious education curriculum planners can articulate their own assumptions and goals more clearly. Considering the scriptural expectation that God's people are to "do justice, to love kindness, and to walk humbly" with God,[96] theological and religious assumptions can undergird such curricular goals. This review of current options to multicultural education, therefore, is intended to stimulate thinking about some of the possibilities for planning multicultural religious-education curricula. One way to use it, of course, is to choose the one approach most suited to a particular faith community and to develop in practical ways the implications of that option. But certainly there are many other ways to employ this framework as a tool for planning because each approach and the goals it embodies contributes to the larger understanding of what multicultural religious education can be, given the multiple forms it may take in diverse settings with distinctive faith communities.

SOME BASIC INGREDIENTS IN FORMING A MULTICULTURAL CURRICULUM IN CHURCHES

It is probably obvious that there is no one best curriculum for multicultural religious education. There is no prepackaged program or set of teaching resources that can put a multicultural curriculum in place in our parishes and congregations with a minimum of effort. Religious educators in each parish and congregation can and should be about the task of forming a multicultural curriculum precisely because no one else can accomplish the task for them.

A curriculum for multicultural religious education is formed by educational leadership in a faith community out of the interplay of its particular verbal, nonverbal, and existential "texts"—the diversity of meanings,

95. Ibid., p. 235.
96. Micah 6:8. Many biblical references might be cited to indicate the high value placed on works of compassion and equity; for example, see Deut 10:17–19.

beliefs, attitudes, values, memories, hopes, life experiences, and gospel visions—that shape the common life they share as Christians. Thus when we speak of forming a multicultural religious education curriculum, we refer to the task of reshaping the common life—the faith community ethos of a congregation or parish—so that it is better able to teach and to nurture a multiculturally Christian people. This section highlights some significant components that have a place in a Christian religious multicultural curriculum. The resource materials religious educators choose, the curricular plans they devise, and the program options they select may be evaluated on the basis of how they introduce these components, as well as others valued by each particular church, into the common life of the faith community.

Begin by Sharing Personal and Corporate Visions

Most persons, in spite of their diverse cultural backgrounds, were formed and educated in monocultural environments and therefore probably have few models for developing a multicultural way of thinking, valuing, and acting. Christians, however, have in their religious heritage moral visions of the multicultural community into which they are called in Christ. As Sara Little reminds us, the church's vision is an appropriate place to begin developing curriculum for parishes and congregations. Little asserts that "the beginning point for a curriculum is not a set of printed resources," but "a vision of what binds a congregation together, of what that congregation in collaboration with other groupings of God's people is called to be and to do." She chooses the term *vision* deliberately because it expresses images that motivate and hopes that empower, "compelling congruence between the 'what is' of tradition and the 'what is to be' of the transforming power of the gospel. Such a vision emerges from the life of the congregation."[97]

Some of these visions arise from the biblical text; others, from Christian theology and doctrine taught, preached, sung, and prayed in faith communities; some, from what we have learned about human beings and their societies. Still other visions are unexpected revelations that confront believers as they wrestle with the diversity that divides Christians instead of uniting them. A basic step in forming a curriculum for multicultural religious education is to nurture congregational imagination so that old and young, male and female, expect to dream dreams and behold visions of community among God's people.

A curriculum plan for multicultural religious education demands a more solid foundation than actions motivated by polite inclusivity or political correctness. A church's moral visions of a religious education that is multicultural must be translated into theological convictions and religious

---

97. Sara Little, "The Place of Education in the Sanctuary Event," in *Tensions Between Citizenship and Discipleship*, ed. Nelle G. Slater (New York: Pilgrim, 1989), pp. 189–90.

attitudes that can be experienced, discussed, embraced, and lived so that the whole faith community can express a shared vision of its calling to engage in multicultural religious education.

Because individual visions in the community are incomplete and partial, opportunity must be given to offer personal visions and to ponder what others in the congregation have experienced. This mutual sharing of visions and experience is not done to choose whose insights and ideas are most promising and true; rather, tentative images and hopes are shared within the community of faith so that God's will may be revealed more fully, and a new vision may emerge from the partial, incomplete visions each has received. In discussing how congregations and parishes educate toward and nurture hope, Charles Foster emphasizes the primary role of the religious imagination in this process: A shared vision capable of infusing the church with hope for the future and energy for faithful response requires a context where people "encounter the creative and redemptive activity of God at work, where the exploration of new images for God's activity is affirmed, and where the exercise of the imagination is deliberately and intentionally nurtured."[98]

Such a nurturing of the congregation's religious imagination will be supported by thoughtfully planned opportunities for worship, Bible study, theological and religious discussion, multicultural encounter and dialogue, and community decision making as multicultural visions are transformed into a multicultural way of life appropriate to particular congregations and parishes. The imaginations of all ages in congregations will be needed to suggest the shape multicultural religious education will take in the church's life and work. The dreams and visions of the faith community may be communicated in a variety of expressive forms appropriate to particular "seers" and the visions that they share, including drama, art, poetry, prayers, sermons, hymns, unanswered questions, goal statements, learning experiences, mission encounters, and, of course, stories.

Creating imaginative stories of a multicultural future is but one way members of parishes and congregations can begin to move from past tradition and present experience to envision what Little names the "what is to be" of the gospel. Vivian Paley offers evocative examples of such envisioning from her multicultural kindergarten class at the University of Chicago Laboratory Schools, where young children often record visions and hopes for the future in the stories they dictate. These stories frequently become the basis of thoughtful conversations in class and at home, as well as informal dramas that the children act out with each other—a kind of embodied vision.

Paley relates how Jeremy's brief story left his father with wet eyes as he read it aloud. "Once there was a black Michael Jordan and a white Michael

---

98. Charles Foster, *Educating Congregations*, p. 122.

Jordan and the black Michael Jordan got the most points but the white Michael Jordan got the most rebounds. So then they were friends and they played together everyday." The sharing of Jeremy's story prompts his father to claim his own vision of a positive multicultural learning context for his son's schooling: "He's got to be comfortable with whites because I'm not. I got a late start. In high school there were a few, but when I got to a white college I nearly flunked out. Culture shock."[99]

Keisha, another of Paley's young students, shares her vision of a multicultural future by dictating to her teacher the story of an imagined past worth emulating. "Once there was a princess who talked only Spanish. . . . This princess is a brown girl. Her name is Annabella. And this princess could talk any language. When she talked Indian she was Indian and when she talked—what does Nadia in the first grade talk?"

"Polish."

"Oh yeah. When she talked Polish she was Polish and when she talked every language she was every person. So she lived happily ever after."

"How could she know all the languages?" Martha [her classmate] asks.

"Because she asked everyone to teach her."[100]

Cultivate Openness to Cultural Diversity

How churches respond to cultural differences is crucial to the formation of a multicultural curriculum. Are cultural differences something church members avoid discussing or are these differences embraced as potential gifts to enrich the faith community? Do members find cultural differences merely interesting or do they expect to discover important insights, values, and attitudes in the culture and the religious practices of other Christians that may deepen their own practice of the Christian life? Does openness to cultural diversity stop at the intellectual level or does it extend to one's attitudes, emotions, and behaviors as well?

Cultivating openness to cultural differences also involves naming our racism or bias and being prayerfully honest about differences that make us defensive and uncomfortable. In the narrative of Peter and Cornelius, openness to persons of another culture went against strongly held convictions on the part of both men; nevertheless they embraced moral visions they did not completely comprehend because of an equally strong experience of God's will and purpose that the visions offered. Openness to cultural difference is, in part, a function of the breadth of the faith vision that impels us toward

---

99. Vivian Gussin Paley, *Kwanzaa and Me: A Teacher's Story* (Cambridge: Harvard University Press, 1995), pp. 22–23. Excerpts from the Paley volume are reprinted by permission of the publisher from *Kwanzaa and Me: A Teacher's Story* by Vivian Gussin Paley, Cambridge, Mass.: Harvard University Press, Copyright © 1995 by the President and Fellows of Harvard College.

100. Ibid., p. 140.

others as we glimpse with increasing clarity God's will that we live as one in Christ.

Cultivating openness to cultural diversity also requires the support of the community. When Peter and Cornelius responded in openness to members of another culture, they did not act alone: each called communities into being for support, encouragement, and, ultimately, for cross-cultural witness and testimony. Actions of openness to diversity that form part of a faith community's multicultural curriculum ought to be acts of cooperative partnership rather than solitary ventures.

Sonia Nieto identifies four levels of support in multicultural programs for embracing pluralism and cultivating an openness to diversity. They are (1) tolerance, (2) acceptance, (3) respect, and (4) affirmation, solidarity, and critique.[101] At the *tolerance* level, cultural differences are not denied; instead they are recognized and permitted as being inevitable in a culturally diverse society. The second level of support is *acceptance* of differences in a manner that acknowledges their reality and importance. At the acceptance level, multicultural programs that feature cultural celebrations in the community may be more prominent. Groups operating at the third level of *respect* for multicultural education tend to honor and esteem differences by explicitly using the diversity of cultural values, attitudes, customs, and experiences to help all learners develop multicultural awareness. At the fourth level, schools and communities *affirm* the cultures and languages of learners and citizens, using cultural diversity as a legitimate source of learning to develop respect and *solidarity* among diverse groups. Learners not only celebrate diversity, they also reflect on and confront it.[102] Nieto's classifications offer the important reminder that openness to cultural diversity in churches will vary and take different forms as congregations and parishes begin to incorporate a multicultural focus into their common life together. A multicultural religious education effort that begins at the second level with churchwide celebrations of the cultures represented in the parish could progress over an appropriate period to a third level of intergenerational learning experiences that build respect and understanding, and finally to a fourth level of age-graded studies of enculturated attitudes, values, traditions, and behaviors that can strengthen or subvert their shared life as a community.

Face Up to Encounter and Dialogue

The experience of cross-cultural encounter and dialogue is another component to consider in fashioning a multicultural religious-education curriculum. The concept of encounter as used here is not to be equated with casual meetings or perfunctory visits that offer little opportunity for significant interaction. Rather, an encounter experience should afford all participants

101. Sonia Nieto, *Affirming Diversity*, pp. 353–57.
102. Ibid., p. 355.

ample opportunity to gain a deepened respect for cultural diversity by becoming more aware of their own cultural commitments, attitudes, and values, as well as by gaining a deepened appreciation of the cultural commitments, attitudes, and values of others.

Some religious educators involved in a search for effective models of transformative education identify encounter experiences, often combined with a "radical change of environment," as crucial components of educative events that stimulate and support behavioral, attitudinal, and cognitive change.[103] William Bean Kennedy concludes that an experience of "intense involvement with the lives of people in their own environment changed radically the provincialism and myopia of the visitors." What might have been learned only cognitively was instead "mediated through real people." Contact with individuals and leaders who previously "had been only abstractions [made] a significant difference in how those people and their situations" were perceived by the learners.[104] Such personal encounter and dialogue may also be effective in challenging stereotypes and previous unexamined assumptions that participants have about each other.

Robert Evans identifies "openness to vulnerability" as a positive factor that is often present in the experience of cross-cultural encounter. He describes this as a willingness to depend on "the care and skills of a person in whom one would normally place no trust, especially regarding personal health and safety."[105] This experience of vulnerability involves a kind of cross-cultural role reversal for both parties to the encounter. People used to being in control within their own culture become vulnerable "guests" dependent on others. Those who take on the "host" role also become vulnerable by assuming responsibility for the well-being of their guests. As a result, hosts and guests may experience the reality of their interdependence as they become vulnerable to each other. Evans reports that often in the context of such direct personal encounter, people voluntarily engaging in cross-cultural immersion feel deep anxiety. Afterward they feel deep appreciation for the support and companionship that result from living through an experience and discovering "the common bonds of humanity and necessary interdependence."[106]

Opportunities for cross-cultural encounter are varied and, with careful planning, appropriate for most age-groups. For example, as young children begin to spend time in church-group settings, day care, preschool, and other contexts outside the home, they may have opportunities to learn about

---

103. See Alice F. Evans, Robert A. Evans, and William B. Kennedy, eds., *Pedagogies for the Non-Poor* (Maryknoll, N.Y.: Orbis, 1987) for descriptions of eight models of transformative education with commentary.

104. Ibid., p. 250.

105. Ibid., p. 277.

106. Ibid.

cultural diversity through experiencing it directly. They also may engage in dialogue with playmates and caregivers who help them name and value differences. Children and adolescents experience cross-cultural encounter and dialogue through camps, conferences, mission trips, and other activities where culturally diverse groups gather to engage in service and to develop interdependence and community. Partner churches may decide to bring adult members of several parishes or congregations together to create a multicultural community around a mission commitment, a retreat, or a special study where opportunities for ongoing encounter and dialogue will be planned.

As a parish or congregation becomes more aware of the incompleteness of its vision, more open to the gifts of cultural diversity, and more conscious of its need to be able to offer perspectives from other cultures on what it means to be one people in Jesus Christ, such a faith community may choose to engage in face-to-face dialogue with culturally diverse Christians. Opportunities to meet and discuss matters of mutual interest in an open, interdependent exchange may do more to remove barriers to cross-cultural understanding than do reams of written data documenting the perspectives and practices of different cultural groups. But face-to-face encounter also involves a certain amount of risk and so demands thoughtful preparation. Attention must be given to what sensitivities and skills are needed to communicate effectively across cultures. Incorporating encounter and dialogue into a curriculum plan is not an easy task, but it is an important element in multicultural religious education.

Seek Multiple Perspectives

The strength of a curriculum designed for multicultural religious education may be analyzed by examining how it encourages persons to seek multiple perspectives on significant issues. Differing perspectives of persons or cultural groups are of great value to multicultural dialogue, and faith communities need to encourage inquiry learning and actively solicit ways of discernment that differ from their own preferred ways of construing social reality.

Multicultural religious education supports the habit of looking at issues from differing points of view so that multicultural exchange will be less a matter of groups justifying the way they each see and value things and more a matter of groups discerning the similarities and differences among their distinctive attitudes and points of view for the sake of what all may learn about God's intentions. Thus, becoming more multicultural in outlook and in lived experience will influence the planning decisions religious educators make about mission and service, the way they teach, the examples they use in the learning situation, the way they worship, pray, and preach in the sanctuary, and the depth of empathy and understanding they share with others.

In Paley's book, Virginia and a colleague, Lorraine, discuss the ways the kindergarten children help each other look at things from the other's perspective. Paley reports how one child explained to another what a "brother" is: " 'You just call someone a brother if they're black, that's all.' " Lorraine observes, "Even kindergartners can inform each other about their own culture. They are most often their own best resource. But sometimes an adult needs to step in and help."

Then Lorraine shares an example of adult intervention. As part of a social-studies unit, a fourth-grade class was talking about the black market. One boy asked, " 'Why are so many bad things called black?' [The teacher] said she could see the black kids' hackles rising." Paley suggests that the question was insensitive. "Shouldn't a fourth grader understand the effect his question would have on a black child?" Lorraine, however, thinks it was a sincere question. "Here is a white boy who suddenly realizes that something is wrong with the way *black* is used."

After describing the power of language and how words "can make you feel wonderful or terrible, strong or weak, ugly or pretty," Lorraine tells the children that *black* has been a very sensitive word for black people. "I told them that before 1960 it wasn't beautiful to be black. Then we talked about expressions like black sheep, a black look, a black day, black magic, black-hearted, and so on. We made a list." She went on to tell the children that "we black people began to realize that we had a lot to be proud of and that black was not ugly, it was beautiful. That's why I still use it, in addition to African American. Once it became beautiful I wanted it to stay beautiful." Then Lorraine asked the children to list some good things called black. "They liked 'black hole' a lot . . . and *Black Beauty* from the book they were reading, black-eyed Susan, blackboard, black belt, black gold, black-tie party, and so on." One fourth-grader said she "didn't realize how damaging ordinary language could be and how important it is to be careful of what you say."[107]

Religious educators should be sure that church volunteers at every level are sensitized to what is communicated by metaphorical language thoughtlessly used to convey religious ideas, for example, by linking sin or evil with blackness and goodness or purity with whiteness.

Learn through Conflict and Public Discussion of Differences

Conflict is a component not often treated seriously as part of the church's religious-education curriculum. More typically in church life, we try to avoid conflict rather than embrace its many educative possibilities.[108] This response to conflict is also prevalent among college professors. Weinstein

---

107. Paley, *Kwanzaa and Me*, pp. 117–19.

108. C. Ellis Nelson, "Some Educational Aspects of Conflict," in *Tensions Between Citizenship and Discipleship*, ed. Nelle G. Slater (New York: Pilgrim, 1989), pp. 209–13.

notes that if professors were left to follow their natural inclinations, many would do everything possible to avoid conflict in the classrooms. He goes on to say, "I know, however, that the most significant learning may result from what is referred to in cognitive development literature as a 'knowledge disturbance' or a disequilibrium and that these disturbances produce conflict essential to human growth and development."[109]

Similarly, in a multicultural religious-education curriculum, conflict generated by diverse cross-cultural perspectives may result in significant learning, producing a positive kind of disruption in knowledge and prodding learners to examine tacitly held cultural stereotypes and racial prejudice that they may not be challenged to confront in monocultural contexts. Such learning is not without discomfort and conflict. Raymond Wlodkowski and Margery Ginsberg, in their work on culturally responsive teaching and learning, use the analogy of living in a different culture to describe teachers and learners who struggle in their effort to alter "long-held viewpoints as they begin to understand and accommodate new perspectives." They observe that many people who move to a culture different from their own are, in time, able to "develop an understanding of and respect for the perceptions, experiences, and values" of the new culture. Wlodkowski and Ginsberg find that there is an initial period in which "sojourners feel dissonance and emotions ranging from fear to excitement as they experience the incongruities between their host culture and their primary culture." However, through processes that involve "actively observing, socializing, and developing friendships within the host culture, they eventually arrive at a more inclusive and integrated world view. Very few people are able to do this without some period of uneasiness."[110]

Exploration of conflicting perspectives, values, and cultural differences through public debate and reflective inquiry often leads to a heightened awareness of what we believe and value, and why. Thus, in forming a multicultural religion curriculum in the parish, planners will want to clarify for themselves and the community the legitimacy of conflict in the learning process and establish public forums where sincere and honest discussion of differences may be practiced as an act of faithfulness for the mutual edification of the body. Nelson suggests a four-step process for such forums in the church's educational program: (1) an encouraging environment for

---

109. Gerald Weinstein and Kathy Obear, "Bias Issues in the Classroom: Encounters with the Teaching Self," in *Promoting Diversity in College Classrooms: Innovative Responses for the Curriculum, Faculty, and Institutions*, New Directions for Teaching and Learning, no. 52 (San Francisco: Jossey-Bass, 1992), p. 47.

110. Raymond Wlodkowski and Margery Ginsberg, *Diversity and Motivation* (San Francisco: Jossey-Bass, 1995), pp. 286–87. See also E. W. Taylor, "Intercultural Competency: A Transformative Learning Process," *Adult Education Quarterly* 44, no. 3 (1994): 154–74.

adults and youth to formulate issues that concern them; (2) a means of
setting up leadership for sustained study—a standing committee or a group
that can help them resolve the issue; (3) an expectation to settle the issue
with a declaration or an action; (4) an evaluation of the events that made
up the educational experience.[111] These and other means of dealing with
conflict need to be planned with sensitivity to the preferences of various
ethnic groups, some of whom may seek less formal and confrontational
venues for exploration and exchange.

Offer and Receive Hospitality

The practice of hospitality may well be the key to an effective multicultural
religious education curriculum. The New Testament term for *hospitality*
refers to more than a host's special concern for the well-being of a guest. It
describes a special quality of joyful expectation that giving and receiving
hospitality will lead to a mutual sharing that strengthens and renews both
host and guest. The practice of hospitality may be understood as "a delight
in the whole guest-host relationship, in the mysterious reversals and gains
for all parties which may take place. For believers, this delight is fueled
by the expectation that God or Christ or the Holy Spirit will play a role in
every hospitable transaction."[112]

Earlier we noted that the service of hospitality surrounds the cross-
cultural interaction of Peter and Cornelius from beginning to end. Even
before he understands why Cornelius seeks him, Peter offers lodging and
hospitality to the Gentile strangers from Caesarea, going against religious
practice (Acts 10:23). He appears to do this largely because of the Spirit's
command not to hesitate to grant the men's request because their presence
at Peter's gate is the Spirit's doing. Peter's offer of hospitality initiates
a "ministry of introduction"[113] by bringing together strangers previously
alienated from each other by cultural differences, so that divisive stereotypes
might be shattered and their particular gifts might be mutually shared. Henri
Nouwen comments helpfully on the importance of mutual sharing that the
context of hospitality enables: "The biblical stories help us to realize not
just that hospitality is an important virtue, but even more that in the context
of hospitality guest and host can reveal their most precious gifts and bring
new life to each other."[114] It is no accident of circumstance that such should
mark the multicultural discipleship to which Christ calls Christians.

---

111. Nelson, "Some Educational Aspects of Conflict," pp. 213–15.
112. John Koenig, *New Testament Hospitality* (Philadelphia: Fortress, 1985), p. 8.
113. Ibid., p. 127.
114. Henri Nouwen, *Reaching Out: The Three Movements of the Spiritual Life* (New York: Doubleday, 1975), p. 47.

In forming the hospitality component of a multicultural religion curriculum for parishes and congregations, religious educators should seek out opportunities to move beyond gathering information about people in other cultures, even beyond face-to-face meetings, to shared meals and conversations, to shared ministry for mutual benefit. The reciprocal nature of hospitality required here is critical. Often the more demanding task is to receive and to make ourselves vulnerable to the hospitality of others. Most church members need to engage in the discipline of receiving as well as giving in a multicultural curriculum. The experience of hospitality fits well with the social-reconstructionist aspects of multicultural education. Activities such as Christians' joining in service with multicultural groups to work together on social issues of common concern are significant ways of giving and receiving hospitality in Christ's name.

BUILDING A MULTICULTURAL CURRICULUM

So far we have dealt mostly with the foundations of a multicultural religious-education curriculum. Biblical, theological, philosophical, psychological, and sociological foundations are essential for all religious-education activity, including multicultural religious curriculum. But no foundation or set of foundations, however valuable or however necessary, can substitute for the actual work of constructing a curriculum and implementing concrete teaching procedures. Put differently, the foundations of education are necessary but not sufficient. One major reason religious education has not attained the success it should be enjoying is that all too often religious-education writers have offered foundations of religious education without concomitantly providing ways to concretely build curricula and devise teaching strategies organically linked to these curricula. With this section of our chapter we hope to remedy this problem by providing religious educators and curriculum developers with some of the basic building blocks for constructing an effective multicultural religious education curriculum.

A multicultural religious education curriculum is not a formal, inert thing. It is not just a cognitive framework printed on paper, which multicultural religious educators can easily forget as they go about their work. Essentially a curriculum is what Peter Rabbett terms a "context for action"—not just any action, not just social action, but most vitally learning action.[115] It is the curriculum that yields teaching, or more precisely, that offers the overall structure and direction through which teaching flows. Consequently,

---

115. Peter Rabbett, introduction, to *Education for Cultural Diversity*, ed. Alec Fyfe and Peter Figueroa (London: Routledge, 1993), pp. 12–14.

constructing and validating a multicultural curriculum is a very important and necessary task for multicultural religious educators.

Basis for Planning for the Multicultural Religious Education Curriculum

"What is the basic rationale for the multicultural curriculum that I wish to build? What do I wish this multicultural religious education curriculum to accomplish for learners?"[116] These are the most fundamental educational questions every curriculum builder and every teacher involved in multicultural religious education must ask.

Since the mid-twentieth century, one rationale has been the dominant influence on curriculum planning. Commonly known as the Tyler Rationale (after its founder, Ralph Tyler), the essence of this rationale for curriculum building is a set of four questions: (1) What educational purposes should the curriculum seek to attain? (2) What educational experiences can be provided by the curriculum that are likely to optimize the attainment of these purposes? (3) How can these experiences be effectively organized? (4) How can educators determine whether these purposes are being attained?

Despite its dominance in curriculum theorizing and curriculum building throughout the United States, the Tyler Rationale has been opposed by a wide assortment of curricular theorists.[117] None of the critics, however, seems to have offered workable and realistic alternatives to the Tyler Rationale. Because it seems congruent with common sense, because it is realistic, because it sees education as the accomplishment of a task, and because it enables educators to evaluate in a valid way the results of a particular curriculum, the Tyler Rationale remains popular. It can prove to be useful to multicultural religious educators in planning the curriculum. Notwithstanding, it is also helpful for religious educators to examine the assumptions underlying the Tyler Rationale to ascertain whether these assumptions are optimally congruent with the goals of multicultural religious education.[118]

Goals and Objectives of the Multicultural Religious Education Curriculum

An educational goal is a broad outcome that the curriculum and the religious educator wish to achieve. An educational objective is a more specific

---

116. George J. Posner, *Analyzing the Curriculum* (New York: McGraw-Hill, 1992), pp. 2–33.

117. Some theorists who question the Tyler Rationale represent a brand of existentialism, while some are followers of the Frankfurt school of critical theory. Others adhere to one or another strand of philosophical deconstructionism, and still others consider themselves humanists resisting the dominance of the technical in life.

118. William E. Doll Jr., *A Post-Modern Perspective on Curriculum* (New York: Teachers College Press, 1993).

outcome, usually conceptualized in terms of performance of one kind or another. An example of a goal in multicultural religious education is that learners acquire the basic ability of successfully introjecting into their own personal faith life those beliefs, attitudes, and lifestyles of other cultures that expand or correct that faith life. An example of an educational objective is that learners acquire a certain set of knowledges about the history of a cultural group other than their own, and be able to display a requisite degree of mastery of these knowledges.

Educational goals and objectives are absolutely essential if any form of intentional education, including intentional multicultural religious education, is to be even minimally successful. After all, inherent in the concept of intentionality is the fact that the intention is organically directed to the attainment of an outcome of one sort or another. Religious educators and others who claim that educational goals and objectives are overly technical, nonhumanistic, or behavioristic should examine their own teaching. Such an examination will show that these religious educators themselves have goals and performance objectives when they teach. There are many legitimate ways of conceptualizing objectives. One of the most famous was developed by Robert Mager.[119] It stresses the precise identification of the objectives of teaching and the concomitant specification of the level of performance that must be met. Other curriculum and instruction specialists proposed different kinds of objectives, including objectives that are more open than the ones that Mager originally proposed. Still other curriculum writers have discounted objectives altogether.[120] Ironically, the very books and articles that propose the abandonment of objectives have clear and precise objectives. In short, it is impossible to have legitimate curricula and teaching activities without performance objectives of one sort or another.

Structural Elements of the Multicultural Religious-Education Curriculum

Once the multicultural religious educator has decided on the basic rationale, the goals, and the objectives of the multicultural religious-education curriculum, the next question becomes selection of the basic structural elements of the curriculum. There are six separate but related elements that together, as a unit, constitute the structure of every curriculum, including the multicultural religious-education curriculum.[121] All must be present in

119. Robert F. Mager, *Preparing Instructional Objectives* (Palo Alto, Calif.: Fearon, 1962).

120. One representative example is Dennis Lawton, *Curriculum Studies and Educational Planning* (London: Hodder & Stoughton, 1983).

121. James Michael Lee, *Principles and Methods of Secondary Education* (New York: McGraw-Hill, 1963), pp. 190–213.

the good multicultural religious-education curriculum. The six elements are design, scope, sequence, continuity, balance (or range), and integration.

While the great preponderance of curriculum writers conceptualize these six structural elements as enacted in formal environments such as the school, they are also present in worthwhile educational activities conducted in informal environments such as home, neighborhood, or vacation resort. The major difference between the structural elements in these two different settings is structural looseness. In informal environments the six elements are deployed with greater structural looseness or fluidity than they are in a more highly structured formal learning environment. It is essential to remember that multicultural religious-education curricula, much like all other components of religious education, are not restricted to formal settings such as the church school, but are present and operative in informal settings as well.

Design: Curricular design is the framework or structural organization used in selecting, planning, and carrying forward a set of learning experiences. Put somewhat differently, curricular design is the plan that the religious educator follows in providing learning experiences. It is the way in which learning experiences are organized and structured as a whole.

There are two chief types or categories of curriculum design: the fragmented pattern and the unified pattern. In the fragmented pattern a subject such as theology or Bible is taught as a separate or distinct unit in isolation from every other subject. The unified pattern, in contrast, is one in which subject-matter lines are broken down—the problem or topic under study unifies the subjects and thus forms an intersubject or interdisciplinary nucleus.

In the case of multicultural religious education, the unified design seems preferable for reasons set forth earlier in the chapter. First of all, multiculturality is above all things multidisciplinary in character, in contrast with, for example, theology in itself or sociology of religion in itself. Second, a social-reconstructionist multicultural outlook is almost always centered on actively addressing a social problem, also something that is by nature multidisciplinary. Third, religion is of itself multidisciplinary, in marked contrast to theology, which is of necessity unidisciplinary.

Religious educators working in multicultural religious education will wish to make sure that the curriculum design they use is a unified rather than a fragmented one. This is often easier to accomplish in an informal teaching/learning environment than in a formal setting such as a school. Notwithstanding, Sunday school and CCD classes can adopt a unified design if the religious educator abandons fixation on theological doctrine and moves to a more realistic, life-centered, experiential form of religious education. Such a move will not weaken theological doctrinal content but will actually help persons learn the doctrine better and more holistically. If Bible study is to truly mirror the Bible, then Bible study in a multicultural vein will be multidisciplinary (or multicognitive), multiaffective, and multilifestyle, since the Bible itself is a glorious tapestry of various disciplines, affective patterns, and life situations woven harmoniously into one beautiful picture of God's interaction with humanity.

During the twentieth century, various forms of curricular design have been proposed and elaborated on. The most familiar to religious educators is the subject-centered design that classifies bodies of information into intrinsically systematic branches of knowledge that form both the organizing force and center of learning, for example, theology, church history, and the like. The subject-centered design is the easiest for the religious educator to teach from. However, for religious education, and especially for multicultural religious education, the subject-centered design is less than effective. Even at the purely cognitive level, this design does violence to reality by compartmentalizing knowledge. Human knowledge is a deeply interconnected web of discrete cognitive disciplines. Furthermore, religion in itself, and also multiculturalism in itself, are not only multidisciplinary (cognitive) but also necessarily involve an intrinsic admixing of various disciplines, attitudes, values, and lifestyles. Thus not only social reconstructionist religious educators, but religious educators of all sorts of orientations might well consider abandoning the fragmented subject-centered design and moving to a more unified pattern.

During the era of progressive education (*c.* 1920–45) the curriculum design favored by many liberal curriculum theorists was the total learner-centered design. This design made a comeback in the years 1965–75 but in response to very different phenomena, notably a form of philosophical existentialism then prevalent is some educational circles in the United States and Western Europe. The total learner-centered curriculum is wholly rooted in the group of learners as they are here and now—their changing needs, purposes, and emotions. This type of design consists not in predetermined subject-matter areas but rather in centers of learner interests and needs which, of course, are always in flux. This form of curricular design has fallen out of favor because of its many limitations. However, some adult educators, espousing what they term "andragogy," seem to adopt a variation of the total learner-centered curriculum design, although andragogy allows considerable place for the leadership of the religious educator as he or she works with the adult learners in a cooperative manner.[122]

The persistent-life-situations curriculum, a kind of unified design, has already been discussed in this chapter. This kind of design, if well planned and implemented, holds significant promise for multicultural religious education in both formal and informal settings.

---

122. R. E. Y. Wickett discusses both andragogical and learner-centered approaches in *Models of Adult Religious Education Practice* (Birmingham, Ala.: Religious Education Press, 1991), pp. 45–52; 93–99.

The core curriculum is a unified design that centers around interdisciplinary (cognitive), interaffective, and interlifestyle tasks of both eternal and personal concern. Cognitive, affective, and lifestyle materials are brought into the learning situation as needed to solve the problem or task under consideration, without respect to precise subject-matter, affective, or lifestyle boundaries. Thus, for example, a study of the problem of the injustice experienced by racial and cultural minorities might bring in such diverse subject areas as the history of various ethnic and cultural groups, their varieties of music, literature on the inhumanity of various groups, religious writings on the issue, and so forth.[123] Because the core curriculum is a unified design, and because it is so natural and lifelike, it holds especial promise for multicultural religious education. Of course the core curriculum requires that religious educators receive a different kind of preservice and inservice preparation than they currently receive.

Scope: Curricular scope is the breadth, variety, and types of educational experiences that are provided to learners. Scope represents the latitudinal axis for selecting learning experiences. Scope deals with the all-important issue: what should be included in the curriculum?

Each of the four kinds of curricular designs mentioned above will specify different kinds of scope. This is why teachers working in multicultural religious education must make a decision about which design they wish to use before proceeding to the other structural elements of the curriculum.

Sequence: Sequence is the order in which educational experiences are developed with, and taught to, the learners. Sequence answers the question "When?" in curriculum development and implementation. The design that multicultural religious educators choose will determine the sequence in which learning experiences occur. The sequence in a subject-centered design flows from the inherent logic and organization of the substantive content material itself. In the core design, by contrast, the sequence is determined by the nature of the problem or task itself, and by the way the religious educator and the learners choose to work on this problem or task. For example, learners in multicultural religious education who wish to tackle the problem of cultural discrimination in America might wish first to learn the basic biblical and Christian principles involved, then move to a study of the history of cultural groups in America, then examine current discriminatory practices in education and other areas, then visit and preferably live for a time with persons of other cultures to learn their affective and lifestyle patterns, then devise concrete ways to help persons from different cultures live a more integrated life together, and finally implement these concrete ways of assisting the target population.

---

123. James Michael Lee, *The Shape of Religious Instruction* (Birmingham, Ala.: Religious Education Press, 1971), pp. 199–200.

Continuity: Continuity is the vertical reiteration of major curricular elements. Because it emphasizes the unity and relatedness of the substantive content, continuity is the curricular guarantor that each sequential learning experience is organically tied in with previous and subsequent learning experiences. This organic tie-in can be primarily logical, as is the case with the subject-centered design, or primarily psychological, as is the case with the core design. Because multicultural religious education is so heavily freighted with psychological learning, the core design, in most instances, is probably more appealing with respect to curricular continuity than is the traditional subject-centered design.

Balance: Balance is the range of educational experiences that the learner encounters in the pedagogical situation. These experiences are designed to help learners grow cognitively, affectively, and in their lifestyle.

In the subject-centered design, balance comes only from the religious educator, as well as whatever reading and audiovisual materials the teacher assigns to the learner. In the core design, balance flows from the range of the problem or task itself. Given the vast range inherent in multiculturalism, it would seem that the subject-centered curriculum is not the ideal design for achieving the broad holistic goals of multicultural religious education. Thus religious educators wishing to teach multiculturalism to learners might give serious thought to using a design other than the subject-centered curriculum.

Integration: Curricular integration refers to the coordination of learning processes and outcomes resulting from experiences in several separate areas of study and experience. Integration is a very important characteristic of a curriculum because it is only through integration that the learners can come to the whole picture and the whole life of multiculturalism. Indeed, the very notion of multiculturalism is an integrated one, namely, a reality that integrates a wide spectrum of cultures into one overall cognitive vision, into one overall set of shared appreciations and affect, and into one overall symphony of variegated patterns of life. The subject-centered design provides no real integration, since in this design the learner, not the curriculum or the religious educator, must provide the curricular integration. However, effective curricula and effective teaching should themselves supply the integration. Therefore, the persistent-life-situations design and the core design are both better able to afford curricular integration for multicultural religious education.

Teaching and the Multicultural Religious Education Curriculum

Curriculum and teaching are intimately and inextricably connected. A curriculum is lifeless unless it is actualized in the teaching act. Conversely, teaching is meaningless and directionless unless it takes place within the overall matrix of the curriculum and with the goals and objectives of the curriculum as its target.

Teaching can be conceptualized in many ways. Among the most famous is the product/process continuum. Product/process research attempts to relate (1) teaching variables to learner achievement and (2) the curriculum planning process to improved teaching and learning.[124]

Another way teaching can be conceptualized is one that holds special promise in terms of blending the teaching dynamic with the overall curriculum matrix. This approach was developed by James Michael Lee in the 1970s and 1980s.[125] Lee spent years empirically examining the components of the here-and-now act of teaching religion. He discovered two discrete but totally interrelated forms of content present in each and every teaching act. The first of these molar contents Lee calls structural content, which is basically the set of procedures the teacher uses in both formal and informal settings.[126] Structural content is authentic content because the way in which religious educators teach is also what these educators teach. Put differently, a learner learns a great deal through the way a teacher teaches.

In empirically analyzing the here-and-now teaching act, Lee discovered that the essence of teaching lies in structuring, or "architechting," the teaching-learning situation. Lee found that there are four major structural variables present in every teaching act: the learner, the teacher, the subject-matter content, and the environment. Teaching consists in initially structuring and then continuously restructuring during the teaching act these four major variables in such a way that the desired learning outcome is produced.

The second form of content present in each and every teaching-learning act Lee calls substantive content. In multicultural religious education, the substantive content is multicultural religion. Each substantive content contains nine molar subcontents: product content, process content, verbal content, nonverbal content, conscious content, unconscious content, cognitive content, affective content, and lifestyle content.[127] The task of the teacher is to structure the teaching process in such a way that each of the nine substantive contents is dynamically and continuously brought into play and replay in such a manner as to facilitate optimum learning outcomes.

---

124. John D. McNeil, *Curriculum: A Comprehensive Introduction* (Boston: Little, Brown, 1985), pp. 367–68.

125. For a summary of Lee's approach, see chapter 1 of this volume, "Goals of Multicultural Religious Education."

126. The second of Lee's trilogy on religious instruction is devoted exclusively to structural content. See James Michael Lee, *The Flow of Religious Instruction* (Birmingham, Ala.: Religious Education Press, 1973).

127. The third volume of Lee's trilogy on religious instruction is devoted exclusively to substantive content. See James Michael Lee, *The Content of Religious Instruction* (Birmingham, Ala.: Religious Education Press, 1985).

Lee's conceptualization holds significant promise for multicultural religious educators who wish to mesh the teaching act with the curriculum in such a manner that the curriculum can be rendered as potent as possible. The richness of structural content and of substantive content as shown by the Lee model is especially suited to the richness, breadth, and enormous variegation of multicultural religious education.

Preparation for Teaching Multicultural Religious Education

All of this requires considerable preservice and in-service preparation for teachers if they are to successfully implement multicultural religious education in their congregations and parishes. Such a requirement necessitates a broadening to multiculturalism from the monoculturalism that is so frequently characteristic of preservice and inservice preparation of religious educators.[128]

An important dimension of this initial and ongoing professional preparation is expanding the attitudes of religious educators toward multiculturalism.[129] This task is often difficult, since many religious educators were raised and taught in a pervasive envelope of monoculturalism and thus sometimes have a tendency to view multiculturalism as strange and even possibly hostile.[130] Religious educators also have to be given considerable information about multiculturalism and diverse traditions, lest they see multiculturalism as a sort of unconventional phenomenon outside the mainstream and otherwise lacking intellectual and affective excellence.[131]

Besides the theory and history of multiculturalism and diverse religious traditions, preservice and in-service work for religious educators should include helping them concretely plan and implement instructional procedures whereby they are able to establish in the learning situation a climate that facilitates the acquisition of desired multicultural outcomes.[132]

---

128. Donna M. Gollnick, "Multicultural Education: Policies and Practices in Teacher Education," in *Research and Multicultural Education: From the Margins to the Mainstream*, ed. Carl A. Grant (London: Falmer, 1992), pp. 218–39.

129. Patricia G. Ramsey, *Teaching and Learning in a Diverse World* (New York: Teachers College Press, 1987), pp. 40–49.

130. On stages of the multicultural process—stages that teachers as well as learners pass through—see Jaime S. Wurzel, "Multiculturalism and Multicultural Education," in *Toward Multiculturalism*, ed. Jaime S. Wurzel, pp. 1–13.

131. Christine I. Bennett, *Comprehensive Multicultural Education: Theory and Practice*, 2d ed. (Boston: Allyn & Bacon, 1990), pp. 13–17.

132. Frances E. Kendall, *Diversity in the Classroom*, 2d ed. (New York: Teachers College Press, 1996), pp. 111–30; Donna M. Gollnick and Philip C. Chinn, *Multicultural Education in a Pluralistic Society*, 3d ed. (New York: Maxwell Macmillan, 1990), pp. 299–300. Thomas J. La Belle and Christopher R. Ward, *Multiculturalism and Education* (Albany, N.Y.: State University of New York Press, 1994), pp. 91–113.

Finally, the preservice and in-service program to help religious educators work in an appropriate multicultural key should include preparation in a wide variety of promising and proven concrete instructional procedures geared to helping learners acquire the desired multicultural outcomes.[133] For maximum impact on learners, religious educators should exhibit and deploy pedagogical competencies in the cognitive, affective, and lifestyle domains.[134] An important pedagogical competency for all religious educators working in multiculturalism is that of communication. Different cultural groups have different ways of communicating, and failure to be aware and competent in these various modes of intracultural and intercultural communication can seriously impede the religious educator's instructional effectiveness with persons of other cultures.[135]

Evaluating the Multicultural
Religious Education Curriculum

To attempt to enact any kind of curriculum, including a multicultural religious-education curriculum, without building an evaluation mechanism into its organic fabric is to court educational disaster. Evaluation is absolutely essential for all kinds of intentional education because it is only through evaluation that educators can gain valid and reliable data on whether the goals and objectives of the curriculum have been actually attained.

History has shown that attention to planning and implementing well-executed systems of evaluation has frequently been seriously neglected in the field of religious education. This indeed is one cause for the failure of religious education to achieve what the church and the people of God have hoped for it during the last one hundred years.

Evaluation begins by examining carefully the goals of the overall multicultural religious education curriculum. It then proceeds to ascertain what are the specific objectives of the various units or elements of the multicultural religious education curriculum.[136] Once the goals of the curriculum

---

133. A helpful book giving many concrete specific teaching procedures for multiculturalism is Michael G. Pasternak, *Helping Kids Learn Multi-Cultural Concepts* (Champaign, Ill.: Research Press, 1979). Although the pedagogical procedures Pasternak offers are intended for children, religious educators can adapt these to learners of all ages.

134. Mira Lanier Baptiste and H. Prentice Baptiste Jr., "Competencies toward Multiculturalism," in *Multicultural Teacher Education: Preparing Educators to Provide Educational Equity*, ed. H. Prentice Baptiste Jr., Mira L. Baptiste, and Donna M. Gollnick, vol. 1 (Washington, D.C.: Commission on Multicultural Education, American Association of Colleges for Teacher Education, 1980), pp. 44–72.

135. K. S. Sitaram and Roy T. Cogdell, *Foundations of Intercultural Communication* (Columbus, Ohio: Merrill, 1976), pp. 1–68; 130–44; 212–36.

136. Ronald C. Doll, *Curriculum Improvement: Decision Making and Process*, 5th ed. (Boston: Allyn & Bacon, 1982), p. 175.

as a whole and the objectives of each phase of the curriculum have been clarified, the curriculum builders devise the mode or modes of evaluation that are best suited to find out the extent to which the curriculum has met the desired goals and objectives.[137]

The various phases of the overall process of curriculum evaluation show once again the organic, intertwined relationship between curriculum and teaching. Evaluation devices can be constructed and implemented to ascertain accurately the extent of the validity and reliability of the multicultural religious-education curriculum. But these devices ultimately will be for naught if in their concrete teaching practices multicultural religious educators themselves do not teach in a way that is congruent with the goals and objectives of the multicultural religious education curriculum. A good multicultural-education curriculum, therefore, should build into its very structure the general and specific ways that religious educators can implement the goals and objectives of the multicultural religious education curriculum.

We cannot overemphasize the essential and inescapable importance of scientific evaluation in the construction and validation of each and every phase of the multicultural religious-education curriculum. Without evaluation, the curriculum builder and the multicultural religious educator are lacking the eyes to see whether the curriculum is accomplishing its intended goals and objectives. In this connection we are reminded of a story that James Michael Lee tells about an incident that happened during an extensive discussion he had in the early 1980s with a highly respected person who was then a leading Catholic figure in religious education. He was born in the same town in the Austrian Alps where Lee's wife was born and raised, took his doctorate in kerygmatic theology under Josef Jungmann at the University of Innsbruck, and served as a missionary to China for many years. He got involved in overt religious education work in the United States relatively late in life. When Lee met him, he was in his late 70s and was working as a religious education expert for an archdiocese. During the course of the extensive conversation Lee asked him what he thought of a particular religious-education curriculum for youth published by a market-driven commercial Catholic religious education publisher. "I like this curriculum," he said. "It resonates well with me. I feel good about it."

"But does it work?" Lee countered. "How do you know whether it will actually accomplish what it claims it will accomplish?"

"That's not really important," responded the religious education expert. "I feel good about it. I'm sure it is a good youth curriculum."[138]

137. Tom Kubiszyn and Gary Borich, *Educational Testing and Measurement*, 4th ed. (New York: HarperCollins, 1993), pp. 36–73.

138. This incident nicely illustrates one of the problems that ensue when religious-education administrators or teachers make their own judgment or their own personal

This kind of response is rather typical of many religious education administrators and teachers. The real issue is not whether it produces its goals
and objectives when taught. Only with well-planned, well-constructed, and
well-implemented scientific evaluation will religious educators be able to
judge the worth, the validity, and the reliability of a curriculum.

Many years ago the distinguished Presbyterian religious-education specialist Ellis Nelson observed that scientific research of all kinds, including research on curriculum evaluation, is absolutely essential in building
and validating religious-education curricula. Noting how many Protestant denominations had spent millions of dollars on building religious-
education curricula without ever scientifically ascertaining if these curricula
were effective, Nelson predicted that "no major Protestant denomination
will ever again" publish curricula without thoroughly evaluating them
scientifically.[139] Some Protestant churches have heeded Nelson's statement;
others have not. Market-driven Catholic publishers of curriculum materials
by and large do not heed Nelson's sage statement. Since maximum financial
gain is the prime goal of commercial publishers, and since there are some
purchasers of Catholic religious-education curricula who do not seem to
be deeply concerned about curricular validation, there is little incentive for
publishers to engage in the time and expense necessary to scientifically
evaluate any religious-education curriculum they produce. What often happens in the end is that vigorous and hardheaded marketing devices replace
scientific evaluation.

Politics and the Construction of Multicultural
Religious Education Curricula

It is impossible to construct a curriculum in a vacuum. A curriculum is
always built within a social context. An unavoidable dimension of this
content is the political.[140] At the essence of politics is power. In itself power
is neutral: it can be a force for good or for evil. Recognizing the evil potential
that power and politics can assume, both ancient Israel (Dan 10:13, 21;
12:1) and the Catholic Church long ago officially recognized the archangel

---

feelings the criteria of the validity and worthwhileness of a curriculum. In spite of the
fact that this distinguished gentleman was in his 70s, had spent most of his life outside the
United States, and had never been involved in youth work, he made his own judgment
and feelings the basis of ascertaining the value of a religious-education curriculum for
youth.

    139. C. Ellis Nelson, "Religious Instruction in the Protestant Churches," in *Toward a
Future for Religious Education*, ed. James Michael Lee and Patrick C. Rooney (Dayton,
Ohio: Pflaum, 1970), p. 178.

    140. John I. Goodlad, "Curriculum Making as a Sociopolitical Process," in *The Politics
of Curriculum Decision-Making*, ed. Frances Klein (Albany, N.Y.: State University of
New York Press, 1991), pp. 9–23.

Michael as patron of the nation and the church respectively. It was Michael, whose name means "Who is like to God?" who led the victorious angelic hosts against Lucifer and his desire for absolute power (Rev 12:7–9). An ancient and most venerable tradition tells us that Michael personally guards the gate of heaven with a fiery sword to ensure that those who lust for power and who are otherwise sinful are banned from entering the divine precincts.

Though history has consistently shown that political power can easily corrupt what it touches, there are still many forces within Christian churches that view their ministry as essentially political in nature. Conservatives and liberals alike sometimes prefer to use power and politics rather than goodness and love to further the work of God here on earth. How do builders of multicultural religious education handle this issue of power and politics?

Those who build multicultural religious-education curricula can minimize this tendency by endeavoring to broadly meet the religious needs of all learners who are impacted by it. Thus the good multicultural religious-education curriculum is one that strives to be as apolitical as possible so that it will serve the religious needs of the entire spectrum of learners. The good multicultural religious-education curriculum studiously avoids advancing any ideological or political agenda as far as possible. The good multicultural religious-education curriculum is consistent with basic biblical and Eucharistic principles and thus does not advocate tenets such as religious relativism and the like. The good multicultural religious-education curriculum does not attempt to take ethnic or racial or cultural or religious groups and put them into a melting pot where all differences are eradicated. The melting pot destroys the distinctive qualities of various groups that give vitality, freshness, and new intimations of the divine, which each and every group possesses. Rather, a good multicultural religious-education curriculum proceeds along the lines of a mosaic in which every ethnic, racial, cultural, and religious group will be encouraged to place its distinctive contributions on the altar of the Almighty so that all other groups can be thereby enriched.

In the end, it is not politics that forms the axis and thrust of a good multicultural religious-education curriculum. On the contrary, it is love, it is a sharing of gifts, it is standing in wonder and admiration of what God has bestowed on other groups that is the thrust of a good multicultural religious-education curriculum.

CONCLUSIONS AND PROSPECTS

Some basic biblical and theological assumptions, outlined at the beginning of this chapter, are worth reviewing at this point. From our view, multiculturalism does not denote a haphazard or relativist blending of traditions and perspectives. The encounter between Peter and Cornelius, for example, has life-changing significance, not because these two men practiced polite, uncritical acceptance of each other, but because they perceived a new, shared reality born out of honest wrestling with their cultural differences. Each was required to bring his own vision to the other, however partial and incomplete. Similarly, one's particular cultural perspective must be "owned," stated, and lived with mindful intentionality. Thus some persons maintain that the Apostles' Creed and the Nicene Creed, for example, may not be universal statements of truth for all Christians everywhere. But for those persons who embrace the contextual and historical traditions that gave rise to them, these creeds, and, more particularly, the theological and religious dialogue out of which the creeds emerged, are at the core of the Christian narrative believed and acted upon in daily life. For those Christian traditions that affirm them, these creedal forms become the basis for continued theological and religious educational dialogue. Some would say they are nothing more, but certainly they are nothing less.[141]

Thus the importance of beginning with basic convictions in multicultural religious education must not be ignored. There is nothing more deadly in multicultural religious encounter than attempting to avoid conflict by not articulating basic beliefs, opting instead to go the route of the least offensive general statements. In such settings, it is virtually impossible to discern the difference between ethnic and religious tradition. Ethnicity tends to shape the perspective of persons and to deny the historical and contextual differences that exist in favor of a bland common ground serves the church not at all.

Are there universal truths of Christian faith that transcend ethnic communities? This question is hotly debated in theology, anthropology, psychology, and sociology. The authors suggest that there are universal truths that transcend cultures for communities that accept God's saving work through Jesus Christ in the power of the Holy Spirit. The theological expressions about God's saving work may take many different forms, for culture shapes perception and expression. But regardless of culture, Christians assert that God is saving the world through Jesus Christ.

Although creeds may express universal truths, no one creedal statement is always normative for the entire global church. All creedal statements are cultural productions and theological expressions in need of constant reformation. Only God's saving work is normative. An ancient pastoral principle in Christianity is *Salus animarum suprema lex*. (The salvation of souls is the supreme law.) We must begin with our limited theological, religious, and cultural expressions in multicultural dialogue because to do otherwise would be to pretend that culture does not shape expression or interpretation. It is because of the incompleteness of our personal visions

---

141. For example, the cultural specificity of trinitarian concepts may be reviewed in Catherine Mowry LaCugna, *God for Us: The Trinity and Christian Life* (San Francisco: HarperSanFrancisco, 1990).

that dialogue with others unlike ourselves is mandatory. Through such dialogue we may begin to see beyond ourselves and to see more clearly the good news of God's saving love.

From hard historical experience, Christians know that it is quite possible for a denomination or other faith group to remain essentially racist and to produce curriculum materials that in the name of God promote racial and ethnic prejudice.[142] Responsible Christians must own these perspectives—these blind spots—as the bases from which dialogue and encounter need to take place. Hostility, fear, and competition are not overcome in the abstract by reading about the history of another ethnic group.

Mutual respect and equality, two basic aims of multicultural religious education in the church, often occur as the result of concrete, face-to-face dialogue and action. Authentic multicultural religious-education curricula cannot be "produced" without cultural encounter and dialogue. This means that conflict-mediation skills, including not only discernment but sensitivity and compassion, will be major gifts of the Christian religious educator in the twenty-first century, for good dialogue never occurs without debate, argumentation, and challenge.[143]

A 1993 conference on multiculturalism held in Atlanta, Georgia, for seminary and university professors discussed the question of national unity built on diversity rather than uniformity.[144] Would a focus on multiculturalism bring national unity, or would it bring destructive, warring factions? Clearly, neither way is an impossibility. This is a crucial and highly emotional issue in the discussion of multiculturalism. It may be a major reason some curriculum experts in the church choose to ignore the multicultural perspective.

---

142. Examples of such materials are discussed in *American Education*, by Lawrence A. Cremin, pp. 222–24, and in *Handbook of Research on Multicultural Education*, chap. 8, "Ethnographic Studies of Multicultural Education in Classrooms and Schools," by H. Mehan, A. Lintz, D. Okamoto, and J. S. Wills, pp. 138–40.

143. One of the finest books available on this topic is David W. Augsburger, *Conflict Mediation Across Cultures: Pathways and Patterns* (Louisville, Ky.: Westminster/John Knox, 1992), esp. pp. 187–220. Multicultural dialogue does not need conflict-reduction or conflict-resolution models. It does need conflict mediation. Mediation, Augsburger says, goes beyond the ability to define and discern; it includes the willingness to absorb tension, to be misunderstood or rejected, and to "bear the pain of others' estrangement." As such, the mediator stands in a precarious but crucial role in the community (p. 191).

144. The multicultural curriculum workshop was called "How We Can Effectively Change Traditional Western (Eurocentric) Curricula in Various Disciplines to Reflect Contributions Made by Different Cultures." It was sponsored by The University Center in Georgia, Council of Academic Deans and Vice Presidents and Human Relations Council, Kennesaw State College, 1 April 1993. The keynoter was Carlos E. Cortes, professor of history at the University of California, Riverside. It is important to note that the postmodernist perspective permeated this event, and that the conference's understanding of multiculturalism included gay, lesbian, and bisexual groups.

In summary, the authors hold that the biblical vision mandates a need for multicultural inclusivity in the church. As long as Christians around the globe presume the biblical texts to be the starting points for theological reflection, religious lifestyle, and faithful discipleship in the church, the vision of "one in diversity" will shape the pattern of relationships in the church. This means that pluralism as the intentional experiencing and valuing of diversity is welcomed as an integral aspect of what the Christian faith is for our day. It does not mean, however, that everyone in the church can believe whatever they want. Christians are not called to cultural relativism, but are called to seek the word of God in the midst of diversity. Beginning with the biblical affirmation of inclusiveness does not presume the ultimate negation of all common value. Instead, our common biblical faith, which welcomes diversity, provides a common context within which our plurality has existence.

The theme of reciprocal hospitality was identified earlier as a significant component of a biblical perspective on multicultural encounter and inclusion. The hospitality and openness to cultural differences that were practiced by Peter and Cornelius in response to what they discerned as the word of God was the beginning point for a deeper understanding of the importance of diversity among Christians. The tangible evidence of their unity was displayed as the Gentiles received the Spirit and were baptized. Hospitality practiced in a faithful and expectant manner is an important way in which Christians seek the word of God in the midst of diversity.

Let us return to the definition of curriculum suggested earlier in this chapter. Curriculum was defined as an interplay of many kinds of existential "texts." The first thing that religious educators who are interested in multiculturalism will need to do is to enable others to understand that the good news of Jesus Christ creates a special place in the world for the practice of pluralism. Different languages, skin tones, habits, music, stories, or ritual practices are to be welcomed as integral parts of the Christian worldview. All of our diversity is brought together on the basis of the gospel. Therefore, no one cultural perspective is religiously normative. Instead, God's word is heard as the people of God in their many diversities faithfully respond to God's saving love through Jesus Christ in the power of the Holy Spirit.

A multicultural Christian worldview is more easily espoused than practiced. For example, what is white, capitalistic, post-Christian culture telling us about the gospel? Many affluent parishes and congregations in the United States presume that there is very little difference between the Gospel and contemporary social reality. Christianity and culture are viewed as one and the same—if it is good for the economy, it is good for the church. The normativity of the dominant culture in the United States is problematic for the gospel at best. Not all our cultural expressions have a positive word to say about what it means to be Christian in our day.

Most churches in the United States tend to be racially and ethnically homogeneous. Such congregations and parishes often feel they have nothing to learn from those that are racially and ethnically different. However, multicultural religious education is not simply learning facts about other ethnic groups. It is not simply "having instructional resources in our own language." Multicultural religious education may include these elements, but it transcends them. At base, multicultural religious education is a disciplined practice of in-depth conversation and experience shared among diverse groups given focus by the gospel of Jesus Christ. Deliberately seeking conversation and interaction with sisters and brothers in Jesus Christ who are different from ourselves is a spiritual discipline. It is within the multicultural interplay of many kinds of "texts" that the curriculum of the congregation is formed. This simple assertion may well prove to be one of the most challenging and controversial statements for Christian religious educators in the twenty-first century.

APPENDIX

Annotated List of Resources for Planning Religious Education Curriculum

There are many fascinating books on the topic of curriculum for religious education. The important resources included in this brief survey list can be considered a guide to those concerned with forming a basis for a multicultural religious education curriculum.

James Michael Lee, *The Content of Religious Instruction* (Birmingham, Ala.: Religious Education Press, 1985). Lee, one of the most insightful of curriculum theorists of the twentieth century, proposes that "there should be three kinds of structural pedagogical relationships situated in every religion curriculum or lesson: (1) relationships between those activities which for one or more reasons constitute religious experience per se; (2) relationships between religious experience and the various academic disciplines or fields of knowledge; (3) relationships between religious experience and human activity of every sort" (p. 12).

Iris V. Cully, *Planning and Selecting Curriculum for Christian Education* (Valley Forge, Pa.: Judson Press, 1983). Cully offers a valuable understanding of curriculum construction and planning based on an interplay of developmental, biblical, and theological foundations.

William Pinar, *Curriculum Theorizing: The Reconceptualists* (Berkeley, Calif.: McCutchan, 1975). This is a solid introductory text for those who know little about different philosophical approaches to curriculum.

Jame R. Gress, ed., *Curriculum: An Introduction to the Field* (Berkeley, Calif.: McCutchan, 1978). This is a fine introductory text.

Howard Gardner, *The Unschooled Mind: How Children Think and How Schools Should Teach* (New York: Basic, 1991). This fine introductory text is destined to become the basis for curriculum theorizing in the early twenty-first century. His idea of "multiple intelligences" brings into question the pervasive "production" model of education in a way that the general public can understand.

Maria Harris, *Fashion Me a People: Curriculum in the Church* (Louisville: Westminster/John Knox, 1989). Harris's approach is congruent with the notion of "text" developed in this chapter. In artistically exciting ways, Harris sees the whole life of the congregation as the curriculum of the church.

Philip H. Phenix, *Education and the Worship of God* (Philadelphia: Westminster, 1961). Phenix, for reasons hard to understand, has been ignored widely by the field of Christian religious education. This brilliant work is developed in five chapters: "Language and the Word of God," "Science and the Wisdom of God," "Art and the Work of God," "Ethics and the Will of God," and "History and the Way of God."

Cooperative Curriculum Project, *The Church's Educational Ministry: A Curriculum Plan* (St. Louis: Bethany, 1965). This is the single most important curriculum statement produced in the twentieth century by an ecumenical Protestant team. It is focused heavily on developmental factors, neo-orthodox theology, and keen insight related to social engagement.

Elliott W. Eisner, "Five Basic Orientations to the Curriculum," in *The Educational Imagination: On the Design and Evaluation of School Programs* (New York: Macmillan, 1985), pp. 61–86. Eisner is a pioneer in the field of curriculum critique. He is at his best when he helps readers understand the hidden and null curricula that educators teach without even noticing. For those wanting an extended reading on the kind of curriculum options discussed in this chapter, Eisner's is the book to read first.

William B. Stanley, *Curriculum for Utopia: Social Reconstruction and Critical Pedagogy in the Postmodern Era* (New York: State University of New York Press, 1992). This is a crucial text for Christian religious educators. It is difficult reading, but well worth the effort. Postmodernism is dealt with in convincing ways, although immediate curriculum implications are elusive. The idea of "textuality" pervades Stanley's volume. For those unfamiliar with such theorists as Derrida, Giroux, Brameld, McLaren, and Habermas, this is the book to read again and again.

Edmund C. Short, ed. *Forms of Curriculum Inquiry* (New York: State University of New York Press, 1991). This gem of a book has a fine chapter by Valerie J. Janesick (pp. 101–19) on ethnography and the curriculum. The chapter is especially relevant for multicultural religious education.

PART IV

CONCLUSION

11

BENEVOLENT TOLERANCE
OR HUMBLE REVERENCE?

A Vision for Multicultural
Religious Education

Virgilio Elizondo

At the very core of a true multicultural religious education program is the original New Testament story of the Christian movement: how the slaves, the disenfranchised, the low merchants, the widows, the unemployed, the immigrants, and the socially downcast found a new and exciting alternative to social life that the world had not imagined possible. In the new community, everyone was accepted with reverence and respect. If the Lord had emptied himself of all social status for them, then they were to do the same for one another. It was the excitement of this new way of life that attracted everyone—even the rich, the righteous, and the mighty. The joyful simplicity of Christians was contagious. Yet it was dangerous, because it dared to transgress all borders for the sake of a new unity.

THE ORIGINALITY OF THE CHRISTIAN MOVEMENT

To best appreciate the challenge and the grace-filled possibilities of multicultural religious education, we need to rediscover and make our own the liberating and life-giving *originality* of the Christian movement. It offered to all peoples, no matter where they came from, a new family name: Christian.

It offered equally to everyone, no matter what their race or nationality, a new, common bloodstream: the blood of Jesus. It flowed through everyone who joined, producing one close-knit unity: the body of the Lord! Thus the body and blood of Jesus, broken and spilled for the sake of humanity, now rehabilitated a broken humanity divided and crushed by the human blood that produces everyone's fundamental earthly identity. Peoples of diverse backgrounds, histories, and heritages could now begin to share in the common story and heritage of Jesus and the biblical heritage of their ancestors in the faith. This new story would not destroy the histories of peoples, but would bring them into a new common space and time. The kingdom of God was now available to everyone.

Christianity produced a new human being who was totally different from the world's nationalities, not by transforming the basic nationality but by transforming the limitations of national identities. The early Christians were considered atheists because they refused to recognize the national gods of any nation. Christians had only one God who was truly Creator and Parent of all. They were respectful of civic authority but refused to accept it as absolute, for they had only one absolute—the unconditional love of God for all human beings regardless of their national or racial identity.

Hence, the Christian identity was the hyphenated identity: Jewish-Christian, Greek-Christian, Roman-Christian. Their identities as Christians made them open to the otherness of others as truly brothers and sisters, all children of the same parent God. The refreshing originality of Christianity is that it transgressed all barriers of separation and division, whether rooted in blood or sacred traditions.

HISTORICAL CHRISTIANITY AS DIVISIVE

The Cultural Reality of the United States

Despite the unity in diversity evident among the earliest Christians, historical Christianity has often served more as a basis of exclusion than of welcome. Multiculturalism is rather new in U.S. churches and in society today, yet it is an unquestioned fact of life. Some see it as the new life of the future while others see it as destructive of all unity—civic, social, and religious. Regardless of how it is understood, multiculturalism is a growing fact of life in the United States. This whole book attempts to break new ground in our understanding of the many aspects and implications of multiculturalism.

The Emergence of a Racist and Segregating Christianity

The U.S. churches are finally coming to grips with the original sin of the great European (and later American) evangelizing efforts that accompanied conquering and colonizing European expansion that began in the fifteenth century. Very simply put, white Europeans saw themselves as godly people while judging all others and their ways as demonic: We, the saved, and they, the damned; we the masters, and they, the servants or slaves; we the true and beautiful human beings, and they, the false and ugly human beings; we the possessors and guardians of truth, and they, who are enslaved by error.

The white Christian invaders had no doubts about the divine righteousness of their invasion, conquest, and colonization of other people. They never questioned their own superiority. Western culture itself became the great idol of our churches. All had to conform or be cast out. It is the pseudodivine status of white Western culture that is finally being revealed as the false idol that must be destroyed. It is not that Western culture needs to be destroyed, but its pseudodivine status that allows it to continue functioning as the unquestioned normative culture and religious expression for all others.

Western theologians still tend to see the Western churches as "the Church," while viewing the churches of other people of the world as "local churches." Western tradition is regarded as "Tradition," while everything else is regarded as local tradition. Western theologies are regarded simply as theology, while the theologies and methodologies of other cultures are regarded as ethnic or particular theologies. The West still keeps to itself the right to be the exclusive ecclesial master of the world and guards this right carefully through its universities and publications.

There is no doubt that in the past, and to a large degree today, most of our churches have been monochurches: monolingual, monocultural, and monoracial. Uniformity and conformity in all things have been the unquestioned norms of acceptance and belonging. These unquestioned norms allowed white churches of the past to justify and legitimize slavery and segregation. In effect, the churches implicitly sacralized fear, dislike, and hatred of others. Separate churches were built to keep diverse people worshiping separately. It has often been observed that eleven o'clock on Sunday mornings is the most segregated hour in America, and that the more churchgoing people are, the more prejudiced they seem to be.

It is out of this scandalous reality of the past that today we are seeking to bring about a new church with a truly multicultural face and heart.

A Graced Opportunity

The undeniable increase in racial and ethnic diversity in the United States poses many potential problems, yet greater than the problems are the opportunities to create something new and life giving on the face of the earth. This volume is an attempt to facilitate a Christian response to the graced opportunities of our multicultural society. However, to promote the emergence of a real multicultural religious experience, we must go from a benevolent tolerance of the otherness of the others to a sincere reverence of others in their otherness.

Before we can embark on a multicultural religious education that is not merely a benevolent tolerance stemming from guilt feelings about the past, we need to undergo a deep cultural conversion from our previously unquestioned Western paradigm of truth itself—that all truth, whether personal, cultural, technical, natural, or religious, is one, absolute, and complete and therefore can be known in terms of either/or: true or false, good or bad, beautiful or ugly. For such a transformation to take place we must all die a bit to our collective self-righteousness so that we may be more willing to listen and learn from the others. As communication between persons, cultures, and nations increases, we are becoming aware that it is not possible to reduce truth to one expression. No one has an absolute and exclusive monopoly on truth. We have much to offer one another, if only we can have the humility to accept it.

A Puzzle Paradigm vs. a Pyramid Paradigm

Ultimate and absolute truth is like a massive puzzle. Each cultural expression of truth, together with its religious expression, is like a large piece of the complete puzzle of God and humanity. But no one piece alone gives us the complete picture. A more complete picture of the true, the good, and the beautiful comes through when all the pieces are together in their proper interconnectedness. Yet the fullness of the mystery of God and of humanity will still lie beyond our human understanding. This alone is the glory of God—no one piece dominating or controlling the others, but all joined together and giving meaning, life, and beauty to one another. This is different from the pyramid paradigm in which one builds on the others to eventually get to the top. In the puzzle all pieces are of equal importance. Only when they are joined together does the whole make sense. This model does not ask who is the best or the most important. It asks how each one fits into the rest for the benefit of everyone.

Multicultural religious education presupposes a truly multicultural church, or at least a church that is striving to be multicultural. But how does Christian multiculturalism come about? How do we build churches that welcome all people as they are, not to the degree that they become like the dominant group of the congregation? Do our churches welcome the diversity of God's humanity? Do we merely tolerate diversity, or do we reject it completely?

The ultimate success or failure of a truly multicultural religious-education program depends on the personality of the local congregation, the person of the religious educator, and the total environment of the church—its people, ministers, decorations, music, church order, and celebrations. It is not just a question of the right materials and the right pedagogical methods, but a totally new attitude about church, ourselves, and others, a new attitude about the way we see and value the otherness of other persons and peoples. In a word, we must decide if we are going to be a tower of Babel or a Pentecost assembly of believers.

MULTICULTURAL CHRISTIANITY AS UNIFYING

My experience at San Fernando Cathedral, an active Mexican parish in San Antonio since 1731, has been an enriching one. Even though our basic identity is very Mexican, we work hard at welcoming others. We have not found this to be divisive in any way. On the contrary, it continues to be very enriching. Last Pentecost Sunday we celebrated our worship service in several languages and had the active participation of thirty-three ethnic groups. It was a great experience of the power of Christ bringing us together in ways no human power is capable of doing. The multicultural experience is not easy, but it is certainly exciting and enriching.

In my experience, a truly multicultural congregation emerges through three phases, or moments—not necessarily one before the other. The three moments are confession, conversion, and construction. But I suspect the first and foremost question is, Does the congregation really want to be a multicultural Christian family? Does it really want to be something new on the face of the earth? Or does it just want to be nice and add new ethnics to its already existing congregation? Does the congregation want continuity with just a bit more color and foreign accents? Or does it really want to be a community of all God's children?

Confession: Naming and Claiming the Sin

The Sin of Dogmatic Ethnocentrism: All of our churches in the United States came out of the great European colonizing enterprise that started in 1492. The church of that period, because of the Reformation and Counter-Reformation, emphasized dogma and looked at any type of difference as heretical and divisive. This emphasis also dogmatized the cultural and racial ideas of the emerging dominant nations of Europe. "White" and "Western civilization" thus became the dogmatically correct image of the dignified, beautiful, and authentic human being. All others would be looked upon as undignified, ugly (except for the young women of the conquered who often appeared to the conquerors as more exotic than their own women), and subhuman.

The Catholic and Protestant churches accepted without question the assumption that white Europeans, especially the Anglo-Saxons in North America, were the superior race, which had been divinely chosen to be normative of the only true humanity possible or desirable by people in their right minds. Everyone else was considered inferior, heathen, and at best underdeveloped! The benevolent looked on the others as children who needed the loving care and discipline of the white Europeans. The ruthless looked on the others as mere beasts of burden. In many ways, this is still the case today.

Europeans and their American descendants fortified their sense of cultural superiority with the religious conviction that they belonged to the one and only true religion. Throughout history they had fought bloody battles among themselves as to which was the dogmatically correct version of this one true religion, but they never questioned that European Christianity was the one salvation for all the peoples of the world. Of course, "Christianity" meant their own particular understanding of it: Catholic, Lutheran, Methodist, Baptist, and so on.

It was this dogmatic certainty intermingled with the European sense of superiority and the European's need for cheap labor that "in good conscience" and with the blessings of religious authorities produced such an incredibly racist and segregated American continent. European immigrants did not hesitate to set up their own churches where they could experience salvation while exploiting and murdering the Natives, the imported Africans, and the conquered Mexicans without any qualms of conscience.

It is true that some church voices protested loudly, and it is true that church movements have been a part of the force that has attempted to bring about change. But in general, the churches sanctified the white, neo-European culture of the Americas and thus sanctioned contempt for people of other races, cultures, and languages.

For a truly multicultural community to emerge, all are called to recognize their specific cultural sinfulness so that they may repent, receive God's forgiveness, and begin to create a new way of relating with each other.

The Sin of Arrogant Pride: White Western Christians need to convert from their sins of arrogance and pride. Their righteous sense of superiority has blinded them to their own inadequacies and sinfulness and has kept them from appreciating the treasures God has bestowed on the peoples of the other races and cultures of the world. This unclaimed sin of arrogant and self-righteous pride still allows them to see themselves as human while seeing the others as "cultural groups" or "ethnics."

There is a deep and unquestioned Western conviction, bolstered by financial, technological, and military superiority, that the West alone knows the truth, the way, and the life. All others either live in ignorance or at best possess only small bits and pieces of the truth. The minorities might be accepted and enjoyed "folklorically," but the West thinks that it alone knows the right way of life for all who want to be correctly human.

The confession of our cultural arrogance will be the beginning of the liberation from the current ethnocentrism that impels us to demand that others conform to our image and likeness. A collective recognition of our limited view of reality, of humanity, and of God will be the beginning of a new enrichment and source of life. It will be the beginning of a new life that, at the present moment, is impossible to imagine.

The Sin of Humiliating Shame: On the other hand, those who have been marginated, brutalized, abused, segregated, put down, ridiculed, or merely tolerated need also to recognize their sin: the sense of inferiority that some come to believe and accept. The victimizer's ultimate triumph is to get the victims to accept the blame for their situation of misery. The sin of the victimized is to accept this as true, resulting in a loss of dignity and self-worth. Attitudes of docility, embarrassment of color or heritage, and the many negative and self-destructive feelings grow out of the inner sense of shame at being who one is.

Even oppressed people who do not believe in their supposed inferiority are forced to live the consequences of inferiority, marginalization, and subservience. This is very painful. It is humiliating and it destroys the inner soul of the person and of a people. The sin of accepting assigned inferiority leads to a distrust of one's own, a disgust with one's culture and language, and a devastating break with the ways of one's ancestors.

Without confession of our cultural singleness, we will at best tolerate one another. We will never enter into a true fellowship among equals, a true family spirit that embraces all as children of the one God. We need to be willing and ready to name and confess our sin so that we may move on the conversion—that is, to a real *metanoia* whereby we will turn our innermost attitudes of life in a radically different direction.

Conversion to the Way of Jesus

Jesus surprised and astounded everyone, rich and poor, sinful and saintly, accepted and rejected, by portraying a totally new vision of the human and the sacred in the very simple and ordinary way in which he related with people and with God in his everyday life. He invited us to share in this new reality that will truly revolutionize our own vision of ourselves, of others, and of God.

Jesus invites us to see ourselves and others in a radically new way through the prism of God's unconditional love for everyone. Through God's love we move from our typical judgmental and conditional tolerance and acceptance of others to the spontaneous joy of discovering our unsuspected sisters and brothers, each one revealing a bit of God's glory. Everyone is invited to convert from pride or shame to a grateful and humble acceptance of who we are and who the other is. This will lead us from either total rejection or benevolent tolerance to a truly humble reverence for one another and an appreciation for the giftedness of each person, nation, and race.

Jesus: The True Image of the Human and of God: The dominant groups of Jesus' day perceived him as an outcast. Being Jewish, he belonged to people who were rejected culturally by the powerful Romans. Being from Galilee, he was from a region scorned socially by Jewish officials in Jerusalem, who frequently viewed their coreligionists from Galilee as unknowledgeable and lax in the practice of their faith. And to make things even more interesting, there were rumors about his dubious parentage and scandals about his friendships with prostitutes and public sinners. Thus did the sacred unseen and untouchable God become visible and touchable in the socially, culturally, and religiously rejected Jesus of Nazareth!

In the very social-cultural-religious human being that God became, Jesus revealed to us the mystery hidden by humanity's sinfulness since the origins of sin itself: that every human being is of infinite dignity, unmeasurable worth, and unique beauty. In its sinfulness, the world constantly creates categories of unworthiness, untouchability, and inferiority, while at the same time creating artificial and often unnatural categories of beauty, importance, dignity, and worth. These sinful categories begin to define the truth of the human and of the divine while in effect hiding (or perverting) the ultimate truth of God and destroying any possibility of human authenticity. Since the escalation of sin (described in Genesis 3–11), this has become the way of the world—the way of men and women throughout history. This was the way Peter was thinking when he wanted a glorious Messiah. This is the way we think when we want only socially acceptable members of the right color and ethnicity in our congregations. But this is not God's way! God creates and loves all of God's children alike.

These human classifications are the sin that brings about the distortion and blindness of the world. In Jesus, God became the nothing of the world so that through Jesus—with him and in him—all might be liberated from their own false notions about themselves and others, and thus come to appreciate people for what they truly are: children of God. There is nothing Jesus condemns more than hypocrisy. Sinful people he deals with compassionately; hypocrites he has no stomach for. People who give in to the world's struggles for superiority, honor, artificial beauty, and the like, lose themselves to the world and are destructive of self and of others.

The New Image of Self and Others: All are invited to convert—to think and feel in a radically new way so as to belong to God's own family. The rich and mighty are invited to give up their wealth and power while the poor and lowly are assured that they will be uplifted and will receive their fill.[1] In other words, those who have considered themselves superior are invited to think less of themselves. The righteous are invited to recognize their sinfulness, and those whom society deems unwanted "public sinners" are invited to become aware of their fundamental worth. Those who think of themselves as trash or as nothing are invited to recognize their strength and

---

1. Luke 1:52–54

independence. Thus all are invited to a change of heart and mind. Through baptism we die to the old self to be reborn with the heart and mind of Jesus. We truly become a new creation within the old creation, and thus we are reborn to a new tension. The great difference is that now we know that ultimate triumph is assured and nobody can take it away from us. Hence we can live in peace even within the context of the tensions and uncertainties of the new life of grace.

It is in the very radical acceptance of our personal and collective mystery of giftedness/lack, wealth/poverty, blessing/curse, health/sickness, understanding/blindness, saintliness/sinfulness, truth/ambiguity, knowledge/ignorance, that we become truly human. It is in the recognition of our innermost existential poverty as persons, as cultures, and as races that we begin truly to appreciate and welcome the wealth of others. It is in this radical acceptance of God's love for us as we are that we receive the courage to accept ourselves as we are and truly rejoice in the acceptance of others as they are, not as we would like them to be.

Division Because of Unity: In the Gospels, the same Jesus who prays "that all may be one"[2] tells us that he has come to bring about division.[3] These statements seem to contradict each other. Yet in practice it is quite obvious what Jesus is speaking about. Precisely because all are invited in an equal way, those who have usually enjoyed status and privilege will not want to come, not because they are not invited, but precisely because now everyone is invited, especially those considered to be unworthy, unwanted, and untouchable. When the club is made available to everyone, those who took pride in belonging to the exclusive, private club will not want to belong to the new one! In the process of working for the unity of the kingdom, we can expect the scandal, criticism, and persecution of those committed to the empires and sacred institutions of this world. The great paradox is that the call to unity so frequently leads to bitter division!

Construction of New Church Bodies

Each local congregation could easily become like a laboratory specimen of the new creation—and is it not in the cell that new life begins? Prayerful insight, patient trust, and a spirit of welcome are the seeds from which the new creation is born, whether at the congregational level or within the dynamics of multicultural religious education.

Prayerful Insight: Because the unity of the church is not one of men and women but of the Spirit, the work of multicultural unity must begin with sincere prayer that God may enlighten and strengthen us to go beyond our own fears and limitations. It is not through the conclusions reached by

---

2. John 17:11
3. Luke 12:51

rational discourse but by the insight revealed through sincere and prolonged prayer that the new church will be built. Without prayer that truly opens up our minds and hearts to the unconditional love of God in all its consequences, even reading Scripture can simply confirm our distorted notions without giving us insight.

Prayer will bring about a new vision of vision itself, a new understanding of understanding itself, and a new truth regarding the reality of truth. Prayer leads us from narrow tunnel vision to a panoramic one, from isolated to more integrated understanding, and from partial to more complete truth. This does not relativize truth; it amplifies it! This is far more objective than the subjective conviction of one cultural group or another.

Patient Trust: The new multicultural fellowship will not come about overnight. It will take patience with ourselves and with others. We are embarking on something new and deeply personal, yet of planetary implications and consequence. It will not be easy. Even when we are committed to doing it, we will not always know just how to bring it about. Cultural misunderstanding is steeped in fear and misunderstanding. Sometimes signals, gestures, or words will be misinterpreted. Insult will be taken when none is intended, and rejection will be easily experienced.

Trust cannot be mandated. It builds up gradually but can be destroyed in an instant. There is no simple pedagogy for building trust. It takes a lot of love, self-giving, and the willingness to hurt with another and to see and feel in ways we are not accustomed to. It comes about through a lot of careful listening, especially to the silence and absence of those who are marginal or newcomers.

It will take time to build up the trust and confidence that people need to truly be themselves. Everyone has to be able to give up a bit of self to receive much from the others. But in the process of giving and receiving, a new and profound commonality will gradually emerge. In this process, all can truly become one body without anyone having to become like all the others simply in order to belong.

The more each one experiences the willingness of each member to die a bit to self for the sake of others, the more this love will become the new commonality and source of unity for the group. The source of unity will no longer be the racial color, the language, the ethnicity, the social class, the sex or sexual orientation, or even precise religious expression, but the love that allows each one to transgress the taboos that separate us. The new language will be that of *agape*, which finds ways of communicating through any and all the languages of humanity.

A Welcoming and Inclusive Home: To be truly multicultural, a local congregation must visibly reflect the various peoples making up the congregation in every aspect of church life. The very physical surroundings should put us in contact with the places of origin of the various members:

pictures, decorations, maps, furniture, and signs in the various languages represented. Efforts should be make to help the members pronounce each other's names correctly. Simple greetings can be learned in one another's languages.

People should be invited to share their personal stories—where they came from, what they left behind, why they came, the struggles it took to get here, how they are getting adjusted, what they miss. Some, like many of our Mexican Americans and Native Americans, never left home but were made foreigners in their own lands. Others might have forgotten the migrations of their previous generations. The story of each one is important. It is by means of personal stories that we break through the stereotypes and begin to know persons as Juan, Mary, Karl, Nindu, Sun Ai, Yong Ting Jin. Through the stories we begin to interconnect on a very personal level.

Religious education activities should explore the various diverse and legitimate religious expressions of our one faith. People can experience the excitement of discovering how each expression enriches the ongoing incarnation of our faith. We need to appreciate the ancestral rites of our Asian Christians, the ancestral traditions of our African Christians, the Mestizo Christian traditions of our Latin American Christians. They include such beautiful customs as the Day of the Dead (which is actually the day of the living), *La Virgen* (which is not understood by North American Catholics or Latin American Protestants), and the crucified Jesus as *el Señor del Poder*; they also include the community dance and meal rituals of our Native Americans, the icons of Eastern European Christianity, the written alphabetic word for Western Christians, the role of the image-painted word for Christians of hieroglyphic cultures.

We must go even further. As Christians, we should lead the way in seeking to truly understand and appreciate all others. If in our minds and hearts we are secure in our own religious conviction, we do not have to be defensive or apprehensive in the face of others. Only one who is insecure will seek to discredit others. Hence, we should present and study the other great religious of the world, not asking whether they are true or false or even if they are a preparation for Christianity, but simply trying to appreciate them as they are. To see the beauty and truth of the others does not deny our own! In fact, it can even strengthen our own and help us to appreciate it more. I have found out in recent years that the more I appreciate the other great religious traditions of the world, the more I come to appreciate and love my own, not because I think we in our faith are better or superior to others, but simply because I have come to a greater awareness of who we are in relation to the others. We need to go beyond the sacralized divisions of the past so that we can become one very diverse and beautiful human family before we destroy one another in the name of the God we confess.

FESTIVE CHRISTIANITY AS PROCLAMATION

The early Christians made many converts through their new life of joy and simplicity. Many of the people Christians encountered had a great deal materially and socially and yet were bored and disillusioned with life. The Christians disregarded social rank and status and were happy because they welcomed everyone alike! All could partake of the table together—master and slave, citizen and foreigner. No matter what their role or status in society might be, within the Christian community they were truly of equal status because here they were brothers and sisters. It was not long before the Christian group was headed by a slave as successor of Peter—Pope Calixtus.[4]

Christians came together not to argue, defend, or try to impose, but simply to sing songs of joy, to tell about the memory of Jesus, to see how they could help one another, and to celebrate their new ritual, the breaking of the bread. In the breaking and sharing of the bread they transgressed the taboos and celebrated what was now begun in them but would only be fully achieved at the end of time—the ultimate unity of humanity. Our multicultural congregations can be the luminous and glorious rainbow whose worship foreshadows the banquet of the eschatological end, anticipating here and now God's ultimate triumph over the divisions of humanity.

---

4. Calixtus I, also known as Callistus, became pope in 218. He was born a slave and died a Christian martyr in 223.

PROFILE OF CONTRIBUTORS

DEBORAH L. BAINER is associate professor of education at Ohio State University, where she coordinates the graduate teacher-education programs at the Mansfield campus. Her teaching responsibilities include pedagogy, multicultural education, and social-studies education. Bainer's research focuses on culturally responsible pedagogy and support behaviors among teachers. She has published in the fields of higher education and multicultural education and is coauthor of the textbook *The Act of Teaching*. She serves as a consultant and facilitator on reentry seminars for international workers for the Christian and Missionary Alliance. Earlier in her career she taught at a school for missionaries' children in Asia and served as chairperson of the education department at Biola University.

RONALD H. CRAM is associate professor of Christian education at Columbia Theological Seminary. He has served as a director of Christian education, and as the director of an ecumenical resource center. He has authored several articles and book chapters and is currently writing a book on the relation of the Trinity to Christian practice. He has served as the review editor of *Religious Education* and is an editorial consultant for the journal *Ex Autitu*. A layperson, he is a member of First Presbyterian Church in Atlanta, Georgia.

VIRGILIO ELIZONDO is the president of the Mexican American Institute and rector of San Fernando Cathedral in San Antonio, Texas. He contributed a chapter to *Ethnicity in the Education of the Church* and has authored many articles and books, among them *Galilean Journey: The Mexican American Promise* and *The Future is Mestizo*.

ESPERANZA GINORIS has taught religion for forty years. She was born in Cuba and studied philosophy and literature at Havana University. She came to the United States in 1961 after Castro's revolution. Ginoris is vice chairperson for the National Advisory Committee for Catechesis with Hispanics of the United States Catholic Conference in Washington, D.C., and a consultant for Hispanics in the Department of Religious Education of the Archdiocese of Miami. She coauthored a textbook for immigrant children, *Una Fe, Una Esperanza*, and her articles have appeared in *Catechetical Sunday, Teacher Journal*, and *Living Light*.

CAROL A. JENKINS serves as professor of sociology at Glendale Community College in Glendale (Phoenix), Arizona. Jenkins's academic preparation included both a doctorate in sociology and a master's degree in religious education. Her research interests concern issues facing American rural ethnic religious minorities and instructional challenges in the multi-cultural classroom at the college level.

DALE KRATT is a doctoral student in the department of sociology at Virginia Polytechnic Institute and State University. He earned his M.A. degree from the School of Intercultural Studies and Biola University. Mr. Kratt's research focuses on issues in comparative sociological thought and international development.

JAMES MICHAEL LEE is professor of education at the University of Alabama at Birmingham. He was born in Brooklyn and is a Catholic layman. He received his doctorate from Columbia University. Three of Professor Lee's many books are his trilogy, which was published by Religious Education Press: *The Shape of Religious Instruction, The Flow of Religious Instruction*, and *The Content of Religious Instruction*. His articles have appeared in many journals, including *Herder Korrespondenz, Religious Education*, and *Living Light*. Professor Lee has taught at the University of Notre Dame, Hunter College of the City University of New York, and St. Joseph's College. He was the recipient of a Senior Fulbright Research Fellowship in Germany and also a Lilly Endowment Fellowship. He is listed in *Who's Who in America, Who's Who in the World*, and *Who's Who in Religion*.

LAURA B. LEWIS is associate professor of Christian education at Austin Presbyterian Theological Seminary in Texas. Her teaching includes courses in selection and use of curriculum in congregations, the ministry of education, and the hermeneutics and pedagogy of the Bible. Her articles, essays, and book reviews have appeared in journals such as *Religious Education*. She is an ordained clergywoman and certified Christian educator in the Presbyterian Church (U.S.A.).

RANDOLPH CRUMP MILLER is the Horace Bushnell Professor of Christian Nurture, Emeritus, at The Divinity School, Yale University, and is editor emeritus of *Religious Education*. From 1936 to 1952 he taught at the Church Divinity School of the Pacific in Berkeley, California. His many books on religious education and related fields include *The Clue to Christian Education*, and, most recently, *Theologies of Religious Education*, which he edited for Religious Education Press.

GREER ANNE WENH-IN NG is associate professor of Christian Education at Emmanuel College, Victoria University, Toronto School of Theology, in the University of Toronto, Ontario, Canada. Besides teaching at Vancouver School of Theology and at Trinity Theological College, Singapore, she has engaged in religious education as curriculum writer and as Conference Christian Development minister for her denomination, the United Church of Canada, of which she is an ordained minister.

JEFFREY W. PECK is assistant professor of education at Gardner-Webb University in Boiling Springs, North Carolina. He received his Ph.D. in school administration and is also an experienced middle-school teacher and religious educator.

DONALD RATCLIFF is associate professor of psychology and sociology at Toccoa Falls College in Georgia. He has published numerous articles on psychology and sociology in scholarly journals. He is the author of *Using Psychology in the Church* and a coauthor of *Introduction to Psychology and Counseling.* Among the many books he has authored or edited for Religious Education Press is the *Handbook of Family Religious Education,* which he edited with Blake J. Neff.

HAROLD DEAN TRULEAR is dean for first professional programs at New York Theological Seminary. His articles have appeared in several journals, among them *American Baptist Quarterly, The Journal of Religious Thought,* and *Religion and Intellectual Life.* Trulear has pastored churches in the New York metropolitan area and was formerly associated with Youth for Christ as an area director and a board member.

JACE WEAVER, of Oklahoma Cherokee and European descent, received his Ph.D. at Union Theological Seminary in New York. He is assistant professor of American studies and religious studies at Yale University. He is author of *Then to the Rock Let Me Fly,* and he has written articles dealing with Native American themes for numerous publications, including *Christianity and Crisis, Native Journal,* and *Wicazo Sa Review.*

BARBARA WILKERSON is a Christian education consultant to churches and an adjunct instructor at Alliance Theological Seminary in Nyack, New York, where she served until her retirement as associate professor of Christian education. She studied Christian education at Princeton Theological Seminary and received her doctorate at Rutgers University. Wilkerson has also been director of Christian education at the Korean American Presbyterian Church in Pearl River, New York. Earlier in her career she taught public school for several years and was later publications editor in the Christian Education Office of the Christian and Missionary Alliance. She is the author of two books on ministry with children, including *Childhood: the Positive Years,* published by Christian Publications.

INDEX OF NAMES

INDEX OF SUBJECTS